Next Generation ABAP™ Development

 PRESS

SAP PRESS is a joint initiative of SAP and Galileo Press. The know-how offered by SAP specialists combined with the expertise of the publishing house Galileo Press offers the reader expert books in the field. SAP PRESS features first-hand information and expert advice, and provides useful skills for professional decision-making.

SAP PRESS offers a variety of books on technical and business related topics for the SAP user. For further information, please visit our website: *www.sap-press.com*.

Horst Keller, Sascha Krüger
ABAP Objects
ABAP Programming in SAP NetWeaver
2007, 2nd, completely new edition, 1059 pp.
ISBN 978-1-59229-079-6

Brian McKellar, Thomas Jung
Advanced BSP Programming
2006, 491 pp.
ISBN 978-1-59229-049-9

Josef Köble
Developing Accessible Applications with SAP NetWeaver
2007, app. 400 pp.
ISBN 978-1-59229-112-0

Horst Keller
The Official ABAP Reference
2005, 2nd, revised and extended edition, 1216 pp.
ISBN 978-1-59229-039-0

Rich Heilman, Thomas Jung

Next Generation ABAP™ Development

Galileo Press

Bonn • Boston

ISBN   978-1-59229-139-7

1st edition 2007

Editor Stefan Proksch
Copy Editor Nancy Etscovitz, UCG, Inc., Boston, MA
Cover Design Nadine Kohl
Layout Design Vera Brauner
Production Iris Warkus
Typesetting Typographie & Computer, Krefeld
Printed and bound in Germany

Contents at a Glance

Contents

Introduction

This book represents 20 years of collective experience from real world ABAP Development projects. When setting out to write this book, our challenge was to share what it was like to be part of a cutting edge ABAP development project with our readers.

Ideally, our goal was for each reader to be able to sit down and observe an entire project from start to finish, and therefore learn the integral techniques of modern ABAP development. They would be able to see the latest ABAP technologies in action, in addition to examining the design and development processes used to maximize these technologies. Unfortunately, few developers ever get the opportunity to observe a project in this way. Too often they have to learn on the job, while dealing with unrealistic deadlines. Therefore, our objective was to allow you, the reader, to see and participate in the evolution of such a project in small incremental steps.

For that reason, this book is not your typical programming guide. Instead of focusing on just the technological aspects of developing in ABAP, we will study a fictional project so you can see how a project is developed. Each chapter will represent a phase or layer of this project's development, as well as one or two new key ABAP technologies. If you're interested in delving into these new technologies straightaway, you're welcome to skip to these respective chapters; however, we, the authors, encourage you to read this book in chronological order so that you'll have an opportunity to see the entire narrative of this project play out.

Fictional Project

Throughout the book, we'll be using a single fictional project for our practice scenario. This project takes place at a university, which is a long time SAP customer who runs their business systems on SAP R/3. For over four years, they've been running SAP R/3 4.6C and have used the Finance and Human Resources modules of SAP R/3 extensively, in addition to custom developing many modules of their own.

This university is in the middle of a typical upgrade cycle. They have begun the process of updating their SAP R/3 4.6C system to SAP ERP 6.0 (formerly named mySAP ERP 2005). SAP ERP 6.0 will run on top of SAP NetWeaver — specifically SAP NetWeaver 7.0 (formerly named SAP NetWeaver 2004s). They are also in the process of implementing the SAP NetWeaver Portal, as well as considering using SAP NetWeaver Process Integration (SAP NetWeaver PI — formerly known as SAP NetWeaver Exchange Infrastructure or SAP XI) and SAP NetWeaver Master Data Management (SAP NetWeaver MDM) in the near future.

This university has a small but strong IT team. Our story will focus on Russel, the lead developer of the IT team at this university. Russel has many years of experience in ABAP development to support the university's systems. Like many developers, he reads about the latest ABAP development technologies and techniques, but is somewhat constrained by the release level of the university's R/3 system. Consequently, he feels that his development skills are not up to date; for example, he has done very little ABAP Object-Oriented (ABAP OO) programming and has virtually no web-based development. Still, Russel is quite excited about the future upgrade to SAP ERP 6.0. He sees this as an opportunity to update his skills and learn about the newest ABAP development techniques.

Little does Russel know that he is about to get a crash course in ABAP development on SAP NetWeaver 7.0. In addition to the upgrade activities, the university is just beginning to offer a new distance learning curriculum. Like new offerings at many universities, this distance learning curriculum will offer online versions of many courses for people looking to complete their degrees, or take part in continuing education without disrupting their current career.

In support of this new curriculum, the university realizes that it will need significant new custom development. Their ERP system will house this development and ABAP will be the language in which the system is developed. This project will enable Russel to build the data access, business logic, and user interface aspects of this new system. This project will also be the first time that Russel will build something that entails *enterprise service-oriented architecture* (enterprise SOA).

Please note again that the context for the project that we're going to study throughout this book is fictional. It does not feature an actual university or SAP customer. The characters that we will meet, like Russel, are not real people; however Russel's experiences and reactions to events are based on our (i.e., the authors) experiences, and hopefully will touch a familiar chord with many of you.

Structure of the Book

The structure of this book reflects the workflow of the development project. The first half of the book focuses on creating the data and application logic layers and then service-enabling them. The second half of the book focuses on creating the user interface layers.

▶ **Chapter 1: Workbench Tools and Package Hierarchy**
Before we begin our project, we will review some of the changes and enhancements to the ABAP Workbench. In this chapter, we will look at the new ABAP Editor, the Refactoring Assistant, the new development tools perspectives in transaction SE80, and the new debugger. Lastly, we will create the packages and package hierarchies for the project.

▶ **Chapter 2: Data Dictionary Objects**
In this chapter, we will model the data relationships and build the corresponding Data Dictionary objects. We'll study the tools for generating table maintenance, creating lock objects, and utilizing foreign keys. We'll also explore the new technology of strings and binary strings within transparent tables.

▶ **Chapter 3: Data Persistence Layer**
In this chapter, we'll build the logic that controls the persistence of application data. We'll start by generating persistent object classes for the underlying data dictionary tables created in Chapter 2. Then, we'll build a set of business object classes to hide the inner technical details of the persistent objects. In addition to the new technology of Persistent Objects, we'll show you how to use ZIP compression on large strings.

▶ **Chapter 4: Consuming a Web Service**
Not all project data will originate from one centralized system. For example, in the sample application, some data will be stored in a legacy system and accessed remotely via Web Services. In this chapter, we will examine the process for generating a Web Service proxy object and integrating this proxy into the data persistence layer.

▶ **Chapter 5: Shared Memory Objects**
After some analysis, it will become apparent that the sample application has some static data that will be accessed repeatedly. In this chapter, we

will describe how you can provide the best performance by structuring the data access for this type of data into an ABAP Shared Memory Object.

▶ **Chapter 6: Model Class**

In this chapter, we will begin to implement the core application logic, which is implemented as a Model Class. This same class will later be used as the business logic layer of all the UI technology examples. This chapter focuses primarily on object-oriented design patterns while introducing techniques for sending email and manipulating XML.

▶ **Chapter 7: ABAP and SAP NetWeaver Master Data Management**

This is the first of our "What-If" chapters. Here, we look at an alternative approach to the project where our master data is modeled and stored in SAP NetWeaver Master Data Management, instead of the local Data Dictionary. This chapter will focus on how we would alter the data persistence layer to read this data via the SAP NetWeaver MDM ABAP application programming interface instead of directly from the local database.

▶ **Chapter 8: ABAP Unit**

Before building any additional objects on top of the existing application logic, this is a good point in the project to unit test what has been completed. In this chapter, we'll look at the built-in unit test tool, ABAP Unit, and examine how unit test classes can be integrated directly into the model class.

▶ **Chapter 9: Exposing a Model as a Web Service**

Not all the logic from the sample model class will be exposed via a user interface. Instead, some of the data was designed to be exposed as a Web Service so that it can be accessible to external systems as well. In this chapter, we'll examine the Inside-Out approach for generating Web Services.

▶ **Chapter 10: Exposing a Model as a Web Service Using SAP NetWeaver Process Integration**

This is the second of the two "What-If" chapters. In the previous chapter, we looked at the Inside-Out approach of generating Web Services via remote enabled function modules. In this chapter, we'll look at the world of Enterprise Service Modeling. We'll show you how the same logic could be modeled in SAP NetWeaver Process Integration and then implemented as a server proxy in ABAP using the Outside-In approach.

▶ **Chapter 11: Classic Dynpro UI/ALV Object Model**

In this chapter, we turn our attention to user interface logic. In the sample application requirements, there are a group of internal users who are full time SAP GUI users and who need powerful reporting tools. Therefore, we'll learn how to build a classic Dynpro screen on top of the Model View Controller, which uses the ALV Object Model for its reporting output.

▶ **Chapter 12: Web Dynpro ABAP**
Since most of the sample application's users are not SAP GUI users, we'll look at how you can build a Web Dynpro user interface for these users. This chapter will focus on real world Web Dynpro applications that contain multiple component usages, ALV integration, and table popins.

▶ **Chapter 13: Business Server Pages**
The next user interface use case is for an Internet-facing application. This user interface needs to be highly customized and stateless for scalability. Therefore, in this chapter, we will use Business Server Pages in order to show the flexibility they provide for highly customized style sheets and AJAX integration.

▶ **Chapter 14: Adobe Forms**
Adobe Forms technology offers an interesting paper-like alternative user interface. In this chapter, we'll look at each of the major types of Adobe Forms — print forms, online interactive forms, and offline interactive forms.

▶ **Chapter 15: SAP NetWeaver Portal**
Although we have focused on ABAP as the primary development environment until now, it is also important to see how some of the SAP NetWeaver Portal technologies can be used with the best aspects of ABAP. In this chapter, we'll explore how to wrap each of our user interface examples in iViews within the SAP NetWeaver Portal and how portal eventing can be used for cross iView communication. We'll also look at how we can use SAP NetWeaver Visual Composer to build code-free applications that consume ABAP services.

▶ **Chapter 16: RSS Feed Using an ICF Service Node**
In this chapter, we'll examine how Internet Communication Framework Service Nodes can be combined with XML processing in ABAP to produce interesting Web 2.0 type projects. As the final example of the book, we'll implement an RSS Feed using these technologies.

▶ **Chapter 17: Closing**
In the final chapter, we will look back on the completed project and review the most important points of what has been discussed.

Prerequisites

Whether you are relatively new to ABAP development or an experienced veteran, there is something in this text for everyone. We do, however, assume that the reader is already familiar with the ABAP Workbench and has some development experience in ABAP as of the 4.x release level. We will primarily focus on new techniques and tools that were introduced in the 6.x and higher releases.

The state of the ABAP development environment described in this book is SAP NetWeaver 7.0 SPS10. As SAP ERP 6.0 has been announced to be the primary release of ERP for customers through 2010, SAP expects this to become the "go-to" ERP release for many years to come. Therefore, capabilities of ABAP in SAP NetWeaver 7.0 will likely become the base-line technology level for most customer development as well.

If you don't already have access to a SAP NetWeaver 7.0 system, you can always download the free trial edition from the SAP Developer Network (*https://www.sdn.sap.com/irj/sdn/downloads*). This trial software has a full ABAP development environment, enabling you to recreate nearly all the examples contained within this book.

To help you follow along with the project as it unfolds in this book, we have also provided you with the source code for all examples in the book, as well as many supporting objects that are not discussed in detail on the accompanying CD. This should help to facilitate your skipping certain chapters if you want, without having to forego the prerequisite objects.

The source code on the CD is available in several different formats:

▶ First, there is a transport file. This is the simplest way to import all the development objects that are discussed in this book in their correct packages.

▶ Not all developers have the necessary security to import a transport file. For this reason, we have also included many of the development objects in SAPlink format (the open source XML based mechanism for exchanging ABAP development objects) and plain text files.

For complete instructions on how to work with each of these import formats, see the *ReadMe.pdf* file in the root directory of the CD or Appendix A.

In case you were wondering, please note that we won't forget about older releases just because our primary focus is on SAP NetWeaver 7.0. The technologies that we'll discuss were primarily released since SAP R/3 4.6C. As we introduce each technology, we will try to indicate in which release it was first introduced, and, what differences, if any, there are between the releases.

As of SAP NetWeaver 7.0, SAP's ABAP foundation developers have not stopped innovating around the ABAP environment. As you read this book, dedicated teams are currently working on additional features and powerful new functions for the ABAP development environment. We will point out these anticipated features throughout the book; however they will simply be identified with the notation "Future Functionality."

With the direction of SAP ERP 6.0, SAP NetWeaver 7.0 will be an established release for many years to come. Therefore, some of this future functionality might find its way into SAP NetWeaver 7.0 via backports of the functionality delivered with support packages. Other new features may be too extensive to deliver in this way, and therefore be postponed until the next major release of SAP NetWeaver, or some other, as yet undetermined, delivery mechanism.

Acknowledgments

I would like to thank my wife, Shonna, for her love and support during the entire project, and for understanding how important this project was to me. Additionally, I would like to thank my kids, Kearston and Gavin, for their unconditional love and understanding while Daddy was working. Thanks for putting up with the laptop on the table during dinner and the shortened play time. Without my family's support, the past few months would have been much more difficult.

Thanks to my parents, for giving me the necessary foundation that enabled me to be successful in life. Thanks to my sister, Angie, for her inspiration and support, which gave me the "can-do" attitude that this project required.

I would also like to thank our editor, Stefan Proksch, for enabling me to share my knowledge with the rest of the world. Thanks to the SDN community for supplying great content that allowed me to learn directly from the experts. Last but certainly not least, I would like to thank my co-author, Thomas Jung, for the opportunity to work together on this project.

York (PA), May 2007
Rich Heilman

I also must start off by thanking my wife, Shari. Without her support, I certainly couldn't have completed the work required to create this book. What is even more amazing to me is that this time, she knew exactly what she was getting herself into and yet, she still agreed to let me work on the project. As with all accomplishments in my life, they simply would not have been possible without her love and support!

To my children, Megan and Madison, I owe my thanks as well. To them, it probably seemed like Daddy was hardly around for the last few months, since most nights and weekends he disappeared into his office.

The main character in the book, Russel, is named after my father. It is ironic that when we are teenagers, we want nothing to do with our parents, but as we grow older, we realize that the greatest compliment is hearing someone say how much we are like our parents. Mom and Dad gave me so much while I was growing up. I only wish they could be here today so that I could thank them.

To my friend, Brian McKellar, thanks for getting me started writing on SDN and giving me the opportunity to learn from you during our first book project together. I do and will carry those lessons with me in everything I do.

To the old gang at Kimball, there certainly is a little bit of each of you in this book, as I learned so much from everyone that I have had the opportunity to work with over the years.

To my new colleagues in SAP NetWeaver Product Management, for a virtual team who only sees one another a few times a year, we are an amazingly close-knit group. Everyone is absolutely wonderful to work with and so willing to share his or her knowledge.

To my friend and coworker, Peter McNulty, even before I decided to come to SAP, I figured if there were people this good in Product Management, then it was certainly an organization of which I wanted to be a part. Peter is always available to pitch ideas off of, and our discussions have influenced more than a few sections of this book.

To our editor, Stefan, thanks so much for giving us the opportunity to create this book. Your guidance and support have been instrumental in its completion.

Lastly, to my co-author, Rich, it has been a real pleasure working with you on this project, and to think it all started because you accepted an invitation to co-present with me at SDN Day at the SAP TechEd in Las Vegas in 2006.

Jasper (IN), May 2007
Thomas Jung

In this chapter, we will meet Russel, the ABAP developer, as he begins to explore his newly upgraded development system. His exploration is cut short, however, as he learns of a new project that will force him to channel his development skills into new directions.

1 Workbench Tools and Package Hierarchy

This is a very exciting day for the ABAP developer, Russel. Today is the first day that Russel gets to log onto and explore his newly upgraded ABAP development system. This is something he has been anticipating for quite some time.

For several years, Russel has worked diligently on his employer's SAP R/3 system. His employer is a university that implemented SAP R/3 over 10 years ago. Originally, they implemented SAP R/3 primarily for Financials. Over the years, they have expanded their use of SAP R/3 into Human Resources and Purchasing.

Russel has worked on all kinds of custom development projects. Early on, he worked primarily on reports and data migration programs for the university. As his skills in ABAP grew, however, he found himself working on increasingly more complex projects. He is quite proud of some of the systems that he has custom developed from scratch in the ABAP environment.

Like many SAP customers, however, the university has stayed with the 4.6C Release of SAP R/3 for many years. Still, Russel has kept up with his reading about the new features that were introduced in SAP Web Application Server (SAP Web AS) 6.10, 6.20, SAP NetWeaver 2004, and SAP NetWeaver 7.0, and he has seen many fine new developments emerge over various ABAP releases. But, because he never had a system or projects to work on at these release levels, he feels a little like he has been looking in from the outside. He can see these great new features, but he never gets the opportunity to try them out for himself.

1.1 Log on and Explore

Like any good ABAP developer would do, Russel went immediately to trans-action SE80 — the ABAP Workbench — when he first logged onto the newly upgraded system. Of course, there are many other interesting capabilities to look at, for example, the *Internet Communication Manager* (ICM) configuration in transaction SMICM or the Service Node Hierarchy in transaction SICF; however, Russel will have to wait until later to further investigate these components.

1.1.1 Workbench Object Browser

When entering the ABAP Workbench for the first time after an upgrade, Russel sees a familiar looking interface (see Figure 1.1).

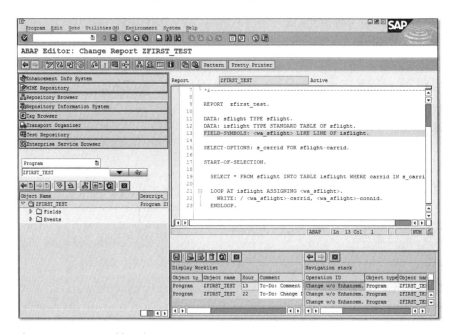

Figure 1.1 ABAP Workbench in SAP NetWeaver 7.0

The classic layout of the object navigation tree on the left side of the page and the object editor on the right side has not changed. You can still navigate through your object view history, up and down the package hierarchy and by drilling into objects via double clicks.

The optional sub-windows for **Display Worklist** and **Navigation stack** are also displayed. Russel had already activated these two features back on SAP

R/3 4.6C, so they are still present with his last entries after the upgrade. Because these features of the ABAP Workbench are optional, they can be activated or deactivated at any time via the **Utilities • Worklist** or **Utilities • Display Navigation Window** menu options.

Like many ABAP developers, Russel likes to use the Worklist to keep track of the items that he still needs to finish or come back to and test. The Navigation stack is another quick way for him to see what objects he has viewed lately. As you will find, for example, when you're using forward navigation to jump between objects frequently, this tool can be very helpful to keep you from getting lost in a deep stack.

1.1.2   Object Browser List

But Russel's attention is drawn to the new *Object Browser* list area (see Figure 1.2). This is the area with rows of buttons at the top, left section of the ABAP Workbench that allow developers to choose their object browser perspective.

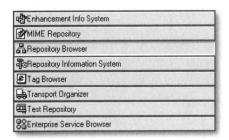

Figure 1.2 Object Browser List

In SAP R/3 4.6C, you basically only had the **Repository Browser** perspective. This view, which allows you to work with core development objects like classes, programs, and data dictionary objects, is still the most commonly used perspective. However, by glancing at the other options, Russel gets a quick preview of some of the expanded functionality now available in the ABAP environment thanks to the upgrade:

▶ **Enhancement Info System and Enterprise Service Browser**
The first and the last options displayed in Russel's Object Browser, as shown in Figure 1.2, were introduced with SAP NetWeaver 7.0 and are specific to new functionality in this release. The **Enhancement Info System** pertains to the new Enhancement Framework (covered in detail in

Chapter 6). Although Russel has only done limited reading about the Enhancement Framework, he can tell that selecting this view causes the Object Browser to display enhancements that have been implemented in his system. To Russel, this seems like a new, easy way to keep track of all of his enhancements in one place.

The other new option introduced in SAP NetWeaver 7.0 is the **Enterprise Service Browser**. Russel suspects that this is the main Object Browser perspective that he would use when working with Enterprise Services. Once someone configures a connection to the *Enterprise Service Repository* of SAP NetWeaver, this browser can be used to get a view of all possible Enterprise Services that can be consumed from ABAP. Russel is fairly certain that he will get an opportunity to use these Enterprise Services in a future project, but little does he know just how soon that will be (see Chapter 4 for more details on using the Enterprise Service Browser).

▶ **Test Repository**

The penultimate option in the list is the **Test Repository**. This item was introduced with SAP NetWeaver 2004. This is a view of your ABAP Unit Test classes. Personally, Russel is a little skeptical about the idea of coding extra unit test classes. He has always done his own "black box" testing informally before handing off any development to the functional owner for extensive integration testing. He has never really put much thought into a more formalized test process. However, with the upgrade, he is open to trying out lots of new ideas and does not want to dismiss the idea of Unit Test classes before he has had a chance to try them out in a first project. Russel's first experiences with Unit Test classes are covered in Chapter 8.

▶ **MIME Repository and Tag Browser**

The remaining options in the Object Browser selection area date back to the early 6.10 Release and 6.20 Release of the SAP Web Application Server. The second and fifth options in the area, **MIME Repository** and **Tag Browser**, come hand-in-hand with the introduction of embedded web functionality in the ABAP environment.

▷ MIME stands for *Multipurpose Internet Mail Extensions* and was a specification originally developed for the transmission of non-ASCII7 characters via SMTP. Although originally conceived as part of the Internet Mail standards, MIME is also the core standard for communicating any non-text data via HTTP as well. For instance, any JPEG images used in the output of a web page would be stored in this repository. Unlike many other web servers, ABAP does not store these MIMEs at the file system level. This would be very complicated, given the multiple application server arrangement of most ABAP-based applications. Instead, the MIMEs are stored in the underlying database. However the **MIME Repository** view in the Object Browser displays the organization of the MIME objects in the familiar File/Folder structure that we are all used to dealing with.

▷ Since web page design is generally based on HTML, it makes sense to also have a **Tag Browser**. Tags are the descriptions of user interface elements that you want to appear in your web page. For instance, an input field is formed by adding the <INPUT> tag to your page's source. In addition to displaying all the standard HTML tags, SAP also uses the **Tag Browser** to organize all the BSP specific tags (*Business Server Pages*, an ABAP specific tool for creating web pages), also known as *BSP Extensions*.

Russel has always been the tried and true ABAP developer focusing on List and Dialog programs. He has never really experimented much with creating web pages, unless you count the time he created an HTML page to share pictures of a family reunion. Nevertheless, he realizes that the time when an ABAP programmer could turn a blind eye to web development has passed. He knows that the future of ABAP development will require him to learn about the new browser-based UI technologies like BSP (see Chapter 13) and Web Dynpro (see Chapter 12).

▶ **Repository Information System and Transport Organizer**
The remaining two options, **Repository Information System** and **Transport Organizer**, are not entirely new tools. Both existed before, but now, they are integrated directly into the ABAP Workbench.

▷ The **Repository Information System** gives you a higher-level view of the organization of ABAP development objects. It allows you to search for objects based on their assignment to an application area, like Materials Management (MM) or Sales and Distribution (S&D). This application area based hierarchy is most useful when trying to find some standard SAP objects that you might want to access or reuse in your own development projects.

▷ The **Transport Organizer** brings the most common functions of the trusty transaction SE10 directly into the ABAP Workbench. For instance, you can now release transport requests or view their contents from the ABAP Workbench. Although this is not state-of-the-art new functionality, the possibilities for integration make this a welcome usability enhancement.

1.1.3 Workbench Settings

Just about the time Russel finished exploring the different Object Browser views, one of his fellow developers, Nathan, stopped by his office and noticed that Russel was exploring the newly upgraded system. Nathan immediately detected that Russel's screen looked quite different than his own, even though they had both been working on the newly upgraded system this morning. Russel explained that it was possible to configure quite a few options about the look and functionality of the ABAP Workbench from the menu options via **Utilities • Settings** (see Figure 1.3).

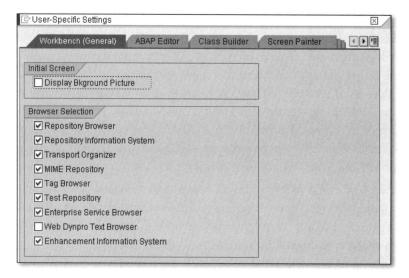

Figure 1.3 Workbench Options — Browser Selection

First Russel showed Nathan how to choose the **Browser Selections** that they want to appear. You can configure the **Object Browser** list that we just looked at in detail, or remove items that you would seldom use.

1.1.4 New ABAP Editor

Russel then asked Nathan if he had an opportunity to try the new ABAP Editor. Although Russel had seen articles on the new editor on SAP Developer Network (SDN, *http://sdn.sap.com*), he might not have realized that there was a new editor in this release if he had not navigated through the **Workbench**

Options screens. In many systems, the new editor is not selected by default; however, after selecting the option for **Front-End Editor (New)** in the **ABAP Editor** tab, sub-tab **Editor**, of the **User-Specific Settings** dialog, as shown in Figure 1.4, he was able to start exploring the new editor.

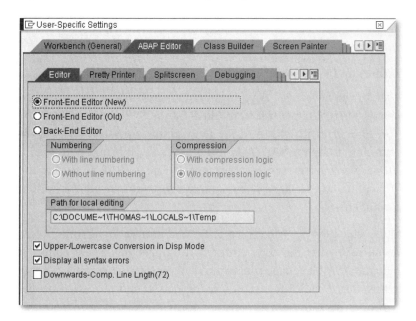

Figure 1.4 Workbench Options — Editor Options

Editor Requirements

First, you should note that the new ABAP Editor is delivered in two parts. The first requirement is the software that runs on the developer's client machine as part of the *SAP GUI for Windows*. This front-end control for the editor was delivered for the 6.40 (and higher) Release of the SAP GUI as of patch level 11. So, before using the new ABAP Editor, you need to ensure that your SAP GUI is up to date.

However, having the correct SAP GUI version alone is not enough. The back-end integration into the ABAP Workbench requires ABAP coding that is delivered along with the ABAP system's release level. The new editor integration into the ABAP Workbench was originally delivered only to SAP NetWeaver 7.0 and higher releases.

This means that our friend, Russel, has the necessary release level and SAP GUI to use the new ABAP Editor.

Editor Backport

However, if you don't yet have SAP NetWeaver 7.0, don't lose hope. Due to popular demand for the new ABAP Editor, SAP has backported the development to SAP Web AS 6.20 and SAP NetWeaver 2004. This backport was delivered to customers via Basis Support Package 59 for SAP Web AS 6.20 and Basis Support Package 18 for SAP NetWeaver 2004.

Editor Features and Functions

Because Nathan had never read anything about the new editor, he asked Russel "So what is so great about this new ABAP Editor?" "Plenty," said Russel. He went on to explain that because the new editor is primarily a piece of software running inside the SAP GUI on the user's PC, it brings with it a lot of user interface enhancements. Furthermore, the new ABAP Editor has the kinds of functionality that have been standard for years in other development environments.

For example, you now have code coloring and syntax highlighting. This front-end control that is the code editor is no longer just a text editor. It understands the ABAP language syntax and contains a mini-compiler. So, as you type, the source code is constantly being parsed and processed on the front-end in order to apply syntax-sensitive formatting.

For instance, you see keywords being formatted with a different text color than comments or data variables. You also have the ability to do code collapse; for example, you can take a complex IF statement and collapse the entire structure. This hides the inner complexity of the statement, making the overall flow of the application more readable. At the same time, you can quickly see the contents of the collapsed area via a popup dialog when you mouse over the area, which is shown in Figure 1.5.

The new ABAP Editor has numerous other usability enhancements such as a built-in split screen view, an extended clipboard, bookmark and breakpoint integration, customizable code templates, and markers to indicate the changed sections since your last save.

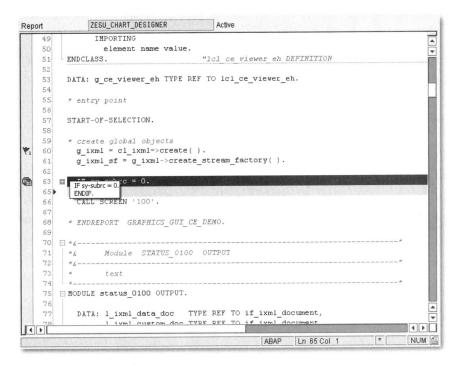

Figure 1.5 New ABAP Editor

Code Completion

Russel doesn't know it yet, but SAP is not finished with the enhancements that they have planned for this new editor. If Russel could peak inside the development offices in Walldorf (i.e., SAP Headquarters), he would see that developers are hard at work to bring extended code completion and quick info to the new editor for a future release.

> **Future Functionality**
>
> These new features will introduce intelligence completion, similar to the pattern insertion functionality that we have today, to the developer with the click of a mouse. This brings the robust object completion or smart insertion found in other development languages to the ABAP environment (see Figure 1.6).
>
> The difference with the ABAP environment is that it uses so many global objects. Inside an ABAP object, you might reference any number of data dictionary objects, function modules, or global classes without the need for any forward declaration. Yet the code completion and quick info of the new ABAP editor is able to make a call from the frontend to talk to the back-end server and retrieve these details on demand.

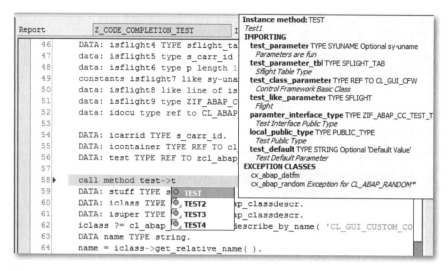

Figure 1.6 Future Functionality — Code Completion

1.1.5 Additional New Workbench Tools

The new ABAP Editor alone was enough to get Russel excited about the upgrade, but he knew that he had other new tools to explore in the ABAP Workbench as well.

Web Dynpro ABAP

The tool that made Russel positively giddy with anticipation was *Web Dynpro ABAP*. He had already read so much about Web Dynpro ABAP. He knew that Web Dynpro ABAP was the new default UI development tool for ABAP going forward. Although Web Dynpro is a tool that creates development objects that can be run within a browser, it isn't tied to just that delivery mechanism. Nor does it require that an ABAP developer learn anything about HTML or JavaScript. All of the inner complexities of the UI coding are hidden behind a simple and uniform meta-model for describing the user interface. Although Russel didn't have time today to navigate throughout Web Dynpro (he'll get his chance in Chapter 12), he saw enough to know that he was looking forward to working on a project that employed this tool.

The screen designer alone, shown in Figure 1.7, made Web Dynpro ABAP development look very appealing. You will note that all the UI elements are in well-defined groups on the left side of the designer. In the middle, you'll see a WYSIWYG editor (*What You See Is What You Get*) of the screen as it is being built. You can even drag and drop UI elements directly on this area.

On the right side of the screen you see the hierarchy of the UI elements. Personally, Russel thinks that the drag and drop from the toolbox is a nice feature, but when working with a complex layout, he realizes that this element hierarchy will be the best way to interact with the design.

Russel is further impressed by the property box for each UI element. Although common in other development environments, this property box is one of the few places where in ABAP you can easily configure all the UI element properties. Ultimately, Russel feels like he can be much more productive designing transactions' screens in the Web Dynpro tools than he is today using the ABAP Dialog Screen Painter.

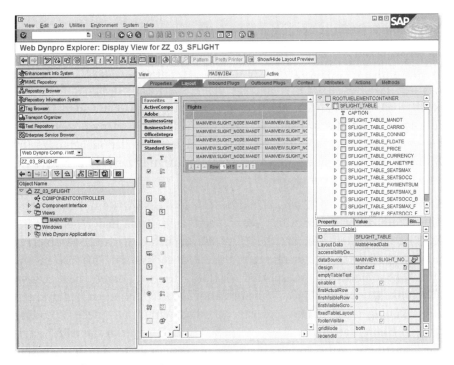

Figure 1.7 Web Dynpro ABAP Designer

Business Server Pages

As it turns out, Web Dynpro ABAP is not the only way to create content in the ABAP Workbench that is targeted for deployment to a web browser. When the Basis layer was renamed to SAP Web Application Server (SAP Web AS) with Release 6.10, it was more than just a name change.

SAP added full web server functionality to the core ABAP stack through the addition of the *Internet Communication Manager* (ICM). This underlying technology is used as the core communication channel for Web Services as well as Web Dynpro ABAP.

But, unlike Web Dynpro, where you can't directly access the generated UI coding, the *Business Server Pages* (BSP) tool is a web-specific development environment. Using this perspective of the ABAP Workbench, you can code custom HTML and JavaScript pages. Later in Chapter 12 and Chapter 13, Russel will get the opportunity to see how both tools can be useful for creating different kinds of browser-based applications.

Extensible Stylesheet Language Transformation

As Russel was navigating through some of the new object types in the ABAP Workbench, he encountered the *Extensible Stylesheet Language Transformation* (XSLT) editor. XSLT is a language that is specifically designed for transformations involving XML. XSLT is not something that SAP invented; instead it is an open standards based language that is found in many development environments. You should think of XSLT as a manipulation language for XML (i.e., it's a way to define an easy path for creating new XML or XHTML structures from an existing XML).

SAP also added the XSLT language processor to the ABAP Kernel and a complete XSLT editor to the ABAP Workbench. One of the major benefits for XLST of being integrated into the ABAP Workbench is that an XSLT object is now stored like any other object in the ABAP repository. This also means that XSLT objects are transported via the *Transport Management System* (TMS) like any other object. Transformations are tightly integrated into the ABAP coding environment and can be called within any piece of coding using the new statement CALL TRANSFORMATION. However in the ABAP environment, there is the added capability of being able to transform native ABAP data types to and from XML as well.

Refactoring

The concept of *refactoring* is not new to the ABAP environment. Every programmer, at one time or another, has had to make changes to a program in order to better organize its structure. In the early days of ABAP, Russel used to have to work with programs that got too large over time. Consequently, he would edit them to move some of the functionality into more manageable forms, and, when necessary, group the forms into separate includes.

All of the aforementioned activities fall under the concept of refactoring; however, refactoring as a normal development practice has really taken root with the advent of object-oriented programming. It is increasingly common to have to refactor your class structures as they grow larger. This often means breaking up a single class into multiple parent/child classes and reassigning the original set of methods among the new class hierarchy.

With the SAP NetWeaver 2004 Release, SAP began introducing some basic refactoring tools within the ABAP Workbench, which is the only available option that enables you to move methods between parent and child objects. You can access the **Refactoring Assistant** within the Class Builder from the menu **Utilities • Refactoring Assistant**.

Future Functionality

With future releases of SAP NetWeaver, SAP plans to expand the toolset offered within the area of refactoring. Figure 1.8 shows some of the new refactoring tools available for standard program code.

One example of this new refactoring functionality will be the ability to rename a method or function module. The **Refactoring Assistant** will do more than simply enable you to perform a **Find and Replace** operation. It will allow you to change all references to the object that is being renamed globally, even if that means changing other development objects. These future refactoring tools will also have a preview option that allows you to gauge the scope of your changes before you make them.

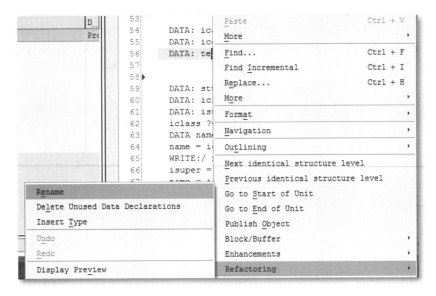

Figure 1.8 Future Functionality — Refactoring Assistant

1.1.6 Debugger

Every developer knows that a critical part of any development environment is its debugger. With SAP NetWeaver 2004, there is a new debugger that keeps up with much of the great new innovation found in the rest of the ABAP Workbench.

Before SAP NetWeaver 2004, the debugger was limited in what kinds of UI controls it could use because the debugger actually ran within the same execution space as the program it was debugging. Therefore, if the debugger contained UI controls that required a control flush or commit work, they could potentially disrupt the flow of the application that was being debugged.

SAP solved this program by making the new debugger a two-process debugger. Therefore, the debugger now runs in a separate work process and remote attaches to the application that is being debugged. This opened up the opportunity for tremendous innovation in a debugger that had seen few changes over time.

When trying the debugger for the first time, Russel noticed that the code was displayed using the new ABAP editor as long as the system met the requirements (i.e., these were described earlier) to have the new editor. The additional functionality provided includes your being able to mouse over a variable and see its type definition and current value (see Figure 1.9).

The new debugger is also modular. There are several preconfigured desktops with a selection of the debugger tools on them; however any developer can choose what tools he or she wants and how he/she wants them arranged on the screen. You can save these custom desktop arrangements of tools for future debugger sessions.

Besides all the traditional tools such as the ability to drill down into structure and internal table values or see ABAP object details, the new debugger also has a suite of highly specialized tools. For instance, internal tables can be downloaded to Microsoft Excel for further comparison. Figure 1.10 shows the built-in comparison tool, accessible via the **Diff** tab in the debugger, which allows you to make some very powerful comparisons, even between two internal tables, without ever leaving the debugger.

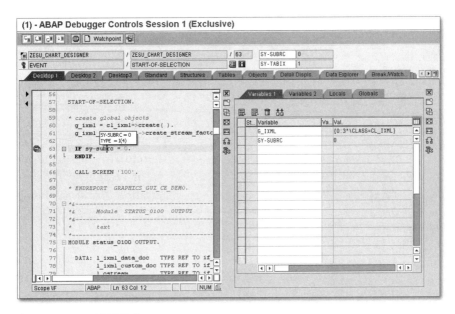

Figure 1.9 New ABAP Debugger

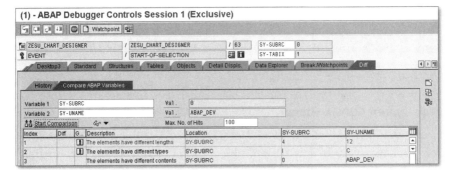

Figure 1.10 ABAP Debugger Variable Comparison

Debugger XML Viewer

XML processing is becoming increasingly more prevalent in normal ABAP programming. Commonly used in web development and Enterprise Services, it is just a matter of time before you will be able to view the contents of an XML stream in the debugger. XML streams are frequently stored in memory as binary strings, making them nearly impossible to interpret in the old debugger. Figure 1.11 shows the capabilities of the new debugger, which includes its ability to not only translate binary strings, but also to display XML streams in a more readable format for users.

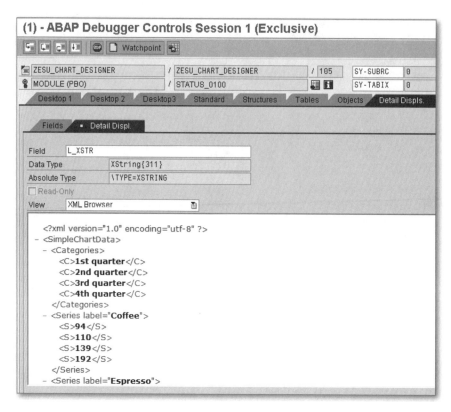

Figure 1.11 ABAP Debugger XML Viewer

Web Dynpro ABAP Debugger

Lastly, with the introduction of Web Dynpro ABAP with SAP NetWeaver 7.0, we have a whole new type of object to potentially debug. Fortunately, the ABAP debugger works just as well within applications that run in a browser. By setting an External Breakpoint, you can debug Web Dynpro ABAP, Web Services, and BSP applications easily and without requiring additional setup on the server.

Web Dynpro goes even farther by introducing a special debugger tool (available as of SAP NetWeaver 7.0 SPS9) for interacting with a Web Dynpro component. Figure 1.12 shows this tool in action. The special Web Dynpro ABAP debugger tools allow you to view the component structure, UI controls and their properties, and even the context at runtime.

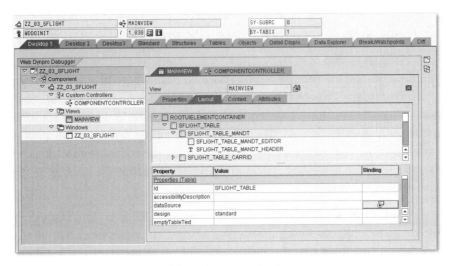

Figure 1.12 Special Debugger Tool for Web Dynpro ABAP

1.2 Package Hierarchy for the Project

Unfortunately Russel's fun exploring the upgrades to the ABAP Workbench had to draw to a close. Along with the SAP ERP 6.0 upgrade, the university that he works for has an ambitious new custom development project. Russel will have to turn his attention to this new project.

Still, he feels that even this brief run through the ABAP Workbench has provided him with a good foundation. In actuality, he hasn't even begun to scratch the surface, given all the new tools that he will be working with over the next few weeks.

When Russel arrived at the project kick-off meeting, he was surprised to see so many people in the room. Since he hadn't heard a thing about this project prior to the meeting, he assumed that his role would be relatively insignificant. The project manager quickly dispelled that idea after announcing that the university had decided to create an online continuing education program. The action items for the ABAP development team were to support this effort with several key pieces of new development.

1.2.1 Project Requirements

First, the students in this new program would have to register for the online program via the existing registration website. The student records would be stored in a separate system that holds the traditional student records as well. Likely some form of interface will have to be written to access this existing, legacy student database.

The new system will require a self-service website where professors can go to maintain details about the courses they will teach and contact information. The professors have also requested an easy means in which to communicate their weekly course assignments to their online students. The administration office also wants a new system to track the course registrations so that they can run some basic accounting reports to gauge the success of the new online program.

The administration workers already are heavy SAP GUI users and want their reports to be integrated with their existing SAP GUI transactions. For all the self-service functions that the professors will use, they want to be able to access these pages via Single Sign-On (SSO) using the new role-based *SAP NetWeaver Portal*. Lastly, any web pages that are externally facing to the students need to run with no assumptions about what Internet Browser the user has. They will need to be able to support a large number of simultaneous users as well.

When Russel left the meeting, he understood that he certainly had his work cut out for him. He had only a few weeks to build this entire online system from scratch. At the same time, he still wanted to use this opportunity to learn as much as possible. He already knew that he wanted to separate the business logic from the user interface layer. By creating a single set of business logic based model classes, he could reuse this same logic throughout the different user interface technologies that he was already imagining would be needed to fulfill all the user requirements.

1.2.2 Package Hierarchy

After returning to his office, Russel wanted to forge ahead and lay down the foundation work for the project while everything was fresh in his mind. Even though he had only been to the kick-off meeting and didn't have detailed requirements yet, he thought that he knew enough to begin structuring his package hierarchy.

On Release 4.6C and before, all ABAP development objects had to be placed into a development class. However this development class really didn't afford much functionality other than the ability to group objects together in a folder like a structure. To further limit the usability of development classes, it was not possible to nest the objects within each other to create any kind of hierarchy.

However, with subsequent releases, the concept of the development class was renamed to the package. This is more than just a name change for semantic reasons, as the package assumes far more functionality and importance than its development class predecessor.

First, *packages* can be nested to create *package hierarchies* and that was exactly what Russel intended to do. He wanted to create one high level package for all the development objects that would make up this online course system. Then he wanted to logically group the remaining objects into separate sub-packages under the main package.

He started out in the ABAP Workbench and chose the option to create a new package, as seen in Figure 1.13, from the **Development Coordination** tab of the **Object Selection** dialog. This first package, ZCOURSE_SYSTEM, would be designated as a **Main Package** in the **Package Type** field. The values in the **Transport Layer** and **Software Component** fields are proposed by the system and almost never changed in customer systems.

The **Software Component** field is primarily used within SAP to separate development objects between layers, such as the separation between Basis and Application objects. The **Transport Layer** is used in development systems that have multiple transport landscapes. This is also extremely rare for all but the largest of SAP's customers, in which case the possible values for the field are customer specific.

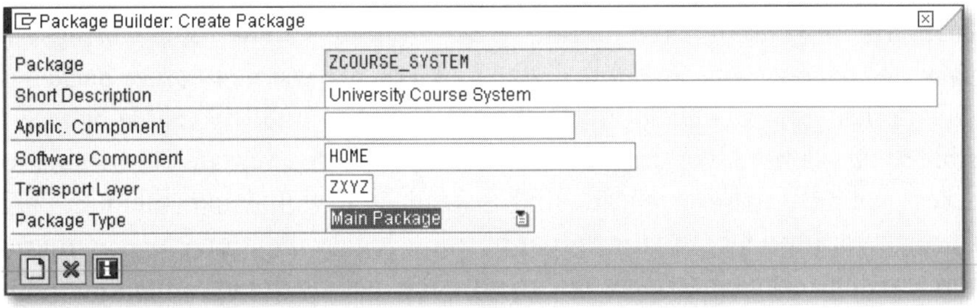

Package Builder: Create Package		⊠
Package	ZCOURSE_SYSTEM	
Short Description	University Course System	
Applic. Component		
Software Component	HOME	
Transport Layer	ZXYZ	
Package Type	Main Package	

Figure 1.13 Package Creation

Figure 1.14 shows the package hierarchy that Russel has initially come up with:

▶ First, he wants to separate out all of his data dictionary objects and the classes that will directly access the data dictionary into the package ZCS_DDIC.

▶ Next, he will establish a separate set of packages for all of his business logic, or model classes called ZCS_MODEL. The sub-package, ZCS_MODEL_ ESOA, under the business logic package, will house the Enterprise Services that will be wrappers for his core business objects.

▶ Lastly, he wants a separate layer of the package hierarchy for the user interface objects. Within this level of the package, ZCS_UI, he can then further segregate between the different UI technologies that he plans to utilize.

Package	ZCOURSE_SYSTEM		Saved

Properties	Use access	Package interfaces	Packages included	Package Hierarchy

Package Hierarchy	Check	Description
▽ ⊞ ZCOURSE_SYSTEM	✖	University Course System
⊞ ZCS_DDIC	✖	University Course System Data Dictionary
▽ ⊞ ZCS_MODEL	✖	University Course System Application Logic
⊞ ZCS_MODEL_ESOA	✖	University Course System - Enterprise Services
▽ ⊞ ZCS_UI	✖	University Course System User Interface
⊞ ZCS_UI_BSP	✖	University Course System - User Interface - BSP
⊞ ZCS_UI_DYNPRO	✖	University Course System - User Interface - Dynpro
⊞ ZCS_UI_WEBDYNPRO	✖	University Course System - User Interface - Web Dynpro

Figure 1.14 Package Hierarchy

"So why," you may ask, "should he go through the trouble of organizing his objects into this hierarchy?" As you know, segregating objects makes the development more organized, which, in turn, helps to support the solution by making it easier to find the individual development object components.

Furthermore, this package hierarchy has additional benefits. By using the package concept, you can control which objects are visible to other packages (i.e., perhaps not all development objects should be publicly visible or accessible). For example, you might not want any outside programs to be able to access your database layer directly. Instead, you would like them to pass through your model class for proper business logic validation. You can therefore create package interfaces that expose the data dictionary objects only to the model class, but still present all the model class objects globally.

With the packages created in advance, Russel has established a sound foundation for the rest of his development. Next, he'll begin the project wholeheartedly by creating his first development objects within these packages.

Russel has his project requirements and is ready to immerse himself in development. Before he starts any coding however, he will outline how he wants to store the data in the database for the project. This will drive the creation of the majority of his data dictionary objects.

2   Data Dictionary Objects

The most important aspect that you need to consider before actually building your data dictionary objects is to figure out the data layout and relationships. For Russel, that means understanding his business requirements.

2.1   Designing Data Relationships

He starts with the basic requirement of tracking information about courses. For now, he knows that everything will revolve around some sort of central course table that will track the details of each course, such as the cost of the course and the scheduled time of the course.

Another known requirement is tracking a long text description of the course and an HTML-formatted syllabus. On his old SAP R/3 4.6C system, these longer text fields would have posed a bit of a challenge; however, as of SAP Web AS Release 6.10, using strings and binary strings in transparent tables is now possible. Russel even toys around with the idea of compressing the HTML syllabi by using application logic, so he plans for this field to be a binary string.

By looking at the required information that he also needs to track about each course, Russel develops a better understanding of what supporting tables he will need. First, each course has to have one faculty member as its owner. Therefore, he will have a relationship where each course has one faculty member assigned to it, but each faculty member record could have none, one, or many courses assigned to him or her.

He will also need a table to hold his student details. Each course will of course have more than one student assigned to it (at least that's what the administration hopes). Most students will also be taking more than one course while at the university. To support these requirements, Russel decides that the best approach is to create a course registration table that will pair the student and course table for each unique registration.

As far as reference tables for the course are concerned, each course must also be part of or applied to a degree major. Therefore, it makes sense to pull out the course majors and their descriptions and insert them into a separate set of tables.

That leaves Russel with two major business requirements that are not yet represented in his data model:

▶ The first requirement is to have a validation during registration that checks to ensure that students have completed all the prerequisites for a course. Since each course could have none, one, or many prerequisites, he decides to create a separate course prerequisite table with a foreign key relationship to the main course table.

▶ He also has a very similar requirement for course assignments. The faculty has requested a way to publish their course assignment details each week, which means that for each course, you will have many separate assignment records. Similar to the prerequisites table, Russel chooses to create an assignment table with a foreign key relationship to the course table.

> **Notice**
>
> Please note that all the development objects that are described in this book are available on the CD that accompanies this book. By no means have we included step-by-step instructions in the text to recreate every object that is part of the solution we are building.

Before Russel jumps into transaction SE80 and starts creating data dictionary objects, he outlines his ideas for his database layout.

2.1.1 Table Relationship Graphic

Different developers use different methods to design their data table relationships. Russel's favorite method has always been just to pull out a piece of paper and sketch the relationships. Later, as he creates the actual data dictionary objects in transaction SE80, the system can generate graphical representations of the relationships he has defined by providing living documentation. Figure 2.1 shows an example of a graph that was ultimately generated for Russel's finished data relationships. You can generate just such a graph from within the data dictionary maintenance of transaction SE80 by clicking on the **Graphic** button on the application toolbar (see Figure 2.2).

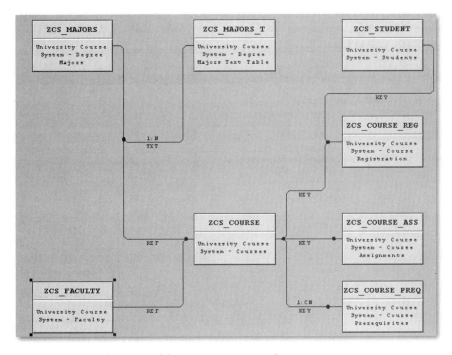

Figure 2.1 Data Table Layout of the Course System Database

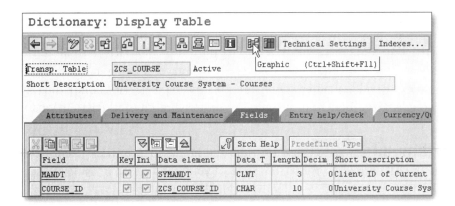

Figure 2.2 How to Generate a Table Relationship Graphic

2.1.2   SAP Data Modeler

Other developers might prefer a more formalized tool. Perhaps Russel's handwritten approach would not work if he had a much larger data model to design. If you want a formal data modeling tool, but still want to stay within the SAP tools environment, you might want to look at transaction SD11 — the SAP Data Modeler (see Figure 2.3).

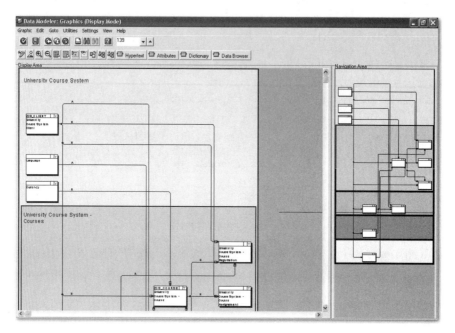

Figure 2.3 Transaction SD11 — Graphical Data Model

Transaction SD11 may not have as elegant a user interface as some third-party tools, but it certainly has the clear advantage of being integrated into the ABAP development environment. This means that you can link directly from your data model objects into the underlying physical data dictionary objects.

There is also forward navigation from the model map to transaction SE80 and the data browser, transaction SE16. If you're interested in using transaction SD11, you should consider exploring the SAP sample model, BC_TRAVEL, which diagrams the well-known SFLIGHT demo tables.

2.2 Data Dictionary Fixed Value Domains

Now that Russel has a good idea of how he wants to store the data, and more importantly, how the relationships should be represented between each section of data, he can start creating the ABAP data dictionary objects. Because Russel has thought through his data dictionary relationships in advance, he can work through the object creation process more systematically. Therefore, he will start by creating many of the more atomic objects first, such as domains and data dictionary elements.

The process for creating domains and data dictionary elements has not really changed much since SAP R/3 4.6C. Russel has quickly assembled data dictionary tables before, but for this project, he wants to be even more meticulous with their design. He knows that he must plan carefully how he creates his objects in order to support the project requirement for easy translation of the user interface into multiple languages. The proper use of certain features in the ABAP data dictionary, even at the domain level, can have a great impact on just how easy it is to translate a system's user interface.

The first level where this proper planning and special techniques come together is with the data element for semesters (see Figure 2.4). The university currently has three separate semesters — Fall, Spring, and Summer. The semester value is going to be an important selection in several different places in the system.

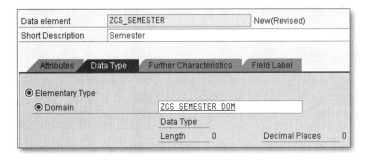

Figure 2.4 Semester Data Element

Russel knows that he needs to have an easily translated description for his semester value since it will be displayed in the user interface. He also knows that the list will be small and fairly static.

It will be a major undertaking to add a new type of semester to the university's offering, so he doesn't have to plan for user-level maintenance of the semester domain values. Given these requirements, he decides that the best approach is to create a fixed value domain for its ease of definition, yet built-in support for value language translation.

2.2.1　Single Value Domains

Russel starts by creating his data element, ZCS_SEMESTER. Typically, when Russel creates a new data element, it is primarily to ensure that he has the translatable field label. Quite often, he doesn't even create a corresponding domain unless he has a value list or needs to set the uppercase/lowercase flag for the stored value, which, by the way, he really wishes SAP would add as an option to the data element-data type definition options. Even on SAP R/3 4.6C, most other settings can be made from the **Data Type** tab of the data element.

One real advantage to using fixed value domains is how nicely they turn out in the user interface. When referencing a field that uses this domain in a drop-down list box, only the descriptions for the current language will be displayed. This allows you to still use short and efficient codes for storage in the database. Since the semester field will be used in several different data tables, Russel decides to go with a single character, numeric character field. Switching to the **Value Range** tab (see Figure 2.5), Russel is able to maintain the possible values for his domain right in the domain creation screen.

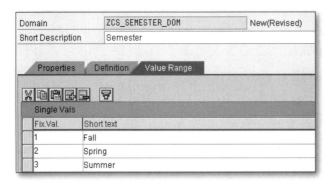

Figure 2.5 Semester Domain Value Range Maintenance

2.2.2　Interval Value Domains

But this is not the only fixed domain that Russel knows that he needs to create in the data dictionary. His first domain used only single values; however, he also has to create a domain for the course year. Since the university stores course information that only dates back to 1970, there is no reason for this domain to go any farther back in time. Russel also doesn't want to get a call in the future requesting that he add more years to the domain. He figures he should be long retired by the year 2060, so that should prevent him from being bothered with any requests (see Figure 2.6).

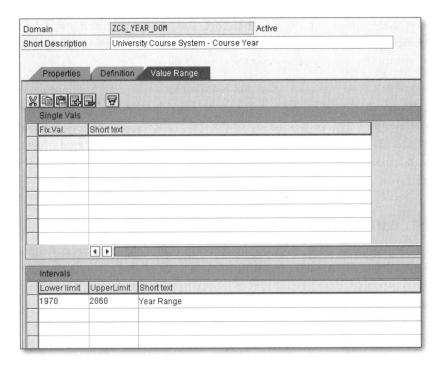

Figure 2.6 Course Year Value Range Domain

This interval will now be used by the ABAP value help systems to automatically generate input help that only accepts values within these limits. You can also add logic in the model class to read the value range intervals from the data dictionary for custom validations.

2.3   Data Dictionary Text Tables

Russel then comes to the first table object for creation in the data dictionary — the offered degree majors. The degree majors have a similar requirement in that they need to be translated into several languages, yet they need to have short codes so that can be stored in the database.

Unlike the semester's domain, the degree majors' value set is much larger. To further complicate the situation, the value listing for degree majors is also far more volatile. The listing of what majors are offered will change from semester to semester. Moreover, the descriptions might need to be changed mid-semester. The requirement is to have a user-accessible maintenance tool for the degree majors; however, the changes need to undergo an approval process that is tightly controlled. Therefore, Russel determines that standard table maintenance will provide the necessary controls, thanks to its integration into the *Transport Management System* (TMS).

Ultimately, Russel wants to have one maintenance transaction where users can create new degree major codes, maintain the descriptions for the codes, and retain the language translation of the descriptions. Although to the end user, this functionality will appear to be available in one integrated object, behind the scenes, Russel will need to create several separate data dictionary objects.

2.3.1   Data Elements and Domains

Russel begins crafting his text table by creating a **Data element** for his degree major code (see Figure 2.7). He wants to use a three-character alpha/numeric code. This provides the flexibility required to have quite a few different combinations, which is necessary because different departments want to have different standards for how they come up with their degree codes.

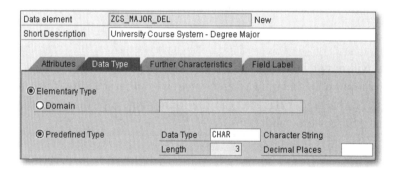

Figure 2.7 Degree Majors Data Element

Next Russel knows that he will need to store a relatively lengthy short text description for each degree major. Part of the requirements he was assigned is that this short text field must accept both uppercase and lowercase letters. Therefore he must create a domain, as shown in Figure 2.8, in addition to the data element for the **Short Description** field since the **Lower Case** flag can only be set at the domain level.

| Domain | ZCS_MAJOR_DESC_DOM | New |
| Short Description | University Course System - Degree Major Description | |

Properties | Definition | Value Range

Format

Data Type	CHAR	Character String
No. Characters	60	
Decimal Places	0	

Output Characteristics

Output Length	60
Convers. Routine	
☐ Sign	
☑ Lower Case	

Figure 2.8 Degree Majors Description Domain

2.3.2 Transparent Table Creation and Relationships

Next Russel will start creating the tables that will hold the majors and their descriptions. That's right; we said *tables*. It's necessary to have two tables in order to create the one-to-many relationship between a major code and each of its description records per language. One table will hold only the major codes. The second table will hold the multiple descriptions for each code.

Key Table: Delivery Class Settings

Russel begins by creating the lead table in this relationship — the one that will store only the codes. The first important setting is on the **Delivery and Maintenance** tab (see Figure 2.9). He sets the **Delivery Class** to **C** for Customizing and the **Data Browser/Table View Maintenance** field to **Display/Maintenance Allowed with Restrictions**.

These two settings are important to the way that Russel wants to allow the data to be maintained in this table. The customizing delivery class setting will classify this data as customizing. Therefore, later, when table maintenance is used to maintain the tables' entries, it will record the entries into a customizing transport request according to the client's TMS settings. Similarly, the second setting also controls whether table maintenance can be generated for this table.

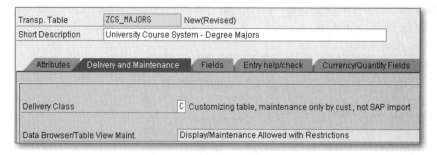

Figure 2.9 Degree Majors Main Table Maintenance Settings

Key Table: Field Definition

Then, he creates the fields for this table (see Figure 2.10). He only needs the client field (MANDT) and the major's code field (MAJOR).

Field	Key	Initi...	Data element	Data Ty...	Length	Deci...	Short Description
MANDT	✓	✓	SYMANDT	CLNT	3	0	Client ID of Current User
MAJOR	✓	✓	ZCS_MAJOR_DEL	CHAR	3	0	University Course System - De

Transp. Table ZCS_MAJORS Active
Short Description University Course System - Degree Majors

Attributes Delivery and Maintenance Fields Entry help/check Currency/Quantity Fields

Srch Help Predefined Type 1 / 2

Figure 2.10 Degree Majors Main Table Fields

Key Table: Technical Settings

But we are not quite finished with the settings on the ZCS_MAJORS table just yet. Russel needs to maintain the **Technical Settings** for this table. Although we recommend setting the **Data class** and **Size category** appropriately for easy classification, what you should really pay attention to in the **Maintain Technical Settings** screen are the **Buffering** settings. Because the values in the Degree Majors table will be changed infrequently, Russel has decided that he wants to take advantage of the built-in data buffering functionality of the SAP NetWeaver Application Server ABAP.

Russel checks **Fully Buffered** for this table (see Figure 2.11) since this table contains only the data keys. Therefore, for the first single record request to go to the database, the system will actually read all the records. The records are placed into shared physical memory on the application server; consequently, a second read from this table will fetch the results from memory, thereby avoiding a trip to the database. You should note that this approach could have tremendous performance improvements for frequently read, but mostly static data.

Dictionary: Maintain Technical Settings

Name	ZCS_MAJORS		Transparent Table
Short text	University Course System - Degree Majors		
Last Change	ABAP_DEV	11/29/2006	
Status	Active	Saved	

Logical storage parameters

Data class	APPL2	Organization and customizing
Size category	0	Data records expected: 0 to 100,000

Buffering

- ○ Buffering not allowed
- ○ Buffering allowed but switched off
- ◉ Buffering switched on

Buffering type

- ☐ Single records buff.
- ☐ Generic Area Buffered   No. of key fields
- ☑ Fully Buffered

☐ Log data changes
☐ Write access only with JAVA

Figure 2.11 Degree Majors Main Table Technical Settings

Description Table: Delivery Class Settings

Now Russel is ready to create the second table in this set, ZCS_MAJORS_T. He sets the **Delivery and Maintenance** settings to the same values that we just discussed for the main table.

Description Table: Field Definition

You can see in Figure 2.12 that Russel has arranged the fields of the table in a very particular order. Like all client-dependent tables in an ABAP system, the first key is MANDT. Then he starts the main keys with the language key (SPRAS) and then the major code (MAJOR). Lastly, he has the description field

(MAJOR_DESC) that he created the domain and data element for earlier. Later, when he maintains the buffering settings for this table, you'll see why the order of the keys is so important.

Transp. Table	ZCS_MAJORS_T	Inactive
Short Description	University Course System - Degree Majors Text Table	

Attributes	Delivery and Maintenance	Fields	Entry help/check	Currency/Quantity Fields

Srch Help   Predefined Type   1 / 4

Field	Key	Initi...	Data element	Data Ty...	Length	Deci...	Short Description
MANDT	☑	☑	SYMANDT	CLNT	3	0	Client ID of Current User
SPRAS	☑	☑	SPRAS	LANG	1	0	Language Key
MAJOR	☑	☑	ZCS_MAJOR_DEL	CHAR	3	0	University Course System - De
MAJOR_DESC	☐	☐	ZCS_MAJOR_DESC	CHAR	60	0	University Course System - De

Figure 2.12 Degree Majors Text Table Fields

Description Table: Foreign Key Relationships

But first Russel needs to create the relationship between his main table and this text table, which he does by creating a foreign key relationship for the MAJOR field of the ZCS_MAJORS_T table.

In the foreign key relationship screen, this special relationship is created by choosing **Key fields of a text table** under the **Foreign key field type** (see Figure 2.13). This little setting has a very powerful impact. It allows the system to automatically use the correct description for the majors' codes when used in value helps and drop-down list boxes.

Description Table: Technical Settings

We now turn our attention to the **Buffering** values on the **Maintain Technical Settings** screen again (see Figure 2.14). Note that when records are read from the main table, they are most likely also going to read a corresponding record from the description table. However, unlike when we read from the main table, we don't necessarily want to buffer the entire table on the first read.

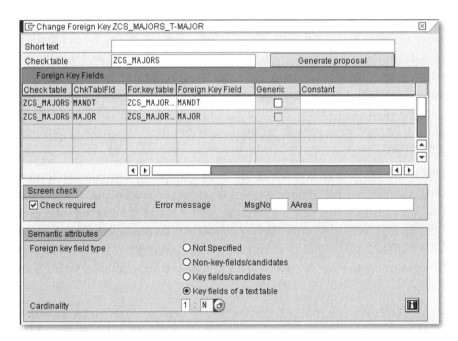

Figure 2.13 Degree Majors Text Table Relationship

Dictionary: Maintain Technical Settings

Name	ZCS_MAJORS_T		Transparent Table
Short text	University Course System - Degree Majors Text Table		
Last Change	ABAP_DEV	11/29/2006	
Status	Active	Saved	

Logical storage parameters

Data class   APPL2   Organization and customizing
Size category   0   Data records expected: 0 to 9,100

Buffering
- ○ Buffering not allowed
- ○ Buffering allowed but switched off
- ◉ Buffering switched on

Buffering type
- ☐ Single records buff.
- ☑ Generic Area Buffered   No. of key fields   2
- ☐ Fully Buffered

☐ Log data changes
☐ Write access only with JAVA

Figure 2.14 Degree Majors Text Table Technical Settings

A user can only be logged onto the system in one language. Therefore, when a user requests a record for a single language, only the rest of the description records for that language need to be buffered. Although this buffer is shared across users, there is no reason to load the descriptions for all languages. Instead, you should wait until the first request for a particular language key to cache all of their values. Therefore, if a particular language is not used, it will not be needlessly consuming precious buffer memory on the application server.

This is also a good reason to set up logon groups on separate application servers organized by commonly used languages. For example, if everyone who uses English logs onto Application Server X and if everyone who uses German logs onto Application Server Y, you will get the most efficient use of table buffering for language-specific tables. Of course this is just one of many factors that come into play with regard to how you should set up your logon groups.

Russel can easily control the buffering ability because of the order in which he places the keys. Because the language key precedes the degree code key, he can set the number of key fields to **2**. In this way, data is buffered based on the values of the client field and the language key only. The first request in client 000 for any degree code in the English language will read and cache all the descriptions for English.

2.3.3 Maintenance View

So now Russel has the individual tables for the degree majors and their relationships defined. Before he can generate a table maintenance transaction for them, however, he needs to create a special type of database view called a **Maintenance view** (see Figure 2.15) via the **Object Selection** dialog on the **Dictionary** tab.

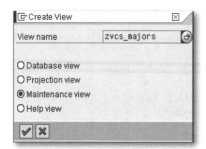

Figure 2.15 Maintenance View Creation

The process for creating a maintenance view is quite similar to a normal view. You manually have to specify the main table of the view, which in this case is ZCS_MAJORS. Then, as shown in Figure 2.16, a list of related tables is displayed.

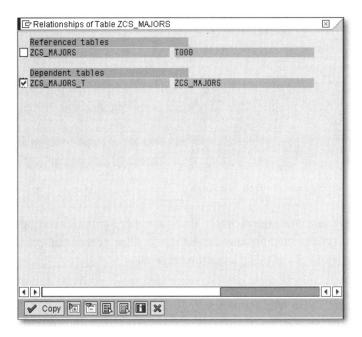

Figure 2.16 Maintenance View Relationships

It is important to note that it was the initial setting of the foreign key field relationship that now enables Russel to choose ZCS_MAJORS_T as his dependent table. If he had not created the foreign key relationship correctly, then ZCS_MAJORS_T would not even appear in this screen.

After selecting the single dependent table, Russel has almost all of the fields that he needs in the view. All the keys from both tables will be pulled into the view by default. He only has to add the **Short Description** field to the **Maintenance view** in order to complete it if he so chooses.

The final setting that must be completed before generating the view is to configure the **Access** settings. This is very similar to the process of setting the **Delivery and Maintenance** tab on the underlying tables. You can use the **Maint. Status** tab, shown in Figure 2.17, to ensure that maintenance is allowed and that changes will be inserted into a customizing request.

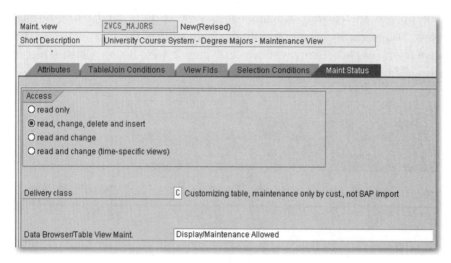

Figure 2.17 Table Maintenance — Maintenance Status

Unlike the **Delivery and Maintenance** tab, there are more granular settings for controlling the type of changes that can be made. This level of control is one of the main advantages of using a maintenance view.

2.3.4 Generated Table Maintenance

Now that Russel is finished creating the transparent tables and the views to support his degree maintenance data, he is ready to start generating the table maintenance. From the change mode of the maintenance view, Russel chooses the menu option **Utilities • Table Maintenance Generator**. The table maintenance generation has not really changed since the upgrade. Russel is still impressed that with just a few selections, a maintenance application can be generated, saving developers a great deal of time for what would be a tedious exercise if they had to code their own basic maintenance screens.

You can set an **Authorization Group**, which is a way to control security on your table maintenance. Since no special security is required for this table, Russel chooses to set the value to **&NC&**, which means no authorization group has been assigned (see Figure 2.18).

The only other setting that has to be made is the name of the **Function group**. The table maintenance generator will write all of its code as function modules in the function group that you specify. Although you can choose any function module within your namespace, even one that already exists, Russel has always followed a personal standard of naming the function group the same as the maintenance view. In this way, it is always easy to find the relationship between the view and the function group by just glancing at the name.

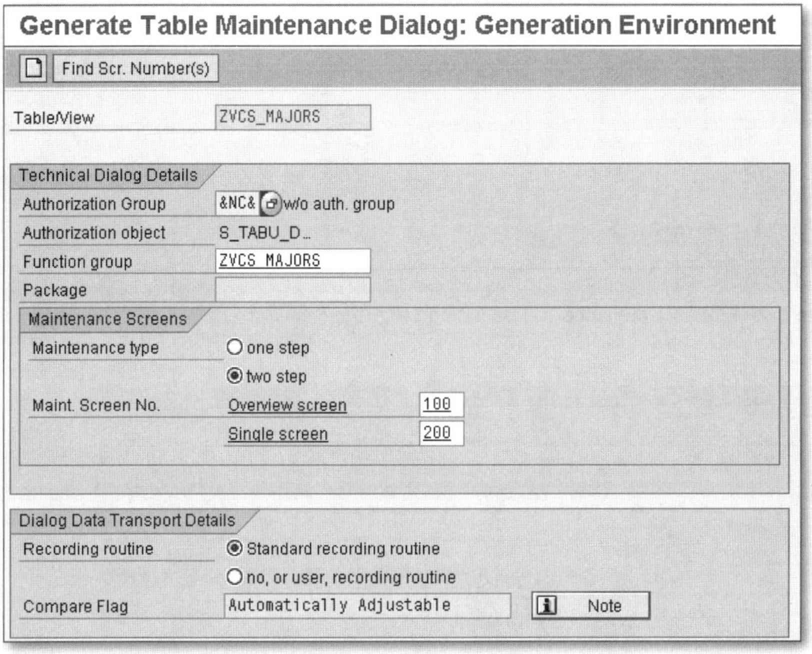

Figure 2.18 Table Maintenance — Generation Environment Dialog

Russel wanted to test the generated table maintenance. So from the maintenance view change mode, he selected **Utilities • Contents**. He entered a few majors and was satisfied that everything seemed to be working well. He also wanted to check the translation capabilities.

Although the translation capabilities were not new to ABAP, Russel had never really worked with anything that needed to be translated to multiple languages before. He discovered that from inside the maintenance transaction, you just have to select your entries and then choose the menu option **Goto • Translation**. Then, you're prompted to choose the language in which you want to work (see Figure 2.19).

The dialog that displayed showed a clean user interface with the key in Russel's logon language and the language that he had selected for translation (see Figure 2.20).

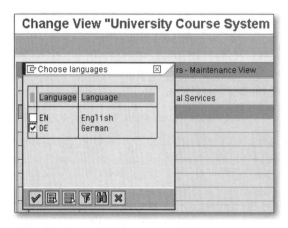

Figure 2.19 Table Maintenance — Translation Language Selection

University Course System - Degree Majors - Maintenance View		
Major	Degree Major Description	

Maintain Texts in Other Languages

D...	Language	Degree Major Description
ART	English	Art
	German	Kunst

Figure 2.20 Table Maintenance — Translation

If, like Russel, you're curious as to what was actually created in the database, you can use the data browser to see the results behind the scenes. When viewing the description table directly (see Figure 2.21), Russel could see two separate records for the degree major key **ART**.

Data Browser: Table ZCS_MAJORS_T Select Entries   4

Check Table...

MAN...	SPR...	MAJ...	MAJOR_DESC
000	EN	ACT	Accounting and Professional Services
000	DE	ART	Kunst
000	EN		Art
000	EN	BIO	Biology

Figure 2.21 New Data Table Viewed from the Data Browser

2.4   Data Dictionary Data Tables

The processing for creating the main data tables has not really changed from SAP R/3 4.6C. The tools are basically the same and the steps that Russel has performed so far to create the degree majors tables will be fairly standard as he creates the rest of his main data tables. The one major difference as of SAP Web AS 6.10 that Russel already knew about as he was designing his tables was the ability to use string and binary string fields directly in the database table. He can now use these complex data types just as he would any of the other basic types.

2.4.1   Enhancements

After Russel saves his first transparent table, a new dialog appears — the **Maintain Enhancement Category** screen (see Figure 2.22). This dialog is new as of SAP NetWeaver 7.0 and is related to the new *Enhancement Framework*.

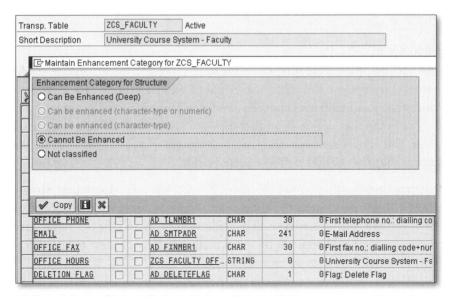

Figure 2.22 Enhancement Category Selection

The Enhancement Framework allows customers to make modifications and additions easily to existing objects. One of the many capabilities of the Enhancement Framework is the option to enhance transparent tables by adding new substructures to them.

In earlier releases, developers could always add *Appends* to existing tables; however, with the Enhancement Framework's new functionality, they have better tractability and control. One area of this additional control captures Russel's attention. With appends, the original developer of the transparent table had no control of when appends could be used. Later, any developer could add appends to almost any transparent table, even though this might have adverse effects on the coding used in the table. With SAP NetWeaver 7.0, the same original developer of the transparent table can classify what future enhancements he or she wants to allow. For example, the developer could choose not to allow any enhancements (**Cannot Be Enhanced**) if the table or structure would be used in a fixed interface and have to remain constant.

Depending on the logic used against the table, the developer might also want to limit the types of fields that can be used in an enhancement. Adding complex data types like strings and binary strings limits the kinds of logic that can be executed across a structure later.

2.4.2 Indexes

After Russel finishes creating all of his data tables, he thinks that he might want to create some indexes. You should think of an index as a secondary copy of the main table that contains a reduced number of fields, with the difference being that the fields in this copy are always maintained in a sorted order. This allows the underlying database system to make faster searches for records that are queried via these sorted fields.

In some development organizations, a separate database administrator (DBA) or Basis person might be the one to create indexes later on. However the university has just a small group of administrators and the developers are used to having to do most of the performance tuning of their own applications — including the creation of indexes.

Nothing can replace the need for good load testing during the application-testing phase. Russel knows that once he is further along with his development, he will need to do some SQL traces during testing for another round of performance tuning. But initially, it seems apparent that some indexes will be required.

One of the most likely places for an index is on the faculty table. Russel already knows that he will have to provide a tool that searches for faculty via the last name. This seems like an excellent place to use an index:

▶ Since this search will be frequently used, a secondary index by last name should have good performance benefits.

▶ Changes and additions to the facility database will also be relatively infrequent, thereby adding to the list of reasons that make this a good candidate.

When creating the index, Russel spots a new feature of SAP NetWeaver 7.0, which is also part of the Enhancement Framework. Before he creates the index, he is prompted to choose between a standard index (**Create Index**) and an extension index (**Create Extension Index**, see Figure 2.23).

Figure 2.23 Create Index or Extension Index

"So why," you ask, "is there a distinction between the two types of indexes?" Prior to SAP NetWeaver 7.0, you could always add indexes, even to SAP delivered tables. In fact, it is a fairly common practice for customers to add their own indexes to the system. SAP delivers many secondary indexes where SAP believes they are most needed. However, because every customer's business runs differently, a table that has very little data and accesses for one customer may see a huge number of hits for a different customer.

The problem with adding these indexes in releases before SAP NetWeaver 7.0 is that they were considered customer modifications. Although they rarely proved to be a dangerous modification, the indexes were often dropped during upgrades if SAP made changes to the delivered table. Customers could recover these indexes after the upgrade, but at the cost of the time it required to rebuild them, which could be substantial for a large data table.

The enhancement index addresses this problem, as well as providing for a better tracking mechanism for all the indexes that customers have added to their delivered data tables. Enhancement indexes will be protected during the upgrade process. As long as SAP has not made changes to the fields that are used by the index, it will not need to be dropped or rebuilt.

The remainder of the process for creating the secondary index is straightforward and has not changed since SAP R/3 4.6C (see Figure 2.24). For a simple index like this, all Russel needs to do is supply the fields that he wants to use. There is even a nifty dialog that can be triggered by clicking on the **Table Fields** button, which allows you to choose your fields.

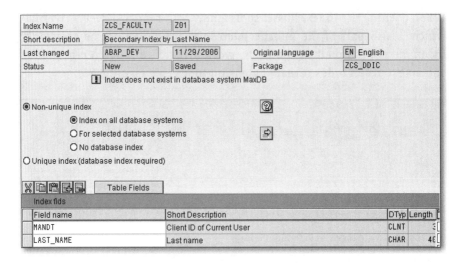

Figure 2.24 Index Maintenance Screen

Russel has read many debates on the SDN forums (*http://sdn.sap.com*) regarding whether you should include the client key (MANDT) in your indexes. One argument is based on the fact that because the majority of production systems rarely have more than one actively used client, the inclusion of the client key has little impact, if any, on performance, and therefore, it doesn't make sense to include it. But, given the small size of the client key, Russel decides to include the client key just to be safe and ensure that performance will not be affected.

2.4.3 Lock Objects

With the addition of indexes to his transparent tables, the main data dictionary objects that will store or organize data are complete. However, Russel's job still isn't done. Because Russel is a responsible developer, he wants to plan ahead for a well-designed system. This means taking table locking into account. In the ABAP environment, you should never count on database level table locking.

For ABAP, the database is just a big data bucket, and other than some basic caching and optimization, all other data integrity — such as locking and relationship checks — happens at the application layer. But don't fret. Supporting good locking mechanisms in your application code doesn't have to be difficult. Fortunately, SAP provides lock objects to make the process easy.

Russel starts by creating a lock object for the main course data table (see Figure 2.25). He names ZCS_COURSE as his primary table and sets the **Lock Mode** to a **Write Lock** since this is a transactional data table.

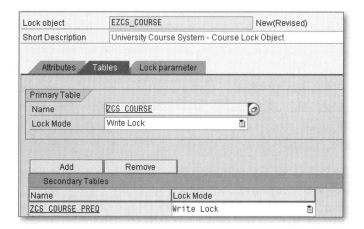

Figure 2.25 Lock Object Maintenance Screen

But, logically speaking, the course table and the course prerequisites should both be locked when creating updates. Data maintenance on these two tables will take place at the same time, so creating this interdependency is as easy as specifying ZCS_COURSE_PREQ as a secondary table.

"What really happens when Russel generates the lock object," you ask. Mostly, a function module will be generated. This generated function module will be called later in Russel's application coding. It contains the functionality to first determine whether an existing lock is in place for the record keys provided, and if that is the case, to return an exception. It will even place the user ID of the person who currently has the foreign lock into the system message variable SY-MSGV1. Assuming no foreign lock exists, the function module continues with the process of placing a lock for the record key(s) supplied. The generated function module provides the complex logic to communicate with the central lock process, ensuring that locks are unique and avoiding deadlocks, even when working with multiple application servers.

This locking process takes place in a separate ABAP work process from the main executing program, further providing for a robust and well performing locking mechanism. You should note that all of this complexity is hidden from the average developer, because SAP handles it all within the generated code.

2.5 Search Helps

The final data dictionary object that Russel needs to address is the search help. The core search help object has not changed since SAP R/3 4.6C; however, it does have a new capability. Web Dynpro ABAP has full support for data dictionary search helps.

This means that the robust functionality that ABAP developers have enjoyed for "free" in classic Dynpro SAP GUI transactions for years now works just as well from the browser. The additional reuse option of search helps within Web Dynpro ABAP means that it is an excellent idea to continue to invest in the creation of these objects.

Russel begins the processing by creating his first **Elementary Search Help**. This first search help will be a search for courses by faculty. He will want to combine details from the course table (ZCS_COURSE) and the faculty table (ZCS_FACULTY) in this search help (see Figure 2.26).

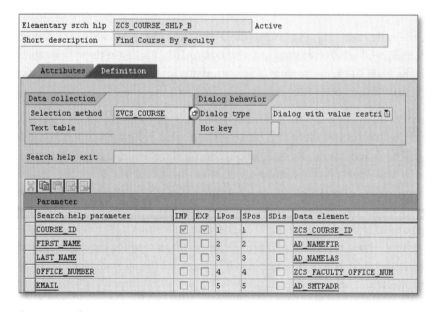

Figure 2.26 Elementary Search Help via Help View

The search help can have one of several different types of data collection options. Usually the most common option is to place a search help directly against a single transparent table. For this search help however, Russel combines data from two different tables to provide an even more powerful search tool for the end users. Therefore, he first creates another view in the data dictionary that creates the join between the two tables. Then, he specifies the table view, ZVCS_COURSE, as his selection method.

Although views and single table selection methods probably cover almost every type of search help that you would want to build, there is the rare exception where more complex logic is needed than what either of these options can provide. For those rare occasions, you can use a search help exit, which is a specially structured function module that affords the developer complete control to program his own data search and retrieve logic. This can be particularly useful if you want to build a search help that contains data from a remote system.

Creating the rest of the search help is easy, once the view has been created and specified as the selection method. Russel chooses the fields that he wants to use in the search help in the **Parameter** section of the screen (see Figure 2.27). He can choose which fields he wants used on the selection screen and which fields he wants used as output on the results list by just setting the position number in the corresponding column. Here, he makes all fields available to both the selection screen and the output list, but, had he wanted, he could have omitted any field from either section of the search help by simply not supplying a position number.

He also needs to supply one or more parameters that will be transported to and from the calling screen. By setting an importing field, you can bring existing values or partial selections from the transaction screen into the search help to initialize the search. Ultimately, of course, the whole point of the search help is to provide a selected value for some form of input field. For that reason, you should always have at least one exporting parameter.

In both classic Dynpro and Web Dynpro, all the screen mechanisms for copying, exporting, and importing values to and from the screen are handled transparently. The application developer doesn't have to worry about how this works. He only has to specify — either directly in the screen parameters or via a data dictionary reference that is connected to the search help — what search help will be used for a field.

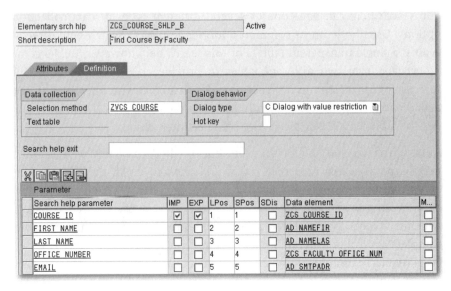

Figure 2.27 Elementary Search Help Field Assignment

But what Russel ultimately envisions for the user interface is a robust search tool for helping faculty, administrators, and students find the courses they need. This means that different types of searches will be required. For instance, a student might want to search for a course by its scheduled time (e.g., most students want to avoid those 8:00 am Monday morning classes). On the other hand, members of the faculty probably want to search for all courses that have been assigned to them.

The search help data dictionary object has a useful mechanism called a *Collective Search Help*, which is for providing just such a grouping of searches. After creating all of his separate elementary search helps for the different types of searches that he wants to support, Russel can combine them all together into a single collective search help. Each of the individual search helps must have at least one parameter in common. In this case, all of these search helps are used to find a course ID. Russel must map the parameter assignment of the COURSE_ID into each elementary search help from the collective search help screen (see Figure 2.28).

The finished user interface will only need to reference the collective search help, ZCS_COURSE_SHLP. When activated, the search help will display the first elementary search help and provide tabs for switching to any of the other related searches. This robust mechanism for collective search helps even works transparently in Web Dynpro ABAP.

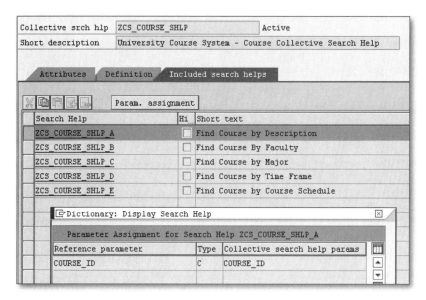

Figure 2.28 Collective Search Help

With Russel's data dictionary layout completed, he can now start writing some code to get data in and out of the database. In this chapter, we'll focus on this lowest level of code that abstracts the data persistence.

3 Data Persistence Layer

Russel plans to take a very systematic approach to his coding. He doesn't intend on simply jumping in and creating web pages or reports. Instead, he wants to incorporate layers of abstraction to protect each layer of his application (Visualization or User Interface verses Application Logic verses Data Access or Data Persistence) from changes that might occur in other layers as much as possible.

This modularized approach to development has many advantages:

▶ It allows smaller, autonomous units to be built so you can test each unit independently, before it is integrated into the larger application.

▶ Although Russel belongs to a small development team and will be creating this entire system himself, using a modular approach will have several benefits for distributed development, for example, different developers can work on different layers simultaneously. As long as the interface between the different layers is clearly defined, developers can make changes within their own object layer without affecting the developers around them.

▶ Long-term maintenance and modifications to the overall system become simpler to make because of this modular approach. Also, the impact of making a change can be clearly identified, because of the direct and documented relationships and separation between the object layers. This can also contribute to localizing changes to just one layer, and therefore limit the amount of testing and work that is required for the other layers.

3.1 Persistent Objects

Following this approach, Russel begins with the absolute lowest layer of coding — the data persistence layer. As of SAP Web AS 6.10, the ABAP environment supports the concept of *Persistent Objects*.

Before we delve into what persistent objects are, we'll look at the classic approach to data access in ABAP. All of the data in your programs — the variables, internal tables, and even object instances and their attributes — are transient. What this means is that when your program is finished with its execution, the memory space and all the values that are held are released. The only type of data in a system that is permanent is the *persistent data*, and this is what is stored in the database.

Essentially, however, there is a clear separation between what is transient and what is persistent. In other words, you have to use SQL statements such as SELECT to read data from the persistent store into transient memory. You can only manipulate and use the data values while in transient memory. But, any changes that you make to the data are not saved unless you use more SQL, like UPDATE or MODIFY, to write the data back into the persistent store.

Perhaps it sounds like we're just using fancy words for what every developer does all the time. As ABAP developers, we all work with the concepts of *Persistent* versus *Transient* data every day, even if we do it only on a very automatic or subconscious level. The idea of performing SQL statements mixed directly into your application logic is quite ingrained in just about every ABAP developer's mind. That can probably be attributed to the strength of the Open SQL integration into the ABAP language.

But the whole idea of *persistent objects* and the *Persistent Object Services* that SAP introduced with SAP Web AS 6.10 is to challenge those old ingrained concepts. By taking an object-oriented approach to persistent data management, you come away with an ABAP object that abstracts the physical data representation, namely, the database table, thereby removing all procedural SQL statements from your application logic.

Quite simply, the persistent object is a new way of representing a database table. We will create a persistent object by defining what database table it should be modeled off of. Then, each field in the database table will be an attribute of the persistent object class. Instead of using SQL statements to access these data fields, you'll use GET and SET methods of the persistent object. Your application logic will then work with instances of a persistent object class instead of rows of data in a table. Although technically the object instance of a persistent class is still transient — in other words, the physical memory is still released when program execution ends — the persistent object services provides a mechanism to map the persistent object attributes (i.e., the data contained within and represented by the instance of the persistent class) back into the database for persistence between executable steps.

3.1.1 Creating the Persistent Object Class

So far, our discussion of what a persistent object is has been rather academic in nature. Russel is the type of developer who likes to see how a new concept like *persistent objects* is used in an actual application, before he can really comprehend it. Because the persistent class is very low level and is actually just an object-oriented abstraction of the database tables, Russel assigns all of the persistent objects to the ZCS_DDIC package (see Figure 3.1). In that way, the persistent object classes can be found adjacent to the data dictionary tables they represent.

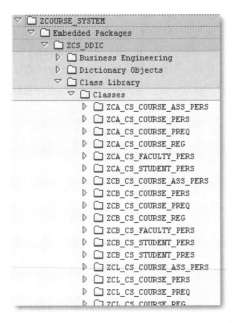

Figure 3.1 Package Assignment of Persistent Objects

The process of creating a persistent object is very similar to creating any other type of global class in ABAP Objects. From the **Create Class** dialog, you simply choose **Persistent class** for the **Class Type** (see Figure 3.2).

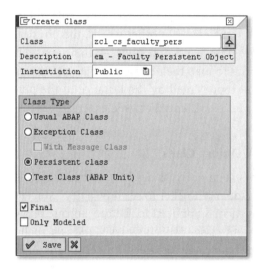

Figure 3.2 Persistent Object Creation Dialog

After the class creation, Russel looks at what the ABAP Workbench has created. In the **Properties** tab (see Figure 3.3), he immediately sees several changes and additions to the basic class definition that have been made because he chose the persistent class type. You'll notice that even though he chose **Public** as the **Instantiation** type in the **Create Class** dialog, the ABAP Workbench has forced this to **Protected** and locked the field against updates.

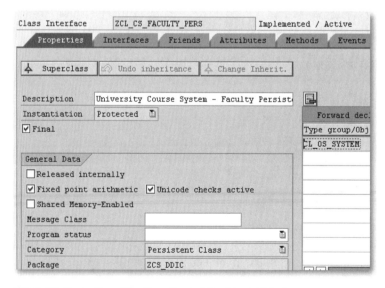

Figure 3.3 Properties of the New Created Persistent Object

This is because more than just this one class has been created. The ABAP Workbench also generated two additional classes:

▶ ZCB_CS_FACULTY_PERS as the Base Class
▶ ZCA_CS_FACULTY_PERS as the Agent Class

3.1.2 Base Classes and Agent Classes

So why did two extra classes get created and what is their relationship to the main class? The main persistent class is what is referred to in object-oriented terms as a *Managed object*. In object-oriented programming concepts, a managed object is an object whose lifetime cannot be controlled directly (i.e., there is a separate object that controls instantiation and access to the managed object).

With ABAP persistent objects, they are always managed by the persistent object services. It is this layer of code that provides the mechanisms to map data to and from the database. This is why the ABAP Workbench changed the instantiation on the persistent class to **Protected**. This means it is no longer possible for just any class to create an instance of the object with the CREATE OBJECT syntax. Only an object that has a relationship to ZCL_CS_FACULTY_PERS can do so.

It is the agent class, ZCA_CS_FACULTY_PERS, which has the ability to create instances of the persistent object. Although there is no direct line of inheritance between ZCL_CS_FACULTY_PERS and ZCA_CS_FACULTY_PERS, the friends definition, which can be seen on the **Friends** tab of the Class Builder, that the ABAP Workbench inserted during object creation (see Figure 3.4) gives the base class, ZCB_CS_FACULTY_PERS, the right to act as though the two classes are related, and thereby gives it access to the protected level of the main class.

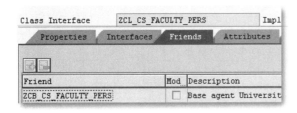

Figure 3.4 Persistent Class Friends Definition

The base class, ZCB_CS_FACULTY_PERS, is an abstract class that has access to much of the functionality of the persistent services. Because it is abstract, the class cannot actually be instantiated. You should think of it almost as a code template. The abstract "template" is made accessible via the agent class, ZCA_CS_FACULTY_PERS. The agent class is a subclass of the abstract base, however, it is marked with a **Private** instantiation.

Ultimately, you may be wondering about the following: What is the purpose of this circle of relationships? Where is the starting point for accessing this chain of **Protected**, **Friends**, **Abstract**, and finally **Private** instantiation?

The need for this complexity is justifiable. If we return to the idea of the managed object for a moment, we understand that in order for a persistent object to work correctly, there must always be some hooks created into the persistent services. These relationships are specifically designed to ensure that the persistent object can only be created in a way that guarantees that the initialization into the persistent object services occurs. Although we have examined the details of these relationships here, in reality, it is not that complicated to work with your persistent object.

As the basic example in Listing 3.1 shows, the agent class, although having a private instantiation, does have a static attribute called AGENT that will return an instance of itself. Access to this static attribute causes the CLASS_CONSTRUCTOR method of the agent class to execute, thereby registering the instance of the agent class with the persistent object services. The agent object then has access to all the persistent object services required to map data from the database and create the persistent object instance.

```
DATA: l_agent    TYPE REF TO zca_cs_faculty_pers,
      l_pers_obj TYPE REF TO zcl_cs_faculty_pers.

  TRY.
      l_agent    = zca_cs_faculty_pers=>agent.
      l_pers_obj = l_agent->get_persistent(
         i_faculty_id = i_faculty_id ).
    CATCH cx_os_object_not_found.
  ENDTRY.
```

Listing 3.1 Persistent Object Instantiation

3.1.3   Persistent Data Mapper

Russel has a persistent object, but it doesn't do much yet because he hasn't mapped any database objects to the class. This is where the *Persistent Data Mapper* comes into play. On the main menu bar in the Class Builder, there is an extra **Persistence** button when you are working with a persistent class (see Figure 3.5). This button will help you to navigate to the Persistent Data Mapper.

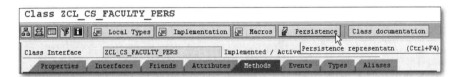

Figure 3.5 Persistent Data Mapper Access

When Russel first enters the Persistent Data Mapper, he is prompted to add a **Table/Structure** (see Figure 3.6). At this point, he specifies exactly what data dictionary object this persistent object will be representing.

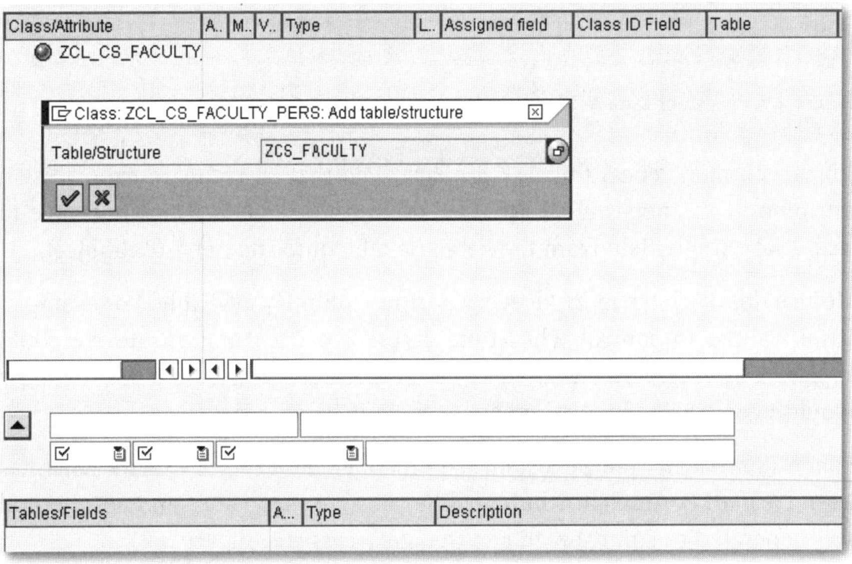

Figure 3.6 Choosing the Persistent Object's Table or Structure

At the top of the screen in Figure 3.6, Russel can see an area with his persistent class and all of its attributes (currently, there are none). At the bottom of the screen, he sees all the possible fields exposed by the data object he just selected.

If he double clicks on a field from the **Tables/Fields** view, it will be loaded into the middle part of the editor (see Figure 3.7). From this area he can change the attribute name, description, visibility (**Public**, **Protected**, **Private**), and read-only flag. Once he has completed selecting these options, he can click on the **Arrow** button to the left of the attribute name to add or update this attribute in his persistent class.

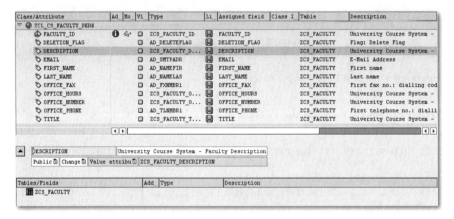

Figure 3.7 Persistent Data Mapper — Attribute Details

Russel can then repeat this task for each field that he wants to expose as an attribute in the persistent class. You should note that he does not have to map every single field from the database table into the persistent object.

He also doesn't have to make every attribute publicly available. For example, if he wanted to control who could access a particular attribute, he could declare it as **Protected** and then any class that needed to access that attribute would need a **Friends** relationship to the persistent object.

When Russel exits the persistent data mapper, he can see exactly what has been created. For each attribute that he chose to map, a GET and SET method was generated to control read and update access (see Figure 3.8).

Class Interface	ZCL_CS_FACULTY_PERS		Implemented / Act

Properties	Interfaces	Friends	Attributes	Methods

☐ Paramet. | 🔲 Excepti. | 🔲 | 🔲🔲🔲 | 🔲🔲 ✂🔲🔲 | 🔲 | 🔲🔲

Method	Level	Vis	Me	Description
SET_OFFICE_HOURS	Instanc	Publi	▶☐	Sets Attribute OFFICE_HOURS
SET_OFFICE_FAX	Instanc	Publi	▶☐	Sets Attribute OFFICE_FAX
SET_LAST_NAME	Instanc	Publi	▶☐	Sets Attribute LAST_NAME
SET_FIRST_NAME	Instanc	Publi	▶☐	Sets Attribute FIRST_NAME
SET_EMAIL	Instanc	Publi	▶☐	Sets Attribute EMAIL
SET_DESCRIPTION	Instanc	Publi	▶☐	Sets Attribute DESCRIPTION
SET_DELETION_FLAG	Instanc	Publi	▶☐	Sets Attribute DELETION_FLAG
GET_TITLE	Instanc	Publi	🔲	Reads Attribute TITLE
GET_OFFICE_PHONE	Instanc	Publi	🔲	Reads Attribute OFFICE_PHONE
GET_OFFICE_NUMBER	Instanc	Publi	🔲	Reads Attribute OFFICE_NUMBE
GET_OFFICE_HOURS	Instanc	Publi	🔲	Reads Attribute OFFICE_HOURS
GET_OFFICE_FAX	Instanc	Publi	🔲	Reads Attribute OFFICE_FAX
GET_LAST_NAME	Instanc	Publi	🔲	Reads Attribute LAST_NAME
GET_FIRST_NAME	Instanc	Publi	🔲	Reads Attribute FIRST_NAME
GET_FACULTY_ID	Instanc	Publi	🔲	Reads Attribute FACULTY_ID
GET_EMAIL	Instanc	Publi	🔲	Reads Attribute EMAIL
GET_DESCRIPTION	Instanc	Publi	🔲	Reads Attribute DESCRIPTION
GET_DELETION_FLAG	Instanc	Publi	🔲	Reads Attribute DELETION_FLA

Figure 3.8 Persistent Object Attribute — GET and SET Methods

3.1.4 Coding with a Persistent Object

There are many things that you can do via the persistent object and the surrounding persistent object services. Russel has already seen how basic instantiation of the persistent object is done via the agent object (see Listing 3.1 above), but now he needs to explore how he would replace the most common SQL commands with functionality from his persistent object.

Create a New Record

When creating a new record (see Listing 3.2), Russel first needs to acquire an instance of the agent class. He can then use the CREATE_PERSISTENT method of the agent class. He has to pass in the new business key for the instance of the object that he wants to create.

```
DATA: l_agent    TYPE REF TO zca_cs_faculty_pers,
      l_pers_obj TYPE REF TO zcl_cs_faculty_pers.

  TRY.
```

```
      l_agent    = zca_cs_faculty_pers=>agent.
      l_pers_obj = l_agent->create_persistent(
        i_faculty_id = i_faculty_id ).
    CATCH cx_os_object_existing.
  ENDTRY.
```

Listing 3.2 Persistent Object — Create New Record

This is similar to performing a SQL INSERT; however, all you know here is the primary key of the record. A persistent object instance for the business key will be returned from the method call, but all other attributes other than the keys will be initial.

The persistent object services provide many different capabilities, but they are not responsible for the generation of new business keys. In all likelihood, Russel might still need to use an ABAP Number Range to generate his next key before calling the CREATE_PERSISTENT method.

The final observation is the use of the TRY...CATCH block around the logic. Since the concept of Exception classes was new in SAP Web AS 6.10, Russel doesn't have much experience with them (see Section 3.2). For now, it will suffice to know that this is the new method for dealing with exception handling. In this case, he is catching the exception CX_OS_OBJECT_EXISTING. This will be raised by the CREATE_PERSISTENT method if the business key specified already exists in the underlying database table.

Read a Record by Business Key

The logic to read a single record (see Listing 3.3) is actually quite similar to what Russel has already coded for creating a record. He just has to call GET_PERSISTENT instead of CREATE_PERSISTENT. The exception that could be thrown, CX_OS_OBJECT_NOT_FOUND, is different as well. This exception means that the business key supplied does not exist.

```
DATA: l_agent    TYPE REF TO zca_cs_faculty_pers,
      l_pers_obj TYPE REF TO zcl_cs_faculty_pers.

  TRY.
      l_agent    = zca_cs_faculty_pers=>agent.
      l_pers_obj = l_agent->get_persistent(
        i_faculty_id = i_faculty_id ).
    CATCH cx_os_object_not_found.
  ENDTRY.
```

Listing 3.3 Persistent Object — Read Single Record

Query for Multiple Records

Now things get a little more interesting when it comes time to reading multiple records. For this operation, Russel will use another part of the persistent object services — the *query service*. The query service basically takes the place of the WHERE construct in SQL. In the example shown in Listing 3.4, Russel is reading all faculty members who have a last name that begins with the letter J.

```
DATA: l_agent    TYPE REF TO zca_cs_faculty_pers,
      l_pers_obj TYPE REF TO zcl_cs_faculty_pers,
      l_objects  TYPE        osreftab.

****Persistent Object Query Interface
  DATA: query_manager TYPE REF TO if_os_query_manager,
        query         TYPE REF TO cl_os_query,
        filter        TYPE REF TO IF_OS_QUERY_FILTER_EXPR.

  TRY.
    l_agent     = zca_cs_faculty_pers=>agent.
    query_manager = cl_os_system=>get_query_manager( ).
    query ?= query_manager->create_query( ).
    filter =
      query->IF_OS_QUERY_EXPR_FACTORY~CREATE_LIKE_EXPR(
      I_ATTR = 'LAST_NAME'
      I_PATTERN = 'J%'  ).
    query->IF_OS_QUERY~SET_FILTER_EXPR( filter ).

    l_objects =
      l_agent->if_os_ca_persistency~get_persistent_by_query(
          i_query   = query ).
    IF lines( l_objects ) = 0.
****Produce an error message
    ENDIF.
    CATCH cx_os_object_not_found.
    CATCH cx_os_query_error.
  ENDTRY.
```

Listing 3.4 Persistent Object — Query for Multiple Records

In this example, Russel uses the Query Manager to create a query object. Then, he uses the query to specify his filter criteria, the same as the WHERE condition in SQL. The query is then used as an input parameter of the GET_PERSISTENT_BY_QUERY method of the agent class.

You should note that the query service does provide quite a few capabilities. You can build sort and filter conditions into the query. However, as of SAP NetWeaver 7.0, there is not a one-to-one replacement for everything that you can accomplish in an ABAP Open SQL WHERE condition. One of the main gaps that still remains is the support for the ABAP IN clause. Therefore, if you have SELECT-OPTIONS or PARAMETERS as part of your query condition, you will have to resort to using SQL.

Update a Record

There really is no implicit UPDATE statement that can be performed on persistent objects. When you instantiate a persistent object either with the CREATE_PERSISTENT or GET_PERSISTENT method, the resulting object is always ready to update the underlying database table. The use of any SET method to change an attribute value has theoretically changed the value at the persistent layer.

However, similar to SQL, the actual changes are not permanent in the physical database until a COMMIT is triggered in the surrounding environment.

Delete a Record

The final operation that Russel considers is the ability to delete a record permanently from the database. This works just like the CREATE_PERSISTENT or the GET_PERSISTENT methods. The name of the method is DELETE_PERSISTENT.

Like the SET methods, it is important to note that actual removal of the record from the database does not happen until an external COMMIT occurs.

3.2   Exception Classes

After spending some time on creating persistent objects for each of his database tables, Russel decides that this would be a good opportunity for him to learn a little more about exception classes. He already knows how they're used since he worked with the generated persistent classes. So, before he proceeds with any more of his own application programming, he decides that he should probably create some exception classes for the course system.

3.2.1   Advantages of Exception Classes

As Russel sees it, there are several main advantages to using the new class-based exception approach to exception handling:

▶ First, the exception class can carry more details about the exception than a simple return code. Because an exception class is instantiated like all ABAP classes, the exception instance can be populated with all sorts of ABAP data types and object references about the exception. This makes the catching of exceptions potentially far more meaningful.

▶ The next advantage is the object-oriented concept of inheritance. Exceptions can be created in hierarchies. When trying to catch an exception, a developer doesn't need to specify the exact exception. If several exceptions are grouped together and all share the same parent exception, the exception can be caught at the parent level. Later, thanks to *polymorphism*, the parent exception can be cast into its more specific child if necessary.

▶ Another advantage is simplification. Because exception classes allow for more than one exception ID, an exception class can actually hold many different types of exceptions. This reduces the complexity, once again, of catching the exception. Gone are the days of large case statements against the system field SY-SUBRC in order to determine the true error situation.

▶ Lastly, exception classes have integration with the ABAP message concept. Message classes and individual message IDs can be mapped directly to an exception class and exception ID respectively. It is also easy to map exception class attributes into the placeholders of the message.

Issuing messages that are produced by exception classes is also greatly simplified (see Listing 3.5). The MESSAGE statement in the ABAP language has been enhanced so that you can directly output a message simply by providing an instance of the exception class.

```
DATA iexp TYPE REF TO cx_transformation_error.
  TRY.
     CALL TRANSFORMATION id
        SOURCE zcs_student = istudents
        RESULT XML  ixml.
   CATCH cx_transformation_error INTO iexp.
     MESSAGE iexp TYPE 'E'.
  ENDTRY.
```

Listing 3.5 Exception Message Output

Web Dynpro ABAP also has excellent support for issuing messages via the exception class (see Listing 3.6). The methods of the Message Manager, shown bolded in Listing 3.6, have the full support of exception class instances, similar to the ABAP statement MESSAGE.

```
DATA iexp TYPE REF TO cx_transformation_error.
  TRY.
      CALL TRANSFORMATION id
        SOURCE zcs_student = istudents
        RESULT XML  ixml.
    CATCH cx_transformation_error INTO iexp.
    DATA: l_current_controller TYPE REF TO if_wd_controller,
          l_message_manager
               TYPE REF TO if_wd_message_manager.
    l_current_controller ?= wd_this->wd_get_api( ).
    l_message_manager =
         l_current_controller->get_message_manager( ).
    l_message_manager->report_exception(
        message_object              = iexp ).
  ENDTRY.
```

Listing 3.6 Web Dynpro ABAP Exception Message Output

3.2.2   Creating an Exception Class

Now let's look at the steps that Russel went through when designing his exception classes. Since exception classes are another type of object that describes the data of his logical objects, Russel decided to create one exception class per main object — Course, Faculty, and Student.

While creating his exception classes, it will also be necessary to create a message class. The single message class, ZCOURSE_SYSTEM, will hold all messages that might be issued anywhere in the system (see Figure 3.9). For the time being, he will define only those messages that he will map directly to his exceptions.

Russel starts the creation of the exception class just like he would any normal class. However, from the **Create Class** dialog (see Figure 3.10), he chooses **Exception Class**. This automatically creates the **Superclass** reference and displays the option to select **With Message Class**.

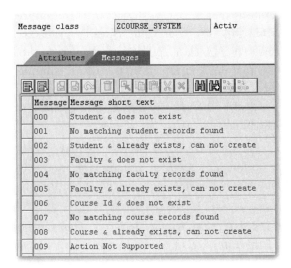

Figure 3.9 Course System Messages

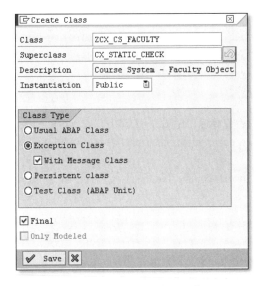

Figure 3.10 Create Exception Class Dialog

Exception Class Type

So what is the impact of these two actions that just occurred? First, the super-class usually determines the way that the exception class can be propagated. You have three main choices:

- ► CX_STATIC_CHECK is for exceptions that must be declared in the interface. It is the most common situation and the default value as well. In this case, any exception class that is raised in a block of coding must be listed in the interface for the block. This situation is enforced by the ABAP compiler and, if not met, will produce a syntax error in your application. Static check-based exceptions must also be handled within a coding block, or propagated to the next coding block.

- ► CX_DYNAMIC_CHECK is for exceptions that don't necessarily have to be declared. These kinds of exceptions are good for situations produced by the runtime system that may or may not be caught by the executing program.

- ► CX_NO_CHECK is for exceptions that must *not* be declared. This type of exception cannot be part of the interface of the coding block. It can be caught in higher level coding blocks. But, if it isn't caught, it is automatically propagated up through the call stack. This type of exception makes the most sense for low-level runtime exceptions that an executing application will have no possible design for or ability to catch. Memory allocation errors, or other resource shortfalls or communications errors are good candidates for the CX_NO_CHECK.

With Message Class Option

The other option, **With Message Class**, was introduced with SAP NetWeaver 2004. When unchecked, there is no connection created between the exception IDs and a message class entry. This might be fine for exceptions that are never intended to produce user interface level messages, such as system runtime exceptions.

Most exceptions do lead to a message of some sort being sent to the user interface. Before SAP NetWeaver 2004, the text of these messages could be maintained directly in the exception class. Although these texts were still translatable, they didn't have the flexibility of the classic message class-based messages. For instance, you couldn't also maintain a long text for an exception message.

Fortunately, by using the **With Message Class** option, you can now create a direct tie between exception IDs and message class IDs. In that way, the corresponding message, including its long text, can be issued directly from the message object as you saw in Listing 3.5 and Listing 3.6.

Message Class Attributes

Earlier we noted that one of the advantages of the class-based exceptions is the ability to hold various pieces of information about the exception in itself. This can be designed by creating attributes for the exception class to retain information such as the FACULTY_ID (see Figure 3.11). This additional information can be used within the exception texts as well, and queried by the catching object at runtime.

Class Interface	ZCX_CS_FACULTY				Implemented / Active		

Properties	Interfaces	Friends	Attributes	Texts	Methods

Attribute	Level	Vis	Rea	Typing	Associated Type		Descripti
<IF_T100_MESSAGE>			☐				
DEFAULT_TEXTID	Constar	Publi	☐			⇨	
T100KEY	Instanc	Publi	☐	Type	SCX_T100KEY	⇨	T100 Key
<CX_ROOT>			☐				
CX_ROOT	Constar	Publi	☐	Type	SOTR_CONC	⇨	Exception
TEXTID	Instanc	Publi	☑	Type	SOTR_CONC	⇨	Key for A
PREVIOUS	Instanc	Publi	☑	Type Ref	CX_ROOT	⇨	Exception
KERNEL_ERRID	Instanc	Publi	☑	Type	S380ERRID	⇨	Internal
NOT_FOUND	Constar	Publi	☐			⇨	
BAD_QUERY	Constar	Publi	☐			⇨	
ALREADY_EXISTS	Constar	Publi	☐			⇨	
FACULTY_ID	Instanc	Publi	☐	Type	ZCS_FACULTY_ID	⇨	Universit

Figure 3.11 Message Class Attributes

Any attributes that you create are automatically mapped into the importing parameters of the exception class constructor (see Figure 3.12). Later, when the exception is created via the RAISE EXCEPTION syntax, what is really happening is that a CREATE OBJECT is being issued for the exception class specified. The CONSTRUCTOR is called during the RAISE EXCEPTION, thereby allowing importing parameters to be specified directly in the statement. Subsequently, any of these attributes will be available to be mapped into the variable placeholders of the message itself.

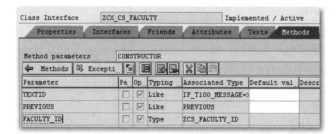

Figure 3.12 Attributes Are Mapped to Constructor Parameters

Exception Class Message Mapping

When an exception is raised, the issuing program can be very specific about the exact situation that produced the error. Each possible situation is represented as separate exception IDs within the exception class.

Now each exception ID can be mapped to a message class and message ID. Figure 3.13 shows that the exception IDs are maintained on the **Texts** tab of the exception in the Class Builder. You can click on the **Message Text** button to maintain the linkage between the exception ID and the message class ID. At the bottom of the assignment dialog, you can also connect attributes of the exception class with variables in the chosen message.

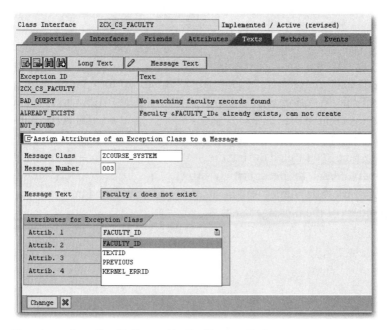

Figure 3.13 Exception ID Mapped to the Message Text

Raising an Exception

Class-based exceptions require the new syntax RAISE EXCEPTION. It is important not to confuse this syntax with the older syntax of just RAISE or MESSAGE ... RAISING. These older forms of the syntax only work for function module and method non-class based exceptions. For new development, you should try to avoid using non-class based exceptions.

In Listing 3.7, Russel is working with his persistent object. He wants to catch the generic persistent object exception, CX_OS_OBJECT_NOT_FOUND, and replace it with something more specific. In the raise exception for ZCX_CS_FACULTY, he first specifies the exception ID via the parameter TEXTID. All exception IDs automatically create a constant for easy reference from outside the class.

```
TRY.
     l_agent   = zca_cs_faculty_pers=>agent.
     l_pers_obj = l_agent->get_persistent(
         i_faculty_id = i_faculty_id ).
   CATCH cx_os_object_not_found.
     RAISE exception TYPE zcx_cs_faculty
       EXPORTING
           textid = zcx_cs_faculty=>not_found
           faculty_id = i_faculty_id.
ENDTRY.
```

Listing 3.7 Raising a Class-Based Exception

Finally you can see the use of the exception class attribute, FACULTY_ID, to provide additional details about the exception. This value can then be used inside any messages issued by this exception.

3.3   Business Object Classes

Russel is now prepared to start creating the next layer of his application, albeit he is not quite ready to begin writing his high-level application logic in the form of model classes. Instead, he would like to supply another layer of abstraction on top of his persistent objects. This is where the *Business Object Class* comes into the picture.

3.3.1 What Is a Business Object Class?

A persistent class, as Russel has already seen, has a very specific purpose. It is designed to be an object-oriented abstraction of the relational database. In other words, it hides all SQL from the developer, and instead provides methods to manipulate each record of data. The persistent object, however, is code that is generated directly from the data dictionary definition so it has a one-to-one match with the underlying database objects.

Conversely, a model class, which Russel will build later on, is not a specific type of ABAP Workbench object. It is simply a logical name for any class that implements the business logic for an application.

For example, in Business Server Pages (BSP), the model class must inherit from a particular superclass, `CL_BSP_MODEL2`. For Web Dynpro ABAP, any class can be used as the model object, but frequently the Assistance class is used because the Web Dynpro ABAP framework controls its lifetime. You can even create and use a model class in classic Dynpro, as Russel will discover in Chapter 11, but there is no framework support or integration into the Workbench. He will have to build the lifetime support into his own screen logic coding (*Process Before Output/Process After Input*, PBO/PAI).

So what is the difference between a model class and the business object class? The model class has the higher-level business logic and is specific to the particular application, but not limited to manipulating a single business object type. Russel's model class will eventually have transactional processing, and the necessary functionality for record copy logic, sending email, exporting to XSLT, and whatever else he needs to support the UI and business applications' requirements.

On the other hand, what Russel wants to build as a business object class really only has *Create, Read, Update, Delete* (CRUD) methods. Therefore, the business object class is just another layer of abstraction. It hides the fact that CRUD commands are being performed via a persistent object, thus further abstracting the final application code and protecting it from changes.

▶ **Flexibility via Abstraction**
Later, as the project progresses, Russel will encounter changes in his requirements that will cause certain pieces of data to no longer come from the local database (via a persistent object). Instead, he will be retrieving some data from a legacy system via Web Services (see Chapter 4). Other data access will include a check against a Shared Memory Object for data caching (see Chapter 5).

The beauty of providing another layer of abstraction is that when Russel makes these changes regarding how and where the data is stored, he can simply substitute the coding in the business object class with methods from Web Services instead of the persistent object.

In actuality, any model classes or other application logic that is already using the business object wouldn't sense any difference because of this change. This concept is integral to *enterprise service-oriented architecture* (enterprise SOA). Many people equate only Enterprise Services with enterprise SOA; however, good business object abstraction is just as critical to ensuring flexibility as is the technology enabler, Enterprise Services.

▶ **Functionality via Abstraction**
Another benefit to having the abstraction layer of the business object is that it allows for a more complex mapping than a one-to-one relationship with the database. This abstraction is what will allow Russel to have ZIP compression built in for the long string fields, without having to introduce any of this complexity into his application logic. The application logic will never even need to know that this level of complexity is happening!

▶ **Simplicity via Abstraction**
The final reason for providing another layer of abstraction is a matter of personal preference for Russel. The persistent object generates GET and SET methods for each field in the database that it is abstracting. This is a well-formatted object-oriented construct that works better in some programming environments than others; for example, in ABAP, it can prove to be quite cumbersome.

Who wants to have 20 or 30 lines of code for setters or getters to interact with all the fields from a database? Russel is used to having simple flat structures and internal tables for such a collection of elements. Therefore, as he designs his business object classes, he will also flatten out the attributes into easy-to-use ABAP structures.

He knows this goes against Object-Oriented (OO) programming design and Kristen Nygaard[1] is probably rolling over in his grave every time someone does this, but sometimes you have to sacrifice pure object orientation for easier programming, given the strengths of a particular development environment. Russel believes that this is one of those instances where such actions are justified.

---

1 Kristen Nygaard is widely attributed to be the father of object-oriented programming due to his co-creation with Ole-Johan Dahl of the programming language Simula in the 1960s.

3.3.2 Business Object Class Structure

The first consideration is that Russel has to determine how he will structure his business objects. Because he needs multiple ways to instantiate the class, a standard object constructor just won't suffice.

You should keep in mind that he wants to hide the persistent object, so the creation methods all need to be separate from what is actually retrieving the initial data. In order to control the instantiation, he sets the classes to allow only **Private** instantiation. This ensures that he can have a constructor that can only be accessed from within static methods of the business object class.

If you look at the methods of one particular business object class, the faculty object for instance, you'll see how the methods are structured to support different types of instantiation (see Figure 3.14). First there are the four **Static** (level) and **Public** (visibility) methods — CREATE_FACULTY, READ_ALL_FACULTY, READ_FACULTY, and READ_FACULTY_BY_LASTNAME. Each of these methods depicts one possible way to access an instance of the business object class.

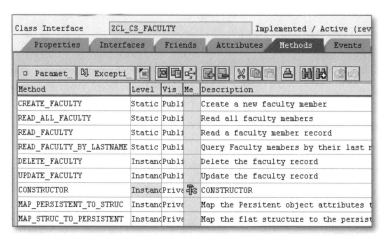

Figure 3.14 Business Object Class Methods

If you look at READ_FACULTY, you'll see that this is a method that accepts the Business Key of FACULTY_ID and returns an instance of its own class, ZCL_CS_FACULTY (see Figure 3.15).

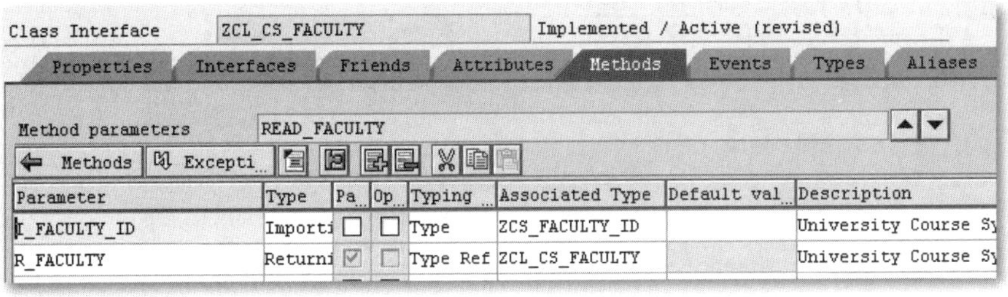

Figure 3.15 READ_FACULTY Method

The coding inside this method should look quite familiar (see Listing 3.8). All that is really happening is that Russel is using the persistent object to load the record for the given business key.

```
DATA: l_agent    TYPE REF TO zca_cs_faculty_pers,
      l_pers_obj TYPE REF TO zcl_cs_faculty_pers.

  TRY.
      l_agent    = zca_cs_faculty_pers=>agent.
      l_pers_obj = l_agent->get_persistent(
         i_faculty_id = i_faculty_id ).
    CATCH cx_os_object_not_found.
      RAISE EXCEPTION TYPE zcx_cs_faculty
        EXPORTING
           textid = zcx_cs_faculty=>not_found
           faculty_id = i_faculty_id.
  ENDTRY.

  CREATE OBJECT r_faculty
    EXPORTING
       i_persistent_object = l_pers_obj.
```

Listing 3.8 READ_FACULTY Method

The CONSTRUCTOR of the business object is designed to accept the instance of the persistent object (see Figure 3.16). But because the CONSTRUCTOR is **Private**, it easily could be changed tomorrow to accept anything else that might hold the data of the record in question. For example, it could accept a flat ABAP structure already loaded with the record from the database, or instead of an instance of the persistent object, it could access a Web Service Proxy class instance.

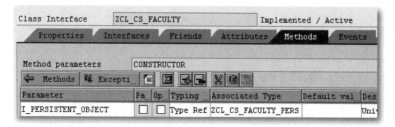

Figure 3.16 ZCL_CS_FACULTY Constructor

The logic inside the CONSTRUCTOR stores the instance of the persistent object in a private attribute (see Listing 3.9). This allows the business object to still have access to the persistent services for this record throughout its lifetime. The CONSTRUCTOR also has a call to the method MAP_PERSISTENT_TO_STRUC. This is how Russel intends to flatten out all the persistent object attributes into a regular ABAP structure.

```
METHOD CONSTRUCTOR.
  me->persistent_object = i_persistent_object.
  me->map_persistent_to_struc( ).
ENDMETHOD.
```

Listing 3.9 ZCL_CS_FACULTY Constructor

Unlike the persistent object, the business object class doesn't expose all the database fields as individual attributes. Instead, you see the attribute FACULTY_ATT, which has the flat structure ZCS_FACULTY just like the underlying database table (see Figure 3.17).

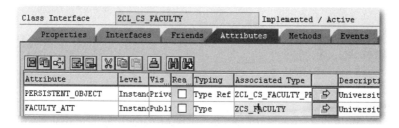

Figure 3.17 ZCL_CS_FACULTY Attributes

The mapping of the persistent attributes to the flat structure is really nothing more than a series of calls to the GET methods of the persistent class, as shown in Listing 3.10.

```
METHOD map_persistent_to_struc.
  faculty_att-faculty_id =
    persistent_object->get_faculty_id( ).
  faculty_att-first_name =
    persistent_object->get_first_name( ).


...
ENDMETHOD.
```

Listing 3.10 Persistent Attribute Mapping

3.3.3 Multiple Object Selection

Russel also has the method READ_ALL_FACULTY. Naturally there are going to be times when you want to work with more than just one business record. Russel decides to try something that was doable with SAP R/3 4.6C, albeit he never had the opportunity to do it, namely, to create an internal table of object references.

First, he creates a line structure in the data dictionary that contains a field, FACULTY, which can hold an object reference to ZCL_CS_FACULTY (see Figure 3.18). Notice the checkmark in the **RTy** column. This declares the component type to be a reference type and is the same as using the TYPE REF TO construct in ABAP code.

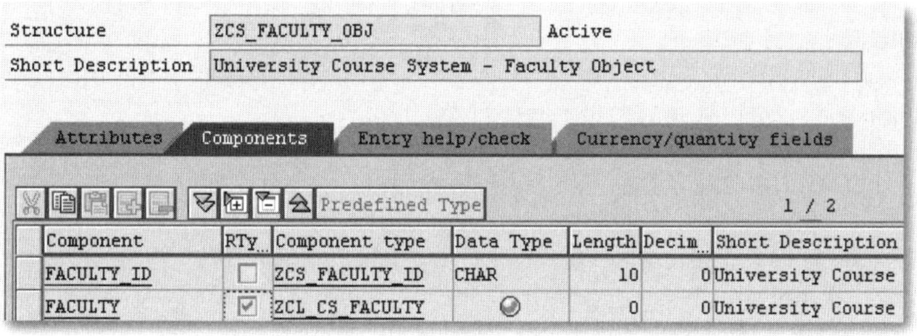

Structure	ZCS_FACULTY_OBJ		Active			
Short Description	University Course System - Faculty Object					

	Attributes	Components	Entry help/check	Currency/quantity fields		

Predefined Type 1 / 2

Component	RTy	Component type	Data Type	Length	Decim	Short Description
FACULTY_ID	☐	ZCS_FACULTY_ID	CHAR	10	0	University Course
FACULTY	☑	ZCL_CS_FACULTY	◉		0	University Course

Figure 3.18 Structure That Contains an Object Reference

If you look at the coding that Russel has created for the READ_ALL_FACULTY method, you'll see that he has a single returning value, R_FACULTY (see Listing 3.11). This returning parameter is a standard table type for the structure ZCS_FACULTY_OBJ that you just saw. His goal is to fill the internal table, R_FACULTY, with all the business keys, FACULTY_ID, and an object instance of his business object class for each key.

```
METHOD READ_ALL_FACULTY.
*Returning@  VALUE( R_FACULTY )  TYPE ZCS_FACULTY_TBL
*Exception@  ZCX_CS_FACULTY

  DATA: l_agent    TYPE REF TO zca_cs_faculty_pers,
        l_pers_obj TYPE REF TO zcl_cs_faculty_pers,
        l_objects TYPE         osreftab.
  FIELD-SYMBOLS: <wa_object>  LIKE LINE OF l_objects,
                 <wa_faculty> LIKE LINE OF r_faculty.

****Persistent Object Query Interface
  DATA: query_manager TYPE REF TO if_os_query_manager,
        query         TYPE REF TO if_os_query.

  TRY.
    l_agent    = zca_cs_faculty_pers=>agent.
    query_manager = cl_os_system=>get_query_manager( ).
    query = query_manager->create_query( ).

    l_objects =
      l_agent->if_os_ca_persistency~get_persistent_by_query(
              i_query   = query ).
    IF LINES( l_objects ) = 0.
      RAISE EXCEPTION TYPE zcx_cs_faculty
          EXPORTING
            textid = zcx_cs_faculty=>bad_query.
    ENDIF.

    LOOP AT l_objects ASSIGNING <wa_object>.
      l_pers_obj ?= <wa_object>.
      APPEND INITIAL LINE
          TO r_faculty ASSIGNING <wa_faculty>.
      <wa_faculty>-faculty_id =
          l_pers_obj->get_faculty_id( ).
      CREATE OBJECT <wa_faculty>-faculty
        EXPORTING
          i_persistent_object = l_pers_obj.
    ENDLOOP.
  ENDTRY.

ENDMETHOD.
```

Listing 3.11 READ_ALL_FACULTY Method

Russel uses the *query service* that was discussed in Section 3.1.4. When we saw the query service before, Russel had built a filter object. However, if you want to read all records via a persistent object, you can simply choose not to supply a filter as Russel has done here.

The GET_PERSISTENT_BY_QUERY method of the agent class of the persistent object returns an internal table of the object references of persistent objects. Russel then loops through all persistent object references, creating an entry in his returning parameter table, R_FACULTY, for each one of them.

So how could we use the returning parameter from this method to get back to a nice flat, structured ABAP internal table? Well, remember that Russel exposes a single attribute with a structure of all his data fields for each business object class. If we keep that in mind, it's a simple process of looping through the table of object references that is returned from READ_ALL_FAC-ULTY and appending this attribute structure to another internal table (see Listing 3.12).

```
DATA: ifaculty_objs TYPE zcs_faculty_tbl,
      ifaculty      TYPE STANDARD TABLE OF zcs_faculty.
FIELD-SYMBOLS: <wa_faculty_obj> LIKE LINE OF ifaculty_objs,
               <wa_faculty>     LIKE LINE OF ifaculty.
* Get data using model class
ifaculty_objs = zcl_cs_faculty=>read_all_faculty( ).
LOOP AT ifaculty_objs
        ASSIGNING <wa_faculty_obj>.
  APPEND INITIAL LINE TO ifaculty
              ASSIGNING <wa_faculty>.
  MOVE-CORRESPONDING
        <wa_faculty_obj>-faculty->faculty_att
                  TO <wa_faculty>.
ENDLOOP.
```

Listing 3.12 Read All Business Object Class Attributes into an Internal Table

3.3.4 Select-Options as a Query Criteria

With the READ_ALL_FACULTY method, you have seen how Russel will handle multiple instances of his business object. Now he has a somewhat bigger challenge ahead of him with the READ_FACULTY_BY_LASTNAME method. What is returned from this method is exactly the same as the READ_ALL_FACULTY. The only difference now is that he will need a more complex way of querying what business object instances are returned.

As he thinks ahead about the needs of his user interface, he believes that he wants to leverage an ABAP SELECT-OPTION for his search by last name. SELECT-OPTIONS are longtime ABAP concepts that are powerful ways for the user to specify their input criteria. They allow for complex combinations of wildcards, NOT expressions, and other patterns. Inside of ABAP report programs, they are commonly used inside SQL statements via the special IN condition of the WHERE clause.

SELECT-OPTIONS are not just limited to dialog programs however. Web Dynpro ABAP also has a reusable component that brings the same concepts to that environment. That said, you couldn't just declare a SELECT-OPTION within a class or Web Dynpro ABAP component as you would in a classic dialog program. In classic Dynpro, when you use the SELECT-OPTION statement, what is actually created (transparent to the user) is an internal table with a very specialized structure. To create this same structure for use in classes and Web Dynpro ABAP, you will need to create a special type of Data Dictionary table type.

Russel begins the process by creating a standard table type in the data dictionary. While in create mode and even before specifying a line type, he chooses the menu option **Edit • Define as ranges table type**. This menu option converts the standard table type into a ranges table type. The ranges table type is the same table type that has always been generated internally by the SELECT-OPTION declaration.

The table type maintenance screen has changed considerably due to the switch to a ranges table type (see Figure 3.19). Russel now only has to specify the data type for which he wants to generate a range, which is akin to specifying the FOR value in an inline coding SELECT-OPTION declaration. At the bottom of the screen, he specifies the name of the row type. This is a structure that will be generated by the ABAP Workbench when he clicks on the **Create** button.

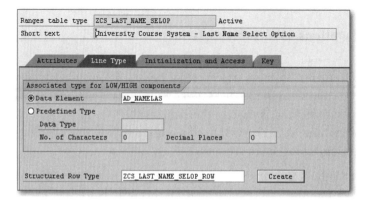

Figure 3.19 Ranges Table Type

This structure (see Figure 3.20) has all the components of the SELECT-OPTION:

▶ SIGN

It has the SIGN field, which specifies if a single criterion is an inclusion (I) or exclusion (E).

▶ OPTION

Next is the OPTION field. This field holds the logical operator of the selection criteria. For instance, it might have the value CP for contains pattern or EQ for equals. The online ABAP documentation lists all the possible values.

▶ LOW/HIGH

The last fields are the LOW and HIGH fields, each of which was generated with the component type that was specified for the range table. These fields will hold values for the field used in the selection criteria.

Structure	ZCS_LAST_NAME_SELOP_ROW		Active			
Short Description	University Course System Last Name Select Option - Row					

Attributes	Components	Entry help/check	Currency/quantity fields

Predefined Type 1 / 4

Component	RTy	Component type	Data Type	Length	Decim	Short Description
SIGN	☐	DDSIGN	CHAR	1	0	Type of SIGN componen
OPTION	☐	DDOPTION	CHAR	2	0	Type of OPTION compon
LOW	☐	AD_NAMELAS	CHAR	40	0	Last name
HIGH	☐	AD_NAMELAS	CHAR	40	0	Last name

Figure 3.20 Ranges Structured Row Type

The range table type definition can now be used directly as the type for the importing parameter, I_LASTNAME, of Russel's method. Once inside the coding, the internal table I_LASTNAME can be used exactly as you would any normal SELECT-OPTION.

If you recall, earlier Russel discovered that the query service has some limitations. It does not yet support the use of SELECT-OPTIONS within the filter. Therefore, to support the SELECT-OPTION, Russel has to make an exception to his use of persistent services and fall back on using some procedural SQL.

He uses a standard SQL statement to retrieve all the business keys, thanks to the use of the IN criteria of the WHERE clause. He still uses the persistent object to load the rest of the data by looping through the internal table of keys returned from his SQL query (see Listing 3.13).

```
METHOD read_faculty_by_lastname.
*Importing@  I_LASTNAME  TYPE ZCS_LAST_NAME_SELOP
*Returning@  VALUE( R_FACULTY )  TYPE ZCS_FACULTY_TBL
*Exception@  ZCX_CS_FACULTY

  DATA: l_agent    TYPE REF TO zca_cs_faculty_pers,
        l_pers_obj TYPE REF TO zcl_cs_faculty_pers,
        l_faculty  TYPE STANDARD TABLE OF zcs_faculty_id.

  FIELD-SYMBOLS: <wa_faculty_key> LIKE LINE OF l_faculty,
                 <wa_faculty> LIKE LINE OF r_faculty.

  TRY.
    l_agent    = zca_cs_faculty_pers=>agent.
    SELECT faculty_id FROM zcs_faculty INTO TABLE l_faculty
     WHERE last_name IN i_lastname.

    IF LINES( l_faculty ) = 0.
      RAISE EXCEPTION TYPE zcx_cs_faculty
        EXPORTING
          textid = zcx_cs_faculty=>bad_query.
    ENDIF.

    LOOP AT l_faculty ASSIGNING <wa_faculty_key>.
      APPEND INITIAL LINE TO r_faculty
        ASSIGNING <wa_faculty>.
      <wa_faculty>-faculty_id = <wa_faculty_key>.
      l_pers_obj = l_agent->get_persistent(
        i_faculty_id = <wa_faculty>-faculty_id ).
      CREATE OBJECT <wa_faculty>-faculty
        EXPORTING
          i_persistent_object = l_pers_obj.
    ENDLOOP.
  ENDTRY.
ENDMETHOD.
```

Listing 3.13 READ_FACULTY_BY_LASTNAME

3.3.5   Complex Business Objects

One of the benefits of using business objects instead of persistent objects that Russel identified is that it allows for more complex object mappings. With persistent objects, you usually have a one-to-one match with the database layer.

However, if you look at the data model that Russel built for his system, you'll notice that the course object has several closely related tables. When accessing this business object, you probably also need details from these other related tables. There are several things that Russel has done to interconnect data from the related underlying tables within his business object class, the first of which is what he decided to expose as attributes of the main business object class.

You should also note that, in addition to the flat structure for the course attributes that are read from the ZCS_COURSE table, he has read-only internal tables with all the course assignments and course registrations (see Figure 3.21).

Class Interface	ZCL_CS_COURSE			Implemented / Active	

Properties	Interfaces	Friends	Attributes	Methods	Events

Attribute	Level	Vis	Rea	Typing	Associated Type	
COURSE_PERS	Instanc	Prive	☐	Type Ref	ZCL_CS_COURSE_PERS	⇨
COURSE_PREQ_PERS	Instanc	Prive	☐	Type	ZCS_COURSE_PREQ_OBJ_TBL	⇨
COURSE	Instanc	Publi	☐	Type	ZCS_COURSE_ATT	⇨
COURSE_ASS	Instanc	Publi	☑	Type	ZCS_COURSE_ASSIGN_ATT_TBL	⇨
COURSE_REG	Instanc	Publi	☑	Type	ZCS_COURSE_REG_ATT_TBL	⇨

Figure 3.21 Attributes of the Course Business Object Class

During the constructor of the course business object, he uses the separate business objects for the course assignments and the course registrations to load all of the detail records (see Listing 3.14). Now Russel is starting to see where his investment in the work to create the business objects is paying off. Already he can see how easily he can reuse logic as objects that are embedded within other objects.

```
METHOD load_supporting_details.
  DATA: course_ass_obj TYPE zcs_course_ass_obj_tbl.
  TRY.
     course_ass_obj =
       zcl_cs_course_ass=>read_all_course_ass(
         i_course_id = course-course_id   ).
   CATCH zcx_cs_course .
  ENDTRY.

  FIELD-SYMBOLS: <wa_obj> LIKE LINE OF course_ass_obj.
```

```
                  <wa_ass> LIKE LINE OF me->course_ass.
      LOOP AT course_ass_obj ASSIGNING <wa_obj>.
        APPEND INITIAL LINE
          TO me->course_ass ASSIGNING <wa_ass>.
        <wa_ass> = <wa_obj>-course_ass->course_ass.
      ENDLOOP.

      DATA: course_reg_obj TYPE zcs_course_reg_obj_tbl.
      TRY.
          course_reg_obj =
            zcl_cs_course_registration=>read_all_course_reg(
              i_course_id = course-course_id   ).
        CATCH zcx_cs_course .
      ENDTRY.

      FIELD-SYMBOLS: <wa_obj2> LIKE LINE OF course_reg_obj,
                     <wa_reg> LIKE LINE OF me->course_reg.
      LOOP AT course_reg_obj ASSIGNING <wa_obj2>.
        APPEND INITIAL LINE
          TO me->course_reg ASSIGNING <wa_reg>.
        <wa_reg> = <wa_obj2>-course_reg->course_reg.
      ENDLOOP.
    ENDMETHOD.
```

Listing 3.14 Load Supporting Details for the Course Business Object

But this is not the only area where he has built in a complex mapping or reused other business objects. If you look at the structure that he is using for the COURSE attribute, you can see that Russel has not created a one-to-one map for the underlying database table, ZCS_COURSE, as he had done with the faculty object (see Figure 3.22).

Instead, here, Russel has used the business object to simplify the access to the main course data by combining information from multiple sources. First, in the database, you'll see that there are technically two separate tables — ZCS_COURSE and ZCS_COURSE_PREQ — because there is a one-to-many relationship. Each table has its own set of persistent object classes; however, Russel has decided to hide that level of complexity by using the business object class.

Inside the business object class, he processes each persistent object individually, but maps all the values of the ZCS_COURSE_PREQ object into an internal table that is stored as a cell in the larger course attribute structure. He creates a nested structure in his attribute that is not technically possible to display directly in the database layer.

You might also notice that there is an object reference in this structure as well — the field FACULTY of component type ZCL_CS_FACULTY. Once more, Russel is able to benefit from his investment in business objects. A faculty member is assigned to each course, but, instead of just having the FACULTY_ ID key present in the course attribute structure, he can expose the entire faculty business object instance, thereby providing easy access to all the associated faculty details.

Dictionary: Hierarchy representation ZCS_COURSE_ATT					
Component	Component type	Short description	DTyp	Lngth	Dec.pla
▽ ▥ ZCS_COURSE_ATT		University Course System - Course Attrib...			
COURSE_ID	ZCS_COURSE_ID	University Course System - Courses - Cou...	CHAR	10	0
COURSE_SDESC	ZCS_COURSE_SHORT_DESCRIPTION	University Course System - Course Title	CHAR	128	0
FACULTY_ID	ZCS_FACULTY_ID	University Course System - Faculty - Id	CHAR	10	0
⇒ FACULTY	ZCL_CS_FACULTY	University Course System - Faculty Object			
SEMESTER	ZCS_SEMESTER	University Course System - Course Semester	NUMC	1	0
COURSE_YEAR	ZCS_YEAR	University Course System - Course Year	NUMC	4	0
MAJOR	ZCS_MAJOR_DEL	University Course System - Degree Major	CHAR	3	0
CREDIT_HRS	ZCS_STUDENT_CREDIT_HRS	Univeristy Course System - Student - Cre...	NUMC	4	0
STUDENT_LIMIT	ZCS_COURSE_STUDENT_LIMIT	University Course System - Student Limit	NUMC	4	0
DELETION_FLAG	AD_DELETEFLAG	Flag: Delete Flag	CHAR	1	0
START_TIME	ZCS_COURSE_START_TIME	University Course System - Course Start ...	TIMS	6	0
END_TIME	ZCS_COURSE_END_TIME	University Course System - Course End Time	TIMS	6	0
COURSE_SCHEDULE	ZCS_COURSE_SCHEDULE	University Course System - Course Schedule	CHAR	2	0
COST	ZCS_COURSE_COST	University Course System - Course Cost	CURR	15	2
CURRENCY	ZCS_CURRCODE	University Course System - Currency	CUKY	5	0
DESCRIPTION	ZCS_COURSE_DESC	University Course System - Course Descri...	STRING	0	0
SYLLABI	ZCS_COURSE_SYLLABI_OUTPUT	University Course System - Course Syllabi	STRING	0	0
▽ ▦ PRE_REQ	ZCS_COURSE_PREQ_ATT_TBL	University Course System - Prerequisite A...			
▽ ▥ Row type:	ZCS_COURSE_PREQ_ATT	University Course System - Prerequisite A...			
PREQ_ID	ZCS_COURSE_PREQ_ID	Prerequisite Counter	CHAR	10	0

Figure 3.22 Structure for Course Business Object Attribute

3.3.6 Modification Operations

Until now, we have just looked at the read-only operations of the business object class. Russel has created the UPDATE and DELETE methods as the only (**Public**) **Instance** methods of the business object classes. Because these are instance methods, this ensures that the persistent object has been loaded for a particular business key and is ready to be used to modify the data in the database as well.

Update

Russel decides not to build transactionality into the business object classes, because he believes that it is better to leave the transaction coordination, record locking, and commits or rollbacks to a higher level of application coding, such as the model class. In this way, the transactionality can be coordinated to best reflect the surrounding user interface.

Consequently, the update method doesn't have much coding within it (see Listing 3.15). It is only required to call the SET methods of the persistent object, thereby mapping the data from the flat structure of the business object attribute into the persistent object attributes. All that is needed is an external commit and the data is then written to the database tables.

```
persistent_object->set_first_name(
    faculty_att-first_name ).
  persistent_object->set_last_name( faculty_att-last_name ).
...
  persistent_object->set_office_hours(
    faculty_att-office_hours ).
```
Listing 3.15 Business Object Update Method

Delete

The DELETE method is another opportunity to showcase the benefits of the business object layer (see Listing 3.16). The DELETE method of a persistent object would of course physically remove the corresponding record from the database; however, it is quite common in business applications to not want to remove a record for tracking purposes.

Instead, in business systems, a deletion operation is really more an act of setting a status flag. You just want to mark a record in some way so that it is excluded from normal operations, but can still be viewed or the deletion action can be reversed. Therefore, a delete in this business object class is only going to set the attribute delete equal to true and then perform an update operation.

```
METHOD delete_faculty.
  faculty_att-deletion_flag = abap_true.
  me->map_struc to_persistent( ).
ENDMETHOD.
```
Listing 3.16 Delete Method

3.3.7 ZIP Compression

There is another area where the abstraction layer of the business object class comes in quite handy. If you recall, there are certain fields in the database that will hold large strings or binary objects. One such example is the SYLLABI field in the main Course table.

The SYLLABI field is designed to hold an entire HTML page. This will allow the faculty to maintain their own richly formatted course syllabi. When the database table was set up, the field was designed to store binary string data.

So why did Russel design the field for binary string data when the contents of an HTML page is just plain text? Ideally, he would have just needed a plain text string field.

Because each syllabus can be a rather large object, Russel decided to take advantage of the ZIP compression technology that has been available in the ABAP environment since SAP Web AS 6.20. This is the same technology used on your PC when you compress a file.

There are two different types of ZIP compression available in ABAP. We will look at how Russel used both of these technologies. The global class is CL_ABAP_GZIP. This library only provides compression. It doesn't have the capabilities to write out ZIP headers or to compress multiple objects into one ZIP stream.

This is all the functionality required for the SYLLABI field. Russel only wants to decompress the stream after it has been returned by the persistent object (see Listing 3.17), and then compress it again before sending it back to the persistent object (see Listing 3.18). That way, any applications using the business object can process the HTML content as a simple string, without having to worry or even know about the underlying compression process.

```
DATA l_syllabi TYPE xstring.
  l_syllabi = course_pers->get_syllabi( ).
  DATA izip TYPE REF TO cl_abap_gzip.
  IF l_syllabi IS NOT INITIAL.
    CREATE OBJECT izip.
    izip->decompress_text(
        EXPORTING gzip_in = l_syllabi
        IMPORTING text_out = course-syllabi ).
  ENDIF.
```

Listing 3.17 Decompress from the Persistent Object

```
  DATA l_syllabi TYPE xstring.
  DATA izip TYPE REF TO cl_abap_gzip.
  IF course-syllabi IS NOT INITIAL.
    CREATE OBJECT izip.
    izip->compress_text(
        EXPORTING text_in = course-syllabi
        IMPORTING gzip_out = l_syllabi ).
  ENDIF.
  course_pers->set_syllabi( l_syllabi ).
```

Listing 3.18 Compress Before Updating

Russel has another more complex task that will also require using compression. This is for the course assignment table. In the database, the course assignments attachments field is defined as a single binary string. This field is intended to allow faculty to upload and attach whatever files they need to support the week's assignments. For each assignment, there may be one file or many different files.

However, we only have the single field to hold all the files. This is where Russel elects to use the more advanced ZIP class — CL_ABAP_ZIP. In addition to performing compression, this library allows you to include separate objects into one ZIP package — more like PC-based ZIP compression utilities. After decompression, the business object will slice the individual components from the ZIP package into separate records in an attachments internal table. The structure that is exposed by the business object for the attachments is shown in Figure 3.23.

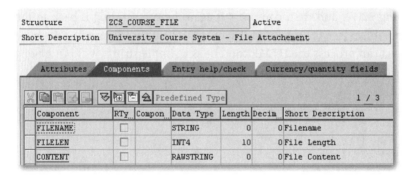

Figure 3.23 Assignment Attachments Structure

The logic for this ZIP library is quite similar to the first library. The main difference is the use of the SPLICE static method to provide an internal table of inner components of the compressed string (see Listing 3.19). Each inner component must be pulled out of the compressed package using the GET method. Russel can then use very similar logic to what he first used with the earlier class in order to compress the data before sending it into the persistent object (see Listing 3.20).

```
CLEAR course_ass-attachments.
DATA: izip TYPE REF TO cl_abap_zip.
DATA: l_attchements TYPE xstring.
DATA: splice TYPE cl_abap_zip=>t_splice_entries.
FIELD-SYMBOLS: <wa_splice> LIKE LINE OF splice,
               <wa_att>    TYPE zcs_course_file.
```

```
l_attchements = persistent_object->get_attachments( ).
IF l_attchements IS NOT INITIAL.
  CREATE OBJECT izip.
  splice = cl_abap_zip=>splice( l_attchements ).
  izip->load( l_attchements ).
ENDIF.

LOOP AT splice ASSIGNING <wa_splice>.
  APPEND INITIAL LINE
    TO course_ass-attachments ASSIGNING <wa_att>.
  <wa_att>-filename = <wa_splice>-name.
  <wa_att>-filelen  = <wa_splice>-length.
  izip->get(
    EXPORTING name = <wa_att>-filename
    IMPORTING content = <wa_att>-content ).
ENDLOOP.
```

Listing 3.19 Slicing and Decompression of Attachments from the Persistent Object

```
DATA: izip TYPE REF TO cl_abap_zip.
DATA: l_attchments TYPE xstring.
FIELD-SYMBOLS: <wa_att>    TYPE zcs_course_file.
CREATE OBJECT izip.
LOOP AT course_ass-attachments ASSIGNING <wa_att>.
  izip->add( name    = <wa_att>-filename
             content = <wa_att>-content ).
ENDLOOP.
l_attchments = izip->save( ).
persistent_object->set_attachments( l_attchments ).
```

Listing 3.20 Compression of Attachments Before Returning to the Persistent Object

3.4   Data Load Programs

Now that Russel has completed all of his business objects, he has all of the interfaces he needs to get data in and out of his database tables. Before proceeding with the development of any of the other layers of logic, he would like to do some testing of what has been developed so far.

3.4.1   Test Data Generator

In order to adequately test his business objects or the underlying persistent objects, he needs to be able to get some test data into the database. Looking at the student database in particular, he needs a way to get some realistic data into the database in order to do good testing. Unfortunately, he doesn't have access yet to any of the real data that will be loaded into the system. He only has a spreadsheet of student names (see Figure 3.24).

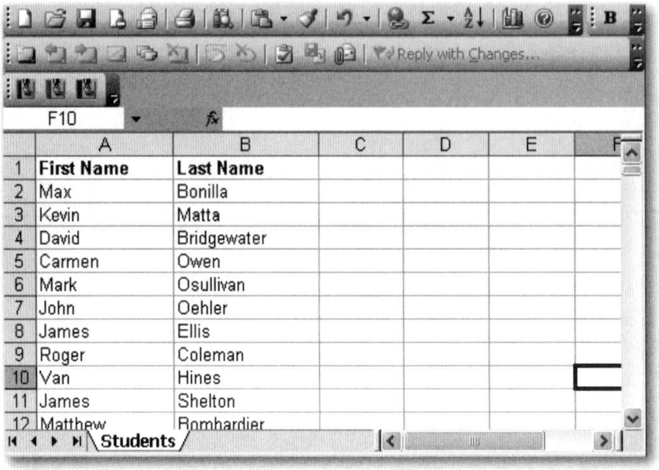

	A	B	C	D	E	F
1	**First Name**	**Last Name**				
2	Max	Bonilla				
3	Kevin	Matta				
4	David	Bridgewater				
5	Carmen	Owen				
6	Mark	Osullivan				
7	John	Oehler				
8	James	Ellis				
9	Roger	Coleman				
10	Van	Hines				
11	James	Shelton				
12	Matthew	Bombardier				

Figure 3.24 Student Name Spreadsheet

Lack of sufficient test data is a fairly common problem for developers. Sometimes you just have to create your own data and that is exactly what Russel decides to do. After all, he sees this generation of test data as another opportunity to try out his business object classes, as he will use them to load the data.

Program Initialization

1. He starts off by creating a basic report that has the ability to query the user for the name of the spreadsheet. He uploads the spreadsheet with the first and last names as the starting point of the generated data:

```
REPORT  zcs_students_generate.

DATA istudents TYPE STANDARD TABLE OF zcs_student.
FIELD-SYMBOLS: <wa_student> LIKE LINE OF istudents.

TYPES: BEGIN OF t_import,
         fname TYPE string,
         lname TYPE string,
       END OF t_import.
DATA: iimport TYPE STANDARD TABLE OF t_import.
FIELD-SYMBOLS: <wa_input> LIKE LINE OF iimport.
```

```
DATA retfiletable TYPE filetable.
DATA retrc TYPE sysubrc.
DATA retuseraction TYPE i.
PARAMETERS filename(300) TYPE c .

INITIALIZATION.

AT SELECTION-SCREEN ON VALUE-REQUEST FOR filename.
  CALL METHOD cl_gui_frontend_services=>file_open_dialog
    EXPORTING
      multiselection     = abap_false
      file_filter        = '*.xls'
      default_extension = 'xls'
    CHANGING
      file_table         = retfiletable
      rc                 = retrc
      user_action        = retuseraction.
  READ TABLE retfiletable INTO filename INDEX 1.
```

File Upload and Processing

2. At the beginning of program execution, he uploads the data from the selected spreadsheet file. Then, he checks to ensure that some data was definitely found in the imported file:

```
START-OF-SELECTION.
  DATA l_filename TYPE string.
  l_filename = filename.
  CALL METHOD cl_gui_frontend_services=>gui_upload
    EXPORTING
      filename           = l_filename
      has_field_separator = abap_true
    CHANGING
      data_tab           = iimport.
  CHECK iimport IS NOT INITIAL.
```

Next he deletes all the data that might currently be in his student table. He could have used the persistent objects to do the mass deletion, but because he opted to do a logical deletion and not a physical one within his business object, he doesn't really feel that this situation warrants testing. Therefore, for maximum performance, he decides to go with the pure SQL operation:

```
DELETE FROM zcs_student.
COMMIT WORK AND WAIT.
```

Data Generation

3. The first test of logic comes at this point. The spreadsheet contains only the first and last names of the students, not their internal student ID. Therefore, he must generate a unique student ID. The business rule used at the university is to take the student's last name and combine it with the first two letters of the first name to create that student's ID. If that doesn't create a unique key, then a counter is added to the end of the ID until it becomes unique:

```
DATA: temp_id TYPE zcs_student_id,
      found_id TYPE boolean,
      id_counter(2) TYPE n.
  LOOP AT iimport ASSIGNING <wa_input>.
  CONCATENATE <wa_input>-lname
     <wa_input>-fname+0(2) INTO temp_id.
     found_id = abap_false.
     id_counter = 0.
     WHILE found_id = abap_false.
       TRANSLATE temp_id TO UPPER CASE.
       READ TABLE istudents TRANSPORTING NO FIELDS
           WITH KEY student_id = temp_id.
       IF sy-subrc = 0.
         id_counter = id_counter + 1.
         concatenate <wa_input>-lname
           <wa_input>-fname+0(2) INTO temp_id.
         temp_id+8(2) = id_counter.
         CONDENSE temp_id NO-GAPS.
       ELSE.
         found_id = abap_true.
       ENDIF.
     ENDWHILE.
```

Next he will start building an internal table of the data that he wants to record to the database. He begins by mapping in the fields, which he read from the database, and the new business key that he has calculated for each student:

```
APPEND INITIAL LINE TO istudents ASSIGNING <wa_student>.
    <wa_student>-student_id = temp_id.
    <wa_student>-first_name = <wa_input>-fname.
    <wa_student>-last_name  = <wa_input>-lname.
```

Now he comes to the **Grade Point Average** and **Credit Hours** field. Since this is just test data, Russel could have simply inserted some dummy value into every record of his spreadsheet. Instead he decides that he will use this opportunity to explore another new feature of the ABAP environment — the random number generator.

Since SAP NetWeaver 2004, the ABAP environment has had a new kernel-based random number generator via the class, CL_ABAP_RANDOM. By using the INTINRANGE method of the CL_ABAP_RANDOM class, Russel even specifies intelligent upper and lower boundaries for his generated results:

```
DATA: random TYPE REF TO cl_abap_random.
DATA: seed TYPE i.
DATA: gpa   TYPE i.
seed = cl_abap_random=>seed( ).
random = cl_abap_random=>create( seed ).
<wa_student>-credit_hrs =
      random->intinrange( low = 0 high = 150 ).
gpa = random->intinrange( low = 1000 high = 4000 ).
<wa_student>-gpa = gpa / 1000.
CLEAR random.
ENDLOOP.
```

Business Object Logic

4. With the final section of the data generation program, Russel gets to put his business object class to work. He uses the business object class to create each new record. They are all written to the database via the persistent object upon the COMMIT WORK statement.

Russel also takes advantage of the powerful new exception class functionality for handling any error conditions, which means no more messy checking of SY-SUBRC codes. Even his error output is cleaner, because he can retrieve the text for the particular message exception directly from the exception class:

```
DATA: student_obj  TYPE REF TO zcl_cs_student,
      iexp         TYPE REF TO zcx_cs_student,
      error_string type string.
LOOP AT istudents ASSIGNING <wa_student>.
  TRY.
      student_obj = zcl_cs_student=>create_student(
          i_student_id = <wa_student>-student_id ).
      MOVE-CORRESPONDING <wa_student> TO
          student_obj->student_att.
      student_obj->update_student( ).
    CATCH zcx_cs_student INTO iexp.
      error_string =  iexp->get_text( ).
      WRITE: / error_string.
  ENDTRY.
ENDLOOP.
COMMIT WORK.
```

3.4.2 Backup and Recovery Program

After several rounds of testing, manually inserting data, and running some of these new mass generation test data programs, it was inevitable that Russel would corrupt some of the data in his course system. This inadvertent corruption of data is almost unavoidable when you're in the early development phases of a new project. ABAP developers don't usually give much thought to backup and recovery of data for the whole system. They leave those kinds of activities to their Basis Administration friends.

Nevertheless, after Russel's first experience with corrupting some of his data and having to type it back in manually, he decides to create his own localized backup and recovery utility applications. You should note that these programs are not intended to be real production-grade backup and recovery, but simply tools to help the ABAP developer in the early phases of development.

Rather than write a complex export utility that would have to be changed if any of the database structures change, Russel considers the feasibility of using XML and XSLT transformations to export and import this database table data.

The CALL TRANSFORMATION statement, which was added to the ABAP language syntax in SAP Web AS 6.10, allows for the direct translation to and from ABAP and XML. It uses a standards-based *Extensible Stylesheet Language Transformation* (XSLT) program to convert internal ABAP data types to their XML counterparts. You can even code your own XSLT programs within the ABAP environment inside of the ABAP Workbench. For this exercise, however, Russel only needs to use the SAP-delivered XSLT programs.

Backup Program

1. Russel begins his backup program by reading all the data from the database that he wants to back up into internal tables:

```
REPORT  zcs_backup_all_data.
DATA: istudents    TYPE STANDARD TABLE OF zcs_student,
  ...
      imajors_t    TYPE STANDARD TABLE OF zcs_majors_t.

START-OF-SELECTION.
  SELECT * FROM zcs_student    INTO TABLE istudents.
  SELECT * FROM zcs_majors_t   INTO TABLE imajors_t.
```

XML Transformation

2. Next you can see how simple it is to convert any structure to XML. No definition must be made in advance to either the export or import structure of ISTUDENTS. The CALL TRANSFORMATION statement reads the structure of the source at runtime and creates the corresponding XML dynamically:

```
DATA ixml TYPE xstring.
DATA xml TYPE string.
CALL TRANSFORMATION id
  SOURCE zcs_student = istudents
  RESULT xml  ixml.
```

ZIP Compression

3. Russel has also decided to take a page from what he has already learned about ZIP compression (see Section 3.3.7) and use the full-featured ZIP library to compress and organize each of his tables into a single ZIP file:

```
DATA izip TYPE REF TO cl_abap_zip.
DATA zip_file TYPE xstring.
CREATE OBJECT izip.
izip->add( name = 'zcs_student.xml'
           content = ixml ).
```

Conversion from Binary String to Binary Table

4. He will then only download the single ZIP file to the client machine. However the ZIP library returns the entire content in a single binary string. Unfortunately, the class that downloads data to the frontend will not accept this format.

So first he must convert his binary string into a binary table by using the function module SCMS_XSTRING_TO_BINARY. Incidentally, the function group SCMS_CONV has many function modules that are useful in conversions between strings, binary strings, character tables, and binary tables:

```
zip_file = izip->save( ).
  DATA binary_tab TYPE STANDARD TABLE OF x255.
  CALL FUNCTION 'SCMS_XSTRING_TO_BINARY'
    EXPORTING
      buffer     = zip_file
    TABLES
      binary_tab = binary_tab.
```

Download to the Frontend

5. The final step is to query the user for the location that he or she wants to save the file to, and then to perform the actual download:

```
DATA: filename TYPE string,
      path     TYPE string,
      fullpath TYPE string.


  cl_gui_frontend_services=>file_save_dialog(
    CHANGING
      filename               = filename
      path                   = path
      fullpath               = fullpath ).


  cl_gui_frontend_services=>gui_download(
    EXPORTING
      filename               = fullpath
      filetype               = 'BIN'
    CHANGING
      data_tab               = binary_tab ).
```

He now has a ZIP file on his PC, which can be opened in any ZIP compatible utility. He can view each of the individual XML files and their content from the PC (see Figure 3.25). All of this was created with just the few lines of code you see above.

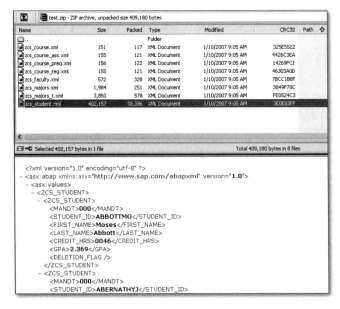

Figure 3.25 Data Backup ZIP File and XML Sample

Of course, what good is a backup program without a corresponding restore application? For the most part, this program is just the opposite of what Russel has just created.

Restore Program

1. He starts off with his data declarations and the logic necessary to allow the user to select a file from the client file system:

```
REPORT  zcs_restore_all_data.

DATA: istudents    TYPE STANDARD TABLE OF zcs_student,
...
      imajors_t    TYPE STANDARD TABLE OF zcs_majors_t.

DATA retfiletable TYPE filetable.
DATA retrc TYPE sysubrc.
DATA retuseraction TYPE i.
DATA input_length TYPE i.
PARAMETERS filename(300) TYPE c .
PARAMETERS merge TYPE boolean AS checkbox.

INITIALIZATION.

AT SELECTION-SCREEN ON VALUE-REQUEST FOR filename.
  CALL METHOD cl_gui_frontend_services=>file_open_dialog
    EXPORTING
      multiselection    = abap_false
      file_filter       = '*.xls'
      default_extension = 'xls'
    CHANGING
      file_table        = retfiletable
      rc                = retrc
      user_action       = retuseraction.
  READ TABLE retfilctable INTO filename INDEX 1.
```

Upload from the Frontend

2. Next he has the logic to upload the file content. Like the download utility, the upload method only returns a binary table. So Russel again resorts to using the function modules of the SCMS_CONV function group in order to perform the conversion:

```
START-OF-SELECTION.
  DATA binary_tab TYPE STANDARD TABLE OF x255.
```

```
DATA ixml TYPE xstring.
DATA izip TYPE REF TO cl_abap_zip.
DATA zip_file TYPE xstring.

DATA l_filename TYPE string.
l_filename = filename.
CALL METHOD cl_gui_frontend_services=>gui_upload
  EXPORTING
    filetype    = 'BIN'
    filename    = l_filename
  IMPORTING
    filelength = input_length
  CHANGING
    data_tab    = binary_tab.

CALL FUNCTION 'SCMS_BINARY_TO_XSTRING'
  EXPORTING
    input_length = input_length
  IMPORTING
    buffer       = zip_file
  TABLES
    binary_tab   = binary_tab.
```

ZIP Decompression

3. He then retrieves each individual component out of the ZIP package by specifying the name of the inner file:

```
CHECK binary_tab IS NOT INITIAL.
  CREATE OBJECT izip.
  izip->load( zip_file ).

  izip->get( EXPORTING name = 'zcs_student.xml'
             IMPORTING content = ixml ).
```

XML Transformation

4. Now this is where the real power comes from. The CALL TRANSFORMATION statement is bi-directional. Therefore, it can easily be used to restore the XML data back into ABAP variables. Furthermore, this works even if the ABAP structure has changed since the data was exported.

New fields in the ABAP destination structure will simply be ignored. Also, extra fields in the XML source won't cause an exception. They just won't be imported:

```
CALL TRANSFORMATION id
  SOURCE xml ixml
  RESULT zcs_student = istudents.
```

Database Update

5. Lastly, Russel writes the data that he has restored to internal tables back into the database tables:

```
MODIFY zcs_course FROM TABLE icourse.
```

Not all of the university's data is stored within their SAP ERP system. Some data is still stored in legacy systems or other third-party systems. In this chapter, Russel will learn how he can use Web Services to retrieve data from these other systems using open standards.

4 Consuming a Web Service

The university has a legacy system where it stores its student master data. Russel needs to access this data and incorporate it into the university course system. Before the upgrade of their ERP system, an interface between the two systems (i.e., in order to read the student data) would likely have entailed a nightly batch exchange of flat files via FTP or a shared file system. If the interface had been really sophisticated, it might have been possible to use the Java or .NET Connector.

All of these pre-upgrade scenarios would have required using file formats or communication protocols that were specific to the particular applications; consequently, changes within one partner in the data exchange could have a huge effect on the other partner. But, in just the last few years, the world of data interfaces has changed considerably. Web Services have revolutionized the way IT shops exchange data in so many ways; still, they have not gained popularity because they're radical departures from existing technologies. In fact, the most important advantage of Web Services is that they're built on a foundation of proven, yet open, technology standards:

- First, Web Services are built on *Hypertext Transfer Protocol* (HTTP) for their communication technology. This is the same technology that already drives the Internet. By choosing HTTP, there are already standards in place for communication encryptions, via Secure Sockets Layer (SSL), and client authentication, via X.509 Certificates.

- The second technology standard that is built into Web Services is *Extensible Markup Language* (XML). Even before Web Services, XML was already being used as a platform-independent way of describing data and data relationships; therefore XML is the perfect tool for structuring the data that will be transmitted via a Web Service.

There are two main parties when working with Web Services (see Figure 4.1):

► There is the *service provider*, who creates the implementation of the Web Service and provides a definition of the Web Service via a *Web Service Definition Language* (WSDL) document. The WSDL document is an XML-based document, which describes the Web Service, including all of its attributes and exposed methods. In addition to the WSDL document, to describe the service, the provider also displays the service itself as an HTTP endpoint, more commonly referred to as a *URL*.

When anyone requests this URL in order to call the Web Service, the documents that are exchanged over HTTP are called *SOAP documents*. SOAP is not a new technology per se. It is an accepted standard for the format and structure of the XML document that is exchanged during Web Service communications.

► The *service requestors* constitute the other party. They want some way to consume the Web Service. They receive the WSDL document, which tells them everything they need to know about calling a particular Web Service. They know the data types, the methods, the parameters, the URLs, etc.

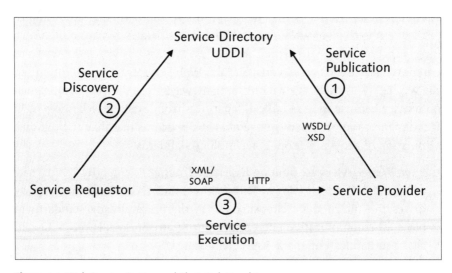

Figure 4.1 Web Service Parties and Their Relationships

If the consumer wanted, he could directly access the Web Service by formulating his own HTTP request and response objects and injecting the XML-formatted SOAP objects into them. But, this would probably entail a lot of low-level work. Instead, most programming environments, ABAP included, provide a simplified approach.

It would be so much easier for the service consuming programmer if they could write programming logic against this remote Web Service object as though it were simply a local object. That is precisely the purpose of a generated client proxy.

The ABAP development environment analyzes the WSDL document. It then generates structures, table types, and programming logic to map between XML and ABAP data types, in the form of *XSL Transformations* (XSLT), and finally an ABAP class to hide all the inner complexities. Ultimately, we recommend understanding what is going on "under the hood" with HTTP, XML, and SOAP; but proxy classes ensure that you rarely see those details when programming with Web Services.

4.1 Proxy Generation

The legacy system at the university that controls the student master data already has the necessary Web Services that expose the needed data. Actually this legacy system is third-party software that was never intended to function as an interface for a SAP ERP system. It runs on the Microsoft platform and was written in .NET. Although Russel's SAP ERP system runs on UNIX, these details become irrelevant due to the open standards upon which Web Services are built.

Russel is ready to start creating his client proxy object for the Web Service. His requirements are to consume the Web Service that retrieves student data from the external system. The client proxy object will provide an interface, which Russel can use in the business object layer of the university course system. The current business object retrieves local data via persistent objects, but will be swapped out to use the client proxy object instead.

4.1.1 Accessing the WSDL Document

In order to consume the Web Service, Russel must first find the WSDL document, which describes the Web Service. There are several ways in which to access a WSDL document. For example, the WSDL could be published to a *Universal Description, Discovery, and Integration* (UDDI) service directory. A UDDI service directory provides functionality for searching for Web Services and accessing the associated WSDL document. This server can be within the service provider's landscape, or could be a public UDDI service directory server. For example, SAP offers a public UDDI service directory at *http://uddi.sap.com*.

Russel could also access the WSDL document using a URL. The URL would have to be provided by the service provider. Similarly, the service provider could send the WSDL document via email and Russel could simply access it as a local file on his PC. In this case, Russel has been in direct communication with his counterparts that manage the hosting system and they have provided him with a direct URL with which to create his client proxy.

4.1.2 Creating the Client Proxy

Now that Russel has the WSDL document he needs, he can create a client proxy. This client proxy will generate a layer of abstraction, hiding the internal workings of the Web Service. The ABAP development environment generates the client proxies as global classes.

1. Russel goes to transaction SE80 to create the client proxy. He selects **Package** from the object list box. He then navigates in the object list to the ZCS_ MODEL_ESOA package. By right-mouse clicking on the **Enterprise Services** folder, a context menu appears from which Russel selects **Create • Proxy Object** as shown in Figure 4.2. Russel could have also used the context menu from the package level by right-mouse clicking on the ZCS_MODEL_ ESOA package and choosing **Create • Enterprise Service/Web Services • Proxy Object**.

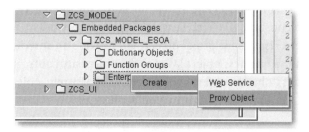

Figure 4.2 Creating the Client Proxy

The creation of a proxy object is actually going to generate a lot development objects. Data dictionary structures, table types, and XSL Transformation programs will all be generated in support of the proxy class itself. Therefore, we recommend that you create a separate package to house all of these objects in order to keep them separate from your main development objects. Since these are generated objects, you don't have to include them in normal maintenance activities, such as language translation.

2. There is also one major criterion that a package must have in order to house a proxy object. If you recall, in Chapter 1, we discussed how the renaming of Development Class to Packages was more than just superficial. Packages can now have interfaces that control which objects can be used from outside the package. Any package that will be the home of a generated proxy object will need access to certain core SAP objects. The package gains this access by declaring a Use Access for the package interface SAI_TOOLS within the package maintenance screen (see Figure 4.3).

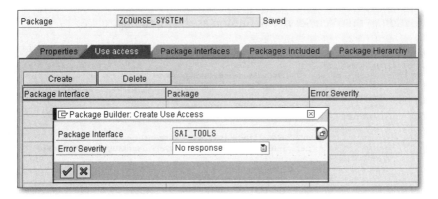

Figure 4.3 Package Use Access

3. Next Russel needs to select the method in which the WSDL document will be accessed. Again, Russel has been provided with the URL, which points to the WSDL document, so he selects the radio button for **URL/HTTP Destination** as shown in Figure 4.4 during proxy generation.

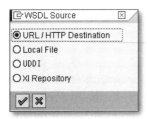

Figure 4.4 WSDL Source

4. Next, Russel pastes the URL into the input field as shown in Figure 4.5.

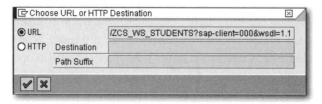

Figure 4.5 URL Destination

5. Russel is a little curious as to what exactly a WSDL file looks like, so he pastes the URL in his web browser to see it. The data is an XML representation of the Web Service definition as shown in Figure 4.6.

```
        <wsdl:part name="parameters" element="tns:ZcsWsGetStudentById" />
    </wsdl:message>
  - <wsdl:message name="ZcsWsGetStudentByIdResponse">
        <wsdl:part name="parameters" element="tns:ZcsWsGetStudentByIdResponse" />
    </wsdl:message>
  - <wsdl:message name="ZcsWsGetStudentsByLname">
        <wsdl:part name="parameters" element="tns:ZcsWsGetStudentsByLname" />
    </wsdl:message>
  - <wsdl:message name="ZcsWsGetStudentsByLnameResponse">
        <wsdl:part name="parameters" element="tns:ZcsWsGetStudentsByLnameResponse" />
    </wsdl:message>
  - <wsdl:portType name="zcs_ws_students">
    - <wsdl:operation name="ZcsWsGetAllStudents">
        <wsdl:input message="tns:ZcsWsGetAllStudents" />
        <wsdl:output message="tns:ZcsWsGetAllStudentsResponse" />
    </wsdl:operation>
    - <wsdl:operation name="ZcsWsGetStudentById">
        <wsdl:input message="tns:ZcsWsGetStudentById" />
        <wsdl:output message="tns:ZcsWsGetStudentByIdResponse" />
    </wsdl:operation>
    - <wsdl:operation name="ZcsWsGetStudentsByLname">
        <wsdl:input message="tns:ZcsWsGetStudentsByLname" />
        <wsdl:output message="tns:ZcsWsGetStudentsByLnameResponse" />
    </wsdl:operation>
    </wsdl:portType>
  - <wsdl:binding name="zcs_ws_studentsSoapBinding" type="tns:zcs_ws_students">
        <soap:binding style="document" transport="http://schemas.xmlsoap.org/soap/http" />
    - <wsdl:operation name="ZcsWsGetAllStudents">
```

Figure 4.6 WSDL File

6. As he continues to create the client proxy, Russel encounters another dialog box. Here he must assign the package and a prefix that will be used by the objects generated for the client proxy (see Figure 4.7). Not only does the prefix allow him to place the generated object within the normal customer name range of objects beginning with Z or Y, but it also enables him to provide a more meaningful name to identify the generated object as a proxy object or a part of a larger project.

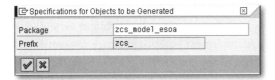

Figure 4.7 Assigning Package and Prefix

7. Russel can now see the proxy object that has been generated. The **Generation** tab displays all of the objects that were created during the generation of the proxy object, including the proxy class, the data elements, structures, and table types. The **Structure** tab, shown in Figure 4.8, displays the structure of the proxy object including all of the methods and the method signatures.

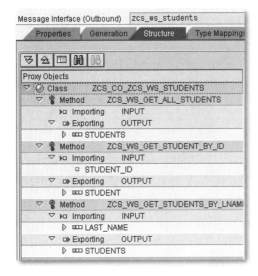

Figure 4.8 Proxy Object Structure

4.1.3 Logical Ports

Before Russel can code against his proxy object, he must first create a logical port. The logical port is used to specify the runtime attributes of the Web Service client proxy. Imagine a typical scenario whereby the system that you are calling the Web Service from probably has at least a development and a separate production system. You have received a WSDL document generated out of just one of those systems. Although it has sent along the set of URLs that you need to call the Web Service, that WSDL document only contains information for one of the two systems.

Similarly, the remote systems' URLs may change over time. You might also need to have different security requirements for each system. The development system probably only needs the most basic of security measures, while the production system might use encryption.

Therefore, it makes sense not to store this level of information within the proxy object itself. By storing this information as a separate object, the logical port, it makes maintenance of the information possible without having to regenerate the proxy class. This also makes it possible to have more than one set of configuration details for the same proxy object.

You can instantiate the Web Service proxy object and specify the logical port via the LOGICAL_PORT_NAME parameter of the CONSTRUCTOR method, but it is not required. If you don't specify the logical port, the system will simply use the default logical port. You must define at least the default logical port. You can have multiple logical ports for a Web Service proxy object, but only one default logical port.

1. Russel goes to transaction LPCONFIG to set up the logical port. He needs to enter the name of the Web Service client **Proxy Class** and the name of the **Logical Port**. Since Russel is creating the default port, he also needs to select the **Default Port** checkbox.

2. The next screen is where Russel will define the attributes of the port. In this case, Russel will simply use the **URL** supplied by the Web Service definition, as shown in Figure 4.9. Later you will see exactly what some of the more advanced functions of the logical port can be used for.

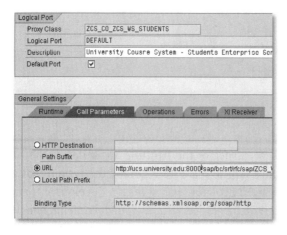

Figure 4.9 Logical Port Definition

3. Lastly, he saves and activates the logical port.

4.1.4 Using the Client Proxy Object

Russel is now ready to test the proxy object that was just created. He starts by writing a simple test program that will leverage the client proxy class, which has been generated. For this test, he will use the ZCS_WS_GET_ALL_STUDENTS method of the generated proxy class.

As shown in Listing 4.1, Russel simply creates an object reference variable for the proxy class ZCS_CO_ZCS_WS_STUDENTS, and calls the method to retrieve the list of students. The output of this program shows the list of students and the associated data. Using the proxy object hides all of the inner workings of the Web Service. Russel doesn't have to worry about any of the communication aspects of consuming a Web Service.

```
report zcs_proxy_test.

DATA sys_exception TYPE REF TO cx_ai_system_fault.
DATA client_proxy  TYPE REF TO zcs_co_zcs_ws_students.
DATA request       TYPE zcs_zcs_ws_get_all_students.
DATA response      TYPE zcs_zcs_ws_get_all_students_re.
FIELD-SYMBOLS <wa_item> TYPE zcs_zcs_student_int_str.

TRY.
    CREATE OBJECT client_proxy.
    CALL METHOD client_proxy->zcs_ws_get_all_students
      EXPORTING
        input  = request
      IMPORTING
        output = response.

    LOOP AT response-students-item ASSIGNING <wa_item>.
      WRITE:/ <wa_item>-student_id,
              <wa_item>-first_name,
              <wa_item>-last_name,
              <wa_item>-credit_hrs,
              <wa_item>-gpa,
              <wa_item>-deletion_flag.
    ENDLOOP.

  CATCH cx_ai_system_fault INTO sys_exception.
    DATA error_details TYPE string.
    error_details = sys_exception->get_text( ).
    RAISE EXCEPTION TYPE zcx_cs_student
      EXPORTING
        textid = zcx_cs_student=>communication_error
```

```
     error_details = error_details.

ENDTRY.
```

Listing 4.1 Client Proxy Test Program

4.1.5   Implementing into the Business Object Layer

Now that Russel feels comfortable with consuming the Web Service, he can implement it within the business object layer of the course system. The READ_ALL_STUDENTS and READ_STUDENT methods of the business object class ZCL_CS_STUDENT were written to retrieve the data from the local system using persistent objects. Russel wants to change this logic to access the data by consuming the Web Service.

> **Note**
>
> It is important to understand that we want to keep the sample code in such a state that the reader can view the original implementation and the versions with Russel's later modifications. That said, the implementation of the Web Service into the business object layer would be done in a copy of the class ZCL_CS_STUDENT on the source code CD that accompanies this book.
>
> In reality, Russel will simply modify the class directly instead of making a copy of it. For the complete example class that utilizes the Web Service, see class ZCL_CS_STUDENT_ES.

Only the implementation of the READ_ALL_STUDENTS method will change. The signature will remain the same. This means that any application that uses the business object class won't know the difference, because the business object class's constructor is private and is accessible only via a factory method.

As shown in Listing 4.2, the method implementation simply uses the proxy object class to retrieve the data via the Web Service and builds an internal table of student objects.

```
METHOD read_all_students.
  DATA sys_exception TYPE REF TO cx_ai_system_fault.
  DATA client_proxy  TYPE REF TO zcs_co_zcs_ws_students.
  DATA request        TYPE zcs_zcs_ws_get_all_students.
  DATA response       TYPE zcs_zcs_ws_get_all_students_re.
  FIELD-SYMBOLS <wa_student> LIKE LINE OF r_students.
  DATA l_student_att TYPE zcs_student.

  TRY.
```

```
        CREATE OBJECT client_proxy.
        CALL METHOD client_proxy->zcs_ws_get_all_students
          EXPORTING
            input  = request
          IMPORTING
            output = response.
        FIELD-SYMBOLS <wa_item>
            TYPE zcs_zcs_student_int_str.
        LOOP AT response-students-item ASSIGNING <wa_item>.
          APPEND INITIAL LINE to r_students
            ASSIGNING <wa_student>.
          MOVE-CORRESPONDING <wa_item> TO l_student_att.
          MOVE l_student_att-student_id
            TO <wa_student>-student_id.
          CREATE OBJECT <wa_student>-student
            EXPORTING
              i_student_att  = l_student_att.
        ENDLOOP.

      CATCH cx_ai_system_fault INTO sys_exception.
        DATA error_details TYPE string.
        error_details = sys_exception->get_text( ).
        RAISE EXCEPTION TYPE zcx_cs_student
            EXPORTING
              textid = zcx_cs_student=>communication_error
              error_details = error_details.
    ENDTRY.
ENDMETHOD.
```

Listing 4.2 READ_ALL_STUDENTS Method Implementation

Similarly, the READ_STUDENT method implementation, shown in Listing 4.3, will use the proxy object class and call the ZCS_WS_GET_STUDENT_BY_ID. In this case, Russel will pass the student ID to the INPUT parameter of the method. This will force the Web Service to provide only a single student record based on the student ID.

```
METHOD read_student.
  DATA sys_exception TYPE REF TO cx_ai_system_fault.
  DATA client_proxy  TYPE REF TO zcs_co_zcs_ws_students.
  DATA student_att    TYPE zcs_student.
  DATA request        TYPE zcs_zcs_ws_get_student_by_id.
  DATA response       TYPE zcs_zcs_ws_get_student_by_id_r.

  TRY.
```

```
        CREATE OBJECT client_proxy.
        request-student_id = i_student_id.
        CALL METHOD client_proxy->zcs_ws_get_student_by_id
          EXPORTING
            input  = request
          IMPORTING
            output = response.
        MOVE-CORRESPONDING response-student TO student_att.
        CREATE OBJECT r_student
          EXPORTING
            i_student_att  = student_att.

      CATCH cx_ai_system_fault INTO sys_exception.
        DATA error_details TYPE string.
        error_details = sys_exception->get_text( ).
        RAISE EXCEPTION type zcx_cs_student
            EXPORTING
              textid = zcx_cs_student=>communication_error
              error_details = error_details.
      ENDTRY.
    ENDMETHOD.
```

Listing 4.3 READ_STUDENT Method Implementation

4.2 Logical Ports

With what Russel has completed so far, he already has a fully working Web Service interface. However, if you return to the **Logical Port Maintenance**, you'll see that there are plenty of other options that can be controlled for Web Service communication. In order to get a better feel for the full range of capabilities in Web Services, it is worth returning to the Logical Port maintenance, transaction LPCONFIG, and exploring these options in detail.

4.2.1 Runtime

The **Runtime** parameters make up the first set of options in the Logical Port maintenance (see Figure 4.10). This section of the maintenance requires you to choose between **Web Service Infrastructure** and **Exchange Infrastructure**.

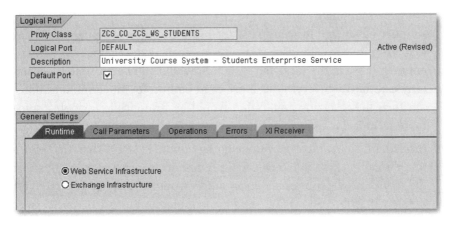

Figure 4.10 Logical Port Runtime Options

So what is the difference between these two runtime options? You've already seen the basic communication structure of normal Web Services. Although a service provider can use a centralized UDDI or Service Repository for sharing the description of its services, the communications at the time of Web Service execution are point to point. In other words, the service provider's system communicates directly and synchronously with the service requestor.

The **Exchange Infrastructure** option — although the application has been renamed SAP NetWeaver Process Integration (SAP NetWeaver PI) from SAP NetWeaver Exchange Infrastructure (SAP NetWeaver XI), there are still many references to XI within the current state of the application — provides a SAP delivered alternative. Instead of using a point-to-point approach, all communications pass between a SAP NetWeaver Process Integration server. Technically, this approach still uses SOAP, HTTP, XML, and all the standard Web Service technologies.

There are several advantages to adding SAP NetWeaver Process Integration (SAP NetWeaver PI) in the middle of your Web Service communications:

▶ **Asynchronous Communications**
First this can allow for asynchronous communications. In point-to-point communications, if, for any reason, the service provider system is offline, the calling system will get a technical connection error and will need to resolve that problem by itself. With SAP NetWeaver PI in the middle, it can store the message and attempt a resend later. It can even serialize the messages so that it ensures that they are transmitted in the original order.

► **Complex Mappings**

Another advantage to using PI is for more complex mappings. Let's say that a service provider uses structures or value codes that are very different than those in the receiving system. It would still be possible to technically call the Web Service via a proxy in point-to-point communications, but then the receiving application would be responsible for doing some more technical mapping so that the data was more usable.

Instead, this mapping can be done in the middle PI layer. Then the service that the calling system interacts with is no longer identical to the one that the service provider offers. A proxy object would actually be generated for the new interface that was created via mapping in PI.

► **One-to-Many Services**

The final advantage is in the one-to-many service situation. This is common with Web Services to an external provider. An example scenario is invoicing. An ERP system might be set up to communicate invoices via Web Services. Chances are good that a company will have more than one customer that they are invoicing via Web Services.

However, they probably don't want the complexity of processing separate proxy objects for each possible customer. Instead there is one Web Service generated in PI and exposed to the ERP system. When passing through PI, the ERP sends along additional information regarding the identity of this particular partner. PI uses this information to determine which Web Service endpoint this communication should be routed to.

This central hub approach can also be combined with the mapping capabilities within PI. In this same scenario, the chances that every customer uses the exact same invoicing Web Service are very slight. You can use PI to map from one standard Web Service interface coming out of ERP to each of the customer specific Web Services.

4.2.2 Call Parameters

The **Call Parameters** are the next set of options (see Figure 4.11). These options are focused on how and where to call the Web Service endpoint. The most common solution is to use the direct **URL** entry. This value is populated when the logical port is created from information that was stored in the WSDL document. This is the Web Service URL that corresponds to the same system that generated the WSDL document.

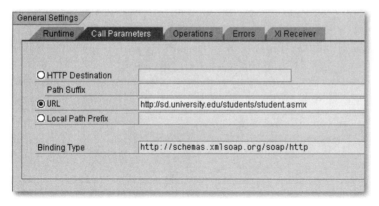

Figure 4.11 Logical Port Call Parameters

We mentioned earlier that logical ports are useful because you can maintain the Web Service URL independent of the proxy object. Since the same proxy could potentially have more than one logical port, there is no reason why you couldn't have a logical port for a service provider's development and production systems. To change the second logical port to reference the second system, you could manually make the adjustment in the **URL** field.

The **Local Path Prefix** is for that rare instance when you want to call a Web Service that exists on the same system as the proxy object. In this case, there is no reason to supply a full URL or connection settings. Only the local path has to be maintained in order to determine which service needs to be called.

The final option is to use the **HTTP Destination**. This option is fairly important once you're ready to move beyond the most basic of Web Service security settings. By using the URL parameter, you can supply a destination but no connection settings. Therefore, if the service requires any kind of authentication, this option will not suffice.

The **HTTP Destination** uses a new type of destination that can be maintained in transaction SM59, which was primarily used to maintain RFC destinations. However, as of the SAP NetWeaver releases, there are two new destination types — **G (HTTP Connection to External Server)** and **H (HTTP Connection to ABAP System)**. Either of these HTTP connections can be used within a logical port. Since Russel's service provider is not another ABAP-based system, he would choose destination type **G**.

The settings in this connection will be used automatically by the proxy object because of the connection that is made by entering the name of the destination in the logical port.

If your proxy object needs to pass through an Internet Proxy, more commonly referred to as a *Firewall*, in order to communicate with a partner outside your network, you can maintain these settings within the HTTP based destination (see Figure 4.12) on the **Technical Settings** tab.

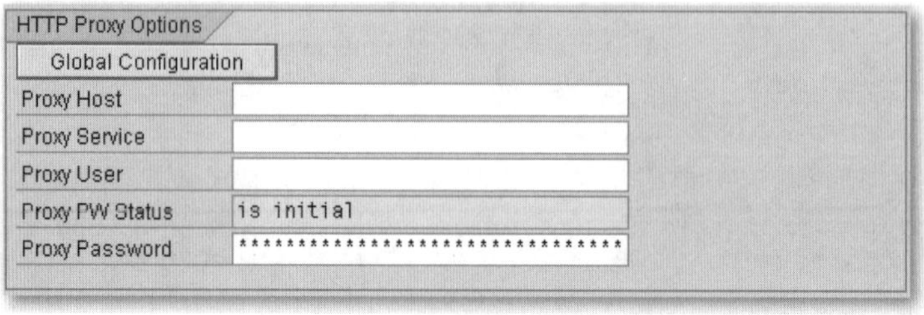

Figure 4.12 HTTP Destination HTTP Proxy Options

The most important options are the settings that you can make on the **Logon & Security** tab (see Figure 4.13). This is where you maintain authentication options.

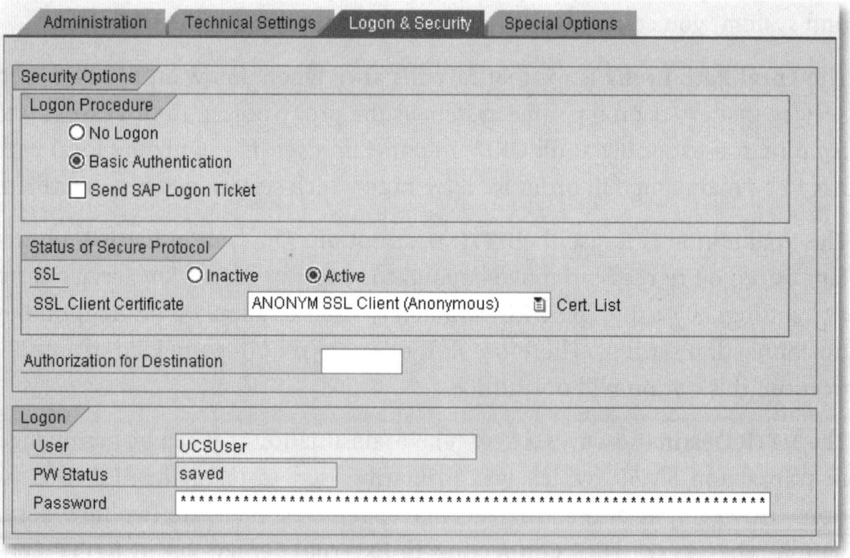

Figure 4.13 HTTP Destination Logon & Security

Logon Procedure

The options in the **Logon Procedure** area control the type of authentication that will be utilized.

▶ **No Logon**
 No Logon indicates that this destination is anonymous and doesn't require any additional authentication settings. This type of connection could be called just by using the URL parameter in the logical port, but even an anonymous connection may still require firewall settings or SSL for encryption of the data.

▶ **Basic Authentication**
 Basic Authentication is a common form of authentication that is integrated into the HTTP standard. The user name and password, which are maintained in the **Logon** area at the bottom of the screen, are transmitted along with the HTTP response header. Unless the entire HTTP stream is encrypted with SSL, this user name and password could potentially be intercepted.

▶ **Send SAP Logon Ticket**
 The final option is the **Send SAP Logon Ticket** option. This is the SAP specific browser cookie that is used as the basis of Single Sign-On (SSO) in the SAP environment. If you're calling a service that is part of another SAP provided solution, it might be useful to set this option and take advantage of SSO.

Secure Protocol

Regardless of which logon procedure you're using, you can combine the option you choose with a secure protocol (i.e., see the **Status of Secure Protocol** area). By activating the **SSL** option, you can switch from HTTP to HTTPS based communication and encrypt the entire communication stream. This can be useful for several reasons:

▶ First, it can protect the user name and password that are transmitted for authentication by encrypting it as well.

▶ Secondly, the entire communication stream is encrypted. Therefore, the business data inside the Web Service message is also encrypted. This might be particularly important if you're transmitting the service request over the Internet to an external partner.

▶ The third and final reason for encryption has to do with the **SSL Client Certificate**. For SSL encryption to work, certificates must be exchanged in order to have the keys to the encryption. Basic SSL can be achieved with an Anonymous Client Certificate. This still means that a user name and password are transmitted, but no additional authorization is required. This approach utilizes SSL as a form of encryption only.

But the **SSL Client Certificate** also lets you choose a client certificate that specifically identifies you. Because a trusted authority has issued it, this client certificate ensures that you are who you say you are. This client certificate will be transmitted along with the request. In addition to forming the keys of the encryption, it is an added layer of protection for the Web Service provider so that they can feel confident with whom they are communicating.

4.2.3 Operations

The **Operations** tab shows each of the methods of the Web Service (see Figure 4.14). For each method, a **SOAP Action** can be maintained. This is a value that will be placed in the HTTP header of the communication stream. It is primarily used to identify the purpose of the method. It can then be analyzed by intermediate systems, like Internet firewalls, for the purpose of filtering Web Service communications.

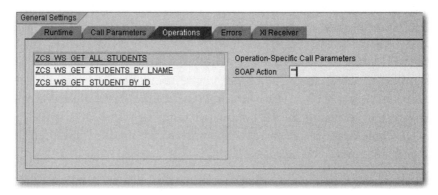

Figure 4.14 Logical Port Operations

4.2.4 Errors

The general rule of computing is that eventually something will go wrong. That is exactly what the **Errors** tab is all about (see Figure 4.15). From here, you can activate tracing and logging and control the level of each.

Tracing, in general, records more details about the communication and stores this information in the RFC developers trace file. They can be viewed in transaction ST11. Logging, on the other hand, records information within the system log.

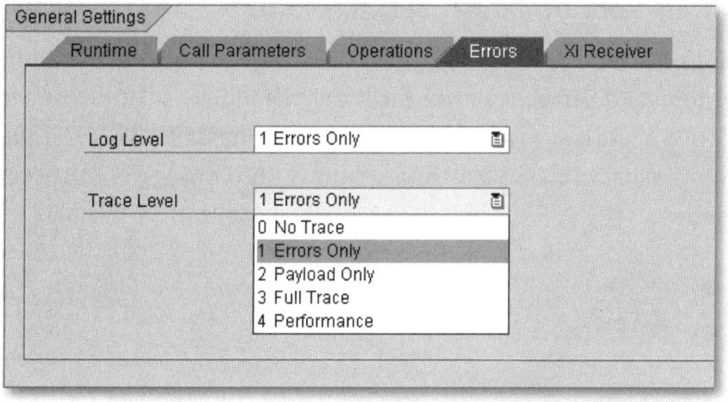

Figure 4.15 Logical Port Errors

4.2.5 PI Receiver

The final tab in the **General Settings** section pertains, **XI Receiver**, once again to the use of SAP NetWeaver Process Integration (SAP NetWeaver PI) during Web Services communication (see Figure 4.16). This area allows you to specify the business keys of the service provider. When using the XI Runtime for hub-based information, these keys will be used for determining the final receiver of the communication request.

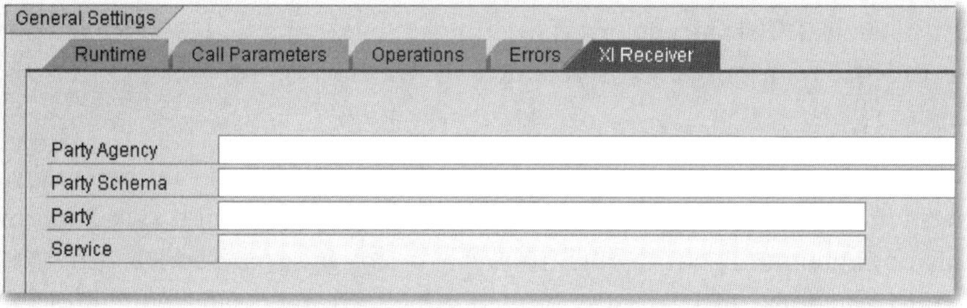

Figure 4.16 Logical Port PI Receiver

However these options can also be used in the Web Service Runtime for point-to-point communications as well. In this situation, a calling application can use the GET_LOGICAL_PORT_FROM_RECEIVER method from the Extended Protocols (see Section 4.3 for details) of the proxy class to determine the true logical port given the same PI Receiver information.

4.2.6 Application-Specific Global Settings

The **Global Settings** of the **Application-Specific Settings** can add a few additional features to the Web Service communication (see Figure 4.17). First the **Message ID** option will add a unique identifier to each message. This unique ID can be useful in ensuring that each transaction is only processed once on the receiving side.

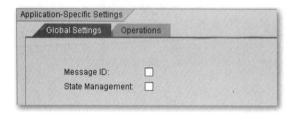

Figure 4.17 Logical Port Application — Specific Global Settings

If communications errors occur, a Web Service message might be transmitted a second time. However on the receiving system, it would be important to ensure that the same business transaction is processed only once, even though it may have been received more than once.

The second option, **State Management**, can activate stateful communications. By default, Web Services, like all HTTP communications, are inherently stateless. That means that if multiple methods of a Web Service need to be called, no information is retained by the service provider during the method calls.

Switching on **State Management** provides HTTP cookies within the communication stream to facility stateful communications, although switching on this option alone is not enough to create a stateful Web Service. The Web Service provider must have also elected to support state management for this particular service.

4.2.7 Application-Specific Operations

The **Operations** tab (see Figure 4.18) of the **Application-Specific Settings** looks a lot like the **Operations** tab in the **General Settings**, which we already discussed (see Figure 4.14). The difference here is that instead of setting a **SOAP Action** for an operation of the Web Service, you can choose a **Web Service Security Profile**.

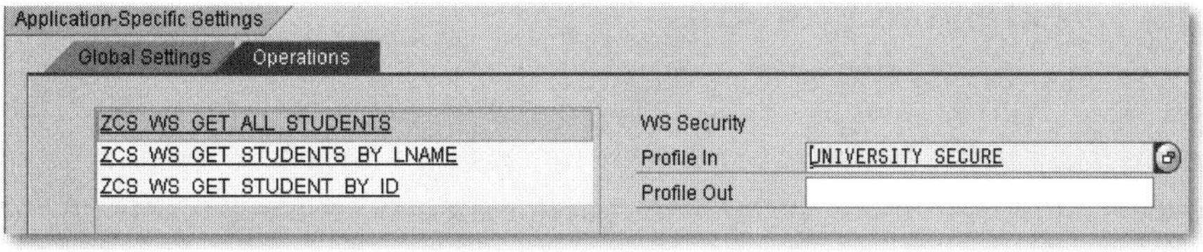

Figure 4.18 Logical Port Application — Specific Operations

But we already discussed Web Service security and how it can be set within the HTTP Destination, right? Well that was just one form of security that can be used with Web Services. That earlier approach secured the communication channel for the Web Service. This means that the entire Web Service document would be encrypted during transmission.

But what happens to the document while it is not being transmitted? What if an intermediate system, such as PI, stores the document for asynchronous communications? The document will no longer be encrypted and any client certificate identification from the SSL stream will be lost.

That is where Web Service security profiles come in. These security profiles are extensions to the Web Services SOAP standards that allow for an additional layer of security to be placed within the Web Service document. You must create Web Services security profiles based on a set of SAP provided templates. The profiles can be created in transaction WSSPROFILE by simply choosing one of the delivered template profiles from the dialog as seen in Figure 4.19.

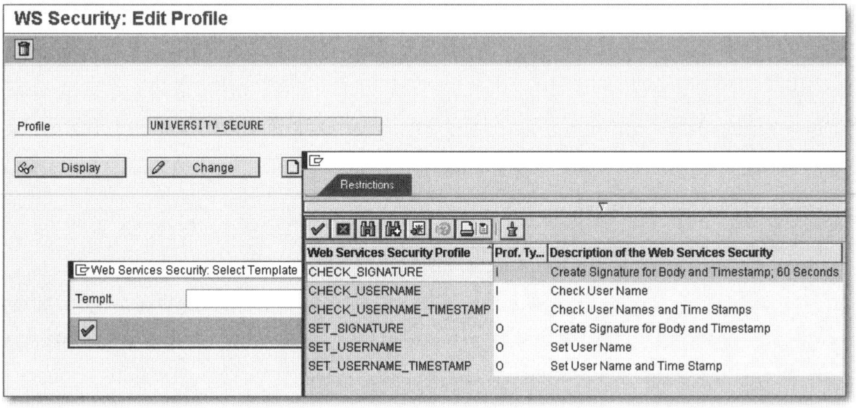

Figure 4.19 Web Service Security Profile Creation

4.3   Extended Protocols

So far, the programming that Russel has done against his proxy object has been fairly basic — he has selected the logical port he will use and initiated synchronous communications with parameters. At its core, this is all the proxy object was designed to do.

However, there are many additional services within the proxy framework. These services are referred to as *Extended Protocols*. It's easy to identify these extended protocol objects, because they all adhere to a naming standard that begins with IF_WSPROTOCOL. Although Russel doesn't have an immediate need to access these additional services in his student service, he wants to be prepared for future projects. So, he decides to spend some time exploring them.

1. First, he wants to learn how to get access to instances of these extended protocol objects. He'll use the example of the *Payload Protocol*. Incidentally, the payload protocol does seem to be one of the most useful of the extended protocols, because it can provide the application access to the entire SOAP message.

2. Russel begins his test application by declaring the objects he will need. After he has his generated proxy class, he uses his generated proxy to gain access to the extended protocol object instances. Next, he has the declaration to the payload protocol object, and lastly, a declaration to the payload object itself:

```
DATA:
    clientProxy      TYPE REF TO zcs_co_zcs_ws_students,
    payload_protocol TYPE REF TO if_wsprotocol_payload
    payload          TYPE REF TO if_ws_payload.
```

3. Next he creates the instance of his proxy object. Remember, no communications are initiated until he accesses one of the methods of the proxy class:

```
CREATE OBJECT clientProxy.
```

The GET_PROTOCOL method of the generated client proxy object can retrieve any of the protocols. The interface IF_WSPROTOCOL has constants that can identify which type of protocol object you want returned:

```
payload_protocol ?=
    clientProxy->get_protocol( if_wsprotocol=>payload ).
```

4. Next Russel calls the proxy object method:

```
client_proxy->zcs_ws_get_all_students(
      EXPORTING  input  = request
      IMPORTING  output = response ).
```

5. After the Web Service communication is complete, Russel can gain access to the payload object via the payload protocol. He can then read either the full XML of the response or request object:

```
payload = payload_protocol->get_sent_response_payload( ).
DATA xml TYPE xstring.
xml = payload->get_xml_text( ).
```

There are various extended protocols available, depending on which SAP NetWeaver release you are using. Some examples are protocols for accessing message attachments, headers, routing information, and the unique message ID. These protocols can also be specific to either the SAP NetWeaver PI or the Web Service runtimes. For instance, as of SAP NetWeaver 7.0, only PI Runtime supports attachments. Also, for accessing the header of a message, there are separate objects, namely, XI_HEADER and WS_HEADER.

A complete listing of the protocols that are available on each release of SAP NetWeaver and the runtimes that they support can always be found on *http://help.sap.com* by searching for "WS Protocols".

Russel has finished the programming for the database access layer. He now wants to optimize the read access to some of the data that is read frequently, but not updated often. For this, he will turn to the new shared memory objects technology that was introduced in SAP NetWeaver 2004.

5   Shared Memory Objects

Shared memory objects are ABAP Object Instances, which can be stored in the shared memory area on an application server. Instead of going to the database to retrieve the required data, the data is accessed through the shared memory, thereby providing faster data retrieval.

This shared memory area can be accessed by all of the ABAP programs running on that application server. Before the upgrade to SAP ERP 6.0, Russel used the EXPORT/IMPORT statements with the SHARED BUFFER or SHARED MEMORY extensions to access a similar memory buffer area. So what are the advantages of using this new functionality?

▸ First, it is read access to shared memory without the need to copy it into user session memory. Technically, an application does a remote attach to the memory segment within shared memory and directly interacts with it.

▸ Secondly, the new shared memory technique is implemented through ABAP Objects; therefore, you are provided with robust tools to interact with shared memory through code. Ultimately, you aren't just buffering raw sets of data; you're also providing a shared mechanism to access the business logic wrapped around this data.

▸ There are also dedicated tools for the monitoring and administration of these shared areas and the objects within them. Transaction SHMM, for example, provides tools to monitor the size and number of objects within a shared area, as well as enabling administrators to force objects out of memory if necessary.

5.1   Getting Started

Russel has spent a considerable amount of time developing the database access layer for this project and wants to ensure that performance is at an optimal level. He decides to leverage the shared memory objects functionality to increase performance when accessing some of the data in the database.

To use this feature of the ABAP runtime environment, Russel will have to create several new types of objects. Shared memory objects are implemented in two parts — the shared object *root* and *area* classes.

- ▶ The root class is the definition of the object that will be stored in shared memory. An instance (or multiple instances) of this class will reside in shared memory. Therefore this class's attributes should represent the data that you want cached and the methods of the class are the way that you access this data.

- ▶ The shared memory area class, on the other hand, will be a generated class. It abstracts a section of shared memory that is set aside for one or more instances of a particular root class. The methods of this area class provide the tools to attach to the shared memory area in order to read or manipulate it. The sole purpose of the area class is to return instances of the root class.

5.1.1   Area Root Class Creation

Russel decides that the ZCS_COURSE table would be a good candidate to create a shared memory object. Shared memory objects should primarily be used for objects that are read often, but updated infrequently. This is due to the locking mechanism that is used by shared objects. Although having multiple read locks across separate user sessions is possible and is the norm, any form of change lock is exclusive (i.e., it doesn't even allow parallel read locks on the same area instance).

This does make ZCS_COURSE a good fit. New courses are rarely created or changed during the school year. All updates are done all at once, before planning for the next semester begins. Technically, this means that this table will have frequent read accesses by students and teachers concurrently, but the data will rarely change.

Russel's first step in implementing a shared memory object to represent ZCS_COURSE is to create the area root class. This class implements the setter and getter methods, which are used to access the data to be stored in the shared memory area. It could also include business logic that further manipulates the data during access operations. For instance, it might include calculations, the results of which could also be stored in shared memory. This is where the value of the shared memory object can extend well beyond the scope of just the buffering of data stored within the database.

Russel creates the class ZCL_CS_COURSE_SHMO_ROOT and assigns it to the ZCS_ DDIC package using transaction code SE80 (see Figure 5.1).

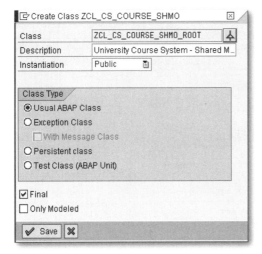

Figure 5.1 Root Class Creation

Russel then sets the **Shared Memory-Enabled** checkbox on the **Properties** tab (see Figure 5.2). This tells the system that the class is eligible to be used as a root class for a shared memory object.

The idea of using shared memory objects is to store data in memory, which can be used at runtime. Therefore, Russel needs to add an attribute to this class that will hold the data retrieved from the ZCS_COURSE database table.

Although it is technically possible to create public attributes of the root class that can be accessed directly from an instance of the class, Russel wants to follow good object-oriented designs and encapsulate all of his attribute accesses within methods. This gives him more control in case he wants to embed other operations within an access to this attribute. Therefore he defines the attribute as a **Private Instance** attribute (see Figure 5.3).

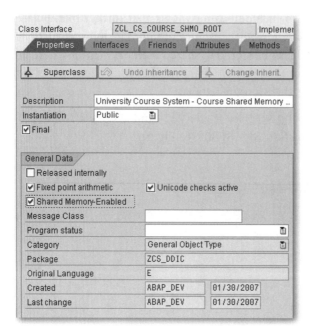

Figure 5.2 Root Class Properties

Figure 5.3 Define Attribute

The class now requires methods that can be used to populate or read this attribute. To start, Russel needs a SET method, which will be used to fill the COURSE_LIST attribute with all records in the database table. This method should be defined as a **Public Instance** method (see Figure 5.4).

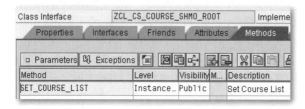

Figure 5.4 Define SET_COURSE_LIST Method

In the implementation of the SET_COURSE_LIST method, Russel leverages the persistent object for database table ZCS_COURSE to fill the instance attribute COURSE_LIST. As shown in Listing 5.1, Russel is simply borrowing some of the persistent object code from the method READ_ALL_COURSES of the class ZCL_CS_COURSE that he wrote in Chapter 3. He then loops through the objects and populates the returning parameter with the values.

```
METHOD set_course_list.
  DATA:  l_agent    TYPE REF TO zca_cs_course_pers,
         l_pers_obj TYPE REF TO zcl_cs_course_pers,
         l_objects  TYPE        osreftab.
  FIELD-SYMBOLS: <wa_object>  LIKE LINE OF l_objects,
                 <wa_course>  LIKE LINE OF course_list.
  DATA: query_manager TYPE REF TO if_os_query_manager,
        query         TYPE REF TO if_os_query.

  TRY.
    l_agent     = zca_cs_course_pers=>agent.
    query_manager = cl_os_system=>get_query_manager( ).
    query = query_manager->create_query( ).

    l_objects =
       l_agent->if_os_ca_persistency~get_persistent_by_query(
           i_query    = query ).
    IF LINES( l_objects ) = 0.
      RAISE EXCEPTION TYPE zcx_cs_course
         EXPORTING
           textid = zcx_cs_course=>bad_query.
    ENDIF.

    LOOP AT l_objects ASSIGNING <wa_object>.
      l_pers_obj ?= <wa_object>.
      APPEND INITIAL LINE TO course_list
        ASSIGNING <wa_course>.
      <wa_course>-syllabi = l_pers_obj->get_syllabi( ).
      <wa_course>-cost = l_pers_obj->get_cost( ).
      <wa_course>-course_id = l_pers_obj->get_course_id( ).
      <wa_course>-course_schedule =
         l_pers_obj->get_course_schedule( ).
      <wa_course>-course_sdesc =
         l_pers_obj->get_course_sdesc( ).
      <wa_course>-course_year =
         l_pers_obj->get_course_year( ).
      <wa_course>-credit_hrs = l_pers_obj->get_credit_hrs( ).
```

```
            <wa_course>-currency = l_pers_obj->get_currency( ).
            <wa_course>-deletion_flag =
                l_pers_obj->get_deletion_flag( ).
            <wa_course>-description =
                l_pers_obj->get_description( ).
            <wa_course>-end_time = l_pers_obj->get_end_time( ).
            <wa_course>-faculty_id = l_pers_obj->get_faculty_id( ).
            <wa_course>-major = l_pers_obj->get_major( ).
            <wa_course>-semester = l_pers_obj->get_semester( ).
            <wa_course>-start_time = l_pers_obj->get_start_time( ).
            <wa_course>-student_limit =
                l_pers_obj->get_student_limit( ).
        ENDLOOP.
    ENDTRY.
ENDMETHOD.
```

Listing 5.1 SET_COURSE_LIST Method Implementation

Russel also needs to define the GET methods, which will be used to retrieve the data. First, Russel needs a GET method to retrieve all the courses. The signature of this method will contain a RETURNING parameter, which is defined as the table type ZCS_COURSES_TT (see Figure 5.5 and Figure 5.6).

Class Interface		ZCL_CS_COURSE_SHMO_ROOT		Implemen
Properties	Interfaces	Friends	Attributes	Methods

| □ Parameters | Exceptions | | | | | | | | | | |

Method	Level	Visibility	M...	Description
SET_COURSE_LIST	Instance...	Public		Set Course List
GET_COURSE_LIST	Instance...	Public		Get Course List

Figure 5.5 Define GET_COURSE_LIST Method

Class Interface		ZCL_CS_COURSE_SHMO_ROOT		Implemented
Properties	Interfaces	Friends	Attributes	Methods E

Method parameters   GET_COURSE_LIST

| ← Methods | Exceptions | | | | | |

Parameter	Type	P...	O...	Typi...	Associated Type
RE_COURSE_LIST	Returning	☑	☐	Type	ZCS_COURSES_TT

Figure 5.6 Define GET_COURSE_LIST Method Signature

Of course as soon as Russel uses a returning parameter, he negates one of the advantages of the shared memory object, namely, the copy free read. Imagine if you had a very large table that could either be exported to shared memory or placed in a shared memory object. In this example, you want to sort the internal table and then read a subset of the records.

With an internal table that was simply exported to shared memory, the entire table would have to be imported before any operations could be performed on it. This entails making a copy of the entire internal table and placing it into the internal session of the running application.

With a shared memory object, however, all of this logic could be placed within the shared object root class and only the resulting few records would be returned. This prevents you from having to copy anything, but the result set, out of shared memory and into the internal session.

In the shared object root class that Russel is building, he needs to support both kinds of accesses. He will eventually build a method that returns a single record, but some applications also need access to the entire course listing. For these applications, it doesn't make sense to keep a constant read attachment to the shared object instance, therefore, he decides to return a copy of the entire internal table attribute. Returning parameters are always marked as **Pass by Value** (see third column in Figure 5.6), making this copy operation happen automatically.

The GET_COURSE_LIST has a very simple implementation. Russel only needs to pass the instance attribute COURSE_LIST to the RETURNING parameter RE_COURSE_LIST (see Listing 5.2).

```
METHOD get_course_list.
  re_course_list = course_list.
ENDMETHOD.
```

Listing 5.2 GET_COURSE_LIST Method Implementation

Additionally Russel needs a GET method, which will be used to get a single course record. By clicking on the **Parameters** button, the signature of the method is displayed. The signature of this method contains an IMPORTING parameter for the COURSE_ID, which will be used to select the specific course. The second parameter is a RETURNING parameter, which will be used to return the course data. This RETURNING parameter is typed like ZCS_COURSE (see Figure 5.7 and Figure 5.8).

Class Interface		ZCL_CS_COURSE_SHMO_ROOT			Impleme

Properties	Interfaces	Friends	Attributes	Methods

□ Parameters	🔍 Exceptions	🔲	🔲🔲🔄	🔲🔲	✂🔲🔲

Method	Level	Visi...	M...	Description
SET_COURSE_LIST	Insta...	Pub...		Set Course List
GET_COURSE_LIST	Insta...	Pub...		Get Course List
GET_COURSE	Insta...	Pub...		Get Course

Figure 5.7 Define GET_COURSE Method

Class Interface		ZCL_CS_COURSE_SHMO_ROOT			Implem

Properties	Interfaces	Friends	Attributes	Methods

Method parameters		GET_COURSE			

← Methods	🔍 Exceptions	🔲	🔲	🔲🔲	✂🔲🔲

Parameter	Type	P...	O...	Typi...	Associated Type
COURSE_ID	Importing	🔘	☐	Type	ZCS_COURSE-COURSE_ID
COURSE	Returning	☑	☐	Type	ZCS_COURSE

Figure 5.8 Define GET_COURSE Method Signature

Again, the implementation for the GET_COURSE method is fairly simple. A simple read statement will read the COURSE_LIST attribute and return the corresponding row based on the IMPORTING parameter COURSE_ID (see Listing 5.3).

```
METHOD get_course.
  READ TABLE course_list INTO course
               WITH KEY course_id = course_id.
ENDMETHOD.
```

Listing 5.3 GET_COURSE Method Implementation

5.1.2 Defining the Shared Memory Area

Russel now needs to create the shared memory area. The transaction code SHMA allows you to create the area and define its properties. When the shared memory area is created, a global class with the same name as the area is created automatically. Therefore, we recommend that you use the standard naming convention for classes, CL_* or ZCL_*, to name the memory area. This shared memory area class inherits from the class CL_SHM_AREA, which is a sub-class of CL_ABAP_MEMORY_AREA, giving it all the necessary methods for accessing area root class.

Russel uses transaction SHMA to create the shared memory area. The subsequent screen allows him to specify the properties of the area as well as the root class that this area will be defined for (see Figure 5.9). For now Russel will leave the default properties that were suggested, no limits on the area size, lifetime, or number of versions. Later you will see how he can use some of these properties to set up automatic initialization of his shared object on the first read request.

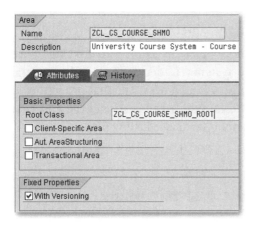

Figure 5.9 Area Properties

Now that the area class has been generated, Russel can look at the public methods that he will use to access the shared memory object (see Figure 5.10). The ATTACH methods will return *area handles*, which are instances of the area class.

Method	Level	Visi...	M...	Description
_HAS_ACTIVE_PROPERTIES	Insta...	Pro...		
CLASS_CONSTRUCTOR	Stati...	Pub...	📑	CLASS_CONSTRUCTOR
GET_GENERATOR_VERSION	Stati...	Pub...		Query Generator Version
ATTACH_FOR_READ	Stati...	Pub...		Request a Read Lock
ATTACH_FOR_WRITE	Stati...	Pub...		Request a Write Lock
ATTACH_FOR_UPDATE	Stati...	Pub...		Request a Change Lock
DETACH_AREA	Stati...	Pub...		Release all locks on all ir
INVALIDATE_INSTANCE	Stati...	Pub...		Active version of one insta
INVALIDATE_AREA	Stati...	Pub...		Active versions of all insta
FREE_INSTANCE	Stati...	Pub...		Deletion of an Instance
FREE_AREA	Stati...	Pub...		Delete all instances
GET_INSTANCE_INFOS	Stati...	Pub...		Returns the names of all
BUILD	Stati...	Pub...		Direct Call of Area Constr
SET_ROOT	Insta...	Pub...		Sets Root Objects

Figure 5.10 Methods of the Area Class

For example, the ATTACH_FOR_READ method will return an area handle, which can then be used to read the shared memory area. Similarly, the ATTACH_FOR_WRITE method will return an area handle, which will allow you to write to the shared memory area. The DETACH_AREA method removes the binding between the area class and the area handle.

5.1.3   Testing the Shared Memory Object

Russel wants to see the shared memory object in action before trying to use it directly in the rest of the course system. He decides to develop several short test programs to get a feel for how it all works. The first program will be a test write program, which will create the area instance of the area root class and place it into the shared memory area (see Listing 5.4).

```
REPORT  zcs_course_shmo_write.

DATA: course_handle TYPE REF TO zcl_cs_course_shmo,
      course_root   TYPE REF TO zcl_cs_course_shmo_root.

TRY.
    course_handle = zcl_cs_course_shmo=>attach_for_write( ).
    CREATE OBJECT course_root AREA HANDLE course_handle.
    course_handle->set_root( course_root ).
    course_root->set_course_list( ).
    course_handle->detach_commit( ).
  CATCH cx_shm_attach_error.
    ...
ENDTRY.
```
Listing 5.4 Write Test Program

Notice that fairly normal conventions are used for creating the COURSE_ROOT instance. Russel still uses the CREATE OBJECT syntax, but now with the new addition AREA HANDLE. These extra statements direct the ABAP runtime to instantiate the root class within shared memory instead of the internal session memory.

Russel writes a second program to test the reading of the data from the shared memory object (see Listing 5.5). This test program will allow Russel to ensure that the GET_COURSE_LIST method and the GET_COURSE method work properly. Before Russel runs this program, he must run the write program to load the memory area. Otherwise, he'll get an ABAP short dump when trying to access an unloaded memory area.

```
REPORT  zcs_course_shmo_read.

DATA: course_handle TYPE REF TO zcl_cs_course_shmo.
DATA: gt_courses TYPE zcs_courses_tt.
DATA: gs_courses TYPE zcs_course.

PARAMETERS: p_rad1 RADIOBUTTON GROUP grp1 DEFAULT 'X'.
PARAMETERS: p_rad2 RADIOBUTTON GROUP grp1.
PARAMETERS: p_csid TYPE zcs_course-course_id.

AT SELECTION-SCREEN.
  IF p_rad2 = 'X'
     AND p_csid IS INITIAL.
    MESSAGE e001(00) WITH 'Enter a course id'.
  ENDIF.

START-OF-SELECTION.

  TRY.
     course_handle = zcl_cs_course_shmo=>attach_for_read( ).
    CATCH cx_shm_attach_error.
  ENDTRY.

  CASE p_rad1.
    WHEN 'X'.
      gt_courses = course_handle->root->get_course_list( ).
    WHEN OTHERS.
      gs_courses = course_handle->root->get_course( p_csid ).
      APPEND gs_courses TO gt_courses.
  ENDCASE.

  course_handle->detach( ).

  LOOP AT gt_courses INTO gs_courses.
    WRITE:/ gs_courses-course_id,
            gs_courses-course_sdesc+0(20),
            gs_courses-faculty_id,
            gs_courses-semester,
            gs_courses-course_year,
            gs_courses-major,
            gs_courses-credit_hrs,
            gs_courses-student_limit,
            gs_courses-deletion_flag,
            gs_courses-start_time,
            gs_courses-end_time,
```

```
        gs_courses-course_schedule,
        gs_courses-cost,
        gs_courses-currency.
```

ENDLOOP.

Listing 5.5 Read Test Program

5.1.4 Shared Memory Monitor

The shared memory monitor provides an interface in which you can monitor the area instances in the shared objects memory. The monitor allows you to view areas, area instances, versions, and locks. Drill-down functionality allows you to drill into these overviews via double-clicking on them.

Russel goes to transaction SHMM to check that the data has been written to the shared memory area by his test applications. He can see that there is one instance of the area class stored in the shared memory area ZCL_CS_COURSE_SHMO (see Figure 5.11). He can also see memory usage, number of instances, number of versions, and the status breakdown of the versions.

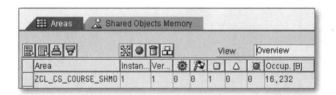

Figure 5.11 Shared Memory Monitor — Areas

If the COURSE_LIST attribute of the area root class was defined as **Public**, Russel could also see the data that is currently stored in the shared memory object. **Private** attributes, however, are not visible. This is also where he can delete shared memory areas.

For developers, the ability to delete a shared memory area within this transaction is probably one of the shared memory monitor's most useful functions. If you make any changes to the coding of the root class and reactivate it, the class will be given a new generation timestamp. The generation timestamp of the root class definition in the database is checked by the area class, whenever an access is made.

Therefore, if you make any changes to the root class after it has been stored within a shared area, this will cause an invalid version exception to be thrown every time you try to access the area. After each change to the root class, you will have to delete any and all versions of the shared memory area before you can test your changes.

5.2   Automatic Preloading

Russel has reviewed what he has learned so far about shared memory objects and realizes that there are some weaknesses in his test applications. For example, it could be problematic if the shared memory area was read before it had been instantiated via a write operation. In other words, reading an unloaded shared memory area will only result in a short dump.

This can occur after the application server has been shut down and restarted. The shared memory areas are all cleared at this time. For the best reliability of his applications, Russel needs to find a way to preload the memory area at the time of the first read. Fortunately, the shared memory object implementation that SAP supplies has just the optional functionality he needs.

5.2.1   Adding the Interface

In order to take advantage of this functionality, he first must add the interface, IF_SHM_BUILD_INSTANCE, to the area root class ZCL_CS_COURSE_SHMO_ROOT. Once the interface is added, the BUILD method appears in the **Methods** tab (see Figure 5.12). This static method is automatically fired if any of the ATTACH methods of the area class are called and the shared memory area has not been loaded.

Class Interface	ZCL_CS_COURSE_SHMO_ROOT			Impleme

Method	Level	Visi...	M...	Description
<IF_SHM_BUILD_INSTANCE>				
BUILD	Static ...	Pub...		Gebietskonstruktor
SET_COURSE_LIST	Instanc...	Pub...		Set Course List
GET_COURSE_LIST	Instanc...	Pub...		Get Course List
GET_COURSE	Instanc...	Pub...		Get Course

Figure 5.12 Build Method

Now Russel can copy and paste the code, which he wrote in the write test program ZCS_COURSE_SHMO_WRITE into the BUILD method (see Listing 5.6). This not only sets up the technical initialization of the root instance within the area, but also provides an opportunity to preload all the data from the database via the call to the SET_COURSE_LIST method.

```
METHOD if_shm_build_instance~build.

  DATA: course_handle TYPE REF TO zcl_cs_course_shmo,
        course_root   TYPE REF TO zcl_cs_course_shmo_root,
        excep         TYPE REF TO cx_root.

  TRY.
      course_handle = zcl_cs_course_shmo=>attach_for_write( ).
    CATCH cx_shm_error INTO excep.
      RAISE EXCEPTION TYPE cx_shm_build_failed
                      EXPORTING previous = excep.
  ENDTRY.

  TRY.
      CREATE OBJECT course_root AREA HANDLE course_handle.
      course_handle->set_root( course_root ).
      course_root->set_course_list( ).
      course_handle->detach_commit( ).
    CATCH cx_shm_error INTO excep.
      RAISE EXCEPTION TYPE cx_shm_build_failed
                      EXPORTING previous = excep.
  ENDTRY.

  IF invocation_mode = cl_shm_area=>invocation_mode_auto_build.
    CALL FUNCTION 'DB_COMMIT'.
  ENDIF.

ENDMETHOD.
```

Listing 5.6 Build Method Implementation

Simply adding the BUILD method is not enough to have it triggered by the area class. Russel must return to transaction SHMM and adjust the properties on his area. He needs to set the flag for **Automatic Area Structuring** and the **Autostart** value for **Area Structure**.

Also he has to define the **Constructor Class**. This is the class where he implemented the BUILD method. Notice that no assumption is made that the BUILD method will be part of the root class. That is a common approach, but the BUILD method can actually belong to any global class.

5.2.2 Modifying the Read Program

Finally Russel needs to modify the read test program ZCS_COURSE_SHMO_READ. Although the static BUILD method of the root class will be called automatically now, it does so asynchronously.

Instead of simply calling the method ATTACH_FOR_READ, Russel needs to take into account the asynchronous BUILD method and modify the program so that it waits for the shared memory area to be loaded by the BUILD method. Then, he needs to call the ATTACH_FOR_READ method again. The BUILD method is actually fired in a different work process, which accounts for needing the WAIT statement (see Listing 5.7).

```
START-OF-SELECTION.
  TRY.
      course_handle = zcl_cs_course_shmo=>attach_for_read( ).
    CATCH cx_shm_no_active_version.
      WAIT UP TO 1 SECONDS.
      course_handle = zcl_cs_course_shmo=>attach_for_read( ).
  ENDTRY.
```
Listing 5.7 Read Program Modification

Russel can now use transaction SHMM to delete any shared memory areas that may still exist. Since Russel has modified the area root class ZCL_CS_COURSE_SHMO_ROOT, he must delete any existing shared memory areas for this root. If this isn't done, Russel will get an ABAP runtime exception stating an inconsistency is present.

Russel can now run the read program directly instead of having to first run the write program. The output proves that the preloading of the shared memory object is working correctly.

5.3 Implementing into the Business Object Layer

Russel has finally completed the programming required for the shared memory object and has tested that it works correctly. The next step is to implement this shared memory object in the business object layer of the course system.

The main goal is to swap out the persistent object code and replace it with the shared memory object code. When the exchange is complete, the changes should have no affect on any developments that use the business object. This allows us to hide any complexities of using the shared memory object from the application logic. Activities like having to wait for the asynchronous BUILD method to complete will all be handled within the business object class now.

Example Source Code

It is important for you to understand that normally Russel (i.e., the developer) would be directly modifying the business object class ZCL_CS_COURSE to implement the shared memory object. In order to illustrate how the business objects change as we delve further into the development of the examples that accompany this book, we will show you how to implement the shared memory object in a copy of the ZCL_CS_COURSE business object class.

For a complete example of all of the changes that you need to make to the business object class ZCL_CS_COURSE, see the class ZCL_CS_COURSE_SHM_ACCESS.

5.3.1 Developing a Test Program

Russel wants to develop a simple program to test data retrieval using the business object class. This simple report program will retrieve all of the courses and write the data out to a standard list display (see Listing 5.8). Later he will use this same program to test the implementation of the shared memory object for the course database.

```
REPORT  zcs_course_obj_read.

DATA: gt_courses  TYPE STANDARD TABLE OF zcs_course_att.
FIELD-SYMBOLS: <gs_courses> LIKE LINE OF gt_courses.
DATA: gt_courses_obj TYPE zcs_courses_tbl.
FIELD-SYMBOLS: <gs_courses_obj> LIKE LINE OF gt_courses_obj.

START-OF-SELECTION.

  gt_courses_obj = zcl_cs_course=>read_all_courses( ).
  LOOP AT gt_courses_obj
          ASSIGNING <gs_courses_obj>.
    APPEND INITIAL LINE TO gt_courses
                  ASSIGNING <gs_courses>.
    MOVE-CORRESPONDING
          <gs_courses_obj>-course->course
                      TO <gs_courses>.
  ENDLOOP.

  LOOP AT gt_courses ASSIGNING <gs_courses>.
```

```
    WRITE:/ <gs_courses>-course_id,
            <gs_courses>-course_sdesc+0(20),
            <gs_courses>-faculty_id,
            <gs_courses>-semester,
            <gs_courses>-course_year,
            <gs_courses>-major,
            <gs_courses>-credit_hrs,
            <gs_courses>-student_limit,
            <gs_courses>-deletion_flag,
            <gs_courses>-start_time,
            <gs_courses>-end_time,
            <gs_courses>-course_schedule,
            <gs_courses>-cost,
            <gs_courses>-currency.
  ENDLOOP.
```

Listing 5.8 Course Object Test Program

5.3.2 Modifying the Business Object Class

Russel has proven that the current business object class ZCL_CS_COURSE works well using the persistent object for the course database. To keep things simple, we'll focus now on only those changes required for the READ_ALL_COURSES method. Listing 5.9 shows that the code for the persistent object has been removed, and the new code to retrieve the data from the shared memory object has been inserted.

```
METHOD read_all_courses.

  DATA: course_handle TYPE REF TO zcl_cs_course_shmo.
  DATA: lt_courses TYPE zcs_courses_tt.
  FIELD-SYMBOLS: <ls_courses> LIKE LINE OF lt_courses,
                 <wa_course>  LIKE LINE OF r_courses.
  TRY.
      course_handle = zcl_cs_course_shmo=>attach_for_read( ).
    CATCH cx_shm_no_active_version.
      WAIT UP TO 1 SECONDS.
      course_handle = zcl_cs_course_shmo=>attach_for_read( ).
  ENDTRY.
  lt_courses = course_handle->root->get_course_list( ).
  course_handle->detach( ).

  LOOP AT lt_courses ASSIGNING <ls_courses>.
    APPEND INITIAL LINE TO r_courses ASSIGNING <wa_course>.
    <wa_course>-course_id = <ls_courses>-course_id.
```

```
    CREATE OBJECT <wa_course>-course
      EXPORTING
        i_course = <ls_courses>.
  ENDLOOP.

ENDMETHOD.
```

Listing 5.9 READ_ALL_COURSES Method

Also notice that the variable being passed to the CREATE OBJECT statement has changed. Instead of passing the persistent object, Russel is now passing a flat structure, which contains the course data. This means that the signature of the CONSTRUCTOR method of the business object class must also be modified. The I_COURSE parameter must be typed like ZCS_COURSE (see Figure 5.13). Because the CONSTRUCTOR is private and only called via static factory methods, this sort of change has no effect on the applications that are using the business object class.

Figure 5.13 Constructor Signature

The CONSTRUCTOR implementation has changed a bit as well. Since Russel is now passing a flat structure to the I_COURSE parameter, the CONSTRUCTOR must do something with this data. Russel has added a new private instance attribute called SHMA_DATA. This attribute will hold the data that is passed from the I_COURSE parameter (see Listing 5.10).

```
METHOD constructor.
  me->shma_data = i_course.
  me->course_preq_pers =
    me->load_course_preqs( i_course-course_id ).
  me->map_shared_to_struc( ).
  me->load_supporting_details( ).
ENDMETHOD.
```

Listing 5.10 Constructor Modifications

Russel has also added a new method called MAP_SHARED_TO_STRUC that replaces the mapping from the persistent object, and will be used to map the data from the SHMA_DATA attribute to the COURSE attribute of the business object (see Listing 5.11).

```
METHOD map_shared_to_struc.

  course-course_id       = shma_data-course_id.
  course-course_sdesc    = shma_data-course_sdesc.
  course-faculty_id      = shma_data-faculty_id.
  course-semester        = shma_data-semester.
  course-course_year     = shma_data-course_year.
  course-major           = shma_data-major.
  course-credit_hrs      = shma_data-credit_hrs.
  course-student_limit   = shma_data-student_limit.
  course-deletion_flag   = shma_data-deletion_flag.
  course-start_time      = shma_data-start_time.
  course-end_time        = shma_data-end_time.
  course-course_schedule = shma_data-course_schedule.
  course-cost            = shma_data-cost.
  course-currency        = shma_data-currency.
  course-description     = shma_data-description.

* Load faculty using business object class
  TRY.
      course-faculty =
        zcl_cs_faculty=>read_faculty( course-faculty_id ).
    CATCH zcx_cs_faculty.
  ENDTRY.

  DATA l_syllabi TYPE xstring.
  l_syllabi = shma_data-syllabi.
  DATA izip TYPE REF TO cl_abap_gzip.
  IF l_syllabi IS NOT INITIAL.
    CREATE OBJECT izip.
    izip->decompress_text( EXPORTING gzip_in = l_syllabi
                  IMPORTING text_out = course-syllabi ).
  ENDIF.

  FIELD-SYMBOLS: <wa_pers> LIKE LINE OF course_preq_pers,
                 <wa_preq> TYPE zcs_course_preq_att.
  LOOP AT course_preq_pers ASSIGNING <wa_pers>.
    APPEND INITIAL LINE TO course-pre_req ASSIGNING <wa_preq>.
    <wa_preq>-preq_id = <wa_pers>-course_preq->get_preq_id( ).
  ENDLOOP.

ENDMETHOD.
```

Listing 5.11 MAP_SHARED_TO_STRUC Method Implementation

5.3.3 Testing the Changes

Now that Russel has completed the changes required to the business object class, he can use the test program, which he created earlier to see whether the data is being retrieved correctly. Again Russel would have directly modified the business object class ZCL_CS_COURSE, so there would be no changes required to the test program to make it work. For our purposes, we have implemented the changes in a copy of the business object class. Therefore, the test program ZCS_COURSE_OBJ_READ must be slightly modified to use the new business object class ZCL_COURSE_SHM_ACCESS.

Listing 5.12 shows that Russel is simply swapping out the table type used to receive the objects from the business object class, and the static call to method READ_ALL_COURSES.

```
REPORT  zcs_course_obj_read.
DATA: gt_courses  TYPE STANDARD TABLE OF zcs_course_att.
FIELD-SYMBOLS: <gs_courses> LIKE LINE OF gt_courses.
*DATA: gt_courses_obj TYPE zcs_courses_tbl.
DATA: gt_courses_obj TYPE zcs_courses_tbl_sma.
FIELD-SYMBOLS: <gs_courses_obj> LIKE LINE OF gt_courses_obj.

START-OF-SELECTION.

* gt_courses_obj = zcl_cs_course=>read_all_courses( ).
  gt_courses_obj =
        zcl_cs_course_shm_access=>read_all_courses().
```

Listing 5.12 Test Program Modifications

Russel has built many parts of his application up to this point, but now he is finally ready to start putting those components together and working toward his final application logic. He will place all this application-specific logic into a model class.

6   Model Class

All the development work that Russel has done so far has laid the ground-work for the final applications that he must ultimately build to complete his business requirements. Now that Russel will begin to actually code the model, he must switch his mode of thinking from the abstract building blocks of the foundation of his application to the specific implementation required for individual elements of his final application.

6.1   Class Overview

Russel has created several different types of classes so far. The shared memory object and persistent objects were special technologies that are supported as separate objects within the ABAP development environment. The business object classes, on the other hand, are not a specific development type. To the development environment, they appear to be just like any other normal ABAP Object class. They only assume a special meaning because of the way that they will be used within the project.

Model classes primarily fall into the latter category, normal classes with special development environment support. Nowhere in the ABAP development environment will you see an option to create a model class, although the Model View Controller (MVC) paradigm is an important aspect of both Business Server Pages (BSP) and Web Dynpro ABAP development. Eventually, Russel will use MVC in all of the applications that he is building for the online university course system.

6.1.1 What Is Model View Controller?

Model View Controller (MVC) is not a specific technology, nor is it unique to the SAP or the ABAP development environments. MVC is a design pattern or paradigm that, like so many modern programming techniques and technologies, originated from the Smalltalk programming language.

The core concept of MVC is the separation and encapsulation of the three major components of an application. The model component represents all application data and the logic necessary to retrieve or manipulate that data. The view is the visual representation of this data, generally regarded as the user interface layer. Lastly, the controller houses the logic that affects the program flow. It is responsible for responding to events and user input, and for dispatching the resulting changes to the view or the model.

Not only does MVC offer a clean organizational structure, but also, by separating the sections logically, it creates better maintenance opportunities. Because the layers of MVC are separated in the way they are, you can make changes to the user interface without having to touch or see the coding of your business logic. Of course the opposite is true as well, since modifications to the business logic can be isolated. Theoretically, this should also reduce the amount of testing required as changes are made.

So far nothing discussed about MVC is specific to web development. Both the traditional *Microsoft Foundation Classes* and the *Java Swing Library* are based on MVC as well. However, the difficulties of managing large modern web applications have pushed MVC into the spotlight and made the design pattern nearly synonymous with web development. Some of the more popular web development frameworks outside of the SAP environment, such as *Java Server Faces*, *Jakarta Struts*, and *Ruby on Rails*, heavily support MVC.

6.1.2 Creating the Model Class

There are several approaches that Russel could take while creating his model class. Russel already knows approximately what kind of applications he is going to create and what user interface technologies he will create them in.

▶ If his applications were significantly different, he could potentially create different model classes for the different types of applications. For instance, he could create a model for the internal facing course data maintenance functionality of the Web Dynpro ABAP application, and then create a completely different model for the external facing course catalog functionality of the BSP application.

▶ On the other hand, if the functionality was going to be similar between the two applications, he might be better off sharing a single model class.

There is no right or wrong answer in this case. Code reuse is a good thing. This has been the motivating factor for creating the generic abstraction layers of the business and persistent objects up till this point. However, once you reach the model class and the application logic, code reuse should not necessarily be your only concern.

Another consideration when designing the model is what special techniques of the particular UI technology you might want to utilize for MVC. Although there is no direct ABAP Workbench support for a special model class type, there are certain things built into both Web Dynpro ABAP and BSP to support model objects.

BSP Models

The ABAP Workbench and the BSP design tools don't really have aspects specific to the model object. To create a model, you create a class in the Workbench just as you would any other class, setting the inheritance from CL_BSP_MODEL2 manually; however this is not a hard requirement. This addition of inheritance from CL_BSP_MODEL2 is only used to provide *Model binding* functionality.

Model binding is an important benefit, yet a part of MVC that many people often overlook. Model binding reduces the amount and complexity of the coding in your typical application, thereby lowering the cost of development and maintenance. The work done by model binding is twofold.

▶ First, when you bind model attributes to BSP extension elements, metadata about the objects is automatically read from the binding. For instance, when you bind an attribute to an <HTMLB:LABEL>, you don't have to supply the label text. If available, the language-specific text will be pulled automatically from the data dictionary definition of the attribute that the element is bound to.

▶ The second reason for binding is the automatic transfer of input and output values between model attributes and elements and their form fields. You no longer have to map values back from the HTTP form fields in input processing. All this logic is performed for you by the MVC runtime and proper placement of the DISPATCH_INPUT controller method.

Web Dynpro ABAP Models

As stated before, MVC is not a specific technology; therefore different development tools will use it in different ways. Both BSP and Web Dynpro ABAP are built using the concepts of MVC, yet each has a very different implementation of those concepts.

Web Dynpro takes a different approach to data binding for instance. All view element data binding is performed against a context instead of a model object. This is not to say that the model has no place in Web Dynpro. It is just as important to separate your application logic properly and not give into the temptation to code any of the application layer within the Web Dynpro component itself.

There is no direct mechanism within Web Dynpro ABAP for the creation of model objects. Early on some developers would use other Web Dynpro components as their models; however, many of them found that where Web Dynpro is well suited for building user interfaces, it is not the ideal tool for housing business logic.

The most popular approach now is to use the *assistance* class as the model object within Web Dynpro ABAP. The assistance class is any ABAP class that inherits from the superclass CL_WD_COMPONENT_ASSISTANCE. The object will be automatically instantiated by the Web Dynpro component and the component will be responsible for its lifetime. This makes for very easy integration into the Web Dynpro environment.

Later when Russel reaches the steps of integrating the model into both BSP and Web Dynpro ABAP, we will see how he technically accomplishes each task. For now, he only needs to plan far enough ahead to know how he wants to design the model class. From what he already knows of his business requirements, he will be accessing similar sets of data in all his different types of user interfaces. Therefore, he is leaning toward creating one reusable model class.

What this means is that he has to choose between fully supporting BSP or Web Dynpro ABAP. Both environments require using a particular superclass for the model class if they are to take full advantage of the special techniques of the environment. Thinking ahead to the application he plans to build in BSP, Russel doesn't believe he will need model binding since the entire course catalog website will be view only. Data binding would be primarily useful in applications that have fields that can be updated. Therefore, he plans to build his single model class to be used primarily in Web Dynpro ABAP. This doesn't preclude the same class from being used within BSP.

Having made these decisions, Russel can finally start to create his model class. He simply creates a normal class within the ABAP Workbench. The only special attribute it will have is the inheritance from CL_WD_COMPONENT_ ASSISTANCE (see Figure 6.1).

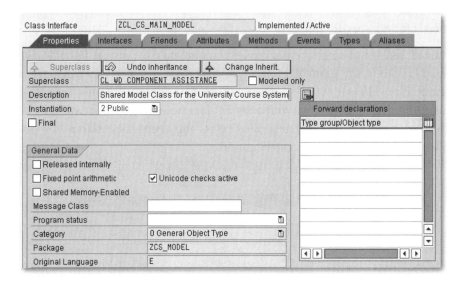

Figure 6.1 Model Class Properties

This superclass only provides two additional methods to the model class that are used by the Web Dynpro framework. These methods will be used later in Web Dynpro when text objects have to be read from the model class (see Figure 6.2).

Method	Visi...	Level	M...	Description
<IF_WD_COMPONENT_ASSISTANCE>				
GET_TEXT	Pub...	Insta...		liefert einen Text der Model-Klasse
<CL_WD_COMPONENT_ASSISTANCE>				
SET_NOT_FOUND_TEXT_KEY	Pro...	Insta...		setzt den Key für den Text bei nicht gefundenem Text

Figure 6.2 Model Class — Web Dynpro ABAP Specific Methods

6.2   Transactional Methods

With all the decisions about how to structure the model class out of the way, Russel can get down to the business of beginning to build application level logic. The first task he wants to tackle will be to build some of the transactional methods. He has his business object classes that abstract the basic *Create, Read, Update, Delete* (CRUD) methods (see Section 3.3), but now he needs to string these together into the actual types of data manipulations he needs for his specific applications.

Russel decides to structure his model class in such a way that he will have read methods for particular pieces of data. For instance, he will have a method called READ_COURSE_DETAILS. These methods will not only be used to read the details associated with a set of data objects, but they will also be used to instantiate the business object class and keep that instance in a private attribute of the model (see Figure 6.3).

Class Interface	ZCL_CS_MAIN_MODEL			Implemented / Active			
Properties	Interfaces	Friends	Attributes	Methods	Events	Types	Aliases

Attribute	Level	Visi...	Re...	Typing	Associated Type		Description
IS_SYUNAME_FACULTY	Instanc..	Priv..	☐	Type	WDY_BOOLEAN	⇨	Supplement for True Boo...
FIRST_NAME	Instanc..	Priv..	☐	Type	AD_NAMEFIR	⇨	First name
LAST_NAME	Instanc..	Priv..	☐	Type	AD_NAMELAS	⇨	Last name
FACULTY_OBJ	Instanc..	Priv..	☐	Type Re..	ZCL_CS_FACULTY	⇨	University Course Syste...
SYUNAME_FACULTY	Instanc..	Priv..	☐	Type Re..	ZCL_CS_FACULTY	⇨	University Course Syste...
COURSE_OBJ	Instanc..	Priv..	☐	Type Re..	ZCL_CS_COURSE	⇨	University Course Syste...
COURSE_ASS_OBJ	Instanc..	Priv..	☐	Type	ZCS_COURSE_ASS_OBJ_TBL	⇨	University Course Syste...

Figure 6.3 Attributes of the Model Class

Russel makes all of the model attributes **Private**. This way no application that uses this model will have direct access to the business object classes and must use the methods of the model to perform any operations on these inner objects. Now the model can control consistency by doing things like making certain that locking methods are called before update methods.

By keeping the instances of the business objects in attributes of the model, they can be initialized during the read methods and then used later for the save methods.

6.2.1 Read Method

As you have already seen, Russel's READ_COURSE_DETAILS method will serve two purposes. First, it will be used to initialize the business object that will be used in a transaction. Secondly, it will be used to pass back all the details about the course that will be needed in the user interface. Both of these requirements are met by the parameters of the method as seen in Figure 6.4.

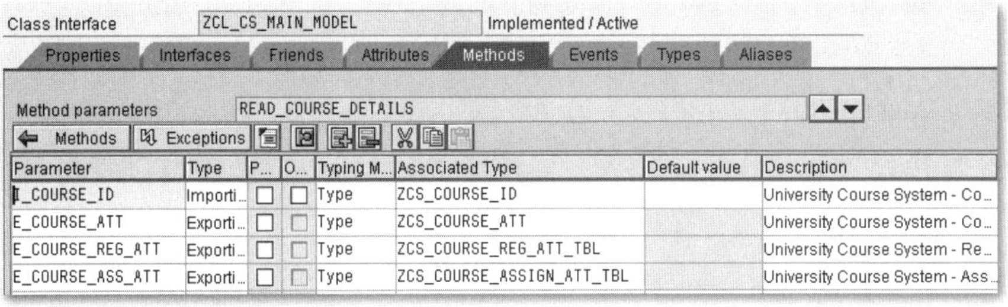

Class Interface	ZCL_CS_MAIN_MODEL			Implemented / Active				
Properties	Interfaces	Friends	Attributes	Methods	Events	Types	Aliases	

Method parameters: READ_COURSE_DETAILS

Methods | Exceptions

Parameter	Type	P...	O...	Typing M...	Associated Type	Default value	Description
I_COURSE_ID	Importi...	☐	☐	Type	ZCS_COURSE_ID		University Course System - Co...
E_COURSE_ATT	Exporti...	☐	☐	Type	ZCS_COURSE_ATT		University Course System - Co...
E_COURSE_REG_ATT	Exporti...	☐	☐	Type	ZCS_COURSE_REG_ATT_TBL		University Course System - Re...
E_COURSE_ASS_ATT	Exporti...	☐	☐	Type	ZCS_COURSE_ASSIGN_ATT_TBL		University Course System - Ass...

Figure 6.4 READ_COURSE_DETAILS Method Parameters

This is really the stage in the project where the abstraction layers that Russel has invested in begin to pay off. What potentially could be a complex method — filled with the logic necessary to read all the related course data from the several underlying database tables — is made quite simple, thanks to the business object class.

The logic in the read method (see Listing 6.1) will mostly involve calling the factory methods of the course business object for whatever COURSE_ID was specified as an input parameter. Then the corresponding course assignment business objects must also be initialized. Once each set of business objects is available, the output parameters of the method can be filled by the public attributes of the business object.

```
METHOD read_course_details.
  CLEAR: me->course_obj, me->course_ass_obj.
  me->course_obj = zcl_cs_course=>read_course(
      i_course_id = i_course_id   ).
  e_course_att = me->course_obj->course.
  e_course_reg_att = me->course_obj->course_reg.
  TRY.
      me->course_ass_obj =
        zcl_cs_course_ass=>read_all_course_ass(
            i_course_id = i_course_id   ).
    CATCH zcx_cs_course.
  ENDTRY.
```

```
FIELD-SYMBOLS: <wa_ass_out> LIKE LINE OF e_course_ass_att,
               <wa_ass_in>  LIKE LINE OF
                                 me->course_ass_obj.
  LOOP AT me->course_ass_obj ASSIGNING <wa_ass_in>.
    APPEND INITIAL LINE TO e_course_ass_att
        ASSIGNING <wa_ass_out>.
    MOVE i_course_id TO <wa_ass_out>-course_id.
    MOVE <wa_ass_in>-week_number
          TO <wa_ass_out>-week_number.
    MOVE-CORRESPONDING <wa_ass_in>-course_ass->course_ass
      TO <wa_ass_out>.
  ENDLOOP.
ENDMETHOD.
```

Listing 6.1 READ_COURSE_DETAILS Method of the Model Class

Even now that Russel has reached the application coding level, he still is not quite ready to have logic to output error messages. Since the techniques for issuing messages vary by which user interface technology he is working with, he wants to leave the output of messages to that final layer.

So once again the model class uses the master exception, ZCX_COURSE_SYSTEM, which encompasses all the more granular exceptions he has created (see Figure 6.5). In this way, any of the course exceptions that might be issued by the inner business objects will simply pass through the model method and can be caught at the user interface coding level.

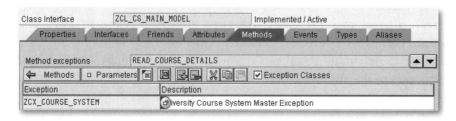

Figure 6.5 READ_COURSE_DETAILS Method Exceptions

Nevertheless, this still provides the opportunity to catch and hide certain errors at this level as well. You should note that the call for the course assignment business objects is surrounded by a TRY...CATCH block. The reason for this is that if no course assignments are found for a particular course, an exception will be raised.

An exception doesn't always have to be equated with an error situation. In the context of this method, it is perfectly fine for there to have been no assignments created yet. Therefore, the logic of the model method catches and then simply ignores this exception, keeping it from ever reaching the user interface layer.

6.2.2 Record Locking Methods

The business object classes had lower level update and delete methods, all of which really should have a lock on the records set before performing them. However Russel has left the locking ownership to his model object. This way the model can be used to lock multiple records simultaneously or lock related objects. This allows much more flexibility in the design of the application.

Initially for the model class however, Russel only needs simple granular locking at the course ID level. Later, if his business requirements expanded to include some sort of mass update, he could just extend the logic of the model class to support mass locking as well.

The granular lock method (see Listing 6.2) will call the generated enqueue function module that was generated by the data dictionary lock object back in Section 2.4.3. The model class method is mostly just a wrapper around the enqueue function module for mapping error conditions to application-specific exceptions.

```
METHOD lock_course.
  CALL FUNCTION 'ENQUEUE_EZCS_COURSE'
    EXPORTING
      course_id      = i_course_id
    EXCEPTIONS
      foreign_lock   = 1
      system_failure = 2
      OTHERS         = 3.
  IF sy-subrc <> 0.
    DATA uname TYPE syuname.
    MOVE sy-msgv1 TO uname.
    RAISE EXCEPTION TYPE zcx_cs_course
        EXPORTING
          textid = zcx_cs_course=>foreign_lock
          course_id = i_course_id
          uname = uname.
  ENDIF.
ENDMETHOD.
```

Listing 6.2 LOCK_COURSE Method of the Model Class

For the reverse, the model class will also support a granular unlock method. This is really only for uniformity, as there are no exceptions that need to be mapped from a dequeue operation.

```
METHOD unlock_course.
  CALL FUNCTION 'DEQUEUE_EZCS_COURSE'
    EXPORTING
      course_id = i_course_id.
ENDMETHOD.
```

Listing 6.3 UNLOCK_COURSE Method of the Model Class

6.2.3 Save Method

To close out the transactionality of the course data, Russel will also need a save method. For the input parameters, Russel will mirror the outputs of the read method. This way the same variables can be used within the user interface and just passed back to the SAVE method with the updated data (see Figure 6.6). Similarly, the logic of the SAVE method mirrors the read method to a great extent. The business object class once again greatly simplifies the processing.

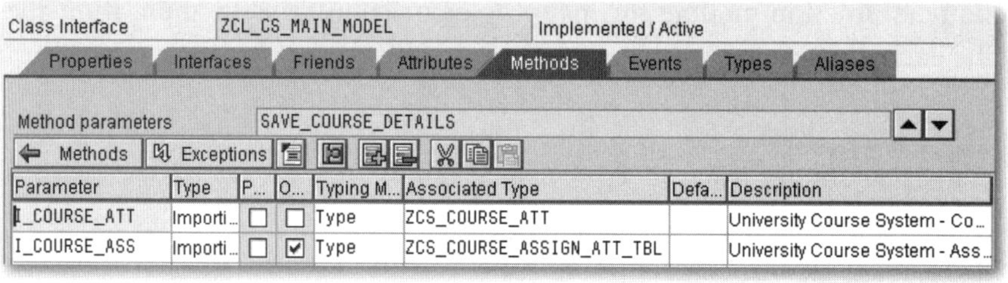

Figure 6.6 SAVE_COURSE_DETAILS Method Parameters

It's interesting to note how the optional course assignment parameter, I_COURSE_ASS, is handled within the code (see Listing 6.4). Optional parameters will be filled with their initial value if they are not supplied to the method call. If Russel passes the empty course assignment table into the business object method, it will delete any existing course assignment records.

```
METHOD save_course_details.
  me->course_obj->course = i_course_att.
  me->course_obj->update_course( ).
  IF i_course_ass IS SUPPLIED.
```

```
    FIELD-SYMBOLS: <wa_ass> LIKE LINE OF i_course_ass,
                   <wa_obj> LIKE LINE OF me->course_ass_obj.
    LOOP AT i_course_ass ASSIGNING <wa_ass>.
      READ TABLE me->course_ass_obj ASSIGNING <wa_obj>
        WITH KEY week_number = <wa_ass>-week_number.
     IF sy-subrc = 0.
        <wa_obj>-course_ass->course_ass = <wa_ass>.
        <wa_obj>-course_ass->update_course_ass( ).
      ELSE.
        APPEND INITIAL LINE TO me->course_ass_obj
           ASSIGNING <wa_obj>.
        <wa_obj>-course_ass =
            zcl_cs_course_ass=>create_course_ass(
                i_course_id   = i_course_att-course_id
                i_week_number = <wa_ass>-week_number ).
        <wa_obj>-week_number = <wa_ass>-week_number.
        <wa_obj>-course_ass->course_ass = <wa_ass>.
        <wa_obj>-course_ass->update_course_ass( ).
      ENDIF.
    ENDLOOP.
  ENDIF.
  COMMIT WORK AND WAIT.
ENDMETHOD.
```
Listing 6.4 SAVE_COURSE_DETAILS Method of the Model Class

A check the parameter to see if it IS INITIAL, won't be able to distinguish between when you want to delete all assignments versus when the parameter is simply not supplied to the method. To avoid this problem, Russel uses the IS SUPPLIED statement, which can be used for optional parameters when just such logic is needed.

Russel's code also has to take into account the creation of new assignments. He kept a cached copy of the assignment table as one of the private attributes of the model class during the read method. He now uses this original copy of the assignment table to determine whether a particular record has been added during processing, and therefore needs the CREATE_COURSE_ASS method of the business object instead of the UPDATE_COURSE_ASS method.

6.2.4   Getters

Because of the design decision to keep the business object instances private within the model class, all other applications won't be able to directly access data from them. Russel may later find parts of his application that require

173

more information than what is returned by the read method of the model. For these occasions, he will build getter methods that expose the data that is required, without giving direct access to the business object instance.

This is also an area where you can see that building the model class is a bit of an iterative process. We recommend that you start with the design and building of the model class before moving to the user interface. This is the foundation of a solid architecture for your application and lends itself to the best reuse of the existing objects. It will also allow Russel to unit test the bulk of his application logic before he even begins to create his user interface.

By building the model class first, however, Russel has to be aware that he might not have included every possible application method. Sure he has thought of all the methods that he will obviously need based on his current business requirements, but new requirements might arise later as he begins to build the user interface. These getter methods are fine examples of additional logic that might need to be added later in order to fill some gap in the originally designed application coding. By segregating the access logic into separate getter methods, he can add to the class without affecting code that is already complete and tested.

For now however, Russel knows that his application will need at least one of these getters later on. He needs a method that can be used to return the currently loaded course ID. For the parameters, he'll use the RETURNING type (see Figure 6.7).

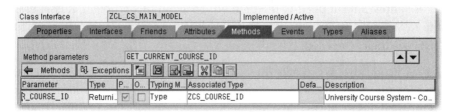

Figure 6.7 GET_CURRENT_COURSE_ID Method Parameter

This will provide for this method to be called in *functional* form, which is quite common for getters. This functional form of a method call is a simplified format that can be used when you have a method with a single RETURNING parameter. These methods can also be called in normal format (see Listing 6.5), or as a functional method (see Listing 6.6).

```
model->get_current_course_id(
  RECEIVING
    r_course_id = course_id ).
```

Listing 6.5 Normal Method Call

```
course_id = model->get_current_course_id( ).
```

Listing 6.6 Functional Method Examples

Future Functionality

The functional style of method calls that is commonly used for getters has an additional benefit in the next release of SAP NetWeaver. This future functionality allows for *method chaining*. So, instead of having to retrieve the value of the first method call into a variable for use in a second method call, the two methods can be chained together using the functional method call as the input parameter into a second method. Listing 6.7 shows an example of this functionality.

```
model->read_course_details(
  EXPORTING
    i_course_id      = model->get_current_course_id( )
  IMPORTING
    e_course_att     = course_att ).
```

Listing 6.7 Example of the Future Functionality of Method Chaining

---

6.3   Utility Methods

Utility methods are those pieces of functionality that don't always pertain to the business data that you're processing in the model class, but are very helpful as reusable sections of code. A more academic discussion of object-oriented design might reveal that utility methods really have no place in a model class, and that instead they should be separated out into some object of their own.

Because Russel has always been a practical programmer, he knows there are times when making these utilities part of the overall application logic makes good sense in order to improve the overall usability of finding and working with these sections of code.

Utility methods are usually declared as STATIC, meaning that the class that they belong to doesn't need to be instantiated in order to call them. This also means that they won't have access to any of the non-static attributes of the class. Russel already has an idea for a utility method. There are several places in his application where he might need to output a label for a field. In a Web

Dynpro ABAP or classic Dynpro screen, the framework will automatically look up the data dictionary definition of a field for you.

But he will need to create an email out of his system. To create the text in the body of the email, no such automatic field label support will be available. Therefore, he plans to build a simple utility method that will accept any data field and return the description for that field, as long as it had been typed from a data dictionary definition. The signature of this method is shown in Figure 6.8.

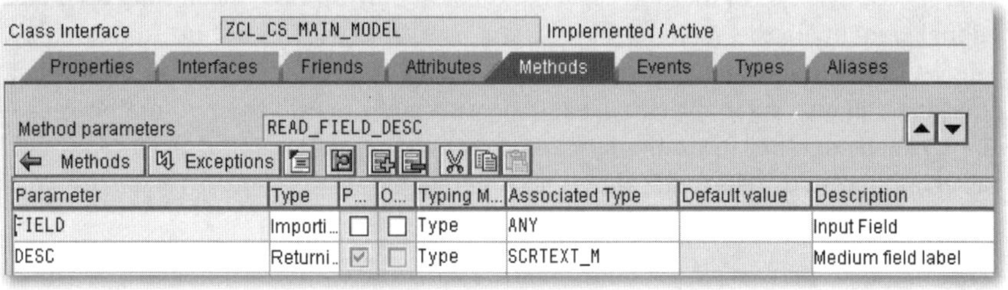

Class Interface	ZCL_CS_MAIN_MODEL				Implemented / Active		
Properties	Interfaces	Friends	Attributes	Methods	Events	Types	Aliases

Method parameters		READ_FIELD_DESC					▲ ▼

← Methods	🔍 Exceptions						

Parameter	Type	P...	O...	Typing M...	Associated Type	Default value	Description
FIELD	Importi...	☐	☐	Type	ANY		Input Field
DESC	Returni...	☑	☐	Type	SCRTEXT_M		Medium field label

Figure 6.8 READ_FIELD_DESC Model Method

Because Russel can generically type a parameter, as he has done with the FIELD parameter of type ANY, he has complete freedom to pass anything into the utility method. Therefore, a calling program can just pass in whatever field they will need a description for regardless of its data type. Listing 6.8 shows an example of how this utility method will be used later on to create the email text.

```
label = me->read_field_desc(
    me->course_obj->course-course_id  ).
concatenate body `<tr><td valign="top"><strong>`
          label
          `: </strong></td><td>`
          me->course_obj->course-course_id `</td></tr>`
          into body.
```

Listing 6.8 Example Usage of the READ_FIELD_DESC Method

Inside the coding of his utility method (see Listing 6.9), Russel will use another new capability of ABAP — namely the *Runtime Type Services* (RTTS). The RTTS provides the capabilities to examine the properties of variables or object instances at runtime.

```
METHOD read_field_desc.
  DATA: el_desc TYPE REF TO cl_abap_elemdescr,
        isddic  TYPE abap_bool,
        field_d TYPE dfies.
  TRY.
    el_desc ?= cl_abap_typedescr=>describe_by_data( field ).
      isddic = el_desc->is_ddic_type( ).
      CHECK isddic = abap_true.
      field_d = el_desc->get_ddic_field( ).
      desc = field_d-scrtext_m.
    CATCH cx_root.     "#EC CATCH_ALL
  ENDTRY.
ENDMETHOD.
```

Listing 6.9 READ_FIELD_DESC Method of the Model Class

In this example, Russel uses the RTTS method CL_ABAP_TYPEDESCR=>
DESCRIBE_BY_DATA to examine the generic data reference that was passed
into the utility method. By casting the return value from this method into an
object of type CL_ABAP_ELEMDESCR, he has already determined that the
parameter is an elemental data type. In other words, if the calling application
had passed in a structure or internal table, this action would have produced
an exception that in turn would have been caught within the CX_ROOT trap.

He will then check to ensure that this data object had been created with reference to a data dictionary type and not a direct type definition via the IS_
DDIC_TYPE method. Next he will retrieve all the data dictionary attributes of
the field with the GET_DDIC_FIELD method. The returned structure, FIELD_D,
will contain all the descriptions, although Russel only needs the medium
length one.

6.4   Emailing

Although Russel has plenty of other logic within his model class, there is one
method that stands out as a rather important piece of functionality worth
looking at in more detail — the method that will send email. Russel's business requirements call for the ability for professors to be able to distribute
information about a course and its weekly assignments to the enrolled students via email. In this way, professors can send out the details of a particular
week's assignment in an email and also attach any support documents.

6.4.1   Email Setup

Before Russel starts coding his email method, he needs to run through some steps to ensure that email is configured correctly in his system. The email interface in Release 6.10 and higher was completely redesigned to take advantage of the native *Simple Mail Transfer Protocol* (SMTP) stack within the SAP Web Application Server (ABAP).

There are many changes from this release on. For one, there is no longer any reliance on external executables to send email. The SAP Kernel now contains native SMTP processing capabilities in the *Internet Communication Manager* (ICM). Moreover, there is a new ABAP interface that can be used, called the *Business Communication Services* (BCS).

Unlike in release SAP R/3 4.6D and lower, there are no external executables to set up. There is no need to configure the Internet Mail Gateway or create any *Remote Function Call* (RFC) destinations. However there is some set up that needs to be done to the ICM in order to activate and configure SMTP processing. As Russel discovered, OSS Note 455140 gives an excellent step-by-step guide to configuring SMTP. But here is a quick checklist that he followed based on the configuration details provided by the OSS Note:

▶ If you are on SAP Web AS Release 6.10 only, you must add the **SMTP Plug-In** entry in your instance profile. This is not required as of SAP Web AS Release 6.20, because the system is delivered with SMTP as an integrated part of the ICM.

▶ In the instance profile, specify the **TCP/IP port** that SMTP will listen on. Port 25 is the default.

▶ If you have multiple clients in your SAP system, you will want to set up a virtual host for each client in order to separate SMTP processing from each client.

▶ Verify in transaction SICF that you have an SMTP node and that it is activated. It should look something like Figure 6.9.

Now that Russel is finished with all the low level setup, he needs to connect the lowest layer, the ICM, to SAP's middle message layer, *SAPconnect*. SAPconnect sits between the application layer, such as the *SAP Business Workplace* (transaction SBWP) or custom applications like Russel's course system, and the lowest layer hiding all the technical details. All of the SAPconnect monitoring and configuration can be reached from one transaction, SCOT.

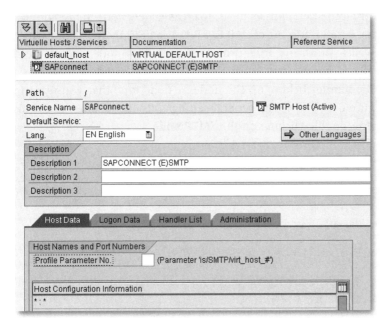

Figure 6.9 SMTP Node in the Service Hierarchy

First SCOT has several different views that can be used. One view shows the jobs that have been set up, another view shows set up by routings, etc. Russel prefers to start SCOT in **system status** view. This view shows a tree with the communication types, the nodes set up for each type, and the number of messages in each status. Figure 6.10 shows this view active within transaction SCOT.

SAPconnect: Administration (system status)

Start of evaluation time: 03/09/2007 00:00

	Completed	Error	In transit	Waiting	Duration In transit ∅ hh:mm	Duration Waiting ∅ hh:mm
(000)	0	0	0	0		
FAX	0	0	0	0	0:00	0:00
INT	0	0	0	0	0:00	0:00
SMTP	0	0	0		0:00	0:00
X40	0	0	0	0	0:00	0:00
RML	0	0	0	0	0:00	0:00
PAG	0	0	0	0	0:00	0:00
PRT	0	0	0	0	0:00	0:00

Figure 6.10 SAPconnect Communication Types Overview

Upon first entry into SCOT, Russel needs to create a new node in SAPconnect for his external email setup. As of SAP R/3 Release 4.6C, there is a fairly nice wizard that walks you through the process of setting up nodes, but you can also control all settings directly in a dialog maintenance window that can be brought up by double-clicking on the node or node type that you want to maintain. Figure 6.11 shows the general settings that Russel entered for his email node after double-clicking on the **SMTP** node.

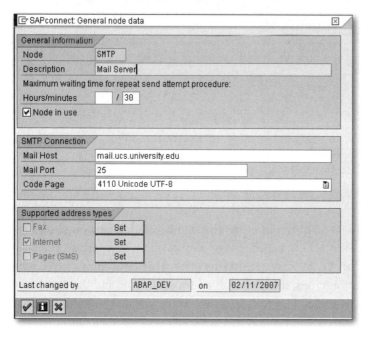

Figure 6.11 SMTP Node General Settings

You can see that all Russel had to do to set up this node is specify the connection information for an external mail server. Here, he gives the host name (**Mail Host**) for his Corporate Microsoft Exchange Server, *mail.ucs.university.edu*. He also supplied the TCP/IP **Mail Port** that the mail server listens on. Port **25** is the default SMTP port and is generally what most mail servers are configured to use. However this value can be altered, so Russel did confirm the setting with the Exchange Mail Administrator.

At this level, Russel can also specify the **Code Page** that he wants all messages converted to before they are sent. He chooses **4110 Unicode UTF-8**, because by converting to UTF-8, he is able to support email outputs in multiple languages regardless of his system settings. You don't have to have a Unicode system to support this functionality. Even a non-Unicode Application Server

ABAP (Release 6.10 or higher) has the capability to convert its current code page to Unicode for outbound communications.

Now Russel begins to configure the Internet address type (see Figure 6.12). He doesn't need to set up any outbound filtering to different nodes. This functionality is mainly used in fax nodes to distribute work based on country code to fax servers, which are regional to the area that the fax needs to be sent to. Therefore the **Address area** is set to the wildcard, namely *.

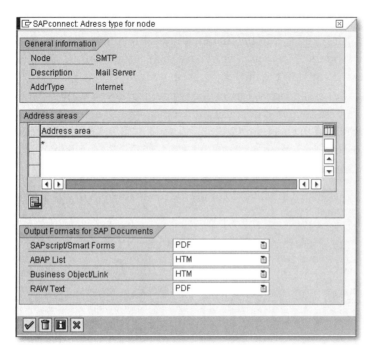

Figure 6.12 Internet Address Type Setup

To comply with the Unicode setting, Russel has all output formats converted to PDF or HTML as OSS note 633265 suggests. Unlike the plain text format, this will ensure that characters in ABAP Lists and RAW Text documents are not corrupted during the conversion to Unicode.

Next Russel needs to schedule a job that will transmit email. Normally, email will only be sent out when this job runs, so Russel wants to schedule it quite frequently. The job-based scheduling is primarily needed for applications that utilize the old SAP R/3 4.6D based email API. It had no capability to send email, except via a background job. But the new Business Communication

Services programming interface that Russel is going to use for his application coding in the university course system can send email immediately as well.

Russel sets up this job to run every five minutes. The job setup can also be done from transaction SCOT. Russel just has to switch his view to **JOBS,** where he can then click on the **CREATE** button to start the process of scheduling a new send job.

6.4.2 Running an Email Test

Russel is just about ready to run his first email test. The only other requirement is that the senders of any email must have their return address set up in their user master. If you don't maintain this data, you will always get an error message during the send process. Russel does know that if you want a standard SAP program that can generate these addresses for you, there is just such a solution documented in OSS note 104263. Also in SAP R/3 4.6C and higher, you can configure the system to generate the sender address automatically if not present. OSS note 320443 provides the details of this solution.

In Figure 6.13, you can see the field that must be maintained in the user master — the **E-Mail** field.

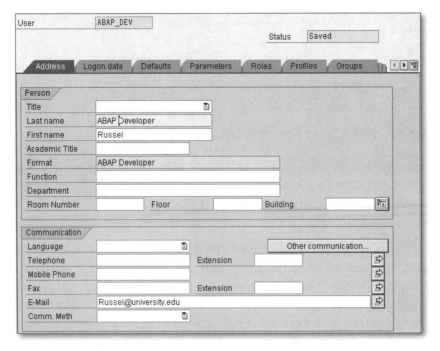

Figure 6.13 User Maintenance of the Sender's Email Address

Finally Russel is ready to test his system setup. First, he uses the SAP short message functionality. He uses menu **System • Short Message** from any transaction. From this system utility, Russel can prepare a short test message. Russel decides not to wait for his batch job to run to determine whether his message went through, so he just jumps back to transaction SCOT. From the **System Status** view, he can choose **Ctrl+F7** or the **Execute** icon to start the send process for the Internet Mail communication type. He receives his test message confirming that the setup is just fine.

> **Troubleshooting**
>
> Let's say that everything is not fine. Where would Russel start troubleshooting? Once again, he would start with the transaction SCOT. The system status shows the overall status overview. Russel can see the number of messages in **Error** or **Waiting** status. If Russel had many messages in **Waiting** status, this might indicate that his send job probably was not scheduled or that the background job was failing for some reason.
>
> The overview screen is adequate, but Russel would probably want more details. From SCOT, he can choose **Utilities • Overview of Send Orders**, or he could jump to transaction SOST to get a more detailed view. This transaction will give a detailed report by address type, status, date, time, and sender. For each message, Russel can view the transmission history, the message, and the trace log. Russel could also try to resubmit the message from here.
>
> If Russel needs to activate tracing, he would have to return to transaction SCOT. He would then choose **Utilities • Trace • Internal Trace**. He could also view all traces from here without having to go through transaction SOST.

6.4.3 Email Method

Now that Russel has confirmed that his system is properly configured for email, he can start coding the email method in his model class. Since the majority of the course data is cached in private attributes of the model class after a call to the read method, the importing parameters of the EMAIL_ ASSIGNMENT method only need to specify what course week that needs to be communicated (see Figure 6.14).

Also the addresses of the recipients of the email are all passed in as parameters as well. Although Russel's original requirement is to send email to all students in a course, he envisions the need to be able to resend a message to one or more students but not the whole class. To provide flexibility within the user interface, he will design this method so that the selection of the users can happen in another block of code.

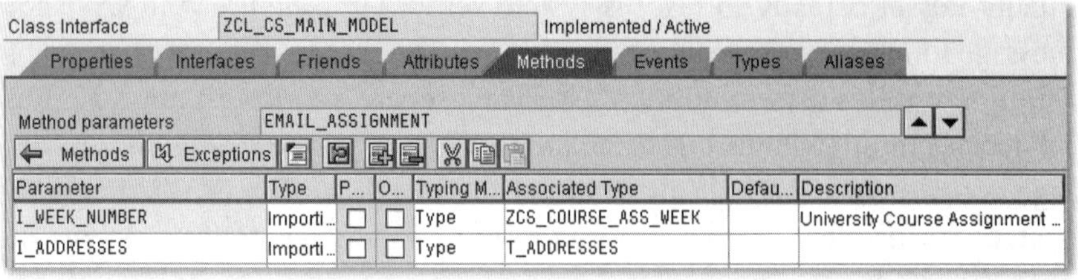

Figure 6.14 EMAIL_ASSIGNMENT Method Parameters

You might have noticed the data type, T_ADDRESSES, that Russel used for the address importing parameter. This did not come from a global type in the data dictionary. Instead, this is an example of how even complex types can be declared directly in a class. The definition of T_ADDRESSES is done within the **Types** tab of the Class Builder (see Figure 6.15).

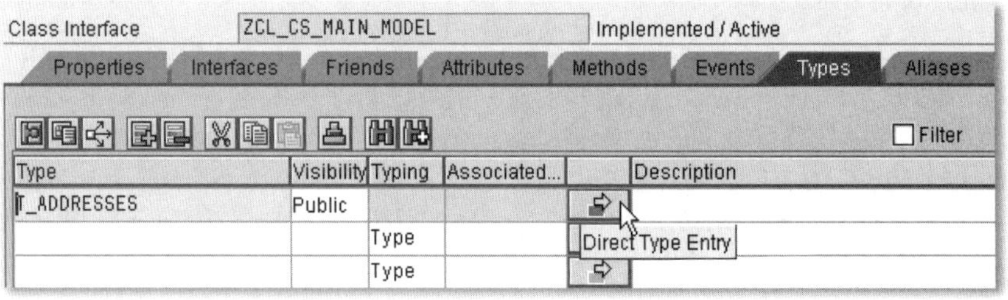

Figure 6.15 Type Declaration within the Model Class

One of the major enhancements to the Class Builder in the more recent releases of SAP NetWeaver is the ability to declare more complex types, such as full internal table statements, directly. This often eliminates the need to leave the Class Builder in order to declare a table type in the data dictionary when you really only need to use it within a class.

When Russel clicks on the **Direct Type Entry** button in the fifth column of the **Types** tab of the Class Builder (see Figure 6.15), he will be taken to the code behind the class definition as seen in Figure 6.16. The direct type entry is powerful, because it not only allows you to define complex types quickly using direct ABAP coding, but also enables you to edit the interfaces of the methods of your class.

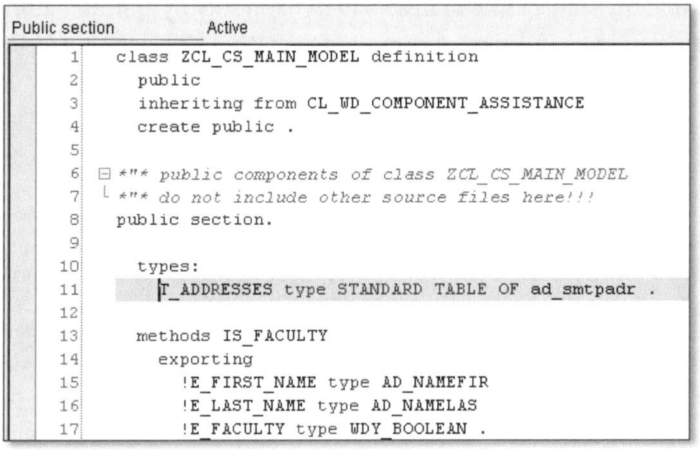

```
Public section          Active
     1    class ZCL_CS_MAIN_MODEL definition
     2      public
     3      inheriting from CL_WD_COMPONENT_ASSISTANCE
     4      create public .
     5
     6  □ *"* public components of class ZCL_CS_MAIN_MODEL
     7  └ *"* do not include other source files here!!!
     8    public section.
     9
    10      types:
    11        |T_ADDRESSES type STANDARD TABLE OF ad_smtpadr .
    12
    13      methods IS_FACULTY
    14        exporting
    15          !E_FIRST_NAME type AD_NAMEFIR
    16          !E_LAST_NAME type AD_NAMELAS
    17          !E_FACULTY type WDY_BOOLEAN .
```

Figure 6.16 Direct Type Entry

If we look at the coding of the EMAIL_ASSIGNMENT method, we can see Russel's first use of the new Business Communication Services (BCS) interface for sending email.

1. Russel begins his processing with a few checks to ensure that at least one address is provided and that the course week is valid; otherwise, there is no point in continuing the processing:

```
METHOD email_assignment.
  FIELD-SYMBOLS: <wa_obj> LIKE LINE OF me->course_ass_obj.
  CHECK i_addresses IS NOT INITIAL.
  READ TABLE me->course_ass_obj ASSIGNING <wa_obj>
    WITH KEY week_number = i_week_number.
  CHECK sy-subrc = 0.
```

2. Next Russel has the data declarations he will need. BCS is a class-based interface as opposed to the old function module-based email application programming interface (API). Therefore, each aspect of the mail process, like the document and the sender, will be separate objects:

```
DATA: send_request TYPE REF TO cl_bcs,
      document     TYPE REF TO cl_document_bcs,
      sender       TYPE REF TO cl_sapuser_bcs,
      recipient    TYPE REF TO if_recipient_bcs.
DATA: l_mailtext TYPE soli_tab,
      l_mailhex  TYPE solix_tab,
      l_subject  TYPE so_obj_des.
FIELD-SYMBOLS: <wa_mail>  LIKE LINE OF l_mailtext,
               <wa_mailx> LIKE LINE OF l_mailhex.
```

3. Russel will build the subject line of his email dynamically by concatenating together text elements and data that he is processing. He used text elements so that even his email could be translated to different languages:

```
CONCATENATE 'Week'(sb1) ` ` <wa_obj>-week_number ` `
            'Assignment for Course'(sb2) ` `
            me->course_obj->course-course_id
            INTO l_subject.
```

4. The BCS is built on the same persistent object technology that Russel took advantage of to build his own Data Object layer (see Chapter 3):

```
send_request = cl_bcs=>create_persistent( ).
DATA body TYPE string.
DATA label TYPE string.
```

5. For the best output format, Russel decides to build an HTML-based email. This is a fairly popular format for email, where instead of sending just plain text, the body of the email is a fully formatted HTML document.

The process is the same as building any regular web page. In fact, to get the look that he wants, Russel first built a simple web page on his PC using a text editor. Then he used his logic to assemble the HTML elements with the data from his course variables, concatenating it all together into one string in memory:

```
CONCATENATE body `<table cellspacing="1" cellpadding="1"`
                 `width="400" border="0">`
            INTO body.
CONCATENATE body `<tbody>` INTO body.
label = me->read_field_desc(
    me->course_obj->course-course_id  ).
CONCATENATE body `<tr><td valign="top"><strong>`
            label
            `: </strong></td><td>`
            me->course_obj->course-course_id `</td></tr>`
            INTO body.
label = me->read_field_desc(
    me->course_obj->course-course_sdesc ).
CONCATENATE body `<tr><td valign="top"><strong>`
            label
            `: </strong></td><td>`
            me->course_obj->course-course_sdesc
            `</td></tr>`
            INTO body.
CONCATENATE body `</tbody></table><br><br>` INTO body.
...
```

6. The BCS will not accept its content as a string or binary string. Instead it needs internal tables of either type SOLI_TAB for character-based data or SOLIX_TAB for binary-formatted data. To convert his string to the internal table format, Russel uses the standard SAP Function Module SCMS_STRING_TO_FTEXT:

```
CALL FUNCTION 'SCMS_STRING_TO_FTEXT'
    EXPORTING  text      = body
    TABLES     ftext_tab = l_mailtext.
```

7. Now Russel creates the main document that will be the email he will be sending via the BCS. He specifies the type to be HTM so that the BCS knows that this is an HTML email body and not plain text. Also, at this point, he passes in the body content via I_TEXT and the subject line via I_SUBJECT:

```
document = cl_document_bcs=>create_document(
    i_type = 'HTM'
    i_text = l_mailtext
    i_subject = l_subject ).
```

8. Next Russel starts taking any course assignment attachments and places those into the email. The attachments are processed within the course system as binary strings; so once again he needs to convert the format to an internal table before adding the content to the BCS document. To go from binary string to binary table, he uses a different function module, SCMS_XSTRING_TO_BINARY:

```
FIELD-SYMBOLS <wa_attach> TYPE zcs_course_file.
LOOP AT <wa_obj>-course_ass->course_ass-attachments
  ASSIGNING <wa_attach>.
  CLEAR l_mailhex.
  l_subject = <wa_attach>-filename.
  CALL FUNCTION 'SCMS_XSTRING_TO_BINARY'
    EXPORTING  buffer     = <wa_attach>-content
    TABLES     binary_tab = l_mailhex.
```

9. When you create a document attachment, you can supply an attachment type. This will be used by the recipients' mail reader to determine what application should be used to open the attachment.

The best information that Russel has to determine the attachment type is the file extension. He uses the new Regular Expressions functionality that was introduced in SAP NetWeaver 7.0 to perform in one line of code the split of the filename and file extension. Russel is pretty impressed by the power of the Regular Expression and decides to explore it in a little more detail after he finishes his work on the email method (see Section 6.5):

```
DATA dot_offset TYPE i.
DATA extension TYPE mimetypes-extension.
DATA attachment_type TYPE so_obj_tp.
FIND FIRST OCCURRENCE OF REGEX '\.[^\.]+$'
   IN <wa_attach>-filename MATCH OFFSET dot_offset.
ADD 1 TO dot_offset.
extension = <wa_attach>-filename+dot_offset.
attachment_type = extension.
TRANSLATE attachment_type TO UPPER CASE.
document->add_attachment(
     i_attachment_type = attachment_type
     i_att_content_hex = l_mailhex
     i_attachment_subject = l_subject ).
ENDLOOP.
```

10. Now Russel can set the document with its attachments as the main document of his send request. To create the sender address, he uses the current logged-on user:

```
send_request->set_document( document ).
sender = cl_sapuser_bcs=>create( sy-uname ).
send_request->set_sender( sender ).
```

11. Next Russel processes through the lists of recipients. The full external email address will be the values that must be passed into this method via the I_ADDRESSES parameters.

    In the previous step, Russel created the sender via the CL_SAPUSER_BCS class because he was working with an internal user ID. Now, because he is working with external addresses, he creates a similar object but via a different class: CL_CAM_ADDRESS_BCS. He can mix and match address objects from different sources, because they all share a common interface within the object model of the BCS:

```
FIELD-SYMBOLS <wa_recipient> LIKE LINE OF i_addresses.
LOOP AT i_addresses ASSIGNING <wa_recipient>.
  recipient = cl_cam_address_bcs=>create_internet_address(
    <wa_recipient> ).
  send_request->add_recipient( recipient ).
ENDLOOP.
```

12. At this point, Russel could send the email and wait for the scheduled batch job to run and process the send request. However, he wants to take advantage of the new capabilities of the BCS interface so he decides to set

the SEND IMMEDIATELY attribute. This will cause the email to process upon a commit work:

```
send_request->set_send_immediately( abap_true ).
send_request->send( ).
COMMIT WORK.
ENDMETHOD.
```

6.5   Regular Expressions

As you've just seen, *Regular Expressions* is another new feature of the ABAP development environment as of SAP NetWeaver 7.0 that is not proprietary to SAP. Regular Expressions are a set of syntax rules similar to a mathematical equation for matching sets of text strings.

Regular Expressions originally gained popularity within the UNIX Operating System environments where the syntax was integrated into system utilities like GREP. System administrators need complex forms of search strings and Regular Expressions filled that gap nicely. Later Regular Expressions began to work their way into core programming languages and can often be used directly within the language syntax to augment basic **Find** and **Replace** functionality.

ABAP is no different in this regard. Regular Expressions are integrated into the syntax of both the ABAP syntax FIND (see Listing 6.10) and REPLACE (see Listing 6.11).

```
FIND {[SUBSTRING] sub_string} | {REGEX regex}
```

Listing 6.10 FIND Syntax Diagram

```
REPLACE [{FIRST OCCURRENCE}|{ALL OCCURRENCES} OF]
  {[SUBSTRING] sub_string} | {REGEX regex}
  IN [section_of] dobj WITH new
        [IN {BYTE|CHARACTER} MODE]
        [{RESPECTING|IGNORING} CASE]
        [REPLACEMENT COUNT rcnt]
        { {[REPLACEMENT OFFSET roff]
           [REPLACEMENT LENGTH rlen]}
        | [RESULTS result_tab|result_wa] }.
```

Listing 6.11 REPLACE Syntax Diagram

In addition to the integration of Regular Expressions within these ABAP syntax elements, SAP also supplies a full Regular Expressions engine in the form of the class CL_ABAP_REGEX. In direct syntax integration, you can either supply a Regular Expression string, like Russel did within his email method, or an instance of the CL_ABAP_REGEX class. The CL_ABAP_REGEX class can also be used as a standalone (see the example of Listing 6.12).

```
DATA: regex    TYPE REF TO cl_abap_regex,
      matcher TYPE REF TO cl_abap_matcher.
    CREATE OBJECT regex
      EXPORTING pattern     = `cat|dog`
                ignore_case = 'X' .
      matcher = regex->create_matcher( text = input_text ).
      IF matcher->match( ) IS INITIAL.
        MESSAGE 'Match Found' TYPE 'S'.
        EXIT.
      ENDIF.
```

Listing 6.12 CL_ABAP_REGEX example

Russel has just learned how powerful Regular Expressions can be, given how quickly he was able to separate the full filename from the file extension in his email method. Even in the simple example used above of `cat|dog`, it would find either cat or dog in a string.

Although the full syntax of Regular Expressions is quite robust and could consume a volume of pages on its own, it is at least worth examining in greater detail how the Regular Expression that Russel wrote works. If you're interested in learning about Regular Expression syntax in general, there are many sources available on the Internet.

Remember that he is trying to find the division between filename and extension as in this typical example, *MyFile.pdf*. The Regular Expression that Russel wrote looked like this:

```
FIND FIRST OCCURRENCE OF REGEX '\.[^\.]+$'
    IN <wa_attach>-filename MATCH OFFSET dot_offset.
```

Here we will break down the Regular Expression into each section:

► Russel starts with this character \. Primarily, we want to search for the period character in the filename; however the period has special meaning in the Regular Expression syntax. It basically functions as a powerful wildcard character. Therefore he must use the escape character, \, in order to tell the Regular Expression interpreter that he really wants the character period and not the special syntax that it could represent.

▶ In the next set, we have a section set off by [ ]. This represents the character class. The caret character (^) beginning the first entry within the square brackets further defines this as a negated character class. The value of the character class is once again an escaped period. So this means that Russel tries to find the first character after the initial match on the period that is not a period itself. This addition to the Regular Expression clause is what causes the FIND statement to position on the *p* in *MyFile.pdf* instead of the period.

▶ Finally the +$ represents a non-greedy repeat of the search. What would happen if the supplied filename had more than one period in the name, e.g., *My.txt.File.pdf*? In this case, you would not want processing to stop at the first period, because that would incorrectly identify the file extension as a text file. The addition of the +$ allows the Regular Expression to read ahead and only stop processing on the final occurrence of the matching condition.

The university that Russel works for has decided to implement SAP NetWeaver Master Data Management. Russel has been asked to include SAP NetWeaver MDM as part of the online course system that he is currently building. In this chapter, we will see Russel begin to explore SAP NetWeaver MDM and how it can be integrated into his custom ABAP development thanks to the MDM ABAP API.

7 ABAP and SAP NetWeaver Master Data Management

SAP NetWeaver Master Data Management (SAP NetWeaver MDM) is a whole new experience for Russel. He was expecting to encounter many new technologies during this project, but he thought they would be primarily new features added to the core ABAP environment with which he was already familiar.

SAP NetWeaver MDM, on the other hand, is going to be a little bit of a departure from what Russel is most familiar with. It is going to require him to do a little research first on just what SAP NetWeaver MDM is. All that he really knows going into this part of the project is that he has been asked to take his main master data table, ZCS_FACULTY, and use MDM instead to house that data.

What If?
This entire chapter is really a "what if" chapter. SAP NetWeaver Master Data Management is an interesting new tool that we are sure many ABAP developers are curious about. However we realize that there are still many companies that have not yet implemented SAP NetWeaver MDM. Also at the date of publication of this book, there is no free trial version of MDM like there is for the core SAP NetWeaver Application Server ABAP and Java. Therefore, we understand that many readers will not have access to an MDM system to recreate these examples. The MDM repository and MDM ABAP API coding that is discussed in this chapter exists right alongside all the other coding for this book on the CD. However, later chapters of this book will not be dependent on the implementation of the MDM examples.

> In that way, everyone can learn something about MDM, but covering this topic
> will not keep you from moving through the rest of the topics.

7.1 What Is Master Data Management?

Russel first needs to learn a little more about MDM. Although we will focus
primarily on the technology of MDM and how it, in particular, impacts
ABAP developers, we will also discuss the business benefits that drive customers to implement MDM in the first place.

The concept of master data is fairly easy to grasp. Every business process has
some core data, like customers or materials, which flow through the entire
process. The same set of material data details can be used in purchasing, sales
order processing, quality management, production, inventory management,
and even finance.

But what happens when this master data must cross technical boundaries
between different IT systems? As enterprise service-oriented architecture
(enterprise SOA really takes root within a company, it will cause more and
more of the business processes to stretch across multiple systems — sometimes even directly to your business partners' systems. Without a good strategy and technology to help you manage your master data consistently, a
company can quickly find itself with disjointed and even broken business
processes.

This is where SAP NetWeaver MDM comes in. It will become your centralized hub for master data. All other systems spread out through a business
process will seamlessly refer back to MDM to ensure that their use and presentation of master data is consistent.

Centralization does more than just provide a single version of the truth. It also
presents the optimal opportunity for companies to harmonize and cleanse
their master data. Therefore, SAP NetWeaver MDM also provides key tools
for duplicate matching and data validation. It also has data quality service
adaptors that allow you to send sections of your master data to third parties,
such as *Dun & Bradstreet* and *Trillium Software*, for additional data cleanup.

7.1.1 Technical Architecture

Although it is an integrated part of SAP NetWeaver, MDM doesn't run on
the ABAP or the Java stack of SAP NetWeaver. Instead, it is built on a custom

technology that provides flexible data modeling combined with high performance analysis. Consequently, developers like Russel almost immediately ask the question, "If it isn't ABAP or Java, how can I access the data in MDM programmatically?"

There are four main ways of accessing the data. First there are three language-specific APIs: one for Microsoft COM based languages (such as the .NET Environment), one for Java, and the one that we are going to look at in the most detail, ABAP. In addition, there are general Web Services built on top of the Java API that provide wide access to MDM based on open standards.

Although SAP NetWeaver MDM uses a database system for long-term persistence, no programming interface accesses the database layer directly. Instead, MDM loads its repositories into memory on the server and all updates and access are done to this in-memory version. It is also interesting to note that MDM is not structured exactly like a database. MDM takes advantage of its focus on only master data to shape the entire environment to the features and techniques that are most efficient for that type of data. General database systems are often tuned much more for working with transactional data and not master data.

Unlike relational databases, MDM is broken down into business objects. Each business object is represented as its own repository (see Figure 7.1). A material repository, for instance, becomes its own autonomous unit. Each repository has its own set of tables, security, and can be stopped and started individually. In traditional relational database concepts, it is almost as if each repository is its own database schema.

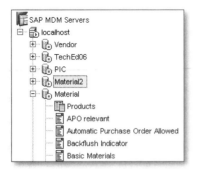

Figure 7.1 MDM Repository Listing — Tables in the Material Repository

Unlike ERP systems, where SAP delivers a fairly fixed definition of the master data structure, MDM is designed so customers can define their data model in accordance with their own specific business needs. SAP delivers example repositories based on ERP data structures as starting points, but customers who want to integrate master data elements and concepts from other parts of their business process are free to do so.

As you will see later, this variation in repository design does affect the way the APIs work. For instance, SAP cannot deliver a dedicated material object in the API, because the structure of each customer's material repository is potentially quite different. Therefore, the APIs must be very generic and allow for any possible data structures.

7.1.2 Clients

Since Russel had already established that SAP MDM runs on a different architecture than other parts of SAP NetWeaver, it wasn't surprising that it would also have a different set of user interface options.

The first way to access MDM is via a set of custom GUI clients. These clients are installed directly on the client machine and, for the most part, are only available for the Windows Environment. These are not tools that the average user would access however. They are designed for power users who spend all of their time working with data in MDM and for system administrators. The two clients that an ABAP developer would primarily work with are the *SAP MDM Console* and the *SAP MDM Data Manager*:

▶ **SAP MDM Console**
The MDM Console, shown in Figure 7.2, is your one stop for all administrative, development, and modelling activities in the MDM environment. From this tool you can create new repositories, add and modify tables in the repository, add and modify fields in a table, and even setup security. Lower level, purely administrative functions like backup and recovery and stopping and starting the server are also present in this tool.

▶ **SAP MDM Data Manager**
The other client is the SAP MDM Data Manager, shown in Figure 7.3. This tool has the ability to create complex queries to find data in your MDM repository. In that respect, it is similar to the ABAP Data Browser — transaction SE16.

However the MDM Data Manager can also be a data entry or data maintenance tool. More importantly, this is where some of the unique and powerful matching and enrichment functionality resides in MDM. Figure 7.3 also shows how easy it is compare multiple records. By simply selecting multiple records, the data is merged together in the detail area. Data that is different between the selected records is displayed in red.

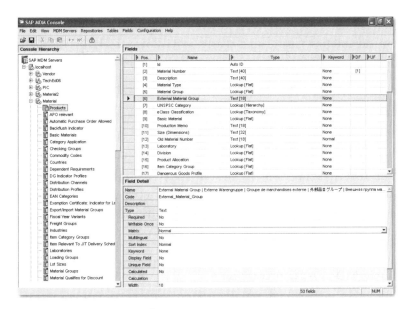

Figure 7.2 SAP MDM Console

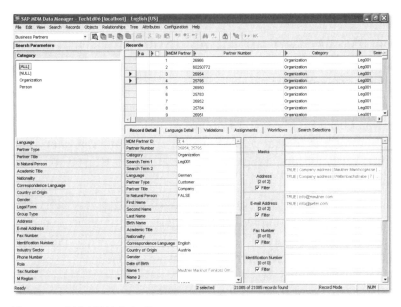

Figure 7.3 SAP MDM Data Manager

197

If power users and administrators use these tools, how might the average business user interact with master data? Well, if everything is done correctly, the fact that the master data originates from the MDM should be transparent to the end user. The end users can continue to use whatever business processes they are using today without having to jump into or out of an MDM specific tool. Behind the scenes, Web Services, the dedicated APIs, and MDM syndication capabilities ensure that master data flows freely between the MDM server and whatever transactional systems need it.

There are times however when an end user might need to interact directly with MDM data. In these cases, you have two options:

▶ You can take advantage of the rich APIs and create a custom user interface.

▶ There is also SAP delivered standard portal content for MDM available. Like the MDM APIs, this content must be structured rather generically in order to adjust to whatever content repository each customer designs. However this can be an excellent tool for basic display or editing of core MDM data.

7.1.3 Basic MDM Administration

Russel has learned enough background information on MDM for his role in this project and he is now ready to start the setup. He launches the newly installed MDM Console on his laptop and is greeted to a similar screen as Figure 7.2. The only difference is that his **Console Hierarchy** is empty.

1. Since this is the first time he has used the MDM Console on his machine, he must first mount a server by right-mouse clicking on **SAP MDM Servers** and choosing **Mount MDM Server**.

2. From this dialog, he must choose the server's host name where the MDM software had been installed. Once connected to the server, he finds that there is not much to look at yet. No one has created any repositories on this server. Lucky for him, it looks like he gets to be the first person to do so.

3. From the **Console Hierarchy**, Russel chooses to create a repository (see Figure 7.4). He will be prompted for the database that he wants to use for this repository. It is important to note that you don't need a one-to-one relationship between MDM servers and database servers.

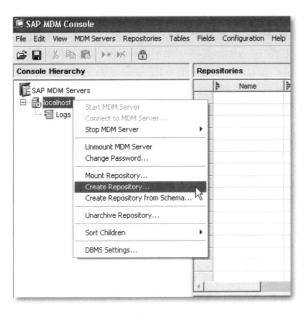

Figure 7.4 Console Hierarchy — Create Repository

4. After specifying the MDM repository name, the **Console Hierarchy** is refreshed. The repository was created with the default structure and a main table named Products (see Figure 7.5). Obviously, Russel will need to model his data structure in the new repository, but first he wants to complete a few other administrative tasks.

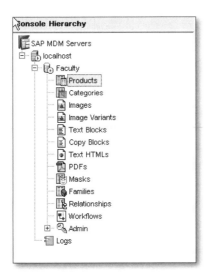

Figure 7.5 Initial Faculty Repository

5. Before he moves on, he wants to set up some additional users in his repository. He opens the **Admin** branch at the bottom of his repository (see Figure 7.6). This allows him to create users and roles. Anyone accessing the MDM repository, even via the APIs later, will need a user account here.

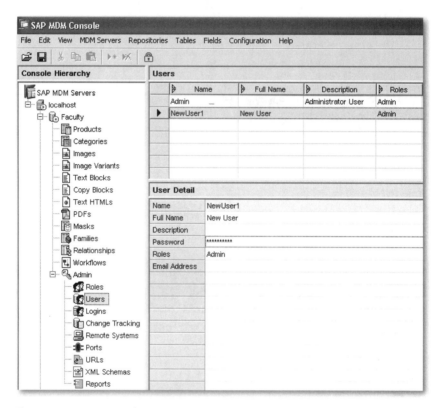

Figure 7.6 MDM User Administration

6. Finally, before he starts his modeling of the repository, Russel decides it would be a good idea to create a backup of what he has created so far. One of the best ways to back up a repository is to choose to **Archive** it via the **Console Hierarchy** context menu. Archiving a repository creates a platform and database-independent version of the structure and content in the repository. This is also an excellent way to move a repository from one server to another.

7.1.4   Modeling in SAP MDM

For Russel's purpose, he doesn't really need to use some of the more powerful aspects of MDM's data modeling. This does make for a simpler example, but should not be considered an indicator of what MDM is capable of. Russel is more interested in the technical aspects of making the API between MDM and ABAP work, so he essentially just creates the same structure in MDM (see Figure 7.7) that he had in his ABAP table, ZCS_FACULT.

Fields

	Pos.		Name		Type		Keyword	DF	UF
	[1]		Faculty Id		Text [10]		Normal	[1]	[1]
	[2]		Title		Text [30]		None		
▶	[3]		First Name		Text [40]		None		
	[4]		Last Name		Text [40]		None		
	[5]		Description		Text Large		None		
	[6]		Office Number		Text [10]		None		
	[7]		Office Phone		Text [30]		None		
	[8]		Email		Text [241]		None		
	[9]		Office Fax		Text [30]		None		
	[10]		Office Hours		Text Large		None		
	[11]		Deletion Flag		Boolean				

Field Detail

Name	First Name
Code	FirstName
Description	First Name
Type	Text
Required	No
Writable Once	No
Matrix	Normal
Multilingual	No
Sort Index	Normal
Keyword	None
Display Field	No
Unique Field	No
Calculated	No
Calculation	
Width	40
Sort Type	Case Sensitive

Figure 7.7 Faculty Repository Main Table Structure

Russel does note a few details that he will need later, mainly that MDM has a **Name** and a separate **Code** attribute for each field. The attribute **Name** is really more of a short description of the field. It can have different language versions as well as contain special characters and spaces. This makes it inappropriate for use in the MDM APIs. Therefore we also have the **Code** attribute. This is the true unique identifier for a field and is what must be used to refer to a field in MDM via the APIs.

7.2 Configuring the SAP MDM ABAP API

The ABAP API for SAP NetWeaver MDM, from here on referred to as *MDM4A*, does the job of mapping all the data types and structures between

MDM and ABAP for the developer. It translates the structures such as data arrays into ABAP constructs like internal tables. It also provides the technical communication layer. Because very high performance levels are needed, MDM4A uses direct TCP/IP port communications. This means that before Russel can begin programming with MDM4A, there are some configuration and installation steps that must be completed.

7.2.1 Installation of the MDM API Add-on

The MDM API Add-on is broken down into several components (see Figure 7.8):

▶ First, there is the **Generic API** layer. This is the only part of the API that ABAP developers will directly interact with. It is represented by a series of generic classes and function modules that are MDM release independent.

A single ABAP system may interface to more than one MDM system. These different MDM systems could potentially be on different releases. Even if you have only one MDM system to work with, over time new features will be introduced by upgrading the MDM system. The MDM4A is built in such a way as to provide compatibility with multiple versions of MDM at the same time.

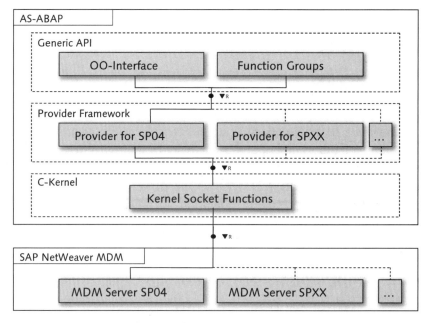

Figure 7.8 Technical Layout of the SAP MDM ABAP API

► Therefore, we have the **Provider Framework** layer. This layer provides release and patch level specific ABAP classes for interaction with MDM. Customers should never access the Provider Framework and instead pass through the Generic API layer.

The Generic API will look up the configuration for the particular MDM repository that you want to communicate with and initialize internally the correct version of the Provider Framework. For instance, to call an MDM SP4 Patch level 0 repository, your program will access the Generic API class, CL_MDM_GENERIC_API, but it, in turn, will actually use CL_MDM_PROVIDER_SP04_PL00. From the same ABAP system, if you wanted to communicate with a different MDM repository that was MDM SP4 Patch level 3, you would still code against CL_MDM_GENERIC_API. Internally though, this class would now call CL_MDM_PROVIDER_SP04_PL03, giving you access to newer features in the API.

It is important to note that the Provider Framework layer is backwards compatible across all supported releases of MDM; however, to use a newer version of MDM requires that you also update the MDM4A Add-on.

► The final layer is the communication libraries within the ABAP kernel. These are C based libraries, not ABAP classes. This **C-kernel** is an integrated part of the Application Server ABAP kernel. The file *dw_mdm.dll* is part of the core disp+work package of the Kernel and is installed into */usr/sap/<SID>/DVEBMGS<Instance Number>/exe*[1] by your Basis Administrators just like the rest of the Kernel. Patching of the MDM API specific C-Kernel layer happens automatically whenever a full ABAP kernel is updated.

The Generic API and Provider Framework layers, being ABAP development objects, are installed like all ABAP Add-ons. This is generally a process done once again by Basis Administrators. They use transaction SAINT to install add-ons and they can apply patches to existing add-ons from transaction SPAM.

Russel, being skeptical, wants to double check and make sure his Basis Administrators have installed and patched the MDM4A Add-on to the correct level in his system. Russel knows of two ways that he can check the release level. First, if he goes to transaction SAINT he would be able to see

---

1 The actual installation directory can be configured and does vary slightly by the OS. However the MDM API portions are stored right alongside wherever the rest of your ABAP kernel is installed.

the release and patch level from the main screen. However, in the development system, he doesn't have access to SAINT. Therefore, he uses the menu option **System • Status** and clicks on the **Component information** button. This also shows you the release and patch level for all components installed in your system (see Figure 7.9).

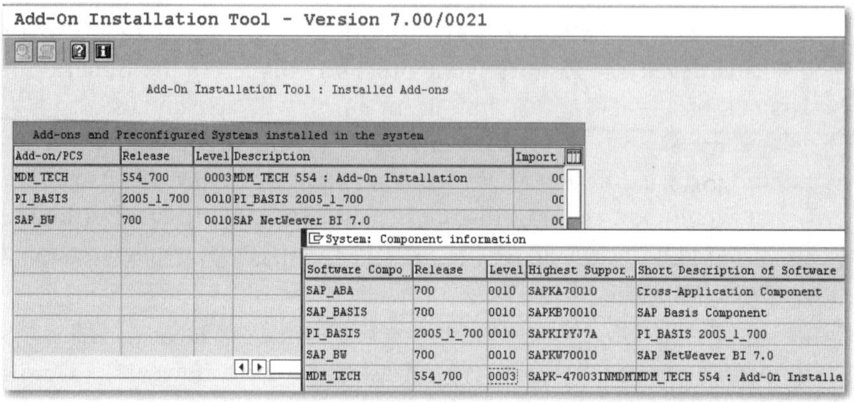

```
Add-On Installation Tool - Version 7.00/0021
```

Add-On Installation Tool : Installed Add-ons

Add-ons and Preconfigured Systems installed in the system

Add-on/PCS	Release	Level	Description	Import
MDM_TECH	554_700	0003	MDM_TECH 554 : Add-On Installation	00
PI_BASIS	2005_1_700	0010	PI_BASIS 2005_1_700	00
SAP_BW	700	0010	SAP NetWeaver BI 7.0	00

System: Component information

Software Compo	Release	Level	Highest Suppor	Short Description of Software
SAP_ABA	700	0010	SAPKA70010	Cross-Application Component
SAP_BASIS	700	0010	SAPKB70010	SAP Basis Component
PI_BASIS	2005_1_700	0010	SAPKIPYJ7A	PI_BASIS 2005_1_700
SAP_BW	700	0010	SAPKW70010	SAP NetWeaver BI 7.0
MDM_TECH	554_700	0003	SAPK-47003INMDM	MDM_TECH 554 : Add-On Installa

Figure 7.9 MDM4A Release Level

7.2.2 Configuring the MDM API Connection

Now that everything is installed, Russel is ready to start configuring the API connections. Later, when he instantiates the API class, he will need to specify a single *Logical Object Name*. This Logical Object Name is a key that will represent all configuration associated with the connection that you want to establish. By specifying this key, you are giving the API what it needs to look up the server name, database name, repository name, and release and patch level of the MDM repository you will be coding against.

SAP provides a transaction code, MDMAPIC, for creating these keys and maintaining all the connection details that go along with it (see Figure 7.10).

There are several different types of configurations that can all be done from this single transaction. Instead of setting up the details for a server within the configuration of each repository, you can, for instance, configure each server just once in the **MDM Server Connections** option on the left side. You can then reuse this logical server key in all the appropriate repository entries.

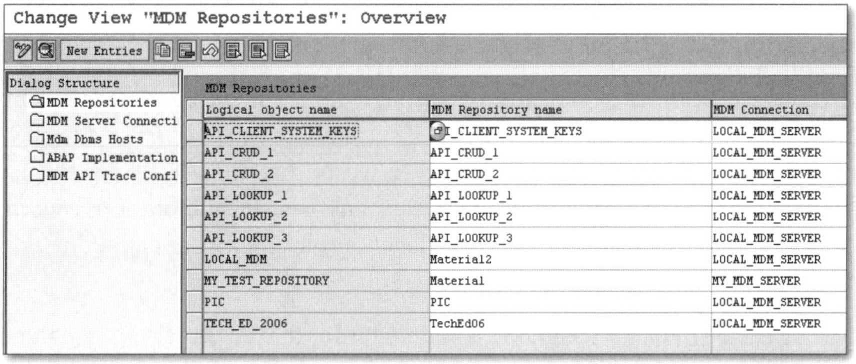

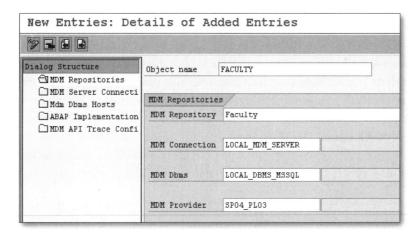

Figure 7.10 MDM API Configuration Screen

If you look at Figure 7.11, you can see the entries that Russel had to set up in order to establish his connection to the Faculty repository. Although a Logical Object Name represents a repository, the names don't have to match, but we do recommend that you logically link the names as closely as possible. The **MDM Repository** name is case-sensitive, whereas the **Logical Object Name** is not.

Figure 7.11 MDM API Configuration for the Faculty Repository

7.2.3 Authentication with the MDM API

When establishing a connection to an MDM repository using the MDM4A, the system will automatically use the same user ID that the current session is running under. This user ID must be set up for the repository in question on the MDM side. There is currently no option to specify a different user ID to use at runtime or via the repository configuration.

Although a user ID is transmitted through the API, no password is sent. Instead the MDM server and the ABAP system must have a *Trusted Connection*. In this situation, the MDM server trusts that the ABAP system has already performed authentication and lets any user in without a password. Users are still only given access to the level of roles that were defined within the MDM repository.

The Trusted Connection can be maintained from the MDM server by editing a few files. The files *allow.ip* and *deny.ip* can be used to specify the IP address of the ABAP servers that you want to maintain trusting relationships for. These files should normally be placed directly into the same folder that holds your *mds.ini* (MDM Server Configuration) file.

If you need to place these files in a different location, perhaps a centralized network share, you can configure their location in the *mds.ini* file. Use the entry `TrustFiles Dir=<directory>` to specify this location. *allow.ip* and *deny.ip* must be flat, text-only files. You can wildcard the entries in *allow.ip* and *deny.ip* using the * character. You cannot just specify a single * to allow all possible IP addresses however; you must specify at least one subnet.

Instead of listing each IP address directly, Russel wants to take advantage of the wildcard. He wants to allow access from all but a few IP addresses, so he will combine the *allow.ip* and *deny.ip* entries. He plans to allow all servers from the 192.168.0.* subnet; however, there is a single "unsafe" machine in this subnet that functions as a network DMZ. To protect against access from this system, he places the IP address of this "unsafe" machine within the *deny.ip* file. The *deny.ip* configuration file can also be useful to keep development or test servers from accidentally updating data in a production repository.

7.3   Coding with the MDM ABAP API

Finally Russel is ready to do some coding. But, before he breaks right into his existing business object class and starts integrating MDM API methods, Russel decides to create some simple test applications so he can get a sense of how some basic operations are performed in the MDM API. He also has seen that there are two different "flavors" of the API — Classes and Function Modules. He wants to have a look at each of these.

7.3.1 Class-Based API

Russel already knows that for the class-based API he will be working with the class CL_MDM_GENERIC_API (see Figure 7.12). The layout is arranged in such a way, however, that there are several subobjects within this class.

Class Interface	CL_MDM_GENERIC_API			Implemented / Active				
Properties	Interfaces	Friends	Attributes	Methods	Events	Types	Aliases	

Attribute	Level	Vis	Rea	Typing	Associated Type		Description
MO_ACCESSOR	Instanc	Publi	☐	Type Ref	IF_MDM_ACCESSOR	⇨	MDM: Accessor interfa
MO_CORE_SERVICE	Instanc	Publi	☐	Type Ref	IF_MDM_CORE_SERVICES	⇨	MDM: Core service int
MO_ADMIN	Instanc	Publi	☐	Type Ref	IF_MDM_ADMIN	⇨	MDM: Administrator in
MO_META	Instanc	Publi	☐	Type Ref	IF_MDM_META	⇨	MDM: Meta data interf
MO_API_CONFIG	Instanc	Publi	☐	Type Ref	IF_MDM_API_CONFIG	⇨	MDM: Configuration in
MO_PROVIDER	Instanc	Priva	☐	Type Ref	CL_MDM_ABSTRACT_PROVIDE	⇨	Abstract provider
MS_MDM_CONFIG_DATA	Instanc	Publi	☐	Type	MDM_CONFIG_INFORMATION	⇨	MDM: Configuration in

Figure 7.12 The Layout of CL_MDM_GENERIC_API

In the Java API, each of these subobjects is a separate class with its own constructors. In ABAP, they are separate classes, but they are all created as attributes of the Generic API class. In this way, you can think of CL_MDM_GENERIC_API as a bit of a factory object. When you create an instance of the Generic API, you must specify the Logical Object Name that you are working with. The Generic API class will validate the configuration and then instantiate all subobjects with knowledge of this configuration information. It also creates the connection between these objects and the specific implementation class via the abstract provider, MO_PROVIDER. The following list describes each of the subobjects of the Generic API:

▶ IF_MDM_ACCESSOR

This object controls the opening and closing of a connection to a repository. For many of the other API methods, you must first have created a connection to a repository via this interface.

▶ IF_MDM_ADMIN

This object provides access to administrative functions similar to those available via the MDM Console. It includes User (creation, password set, role maintenance) and Repository (Mount or Load Repositories) level administration.

▶ IF_MDM_API_CONFIG

This interface allows you to read the configuration entries from transaction MDMAPIC for one repository or for all of them at once. You can view the Data Dictionary structures MDM_REPOSITORY, MDM_CONNECTION, MDM_DBMS, and MDM_PROVIDER to get an idea of the data supplied by this object.

▶ IF_MDM_CORE_SERVICES

This is the main object to directly manipulate the data within a repository. It includes Check In/Out, Client System Keys, Update, Delete, Creation, Attribute Creation, and Query of data methods.

▶ IF_MDM_META

This object provides methods that allow you to change the metadata of a repository. Many of these methods require that the repository be unloaded before they can be performed.

Now Russel is ready to try and code a connection to his Faculty repository.

1. He starts by creating an instance of the Generic API for the language and repository key he wants to work with:

```abap
DATA api TYPE REF TO cl_mdm_generic_api.
DATA log_object_name TYPE mdm_log_object_name.
DATA language        TYPE mdm_cdt_language_code.
DATA exception       TYPE REF TO cx_mdm_main_exception.

log_object_name   = 'FACULTY'.
language-language = 'eng'.
language-country  = 'US'.
language-region   = 'USA'.

TRY.
    CREATE OBJECT api
      EXPORTING
          iv_log_object_name = log_object_name.
```

2. He then uses the MO_ACCESSOR object to create the connection:

```abap
        api->mo_accessor->connect( language ).
```

3. To test that he has a good connection, Russel outputs some configuration data and then disconnects from the repository:

```abap
****Do Something
      WRITE: / api->ms_mdm_config_data-repository_name.
      api->mo_accessor->disconnect( ).
```

There are several different class-based exceptions that might be thrown by the MDM4A API; however they all share one parent class, CX_MDM_MAIN_EXCEPTION. Russel doesn't care which exception caused an error, because he can catch any of them by looking for the parent exception.

If there is an exception, he doesn't want to leave an open connection to the MDM repository. This will keep resources within the kernel and on the MDM server locked until they time out.

4. He uses the CLEANUP event for the exception to execute some logic before exiting the routine. As with many MDM exceptions, however, the situation might have occurred because there is no valid connection already established. Therefore, it is wise to also catch all exceptions that might be thrown within the CLEANUP logic via CX_ROOT:

```
CATCH cx_mdm_main_exception INTO exception.
CLEANUP.
  TRY.
      api->mo_accessor->disconnect( ).
    CATCH cx_root.
  ENDTRY.
ENDTRY.
```

5. Finally, for test purposes, he outputs the error message associated with whatever exception was raised:

```
IF NOT exception IS INITIAL.
  MESSAGE exception TYPE 'E'.
ENDIF.
```

7.3.2   Function Module Based API

For all the functionality contained in the Generic class of the MDM API, there are equivalent Function Modules (see Table 7.1 for a cross-reference listing). The processing logic is quite similar for the two different approaches to the API. So why, you might ask, did SAP provide both?

The main advantage is that all the function modules are remote-enabled. This makes it possible to quickly generate Web Services for each API action. Also the MDM4A API is only available on SAP NetWeaver 2004 and higher. If you have an older ABAP system, you cannot install the Add-on. You could, however, access these function modules via RFC on another SAP NetWeaver based system.

Function Group	Class-Based Interface
FG_MDM_ACCESSOR	IF_MDM_ACCESSOR
FG_MDM_ADMIN_API	IF_MDM_ADMIN
FG_MDM_CONFIG_MONITOR	IF_MDM_API_CONFIG
FG_MDM_CORE_SERVICE_API	IF_MDM_CORE_SERVICES
FG_MDM_META_API	IF_MDM_META

Table 7.1 Mapping of API Function Groups to Class Interfaces

The function modules are really just wrappers around the class-based API. The main difference is that they map the class-based exceptions to classical exceptions. Also, the Logical Object Name must be specified as an input parameter into each function call within an application.

If you look at a connection example that is similar to the earlier class-based one, you can see how a function module is used in place of the classes (see Listing 7.1). Notice that the exception handling does become a bit more complicated because of the switch to classic exceptions.

```
DATA log_object_name TYPE mdm_log_object_name.
DATA language        TYPE mdm_cdt_language_code.

log_object_name = 'FACULTY'.
language-language = 'eng'.
language-country  = 'US'.
language-region   = 'USA'.

CALL FUNCTION 'MDM_ACCESSOR_CONNECT'
  EXPORTING
    iv_log_object_name    = log_object_name
    is_repository_language = language
  EXCEPTIONS
    ex_api_usage_error    = 1
...
    OTHERS                = 6.
IF sy-subrc <> 0.
  WRITE: / 'Error during connect: ', sy-subrc.
  EXIT.
ENDIF.
```

Listing 7.1 Function Module Based API Connection

Even in the DISCONNECT command (see Listing 7.2), you must again specify your Logical Object Name:

```
CALL FUNCTION 'MDM_ACCESSOR_DISCONNECT'
  EXPORTING
    iv_log_object_name = log_object_name
  EXCEPTIONS
    ex_api_usage_error = 1
...
    OTHERS             = 6.
IF sy-subrc <> 0.
* MESSAGE ID SY-MSGID TYPE SY-MSGTY NUMBER SY-MSGNO
*         WITH SY-MSGV1 SY-MSGV2 SY-MSGV3 SY-MSGV4.
ENDIF.
```

Listing 7.2 Function Module Based API Disconnect

7.3.3 Non-Unicode ABAP Systems

MDM servers are always Unicode. In the ABAP environment, however, you may encounter single code page or Unicode-based systems.[2] Unicode-based ABAP systems won't have any problems communicating with MDM via the MDM4A API. But, single code page systems must convert all data communications to Unicode.

Fortunately, all the conversion mechanisms take place within the API. Still, you can request data from MDM that is outside the current code page of the ABAP systems. For example, if you logged into the ABAP system in English, but when you queried from MDM, you requested data that had Polish language elements, an error would occur. This error would produce the CX_SY_CONVERSION_CODEPAGE exception.

The best way to avoid this error is by ensuring that you fully maintain the language parameter while you're establishing a connection to the repository:

```
DATA ls_language TYPE mdm_cdt_language_code.
ls_language-language = 'eng'.
ls_language-country  = 'US'.
ls_language-region   = 'USA'.
lr_api->mo_accessor->connect( ls_language ).
```

---

2 Technically, there is a third option — *Multiple Display Multiple Processing* (MDMP). MDMP is a pre-Unicode technology that allowed for switching between multiple code pages. Since this technology is no longer supported as of SAP NetWeaver 7.0, we will not include it in our discussion.

7.3.4 Simple Read

Many of the Core Services have a second method that ends in _SIMPLE. For instance, there is UPDATE and UPDATE_SIMPLE. These "simple" methods accept data dictionary structures that match the format of the repository table that you want to manipulate. This provides an easier interface into the API, but requires the creation of a matching structure in the ABAP Data Dictionary. The field names in the ABAP Data Dictionary Structure must be the same as the CODE attribute for the field in the MDM repository. You're also restricted to using primarily the MDM API data types.

You should keep in mind that in ABAP there is no NULL state for a value. Any NULL value from MDM will be returned through the simple data types using the initial value for the underlying data dictionary domain. Use of the specific methods instead of the SIMPLE ones will help you to avoid this issue by returning an empty data reference for the value.

So, before Russel can use the READ_SIMPLE method against his repository, he must create a data dictionary structure that matches his repository structure (see Figure 7.13). He started by copying from the original database table structure, ZCS_FACULTY. He then had to adjust some of the field names to match the ones in the repository; for example, he had to use FACULTYID instead of FACULTY_ID. The MDM API is going to fill the structure by matching names and not the field position. This gives you the flexibility to not retrieve fields from MDM by simply not adding them to your data dictionary structure.

Structure	ZCS_FACULTY_MDM			Active		
Short Description	University Course System - MDM Faculty Structure					

Attributes Components Entry help/check Currency/quantity fields

Predefined Type 1 / 11

Component	RTy	Component type	Data Type	Length	Decim	Short Description
FACULTYID	☐	ZCS_FACULTY_ID	CHAR	10	0	University Course Syste
TITLE	☐	ZCS_FACULTY_TITLE	CHAR	30	0	University Course Syste
FIRSTNAME	☐	AD_NAMEFIR	CHAR	40	0	First name
LASTNAME	☐	AD_NAMELAS	CHAR	40	0	Last name
DESCRIPTION	☐	MDM_E_CONTENT	STRING	0	0	MDM: Key content
OFFICENUMBER	☐	ZCS_FACULTY_OFFIC	CHAR	10	0	University Course Syste
OFFICEPHONE	☐	AD_TLNMBR1	CHAR	30	0	First telephone no.: di
EMAIL	☐	AD_SMTPADR	CHAR	241	0	E-Mail Address
OFFICEFAX	☐	AD_FXNMBR1	CHAR	30	0	First fax no.: dialling
OFFICEHOURS	☐	MDM_E_CONTENT	STRING	0	0	MDM: Key content
DELETIONFLAG	☐	MDM_E_BOOLEAN	CHAR	1	0	MDM: Boolean data eleme

Figure 7.13 MDM-Specific Data Dictionary Structure for the Faculty Repository

You'll also notice that Russel has had to use the MDM-specific data elements on some fields. For the Boolean field, he has switched to MDM_E_BOOLEAN. For the strings, he has switched to MDM_E_CONTENT. What follows is a detailed breakdown of the full logic required to read from an MDM repository.

1. Although this is a bit more complicated than the simple connection example from before, Russel begins with basically the same logic in order to establish his connection to the repository:

```
DATA result_ddic   TYPE STANDARD TABLE OF zcs_faculty_mdm.
DATA api           TYPE REF TO cl_mdm_generic_api.
DATA log_object_name TYPE mdm_log_object_name.
DATA language      TYPE mdm_cdt_language_code.
DATA keys          TYPE mdm_keys.
DATA exception     TYPE REF TO cx_mdm_main_exception.

log_object_name = 'FACULTY'.
language-language = 'eng'.
language-country  = 'US'.
language-region   = 'USA'.

TRY.
    CREATE OBJECT api
      EXPORTING
        iv_log_object_name = log_object_name.
    api->mo_accessor->connect( language ).
```

2. Most of the core operations on the repository (Read, Update, Delete, etc.) require that you pass in an internal table of the MDM internal record keys. Generally, you use the QUERY method to specify some search criteria. A table of internal keys is then returned. In this case, Russel wants to read all records from the repository so he doesn't specify any criteria for his QUERY method.

   You'll notice that in many of the methods, you must supply the specific table that you want to operate from. We have only made a connection to the MDM repository. Each operation can therefore be performed on any of the tables. In this case, the value **Faculty** for the parameter IV_OBJECT_TYPE_CODE is not referring to the repository name, but to the main table of the repository that happens to have the same name. Table names are case-sensitive as well:

```
DATA: result_set TYPE mdm_search_result_table.
CALL METHOD api->mo_core_service->query
  EXPORTING
```

```
       iv_object_type_code = 'Faculty'
  IMPORTING
     et_result_set       = result_set.
```

3. The internal records' keys are returned in a deep structure. So now Russel must move those out to his own structure. He can then use this as input to the RETRIEVE_SIMPLE method. In the RETRIEVE_SIMPLE method, he just specifies a variable with his data dictionary structure to the importing parameter ET_DDIC_STRUCTURE. The API will analyze this variable at runtime to determine the data dictionary structure that should be used in the API call:

```
DATA: result TYPE mdm_search_result.
READ TABLE result_set INDEX 1 INTO result.
IF sy-subrc = 0.
  keys = result-record_ids.
ENDIF.
CALL METHOD api->mo_core_service->retrieve_simple
  EXPORTING
     iv_object_type_code = 'Faculty'
     it_keys             = keys
  IMPORTING
     et_ddic_structure   = result_ddic.
```

4. Russel receives a standard ABAP internal table with a nice flat structure (see Figure 7.14). It is easy to then access the values returned from MDM. In a moment, we will look at how vastly different this step is with the full RETRIEVE method:

```
api->mo_accessor->disconnect( ).
FIELD-SYMBOLS: <wa_result> LIKE LINE OF result_ddic.
LOOP AT result_ddic ASSIGNING <wa_result>.
  WRITE: / <wa_result>-title, <wa_result>-firstname,
           <wa_result>-lastname.
ENDLOOP.

CATCH cx_mdm_main_exception INTO exception.
...
```

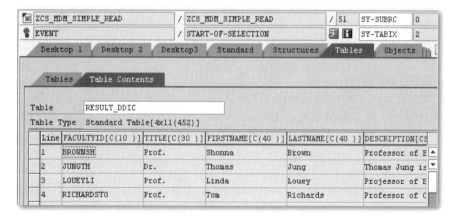

Figure 7.14 Flat Structure Results from the RETRIEVE_SIMPLE method

7.3.5 Full Read

Although the _SIMPLE methods do provide much easier coding, they are limited by needing existing data dictionary structures. This has the disadvantage of having to keep the data structures in sync between the ABAP system and MDM. A change on one side without communicating that change to the other side could result in applications terminating or producing incorrect results.

The full methods, on the other hand, don't require any data dictionary structures. They return the data in a rather complex format whereby each cell in the array of data is represented by its own internal table record. Moreover, the values themselves are returned as TYPE REF TO DATA. In other words, they are just generically typed. Before they can be processed by ABAP, they must be cast into more specific data types.

1. The more complex logic requires a few more variables, but the connection coding that Russel creates is still the same:

```
DATA result_set_def      TYPE mdm_field_list_table.
DATA result_set          TYPE mdm_result_set_table.
DATA api                 TYPE REF TO cl_mdm_generic_api.
DATA log_object_name     TYPE mdm_log_object_name.
DATA language            TYPE mdm_cdt_language_code.
DATA keys                TYPE mdm_keys.
DATA exception           TYPE REF TO cx_mdm_main_exception.
FIELD-SYMBOLS <field_value> TYPE simple.
FIELD-SYMBOLS <wa_result_set_def>
        LIKE LINE OF result_set_def.
```

```
FIELD-SYMBOLS <wa_result_set> LIKE LINE OF result_set.

log_object_name = 'FACULTY'.
...
    api->mo_accessor->connect( language ).
```

2. With the _SIMPLE methods, Russel could reduce the number of fields returned by MDM simply by not specifying the fields in the data dictionary structure. With the full methods, he must fill an internal table with the fields he wants returned:

```
APPEND INITIAL LINE TO result_set_def
    ASSIGNING <wa_result_set_def>.
<wa_result_set_def>-field_name = 'FacultyId'.
APPEND INITIAL LINE TO result_set_def
    ASSIGNING <wa_result_set_def>.
<wa_result_set_def>-field_name = 'FirstName'.
APPEND INITIAL LINE TO result_set_def
    ASSIGNING <wa_result_set_def>.
<wa_result_set_def>-field_name = 'LastName'.
```

3. The logic to perform the query for record keys is the same as before as well. Even the call to the RETRIEVE method is similar:

```
DATA: search_set TYPE mdm_search_result_table.
CALL METHOD api->mo_core_service->query
...
    IF sy-subrc = 0.
      keys = search-record_ids.
    ENDIF.
    CALL METHOD api->mo_core_service->retrieve
      EXPORTING
        iv_object_type_code      = 'Faculty'
        it_result_set_definition = result_set_def
        it_keys                  = keys
      IMPORTING
        et_result_set            = result_set.
    api->mo_accessor->disconnect( ).
```

4. Now Russel comes to the complex part of the processing. The result set is almost like an internal table turned on its side. Each row in the table has another internal table inside of it called NAME_VALUE_PAIRS. This internal table has each column of returned data as a separate row. This structuring of the returned information is most easily seen in the debugger (see Figure 7.15). Therefore, he has to loop through the result table and then process the inner table, NAME_VALUE_PAIRS, just to drill down to the individual cells.

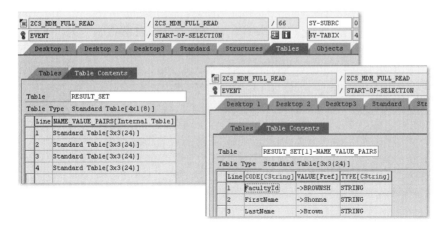

Figure 7.15 Results from a RETRIEVE Method Call

Now the value field in the NAME_VALUE_PAIRS table is TYPE REF TO DATA. This means that this single field could hold any possible data type — even a complex one such as an internal table. You can use the field TYPE in NAME_VALUE_PAIRS to determine what data type the value actually is.

5. In this example, Russel is only reading character fields, so he can cast everything in a field symbol of type STRING:

```
FIELD-SYMBOLS <wa_pair> LIKE LINE OF
     <wa_result_set>-name_value_pairs.
LOOP AT result_set ASSIGNING <wa_result_set>.
   READ TABLE <wa_result_set>-name_value_pairs
     INDEX 1 ASSIGNING <Wa_pair>.
   ASSIGN <wa_pair>-value->* TO <field_value>.
   IF sy-subrc = 0.
     WRITE: / <field_value>.
   ENDIF.
ENDLOOP.
```

7.3.6 Integrating the MDM Repository into Your Business Object Class

Russel feels comfortable enough with the MDM API to begin integrating it into his business object class. Remember part of the power of using a business object class is that you can hide the inner coding. Using this functionality to his advantage, Russel is able to make changes to swap out the processing from *persistent object* to MDM API without affecting all of the programs that are using the business object class.

1. To get an idea of the changes that Russel has to make to his business object class in order to adapt it to MDM, let's look at one method, READ_FACULTY. Originally, this method would perform a persistent object query that returns a persistent object instance. Russel replaces the query service with a call to the query method of the MDM API:

```
DATA result_ddic  TYPE STANDARD TABLE OF zcs_faculty_mdm.
DATA api          TYPE REF TO cl_mdm_generic_api.
DATA log_object_name TYPE mdm_log_object_name.
DATA keys         TYPE mdm_keys.
DATA exception    TYPE REF TO cx_mdm_main_exception.
  log_object_name = 'FACULTY'.
  try.
      api = zcl_cs_mdm_conn_pool=>get_mdm_connection(
      repository = log_object_name ).
      DATA: query TYPE mdm_query_table,
            ls_cdt_text  TYPE mdm_cdt_text,
            ids          TYPE string.
```

2. The query logic is a bit more complex than his earlier API call that read all records. Now Russel just tells the API what kind of query he wants to perform, field search, and what data type the field he will search on has text:

```
FIELD-SYMBOLS: <wa_query> LIKE LINE OF query.
APPEND INITIAL LINE TO query ASSIGNING <wa_query>.
<wa_query>-parameter_code = 'FacultyId'.
<wa_query>-operator       = 'EQ'.       "Equal to
<wa_query>-dimension_type  =
    mdmif_search_dim_field.             "Field search
<wa_query>-constraint_type =
    mdmif_search_constr_text.           "Text Search
```

3. Next Russel has to pass the input value for his query, which is the FACULTY_ID in this case, into the API. Similar to the full read method, this variable is a TYPE REF TO DATA in order to accept any data type. To move a fully typed variable into a TYPE REF TO DATA reference variable, you must use the GET REFERENCE OF syntax:

```
MOVE i_faculty_id TO ids.
GET REFERENCE OF ids INTO <wa_query>-value_low.
DATA: result_set TYPE mdm_search_result_table.
CALL METHOD api->mo_core_service->query
  EXPORTING
    iv_object_type_code = 'Faculty'
    it_query            = query
```

```
        IMPORTING
          et_result_set        = result_set.
```

4. The faculty structure should remain static, so Russel decides to use the simple version of the RETRIEVE method:

```
        DATA: result TYPE mdm_search_result.
        READ TABLE result_set INDEX 1 INTO result.
        IF sy-subrc = 0.
          keys = result-record_ids.
        ENDIF.
        CALL METHOD api->mo_core_service->retrieve_simple
          EXPORTING
            iv_object_type_code = 'Faculty'
            it_keys             = keys
          IMPORTING
            et_ddic_structure   = result_ddic.
        DATA wa_result LIKE LINE OF result_ddic.
        READ TABLE result_ddic INDEX 1 INTO wa_result.
```

5. To keep the exceptions specific to the business object, Russel catches any exceptions thrown by the MDM API and produces the ZCX_CS_FACULTY exception instead:

```
        IF sy-subrc NE 0.
          RAISE EXCEPTION TYPE zcx_cs_faculty
            EXPORTING
              textid = zcx_cs_faculty=>not_found
              faculty_id = i_faculty_id.
        ENDIF.
      CATCH cx_mdm_main_exception INTO exception.
        RAISE EXCEPTION TYPE zcx_cs_faculty
          EXPORTING
            textid = zcx_cs_faculty=>not_found
            faculty_id = i_faculty_id.
    ENDTRY.
```

6. Finally, Russel creates the instance of the object and that is what is returned from the static method. Everything appears exactly the same from the outside. Russel has adjusted the signature on his private constructor to remove the importing parameter of the persistent object and accept the flat structure of data returned from the MDM API call:

```
        CREATE OBJECT r_faculty
          EXPORTING
            i_mdm_data = wa_result.
```

In this chapter, Russel will explore the ABAP Unit tool, which will allow him to implement test code directly into his programs. He feels that testing is a very important part of the application development process and wants to leverage the new ABAP tools as much as possible.

8 ABAP Unit

Like most developers, Russel's least favorite part of developing applications is testing. Many developers unit test their programs using small modularized sections of code; for example, writing code in FORM routines and checking the results. Also, many developers leverage the ABAP Debugger to track exactly what is happening during execution of the code.

As of SAP NetWeaver 2004, developers have another tool known as *ABAP Unit* to help them with testing. ABAP Unit takes the ideas of JUnit from the Java environment and applies them to ABAP.

ABAP Unit is a testing tool used by developers to implement test logic directly into their programs. ABAP Units are directly integrated into the ABAP runtime environment and are implemented using the ABAP language. Therefore, there is no need to learn any additional test scripting language.

8.1 Overview of ABAP Unit Tests

Russel has completed a lot of the low level coding in the previous chapters for the university course system and has done some testing using simple test programs, but he is curious about the new ABAP Unit testing tool. Using ABAP Unit would create reusable test scenarios that are directly connected to the objects they test, unlike the little test programs he has been building.

He feels that it would be worthwhile to explore this testing tool further and see how it could help him with this and future developments. Before Russel can start implementing ABAP Unit tests, however, he must first understand the basics of using this tool.

8.1.1 Test Classes

ABAP Unit test classes are defined by using the FOR TESTING addition to the CLASS DEFINITION statement as shown in Listing 8.1. ABAP Unit tests are implemented as local classes within the object they will be testing.

```
CLASS my_test DEFINITION FOR TESTING.

ENDCLASS.
```

Listing 8.1 Test Class Definition

These local classes can be defined in executable programs, function groups, class pools, subroutine pools, and module pools. Test classes are not generated in productive systems and therefore cannot be executed. This keeps anyone from accidentally running a test and deleting or creating production data.

This generation of the unit test classes is controlled using the profile parameter **abap/test_generation**. By default, in customer systems, this profile parameter is set to disable the generation of test classes. Also the test framework checks the client settings in transaction SCC4. If the **Client role** is marked as **Production**, the test classes might be generated but the test framework will not allow their execution.

As of SAP NetWeaver 7.0, test classes can be implemented using global classes. These global classes are abstract and can only be used in local test classes. The instance methods of a global test class are always marked as test methods by default. Given the restrictions on global test classes, they are really only usable as templates for groupings of similar tests. They might also contain reusable utilities, such as methods for the loading of initial test data.

8.1.2 Test Attributes

Test attributes are attributes of the test class, which are used during the execution of the test. Currently there are two test attributes that can be defined: *risk level* and *execution duration*. The test attributes of local test classes are defined by using comments known as *pseudo comments* in the CLASS statement immediately following the FOR TESTING addition. The following is the syntax for the pseudo comments:

```
"#AU Risk_Level Critical|Dangerous|Harmless
"#AU Duration    Short|Medium|Long
```

A simple example of this syntax used in a test class definition is shown in Listing 8.2.

```
CLASS my_test DEFINITION FOR TESTING
     "#AU Risk_Level Harmless
     "#AU Duration Short
     .
ENDCLASS.
```

Listing 8.2 Test Attributes Definition

There are a few things to remember when using the pseudo comments. First, you can only specify one pseudo comment per line, and second, they are case-sensitive. For example, if it is necessary to define both risk level and duration for the test class, the CLASS statement must be separated into two lines. Test attributes of global test classes are defined as attributes of the class, which can be defined on the **Attributes** tab within the Class Builder.

Risk Level

The risk level test attribute defines how the test can affect the data consistency of the system. This is used to protect the system from unwanted changes to the data, system settings, or customizing. There are three settings for the Risk_Level test attribute:

▶ **Critical**
Test could change system settings or customizing

▶ **Dangerous**
Test could change data

▶ **Harmless**
Test has no effect on system settings or data

The risk level determines whether a test can be executed based on the risk level setting in the IMG implementation guide. The transaction SAUNIT_CLIENT_SETUP can be used to raise or lower the maximum risk level for that system.

Execution Duration

The execution duration test attribute is used to define the expected runtime duration of all of the test methods of the test class. There are three settings for the Duration test attribute:

▸ **Short**
Expected runtime less than 1 minute

▸ **Medium**
Expected runtime between 1 minute and 10 minutes

▸ **Long**
Expected runtime between 10 minutes and 60 minutes

The function of the execution duration is to prevent such things as endless loops and extremely long runtimes. The time limits mentioned above are only default values and should be changed to adapt to the hardware configuration of the application server. The runtime limits associated with each setting are defined by using the transaction SAUNIT_CLIENT_SETUP. These settings can be modified directly, or the system can propose the values via the **Proposal** button as shown in Figure 8.1.

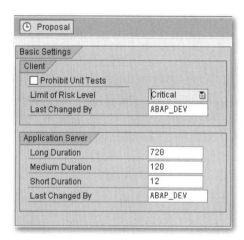

Figure 8.1 Transaction SAUNIT_CLIENT_SETUP

Future Functionality

After reading about the test attributes, Russel is a little puzzled as to why the test attributes were implemented using comments. He feels that it would be far better if they were implemented in such a way that the ABAP syntax checker could see these attributes.

Unbeknown to Russel, in a future release, he will be able to define these test attributes directly into the CLASS statement instead of using the pseudo comments. The ABAP syntax checker will then be able to see these attributes and validate the settings. Also included in this future release is an enhanced Test Class Generator Wizard.

So, in this future release, the class declaration would look as follows:

```
CLASS lcl_unit_test DEFINITION
  FOR TESTING DURATION MEDIUM RISK LEVEL HARMLESS.
```

8.1.3   Test Methods

Test methods are methods of the test class, which are used to trigger an ABAP Unit test. Each method corresponds to one single ABAP Unit test. These test methods do not have a signature and are defined as instance methods. You define these methods as test methods by adding the FOR TESTING addition of the METHODS statement in the CLASS definition block as shown in Listing 8.3.

```
CLASS my_test DEFINITION FOR TESTING
      "#AU Risk_Level Harmless
      "#AU Duration Short
    .
  PRIVATE SECTION.
    METHODS my_test_method FOR TESTING.
ENDCLASS.
```

Listing 8.3 Test Method Definition

The function of a test method is to trigger some block of productive code in the object you are testing, for example, a method of a class, and check the results of the execution using the ASSERT methods of the class CL_AUNIT_ASSERT.

In some cases, *fixtures* are used to set certain conditions, which will be used only during the test execution. Fixtures are nothing more than private methods defined in the test class, which are used to set up specific conditions for the test. These method names are reserved and are triggered automatically by the ABAP runtime. The SETUP fixture is triggered at the start of each ABAP Unit test. This method can be used to set up test data or create instances of classes required for the test. The TEARDOWN method is triggered at the end of the ABAP Unit test and is used to destroy anything that was created in the SETUP method.

8.1.4   Assertions

The test methods are used to make some assertions or specific checks about the data. The class CL_AUNIT_ASSERT provides methods to check the expected results. For example, the method ASSERT_SUBRC can be used to check the value of SY-SUBRC. The method parameters allow you to pass the actual value via parameter ACT and the expected value via parameter EXP. If the assertion fails, the error is written to the unit test log. Figure 8.2 shows the complete listing of the public static methods of class CL_AUNIT_ASSERT.

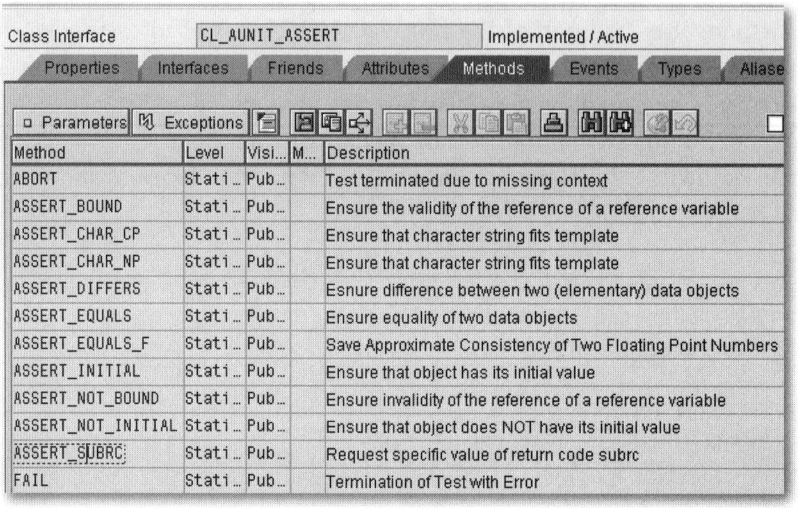

Method	Level	Visi...	M...	Description
ABORT	Stati...	Pub...		Test terminated due to missing context
ASSERT_BOUND	Stati...	Pub...		Ensure the validity of the reference of a reference variable
ASSERT_CHAR_CP	Stati...	Pub...		Ensure that character string fits template
ASSERT_CHAR_NP	Stati...	Pub...		Ensure that character string fits template
ASSERT_DIFFERS	Stati...	Pub...		Esnure difference between two (elementary) data objects
ASSERT_EQUALS	Stati...	Pub...		Ensure equality of two data objects
ASSERT_EQUALS_F	Stati...	Pub...		Save Approximate Consistency of Two Floating Point Numbers
ASSERT_INITIAL	Stati...	Pub...		Ensure that object has its initial value
ASSERT_NOT_BOUND	Stati...	Pub...		Ensure invalidity of the reference of a reference variable
ASSERT_NOT_INITIAL	Stati...	Pub...		Ensure that object does NOT have its initial value
ASSERT_SUBRC	Stati...	Pub...		Request specific value of return code subrc
FAIL	Stati...	Pub...		Termination of Test with Error

Figure 8.2 CL_AUNIT_ASSERT Methods

The program shown in Listing 8.4 provides a very straightforward example of using the ASSERT methods. Here we have a simple local class with a static attribute SUBRC and a static method SET_SUBRC. This program also has a test class, which will just call the static method SET_SUBRC and check the results. When calling the ASSERT_SUBRC method, you can specify a message that is to be logged as well.

```
REPORT zaunit_test.

CLASS my_class DEFINITION.
  PUBLIC SECTION.
    CLASS-DATA subrc TYPE sy-subrc.
    CLASS-METHODS set_subrc.
ENDCLASS.

CLASS my_class IMPLEMENTATION.
  METHOD set_subrc.
    subrc = 4.
  ENDMETHOD.
```

```
ENDCLASS.

CLASS my_test DEFINITION FOR TESTING
      "#AU Risk_Level Harmless
      "#AU Duration Short
  .
  PRIVATE SECTION.
    METHODS my_test_method FOR TESTING.
ENDCLASS.

CLASS my_test IMPLEMENTATION.
  METHOD my_test_method.
    my_class=>set_subrc( ).
    cl_aunit_assert=>assert_subrc( act = my_class=>subrc
                                   exp = '0'
                                   msg = 'Sy-Subrc <> 0' ).
  ENDMETHOD.
ENDCLASS.
```

Listing 8.4 Simple ABAP Unit Test

8.2   Creating ABAP Unit Tests

Now that Russel has had a chance to review the basic functionality of the ABAP Unit tool, he can start implementing ABAP Unit tests in his existing code. He plans to implement tests for just a few methods of the main model class ZCL_CS_MAIN_MODEL.

8.2.1   Creating the ABAP Unit Test Class

Russel must first create the local test class within the class ZCL_CS_MAIN_MODEL. He has learned that there is a test class generation tool, which is built directly into the ABAP Workbench. He will leverage this tool to quickly build the basic framework of the ABAP Unit test class. This tool can be accessed via the menu path, **Utilities • Test Class Generation**, in the Class Builder.

The dialog shown in Figure 8.3 gives Russel a few options when generating the local test class. He can allow the system to generate the method calls as well as the ASSERT_EQUALS statements for the IMPORTING parameters of those methods. There is also a section where Russel can define the risk level and execution duration for the test class. Finally there is a list of methods, which can be selected for test methods.

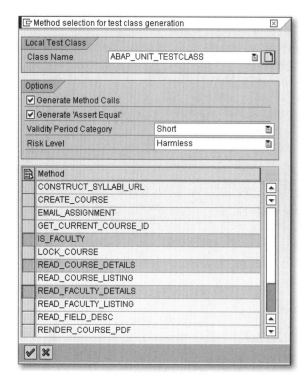

Figure 8.3 Test Class Generation

As shown in Listing 8.5, the system generates the local test classes based on the options that Russel has selected in the previous dialog. The SETUP and TEARDOWN methods are automatically declared, as well as the test methods that were selected. The tool has also defined a reference variable M_REF for the main model class ZCL_CS_MAIN_MODEL.

```
CLASS abap_unit_testclass DEFINITION FOR TESTING
  "#AU Duration Short
  "#AU Risk_Level Harmless
.
  PUBLIC SECTION.

  PROTECTED SECTION.

  PRIVATE SECTION.
    DATA:
      m_ref TYPE REF TO zcl_cs_main_model.

    METHODS: setup.
```

```
    METHODS: teardown.
    METHODS: is_faculty FOR TESTING.
    METHODS: read_course_details FOR TESTING.
    METHODS: read_faculty_details FOR TESTING.
ENDCLASS.        "Abap_Unit_Testclass
```

Listing 8.5 Test Class Definition

8.2.2 Fixture Implementation

Earlier you learned that fixtures could be used to simulate certain conditions within the test class; for example, setting up data or creating instances of the classes that are to be used during the test. In this example, Russel has implemented very simple tests. The SETUP fixture will create an object reference variable M_REF for the main model class ZCL_CS_MAIN_MODEL as shown in Listing 8.6.

```
METHOD setup.
  CREATE OBJECT m_ref.
ENDMETHOD.        "Setup
```

Listing 8.6 Setup Fixture

8.2.3 Test Method Implementations

The test class generation tool has already generated some code for the implementation of each of the test methods, but Russel still needs to modify them in order to make them fit his requirements.

The test method IS_FACULTY, shown in Listing 8.7, simply calls the IS_FAC-ULTY method of the object reference M_REF and tests to see if the current user ID is a valid faculty member. Russel uses the ASSERT_EQUALS method of the class CL_AUNIT_ASSERT to verify whether the value of E_FACULTY is ABAP_TRUE. If the user is a faculty member, the test method will execute the remaining tests to determine whether the first and last name of the faculty member has been retrieved from the database successfully.

```
METHOD is_faculty.

  DATA e_first_name TYPE ad_namefir.
  DATA e_last_name  TYPE ad_namelas.
  DATA e_faculty    TYPE wdy_boolean.

  m_ref->is_faculty(
    IMPORTING
```

```
        e_first_name = e_first_name
        e_last_name = e_last_name
        e_faculty = e_faculty ).

    cl_aunit_assert=>assert_equals(
      act   = e_faculty
      exp   = abap_true
      msg   = 'User is not a valid faculty memeber' ).

    cl_aunit_assert=>assert_not_initial(
      act   = e_first_name
      msg   = 'First name not retrieved from database' ).
    cl_aunit_assert=>assert_not_initial(
      act   = e_last_name
      msg   = 'Last name not retrieved from database' ).

  ENDMETHOD.         "Is_Faculty
```

Listing 8.7 IS_FACULTY Test Method Implementation

The next test method READ_COURSE_DETAILS, shown in Listing 8.8, calls the method READ_COURSE_DETAILS of the object reference M_REF and attempts to retrieve the course details. Russel uses the static method ASSERT_NOT_INI-TIAL of the class CL_AUNIT_ASSERT to ensure that the data was actually retrieved successfully.

```
  METHOD read_course_details.

    DATA i_course_id      TYPE zcs_course_id VALUE 'IFS200'.
    DATA e_course_att     TYPE zcs_course_att.
    DATA e_course_reg_att TYPE zcs_course_reg_att_tbl.
    DATA e_course_ass_att TYPE zcs_course_assign_att_tbl.

    TRY.
        m_ref->read_course_details(
          EXPORTING
            i_course_id = i_course_id
          IMPORTING
            e_course_att = e_course_att
            e_course_reg_att = e_course_reg_att
            e_course_ass_att = e_course_ass_att ).
      CATCH zcx_course_system.
    ENDTRY.

    cl_aunit_assert=>assert_not_initial(
```

```
      act   = e_course_att
      msg   =
     'Course Data could not be retrieved from database'
      quit  = cl_aunit_assert=>no ).
   cl_aunit_assert=>assert_not_initial(
      act   = e_course_reg_att
      msg   =
     'Course Registration could not be retrieved from database'
      quit  = cl_aunit_assert=>no
      level = cl_aunit_assert=>tolerable ).
   cl_aunit_assert=>assert_not_initial(
      act   = e_course_ass_att
      msg   =
     'Course Assignments could not be retrieved from database'
      quit  = cl_aunit_assert=>no
      level = cl_aunit_assert=>tolerable ).
  ENDMETHOD.        "Read_Course_Details
```

Listing 8.8 READ_COURSE_DETAILS Test Method Implementation

The final test method READ_FACULTY_DETAILS, shown in Listing 8.9, calls the READ_FACULTY_DETAILS method of the object reference M_REF and attempts to retrieve the faculty details from the database.

```
  METHOD read_faculty_details.

    DATA i_faculty_id TYPE zcs_faculty_id VALUE 'RICHARDSTO'.
    DATA r_faculty_att TYPE zcs_faculty.

    TRY.
        r_faculty_att =
          m_ref->read_faculty_details( i_faculty_id ).
      CATCH zcx_course_system.
    ENDTRY.

    cl_aunit_assert=>assert_not_initial(
      act   = r_faculty_att
      msg   = 'Faculty Id is not valud' ).
  ENDMETHOD.        "Read_Faculty_Details
```

Listing 8.9 READ_FACULTY_DETAILS Test Method Implementation

8.3 Executing the ABAP Unit Test

Russel has completed all of the coding required to implement his unit tests and is now ready to run the tests. Again, it is important that the system is configured in such a way that it allows the ABAP Unit tests to be performed. This means completing the configuration in transaction SAUNIT_CLIENT_ SETUP, as well as setting the profile parameter **abap/test_generation** equal to ON. This profile parameter should be defined by the SAP NetWeaver administrator for the system.

Russel has ensured that the prerequisites have been completed and he can now run the tests. He runs the tests directly in the Class Builder using the menu path **Class · Unit Test**. When the tests are complete, the results screen is displayed as shown in Figure 8.4.

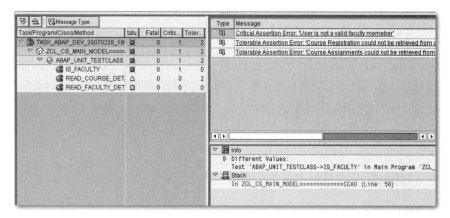

Figure 8.4 ABAP Unit Results Display

The overview section, shown in Figure 8.5, provides a simple overview of all of the tests that were executed and includes the aggregate status of each test. It also gives the number of assertions and the assertion error level for each test. For example, the READ_COURSE_DETAILS test resulted in two tolerable assertion errors while the IS_FACULTY test resulted in only one critical assertion error.

Task/Program/Class/Method	Status	Fatal	Critical	Tolerable
▽ 🔲 TASK_ABAP_DEV_20070227_185942_	⊚	0	1	2
▽ ◇ ZCL_CS_MAIN_MODEL=========	⊚	0	1	2
▽ ◎ ABAP_UNIT_TESTCLASS	⊚	0	1	2
🔘 IS_FACULTY	⊚	0	1	0
🔘 READ_COURSE_DETAILS	△	0	0	2
🔘 READ_FACULTY_DETAILS	☐	0	0	0

Figure 8.5 ABAP Unit Test Overview

The messages section, shown in Figure 8.6, provides a listing of all of the assertion messages that were logged during the test. The messages shown here come from passing the text to the MSG parameter when calling one of the ASSERT methods. By double-clicking on an entry, the detail of the assertion message is shown in the detail section (see Figure 8.7), which provides the details for each assertion message. By clicking on the link in the **Stack** node, you can drill down directly into the source code that logged the message.

Type	Message
🔳	Critical Assertion Error: 'User is not a valid faculty memeber'
🔳	Tolerable Assertion Error: 'Course Registration could not be retrieved from database'
🔳	Tolerable Assertion Error: 'Course Assignments could not be retrieved from database'

Figure 8.6 ABAP Unit Assertion Messages

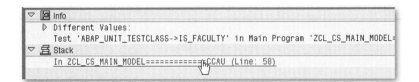

Figure 8.7 Message Detail

Russel needs to expose some functionality from the model class as a Web Service. In this chapter, he will explore how to create a Web Service definition and how to release it to external systems using the Web Service wizard.

9   Exposing a Model as a Web Service

As we discussed in Chapter 4, the ABAP environment has the capability to consume a Web Service using a client proxy object. This gives ABAP a whole new world of integration possibilities founded on the widely accepted and standards-based technology of Web Services.

By the same token, ABAP can also expose some functionality as a Web Service. This functionality could be implemented in a remote function call (RFC) enabled function module or Business Application Programming Interface (BAPI), a function group, or even a message from SAP NetWeaver Process Integration (SAP NetWeaver PI). The Web Service can then be accessed locally or by external systems, within the landscape or outside it.

There are usually two separate roles when dealing with exposing a Web Service. First, there is the Web Service developer, who is responsible for creating the Web Service definition. Additionally, there could be a Web Service configurator, who is responsible for releasing the Web Service and configuring the runtime attributes. These roles could also be combined. At the university, Russel has the role of Web Service developer and needs to expose an RFC-enabled function module as a Web Service.

9.1   Web Service Definition

Russel's first step in exposing a Web Service is to create the development object that the Web Service will use. Russel has already created the function module, ZCS_WS_GET_COURSE_DETAILS, which was specifically developed to be exposed as a Web Service. This function module retrieves the course data, as well as the course registration data using the main model class ZCL_CS_MAIN_MODEL.

9.1.1 Service Definition Wizard

From transaction SE80, Russel navigates to the ZCS_MODEL_ESOA package. From here, he right-clicks on the package name and chooses **Create · Enterprise Service/Web Service · Web Service**. This will start the Web Service wizard. The wizard will take Russel through all of the steps required to expose his function module as a Web Service.

1. As you can see in Figure 9.1, the first screen is a simple overview, which shows you which development objects can be exposed as a Web Service. Russel can see that the objects are primarily related to function modules. He knows that his job is to expose a function module, so he simply clicks on the **Continue** button.

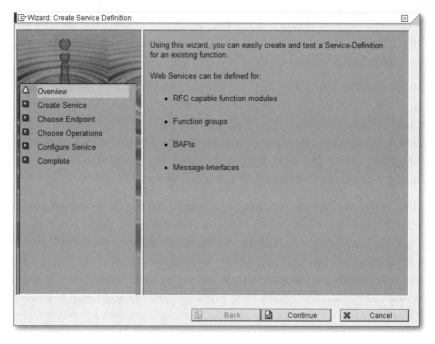

Figure 9.1 Service Definition Wizard — Overview

2. The next step in the wizard is the **Create Service** step. This is where Russel will supply a service definition name, a description of the Web Service, and finally the endpoint type. The endpoint type is the development object that is being exposed. In this case, Russel chooses **Function Module** as the endpoint type, as shown in Figure 9.2.

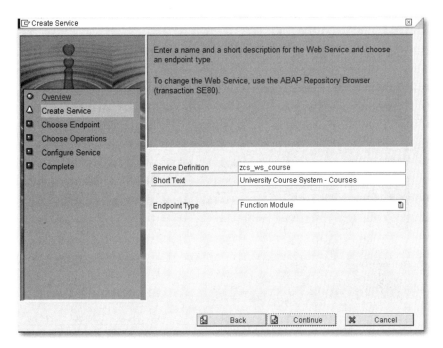

Figure 9.2 Service Definition Wizard — Create Service

3. The **Choose Endpoint** step is the next step (see Figure 9.3). Because Russel chose **Function Module** as the endpoint type in the previous step, he must now enter the name of the function module, which will be exposed as a Web Service. If he had selected **Function Group** or **BAPI** as the endpoint type in the previous step, Russel would have to enter the function group name or the BAPI name instead.

   There is also a **Name Mapping** checkbox. As it states in the text at the top of the screen, the existing descriptions of the endpoints are applied with the initial letters capitalized and the underscores removed. You will see how this is applied later in this section.

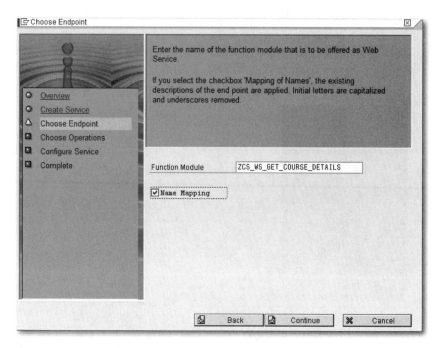

Figure 9.3 Service Definition Wizard — Choose Endpoint

4. The **Configure Service** step allows Russel to choose the security level of the data transfer and the type of communication. There are two profiles from which to choose:

▶ The **Basic Authorization: SOAP Profile** uses a user name and password for authentication, but provides no encryption of the user name/password or the data being transferred.

▶ The **Secure SOAP Profile** uses client certificate authentication and transfers the encrypted data via the *Secure Sockets Layer* (SSL) protocol.

It is not uncommon for developers to use the Basic Authorization profile when the Web Service is to be exposed and consumed within the same corporate landscape. Russel trusts that his corporate network is secure, so he simply accepts the default **Basic Authorization: SOAP Profile** as shown in Figure 9.4.

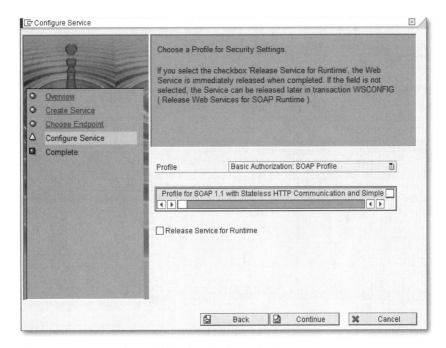

Figure 9.4 Service Definition Wizard — Configure Service

There is also a **Release Service for Runtime** checkbox. If you select this checkbox, the Web Service will automatically be released. It is not uncommon for a company to prohibit its developers from releasing Web Services directly. Sometimes a member of the SAP NetWeaver administration team, who will review the security settings and modify them accordingly, takes this action. Later, we will explore how to release the Web Service via transaction WSCONFIG, but, for now, Russel will not select this option.

5. The last step of the wizard is the **Complete** step (see Figure 9.5). This is simply an informational screen that states that the Web Service definition has been created successfully. Once Russel has clicked on the **Complete** button, the wizard will end, and the service definition will be displayed.

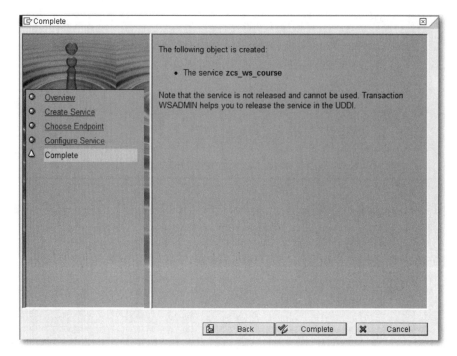

Figure 9.5 Service Definition Wizard — Complete

9.1.2   The Service Definition

Now that the service definition is complete, Russel can examine what has been generated. The first thing Russel notices is that the label next to the service definition name is **Virtual Int.** Now he is thoroughly confused.

So what is a *Virtual Interface* and what does it have to do with the service definition? In SAP NetWeaver 2004, the creation of a service definition actually involved two separate steps. First, you had to create the virtual interface. Then, you would create the service definition. You would specify the virtual interface to be used when creating the service definition.

As of SAP NetWeaver 7.0, the creation of the virtual interface has been absorbed into the process of creating the service definition. Transparent to the developer, there are still two development objects that are generated via the wizard, but both are created at one time. In some cases, the virtual interface terminology is still seen in documentation, error messages, and of course, in the service definition screen. In the future, SAP will probably eliminate the separation between service definitions and virtual interfaces and have one unified development object instead.

The **Interface** tab, shown in Figure 9.6, displays the associated service interface, including the operations as well as the parameters of the operations. The operations are directly related to the function modules included in the Web Service definition.

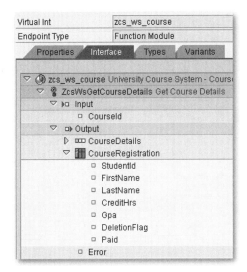

Figure 9.6 Service Interface

If Russel had chosen to create the Web Service using a function group, all function modules of that group would be translated into operations in the service definition. Furthermore, Russel can now see what affect the **Name Mapping** checkbox in the **Choose Endpoint** step of the wizard had on the naming of the ZcsWsGetCourseDetails operation and its parameters. It has the same name as the function module, but the initial letters are capitalized and the underscores have been removed. Similarly, the parameters of the operation have had the same formatting applied.

9.1.3   Releasing the Web Service

Russel must now release the Web Service in order for it to be used. As discussed earlier, this job may be better suited for the SAP NetWeaver administration team. They should know all of the rules and regulations mandated by the company with regard to security and protecting data that may be sent outside the company landscape. Since Russel knows that this Web Service is to be exposed and consumed within the university's landscape, he simply checks with his SAP NetWeaver administration team and verifies that he has the authorization to release this Web Service.

Now that he has permission, Russel goes to transaction WSCONFIG. A screen prompts him to enter the service definition name and the variant name. In previous releases, a service definition could have several variants. This is no longer the case, so there is always a default variant created when generating the service definition (see OSS note 908578). This variant is always named the same as the service definition.

As shown in Figure 9.7, Russel enters the name of the service definition and copies this name to the **Variant** field as well. He then clicks on the **Create** icon to navigate to the next screen.

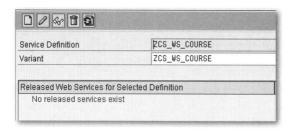

Figure 9.7 WSCONFIG Initial Screen

Finally, Russel can check and verify the default settings and click on the **Save** icon to release the Web Service (see Figure 9.8). Russel also notices a button on the **Web Service Settings** tab labeled **ICF Details**. This button can be used to navigate directly to the ICF (*Internet Communication Framework*) service node.

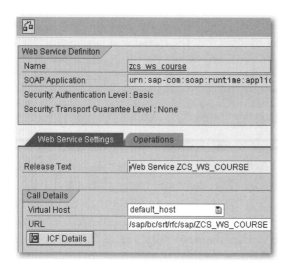

Figure 9.8 WSCONFIG Settings

He could also navigate to this service node using transaction SICF. The ICF service node allows you to configure things such as logon settings, error handling, and security settings. This is also where Russel would activate the service node if it had not already been activated. This is important because when transporting your Web Service definition to productive systems, the service node is inactive by default. This is a security mechanism and you must activate the service node manually after transporting the service definition.

9.2 Testing the Web Service

Russel knows that the logic, which is implemented in the function module behind his Web Service, works well. But he still feels that it is important to test the Web Service. Of course, he could create a client proxy object based on the WSDL as discussed in Chapter 4, but he wants to test his Web Service from outside the local system. He can do this using the *Web Service Homepage*, which has been provided by SAP. Since this testing tool is a *Java Server Page* (JSP) application, you must have a SAP NetWeaver J2EE Engine installed somewhere in your landscape, either as a standalone engine or as an ABAP stack add-on.

9.2.1 Web Service Administration

Before Russel can test the Web Service using the Web Service Homepage, he must tell the ABAP system what J2EE Engine to use.

1. This can be done through the Web Service Administration transaction WSADMIN. Russel runs this transaction and chooses **Go To • Administration Settings.** As shown in Figure 9.9, a dialog where he can enter the URL of the J2EE Engine opens.

Figure 9.9 Web Service Administration Settings

2. Next Russel launches the Web Service Homepage by selecting the Web Service from the tree structure and clicking on the **Web Service Homepage** icon (fourth icon from the left) in the application toolbar (see Figure 9.10).

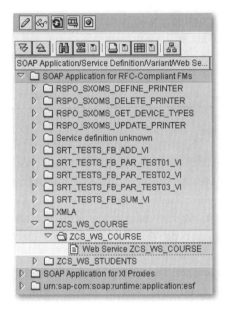

Figure 9.10 Launching Web Service Homepage

3. The dialog that appears when clicking on the **Web Service Homepage** icon is simply the settings for how the WSDL file is generated. Russel accepts the default values and continues.

4. Instead, he could have also used the menu path **Web Service • Web Service Homepage**. Russel can also view the WSDL file from this transaction by selecting the Web Service and clicking on the **WSDL** icon (fifth icon from the left) on the application toolbar.

9.2.2 Using the Web Service Homepage

After configuring the J2EE server in transaction WSADMIN and launching the Web Service Homepage, Russel can now use the testing functionality supplied within.

1. The first screen that Russel sees is the authentication screen (see Figure 9.11). Russel must provide credentials in order to proceed with accessing the Web Service.

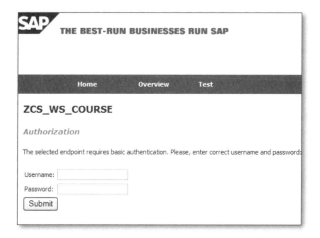

Figure 9.11 Web Service Homepage — Authentication

2. Once Russel has provided his user name and password, a basic Web Service overview screen appears, as shown in Figure 9.12. This screen provides general information about the Web Service, including the URL of the WSDL file. Russel can also view the contents of the WSDL file simply by clicking on the link on this page. Russel clicks on the **Test** link to test his Web Service.

Figure 9.12 Web Service Homepage — Overview

3. The next screen provides a list of operations for the Web Service (see Figure 9.13). If there had been multiple operations for this Web Service, all operations would be displayed here. In this case, Russel has only one operation to choose from, so he simply clicks on the link.

Figure 9.13 Web Service Homepage — Operations

4. In the next screen, the parameters of the operation are displayed. Here, Russel can enter the input parameters that will be passed as a request (see Figure 9.14). Russel clicks on the **Send** button to execute the Web Service.

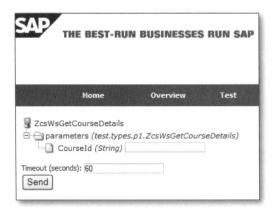

Figure 9.14 Web Service Homepage — Input Parameters

5. A request is then sent to the application server, which triggers the call to the Web Service. As shown in Figure 9.15, the Web Service homepage

testing tool then sends back a response, including all of the data retrieved by the underlying function module.

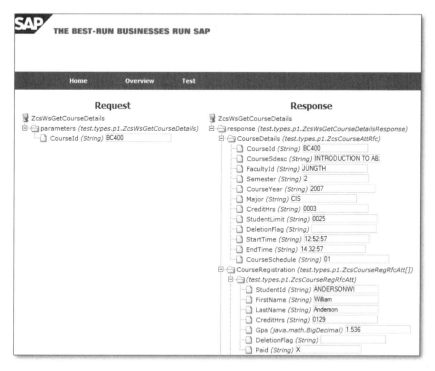

Figure 9.15 Web Service Homepage — Request/Response

6. Russel can clearly see that the Web Service is working perfectly. The data is being sent back correctly. When Russel scrolls down to the very bottom of the page, he can review the actual SOAP messages that were sent as the request and received as the response (see Figure 9.16).

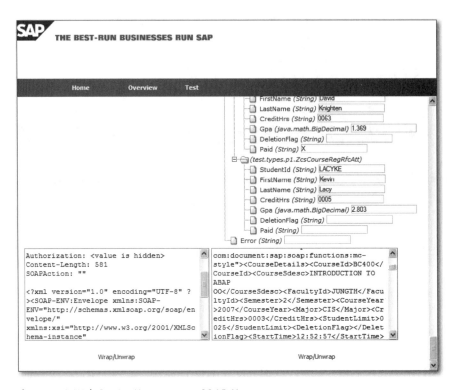

Figure 9.16 Web Service Homepage — SOAP Message

In the last chapter, we saw Russel create a Web Service by exposing an existing function module. There are two approaches to creating Web Services in the SAP environment, however. In this chapter, he will look at an alternative approach that involves using SAP NetWeaver Process Integration to model the service in a language-independent format and then implement the Web Service as an ABAP server proxy.

10 Exposing a Model as a Web Service Using SAP NetWeaver Process Integration

What Russel did in the previous chapter was to use an existing remote-enabled function module to quickly create a Web Service. This approach is generally referred to as *Inside-Out*. In other words, you start with existing functionality and interfaces from inside your system and use these as the basis of your new service. This approach has the advantage of allowing you to reuse your existing investments easily, but there is a downside. The interface of the new service is directly tied to the interface of the underlying function module. This does not give you the flexibility you need to easily move this service definition to another platform for a different implementation.

There is a second option for creating Web Services. This approach is known as *Outside-In*, because you start by modeling the service outside the system in which it will ultimately be implemented in. You have already seen in Chapter 4 that the SAP NetWeaver Process Integration or SAP NetWeaver PI (formerly known as SAP NetWeaver Exchange Infrastructure or SAP XI) can optionally be used as the Web Service Runtime. But there is another separate role that it can play as well. When taking the Outside-In approach, the *Integration Builder* within SAP NetWeaver PI is used to model your service in a language-independent manner. This modeling will produce an XML representation of the service interface in the form of a WSDL document. This WSDL document can then be used as the basis to generate a server proxy to implement the service in either ABAP or Java.

Although Russel has already implemented his Web Service using the Inside-Out approach and has met his business requirements, he is curious about what the corresponding steps would have been to implement the service using the Outside-In approach.

> **What If?**
>
> This entire chapter is really just another "what if" chapter. The implementation of a Web Service via the Outside-In approach requires access to a SAP NetWeaver Process Integration system. We realize that not all readers will have easy access to such an environment.
>
> We still feel that this is a critical part of the development process and will become more common in the near future. Therefore, we decided to include this chapter, but it is not implemented directly within the code samples that reside on the CD that accompanies this book. Therefore, everyone can still complete the remaining sample applications that are built on the code that has been introduced so far.

10.1 Modeling a Service in SAP NetWeaver Process Integration

Although all the modeling will be done within SAP NetWeaver PI, Russel starts his work from the ABAP Workbench. Russel switches his Object Browser to the **Enterprise Service Browser** perspective. If you recall, in Chapter 1 we said that the listing of perspectives is configurable and the Enterprise Service Browser is not a perspective that is displayed by default.

If your system is properly configured with a connection to a repository, the contents of the repository will be displayed in the Object Browser. You can test the repository connection with the menu option **Goto • Connection Test**.

To begin the service modeling process, Russel will need to launch a connection to the **Enterprise Services Repository**. On SAP NetWeaver 7.0, the PI Integration Builder serves as both the modeling environment and the repository. When Russel clicks on the **Enterprise Service Repository** button in transaction SE80 (see Figure 10.1), a browser window launches and begins to load the PI Integration Builder application.

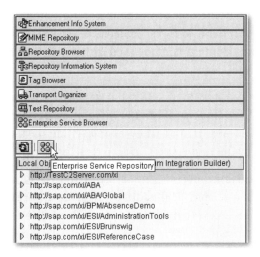

Figure 10.1 Launching the PI Integration Builder from Transaction SE80

10.1.1 Integration Builder

After logging in, Russel sees the opening screen of the Integration Builder (see Figure 10.2). Russel is not a PI expert; nor does he expect to become one just by walking through this sample implementation. But, as Russel will learn, you don't have to be a PI expert to model a service within the tool.

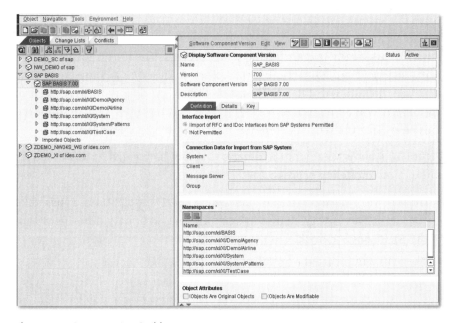

Figure 10.2 PI Integration Builder

The first thing Russel notices is that all the objects in the Integration Builder are organized in *Application Component* and *Software Component Versions*. For example, some of the SAP delivered content is embedded in the SAP_BASIS software component.

These high level organizational units are defined within the *System Landscape Directory* (SLD) and have already been imported into the Integration Builder from the SLD by Russel's system administrators. They have even defined a separate application component for the university's custom development.

Before Russel can create new custom objects, he must define a new namespace in which to place all the objects. He maintains his **Namespaces** from the **Definition** tab of his selected **Software Component Version** (see Figure 10.3). This namespace entry will become the namespace of all the WSDL documents that are generated by the modeling process. Russel creates a namespace from the combination of the university's primary domain (*university.edu*) and a description of his current project (*UniversityCourseSystem*).

Figure 10.3 Creating a Namespace for This Project

Russel is now ready to start the modeling process. The idea is to start with a blank slate and model everything necessary to describe a complete service interface, including drilling down to the individual data type level. Each of the objects will all be modeled separately with their own XML description. This allows for the reuse of common interface objects across services.

Figure 10.4 shows many of the objects that will be created as Russel moves through the modeling process:

▸ He will first need to create the lowest level simple **Data Types**, like CourseId. This is very similar to creating data dictionary domains within the ABAP environment.

▸ Then he will create the complex **Data Types**, like CourseRegistrations. These will be structures with several inner data types. These data types can also form repeating structures, which would be the equivalent of an ABAP data dictionary table type.

▶ Russel can also model **Fault Message Types**. These are similar to system or application exceptions. Later in the server proxy implementation, these object types will be mapped directly to ABAP Exception classes.

▶ Next Russel will model his **Message Types**. Message types are the input and output parameters for the eventual Web Service Operations. In this case, he will model a single input Request (`GetCourseDetails`) and an output Response message type (`GetCourseDetailsResponse`).

▶ Finally, Russel will pull all of these objects together as he builds the **Message Interfaces**. The one needed here, `GetCourseDetails`, will become the Web Service Operation and Server Proxy Method.

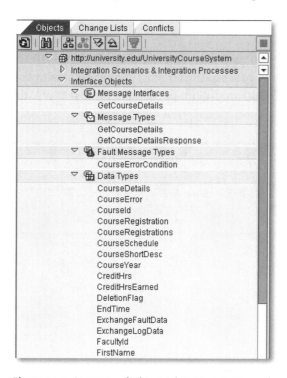

Figure 10.4 Overview of Objects That Must Be Created

10.1.2 Simple Data Types

Russel starts his modeling with the most atomic of the individual objects — the simple data type.

1. He just has to right-click on the **Data Types** category and then choose **New** from the context menu (see Figure 10.5).

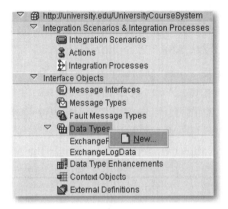

Figure 10.5 Creating New Data Types

2. Each type of object will present its **Create Object** dialog (see Figure 10.6). In the first step of the creation process, Russel must supply a **Name** to the new object, a **Namespace**, a **Software Component Version** that it will be grouped within, and lastly, a short **Description** for the object.

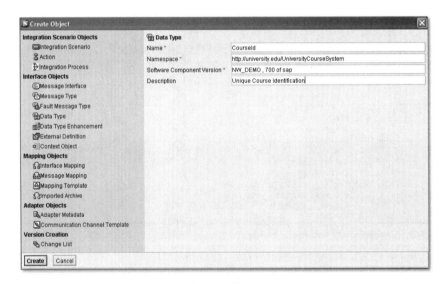

Figure 10.6 New Data Type Create Object Dialog

3. The real inner details of any object cannot be maintained until after completing the entries in the **Create Object** dialog. Figure 10.7 shows the detailed **Type Definition** edit window.

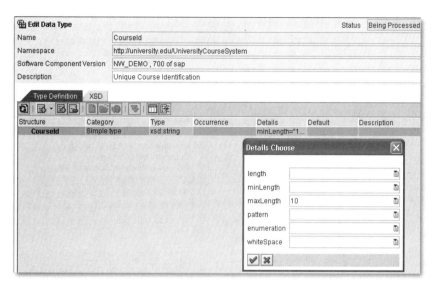

Figure 10.7 Detail Definition of String Data Type

Most of the object options can be completed in the table. Russel chooses his data type of xsd:string from a drop-down listing of possible data types. When Russel double-clicks on the **Details** cell, a popup window appears, allowing for the entry of multiple fields that all correspond to the **Details** column.

It is here that you can set many of the powerful options that control the details of a particular **Type Definition**. For instance, Russel uses the **max-Length** detail option to restrict this data type to match the length of the corresponding field in his ABAP data dictionary definition.

4. Every one of the objects that Russel is going to model can be documented within the Integration Builder as well (see Figure 10.8). The documentation tool provides a simple **HTML Editor** and **Preview** area for immediate feedback on the look of the formatting options.

5. Before any of these objects can be used outside the Integration Builder, they must be activated. This is similar to the activation process for all ABAP repository objects.

Russel can activate any of his objects by right-mouse clicking on them and then choosing **Activate** from the context menu (see Figure 10.9). A worklist of all inactive objects is displayed. By default, only the object that Russel right-mouse clicked on will be checked for activation. Still, you can select more than one item at a time for activation if you so choose.

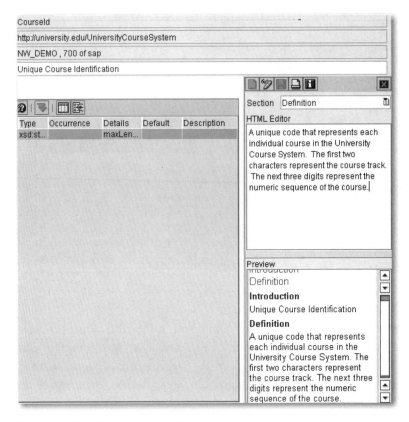

Figure 10.8 Data Type Documentation

Figure 10.9 Object Activation

Russel is already aware of the data model that he has implemented within the ABAP data dictionary for this project. This may not generally be the case, however, when starting from the Integration Builder and then creating proxy objects within the implementing system. Normally you would start by modeling your business processes and global data types first within a tool like the Integration Builder.

So, instead of having to work directly from the business requirements to model his service, he is able to closely follow the structure of the objects already defined for the project within the ABAP development environment. Of the simple data types, most have used the string elemental type with only the most basic of detail settings.

But Russel has now reached his first all-numeric field — the **Semester** code.

1. For this field, he will still choose the xsd:string type. This will correspond best with the numeric character data type originally used within the ABAP data dictionary. He still needs some way to place a rule on the field in order to restrict it to only number data types.

2. He uses the **pattern** detail option for this task (see Figure 10.10). This is the input pattern that will be allowed for this field. It is based on the syntax of Regular Expressions (see Section 6.5). Later, any proxy classes that are generated to consume this Web Service should use these patterns for basic validation on this field.

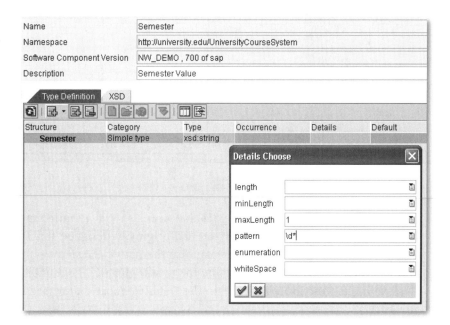

Figure 10.10 Numeric-Only Fields Using a Pattern

This numeric character field was just one simple example of what you can do with the **pattern** option. The next simple data type that poses a challenge for Russel is the **StartTime**. There are native date and time formats supported by WSDL, but Russel infers that this probably will not match up very well with the way ABAP splits date and time into two separate fields and internally processes them as numeric characters.

3. So Russel decides to follow a similar approach to what he has already done with the **Semester** type. He goes ahead and declares the **StartTime** type as an xsd:string. Once again, he uses a **pattern**, this one being just a bit more complex so as to allow for the external format of an ABAP time field (see Figure 10.11).

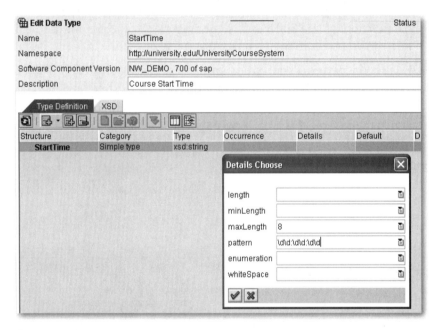

Figure 10.11 Date Data Types Using a Pattern

4. The final one of the simple data types that needs special attention is the **GradePointAverage**. Within ABAP, he had originally designed this field as a decimal data type. For this, he can use the native xsd:decimal type format. Then, he only needs to define the **totalDigits** and the number of decimal digits (**fractionDigits**) within the **Details Choose** dialog (see Figure 10.12).

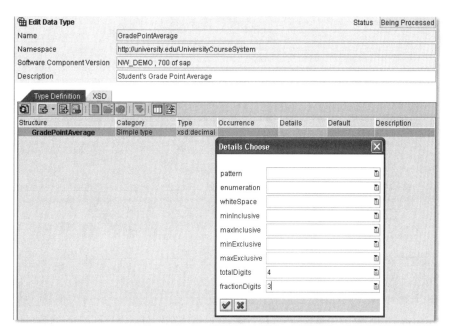

Figure 10.12 Decimal Data Type

10.1.3 Complex Data Types

For the final output parameters of the Web Service, Russel needs to return a single structure with all the details of the selected course records. He also needs to return the array of records that represents all the students that are registered to take the course.

In ABAP, this is the point where you would create structures and table types within the data dictionary to group the individual fields together. The process within the Integration Builder is quite similar. Russel must continue building data types, but in the data type editor he can begin to nest elements.

1. Figure 10.13 shows the three insertion options: He has the ability to insert elements at the same level as the current element, or to create nested structures by inserting the next element as a subelement. He can also maintain the fields within his structures by inserting attributes.

2. This gives Russel the ability to create a CourseRegistration **Complex Type** by combining the simple data types that he created previously (see Figure 10.14). He can even drag and drop simple elements from the objects window on the left side of the screen directly into the **Type Definition** edit area on the right side of the screen.

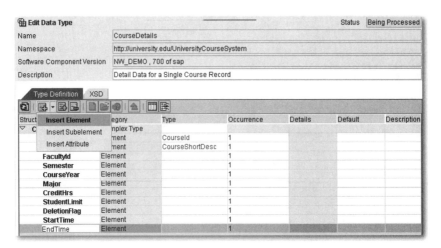

Figure 10.13 Complex Data Types

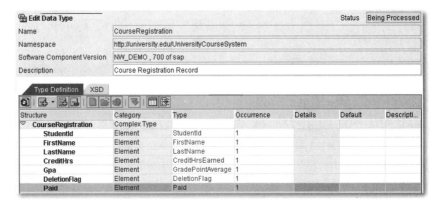

Figure 10.14 Complex Type Structure

3. For the Course Registrations, Russel needs more than one occurrence of the structure to create the array of records. Complex data types can be nested within one another as well. So he creates the new **Complex Type** CourseRegistrations and assigns a single element of the type Course-Registration that he just created.

4. He can then make this element repeating by setting the **Occurrence** attribute (see Figure 10.15). The maximum value of **unbounded** is generally used to represent a corresponding ABAP internal table since this means that any number of rows are allowed.

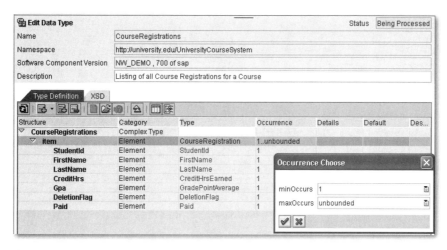

Figure 10.15 Complex Type with Occurrence

10.1.4 Message Types

Message Types are the input and output parameters of a Service Operation. At this point, the investment that Russel has made in defining his lower level elements begins to pay off. He can build his `Request` and `Response` message types just by combining many of the existing Complex Types that he has already defined.

1. For easy assignment to the Message Types, Russel first needs to create one final Complex Data Type for each Message Type. Figure 10.16 shows the Complex Type that he has designed for the Response. He has pulled together all the inner types to form the complete output parameter of his Web Service Operation.

2. The assignment of the Data Type to the Message Type is done from the **Data Type Used** section of the Message Type maintenance (see Figure 10.17).

3. The complete structure of the hierarchy of elements within the assigned data type is displayed at the bottom of the maintenance screen. However, at this point, this is a display-only view. If Russel needed to edit any of the Message Type parameters, he would have to return to the individual data type maintenance.

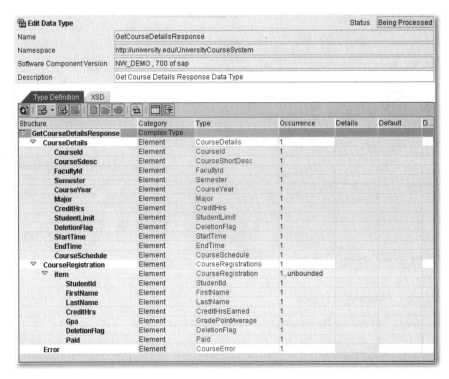

Figure 10.16 One Final Complex Type for the Message Type

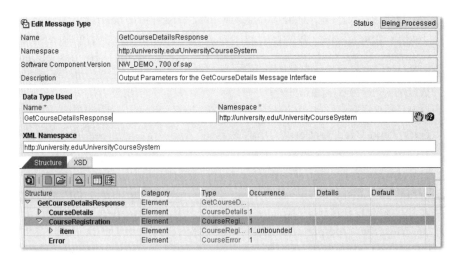

Figure 10.17 Assignment of the Data Type to the Message Type

10.1.5 Message Interface

Now it is time for Russel to pull all of his modeled elements together into what will become the final Web Service. This consolidating object is called the *Message Interface* (see Figure 10.18).

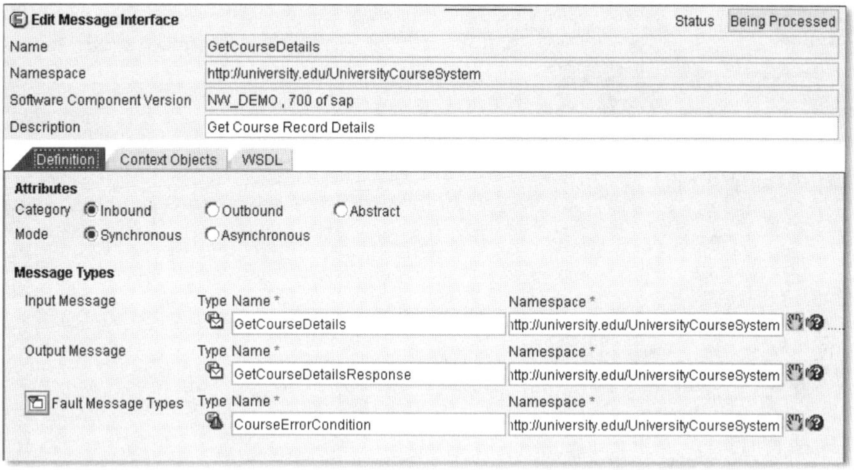

Figure 10.18 Message Interface Definition

You can model both inbound and output message interfaces. Russel is building a Web Service that will run from his ERP system and can be called from any other system. Therefore, the communications request relative to the ERP system is **Inbound**. In other words, other systems will initiate an inbound request to which the Web Service will respond.

From the Message Interface, Russel must also choose a communication mode. In Chapter 4, we discussed the two different Web Service runtimes. Although we are modeling the object within SAP NetWeaver PI, we are not required to use the PI runtime. The final server proxy implementation could still be a point-to-point service, however, only PI runtime services can support **Asynchronous** mode. Defining the parameters of the message interface is as simple as assigning the message types that were created in the previous step to the correct direction. Russel can also assign one or more fault messages for the handing of exceptions.

At this point, Russel has fully described the final Web Service. In fact, he is able to turn to the **WSDL** tab of the Message Interface and see what the complete WSDL document would look like for this would-be service (see Figure 10.19). It is this WSDL document, which has been generated from his modeling efforts, that will be interpreted by the ABAP development environment to generate the server proxy class.

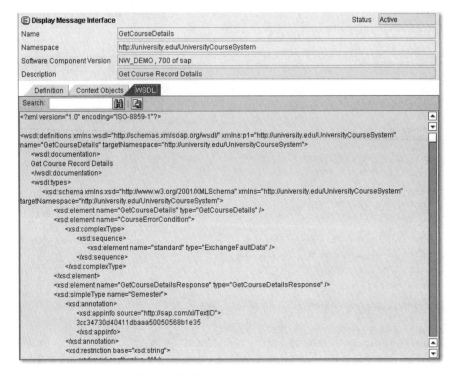

Figure 10.19 WSDL Definition of the Message Interface

10.2 Implementing the Service as a Server Proxy

SAP NetWeaver PI is a great tool for designing services, but it is not intended to be used to actually implement them. The technical implementation of the services should be done within the business systems that house the existing business logic and data.

In Russel's case, he has modeled his service in the university's separate PI system landscape. Now he returns to the ABAP development environment on the university's ERP system to complete the service definition and implementation. Upon returning to transaction SE80 in his ERP system, Russel refreshes the view in the Enterprise Service Repository. He can now see all the objects that he just finished modeling (see Figure 10.20).

Figure 10.20 Service Browser within SE80

But all the objects have the red and white **Hazard** icon next to them. This is to signify that although the definitions of the objects have been modeled, no implementation of them exists yet.

1. For that, Russel needs to start the generation of a server proxy by selecting **Create Proxy** from the context menu (see Figure 10.21).

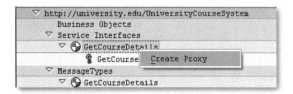

Figure 10.21 Creating the Server Proxy

A server proxy is really quite similar to the client proxy that Russel built in Chapter 4. They are both classes and associated objects that are generated off of a WSDL document. The only real difference between the two proxies is the direction of the communication streams.

▷ *Client proxies* are local representations of a service that is implemented on another machine. They contain no business logic, just the technical details of how to map from ABAP data types to XML, and then how to call the remote service passing it the necessary parameters.

▶ *Server proxies*, on the other hand, represent Web Services that will be served out of the local system. These proxies are only generated for the service interface definition that was modeled outside the current application. They are still responsible for the technical implementation of the inner business logic.

2. Since this is once again a generated object, the first dialog requires information about the **Package** in which the object will be generated and the **Prefix** for the main proxy class (see Figure 10.22).

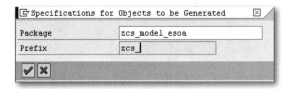

Figure 10.22 Object Generation Settings

3. As you can see in Figure 10.23, the results of the generation process look remarkably similar to the client proxy generation. It is also clear that all the details, such as the **Namespace**, have been brought over from the PI modeling process.

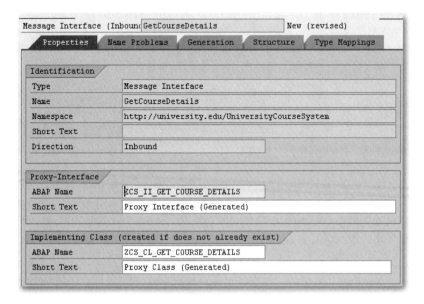

Figure 10.23 Generated Message Interface Properties

4. The **Structure** tab still shows the inner details of the input and output parameters (see Figure 10.24). The mapping from the XML-based modeled data types to the native ABAP data types has already been performed, and the results are shown in the right-hand side of the screen.

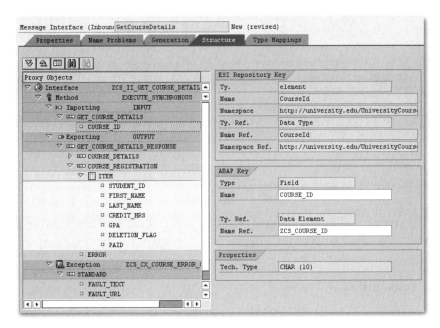

Figure 10.24 Generated Interface Structure

5. The implementation of the server proxy is done via the generated objects. Figure 10.25 shows the **Interface**, ZCS_II_GET_COURSE_DETAILS, and the implementing class, ZCS_CL_GET_COURSE_DETAILS. It is in the method, EXECUTE_SYNCHRONOUS, that Russel will put the code that will be executed when the Web Service is called.

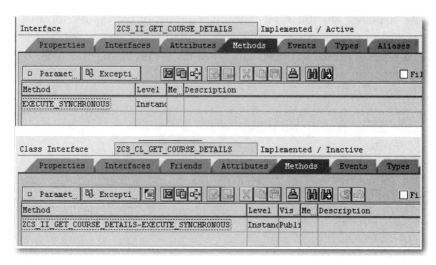

Figure 10.25 Implementing Interface and Class

The coding within this method will be similar to the function module that was used as the basis of the original Web Service in the previous chapter.

1. Russel begins his coding with the necessary data declarations and the instantiation of the model class:

```
METHOD zcs_ii_get_course_details~execute_synchronous.
  DATA model TYPE REF TO zcl_cs_main_model.
  DATA o_excep TYPE REF TO zcx_course_system.
  DATA course_id TYPE zcs_course_id.
  course_id = input-get_course_details-course_id.
  CREATE OBJECT model.
```

2. Next Russel calls the READ_COURSE_DETAILS method of the model class passing in the input COURSE_ID from the service parameters:

```
TRY.
    DATA course_att TYPE zcs_course_att.
    DATA course_reg_att TYPE zcs_course_reg_att_tbl.
    model->read_course_details(
        EXPORTING   i_course_id      = course_id
        IMPORTING   e_course_att     = course_att
                    e_course_reg_att = course_reg_att ).
```

3. He then must map the values that were returned by the model method to the exporting parameters of the service operation. The structure of the request and response parameters of the service operation are nested just as they were when he worked with a client proxy object:

```
MOVE-CORRESPONDING course_att TO
  output-get_course_details-course_details.
FIELD-SYMBOLS: <wa_source> LIKE LINE OF course_reg_att,
               <wa_dest>   TYPE zcs_course_registration.
LOOP AT course_reg_att ASSIGNING <wa_source>.
  APPEND INITIAL LINE TO
  output-get_course_details-course_registration-item
  ASSIGNING <wa_dest>.
   MOVE-CORRESPONDING <wa_source> TO <wa_dest>.
   MOVE-CORRESPONDING <wa_source>-student->student_att
     TO <wa_dest>.
ENDLOOP.
```

This is the only area of the coding where Russel has to perform any special logic associated with this being a server proxy. Remember the message fault that Russel modeled within SAP NetWeaver PI. This has generated a corresponding ABAP Exception Class, ZCS_CX_COURSE_ERROR_CONDITION.

Fault messages are a standard way of announcing some form of incorrect or unexpected processing from within a Web Service. Although SAP supports this portion of the Web Service standard, it often does not supply the level of detail of an error condition that is necessary in business applications. Therefore, you will often see that standard SAP services only raise the message fault exceptions with the CX_AI_APPLIATION_FAULT ID, as Russel has done. This generically reports that an application error has occurred as opposed to some low level technical error.

SAP applications then write out a more detailed log of the error within a normal response parameter. Russel has followed this approach as well, by outputting the full description of his actual exception into a field in his response he has named ERROR (see Listing 10.1).

```
CATCH zcx_course_system INTO o_excep.
   output-get_course_details-error = o_excep->get_text( ).
   RAISE EXCEPTION TYPE zcs_cx_course_error_condition
     EXPORTING
       textid =
   zcs_cx_course_error_condition=>cx_ai_application_fault.
ENDTRY.
ENDMETHOD.    "zcs_ii_get_course_details~execute_synchronous
```

Listing 10.1 Server Proxy Implementation

10.3 Creating a Service Definition

Russel has completed the server proxy implementation, but he still doesn't have a callable Web Service. Just like the function module based Web Services, he still needs a released service definition. He starts the *Service Definition Wizard* from within the Message Interface maintenance view.

The overall flow of the wizard looks very much like the wizard Russel used in the last chapter to wrap his function module in a Web Service. In fact, the object that is created at the end of the wizard is almost indistinguishable from a function module based service definition.

1. The first step of the wizard requires that Russel supply the name of his **Service Definition**. The **Endpoint Type** selection is disabled, because he started the wizard from within a message interface (see Figure 10.26).

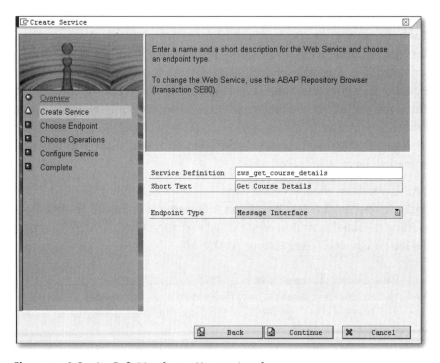

Figure 10.26 Service Definition from a Message Interface

2. In the next step, the **Service Interface** that will be used as the endpoint of the service definition is displayed (see Figure 10.27). If Russel had not had this particular message interface loaded into transaction SE80 before he

started the wizard, this field would not be disabled. He would instead have to choose the service interface from the selection field.

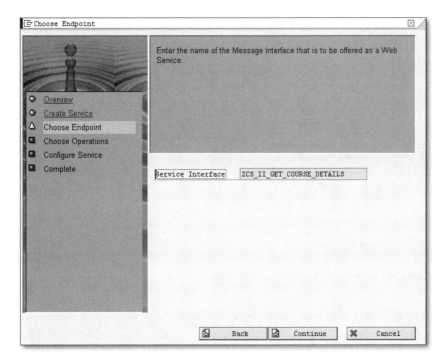

Figure 10.27 Service Interface as the Endpoint

3. The final service definition shows the interface parameters that were generated from the server proxy object (see Figure 10.28). The **Variants** tab still allows for the definition of the required **Authentication Levels** and the **Transport Guarantees**. All of the same security measures and authorization types that were available to the function module based Web Service can be applied to the server proxy version.

4. When Russel navigates to transaction WSADMIN, he now finds a second set of folders (see Figure 10.29). This second grouping contains all the PI based proxy objects. Other than having a slightly different URL than its function module based counterpart, all the same options that were discussed in Chapter 9 for service node setup — WSDL viewing and testing within the J2EE Web Service Homepage tool — still exist for this new type of entry.

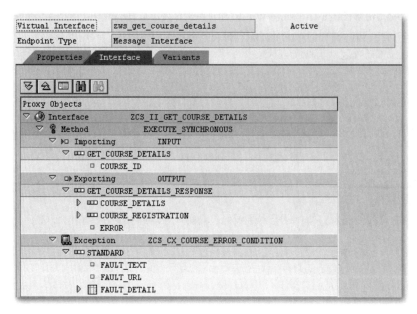

Figure 10.28 Service Definition for the Message Interface

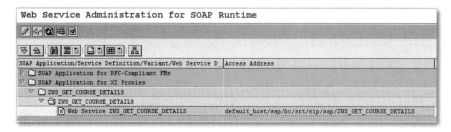

Figure 10.29 Service Administration for PI Proxies

In this chapter, Russel discovers the new ALV Object Model. He quickly realizes that this new model can help him to develop robust reporting applications. In addition, Russel will be coding once again in classic Dynpro. This is a chance for him to leverage the skills he has already mastered from working in the SAP R/3 4.6C environment, while applying some of the new object-oriented constructs.

11 Classic Dynpro UI/ALV Object Model

Russel has learned a lot while exploring his new ABAP development environment. Since the university has upgraded to SAP ERP 6.0, he now has the opportunity to leverage powerful development tools such as the new *ALV Object Model*, which was introduced in SAP NetWeaver 2004. Russel has been successful in implementing *SAP List Viewer* (ALV) technology in the past, using the older tools, and he feels confident about using the new ALV Object Model tool.

The university administrators have handed down a requirement for a report, which gives details about the courses, the course prerequisites, and the registered students for these courses. When Russel reads through the technical specification that his functional analyst gives him, he immediately thinks about using the new ALV Object Model to satisfy the requirements of the report.

Russel decides to use the most basic tool, the two-dimensional grid, with the full-screen grid display type. The requirement calls for one basic list to present the courses, and the ability to select a course and display the prerequisites or the registered students by clicking on a button on the application toolbar.

11.1 ALV Object Model Overview

Russel has been reading the online help provided by SAP about the ALV Object Model. He studies the documentation completely in order to give himself a basic understanding that he can build on. In previous releases, Russel used function module based ALV tools, such as `REUSE_ALV_GRID_DISPLAY`, to create the ALV output. The new ALV Object Model is an encapsulation of these pre-existing ALV tools using object-oriented concepts. It was developed to give the developer a unified API for all ALV tools, including the two-dimensional table, the hierarchical-sequential list, and the tree structure.

Each ALV tool has its own main class that you use to implement the tool:

▶ `CL_SALV_TABLE`
used for two-dimensional table

▶ `CL_SALV_HIERSEQ_TABLE`
used for hierarchical-sequential list

▶ `CL_SALV_TREE`
used for tree structures

Each main class has similar methods that you will use to modify the attributes of the ALV output. The methods and the method parameters may vary slightly when tool-specific features are to be implemented.

11.1.1 ALV Tool Overview

There are three basic ALV tools for displaying data to the end user. The data that is to be displayed usually will dictate which ALV tool will be used.

▶ The *two-dimensional table display,* shown in Figure 11.1, is a tabular representation of the data. It can contain any number of lines, but the structure must remain constant throughout. This is the most basic tool of the three.

Column Headings ⟶

Airli...	Flight N...	Country	Depart	Country	Target	Flight time
AA ⊡	17	US	JFK	US	SFO	6:01
AA	64	US	SFO	US	JFK	5:21
AZ	555	IT	FCO	DE	FRA	2:05
AZ	788	IT	FCO	JP	TYO	12:55
AZ	789	JP	TYO	IT	FCO	15:40
AZ	790	IT	FCO	JP	KIX	13:35
DL	106	US	JFK	DE	FRA	7:55
DL	1699	US	JFK	US	SFO	6:22
DL	1984	US	SFO	US	JFK	5:25

Data Rows

Figure 11.1 Two Dimensional Table

▶ The *hierarchical-sequential list*, shown in Figure 11.2, provides output with hierarchy levels. There can be only two levels: a header level and a detail level. There can be any number of header level lines with any number of detail level lines beneath.

The structure of the header level and the detail level can be totally different. The only restriction is that the data of each level must have some relationship. In other words, there must be some field that ties the two levels together, like when an order header and any number of order items all share the same order number field.

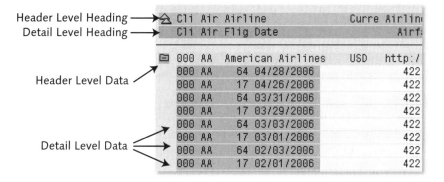

Figure 11.2 Hierarchical-Sequential List

▶ The *tree structure display*, shown in Figure 11.3, allows you to format your tabular data into any number of hierarchical levels. Each hierarchical level is referred to as a node. Unlike, the hierarchical-sequential list tool, each node of the hierarchy must contain the same data structure.

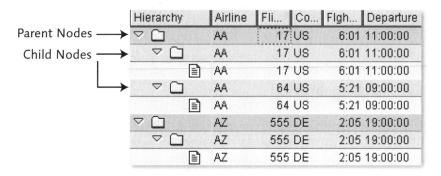

Figure 11.3 Tree Structure

11.1.2 Display Types

The ALV Object Model provides three different ways to display the output: Classical ABAP List, Full Screen, and GUI Container. The display type defines how the specific ALV tool is implemented into the screen. For example, the ALV output can be displayed in a container within the screen, or as a full screen display. This is one of the main benefits of the ALV Object Model over its predecessors. In the past, we had very different coding methods for each of these different display types. Now, however, the ALV Object Model unifies all of these different display types into a similar programming model, making it easier to choose the correct display type for the need at hand:

▶ **Classical ABAP List**
This list display is similar to the list output, which is displayed when using WRITE statements in a report program. It consumes the entire screen and implements the toolbar in the application toolbar.

▶ **Full Screen**
The full screen display is a graphical grid, which allows the user to drag and drop columns. This display type uses the entire screen and also implements the ALV toolbar in the application toolbar.

▶ **GUI Container**
The GUI container display type is also a graphical grid, but is implemented inside of a container control embedded in the screen. This allows you to put multiple ALV grids in one screen, as well as other GUI controls. The ALV toolbar is implemented inside of the container along with the ALV grid rather than in the application toolbar.

In some cases, the ALV tools can only use certain display types. For example, the hierarchical-sequential list tool cannot use the full screen grid display type nor can it be displayed in a GUI container. The reason is that it is rendered using the classical list display.

11.2 Getting Started

Now that Russel has read through the online help, which discusses the ALV Object Model in greater detail, he is confident that he can begin developing the reports that are targeted for his SAP GUI users.

11.2.1 Package Selection

Russel starts transaction SE80 and begins to develop his reporting application. The first thing Russel wants to do is determine where his application falls in the package hierarchy. He selects **Package** from the object list box and enters the main package name ZCOURSE_SYSTEM. Since his application will use regular classic Dynpro technology, Russel decides that the best choice here is the package ZCS_UI_DYNPRO, as seen in Figure 11.4. Then, he creates the new report program as ZCS_COURSE_RPT and assigns it to a transport request.

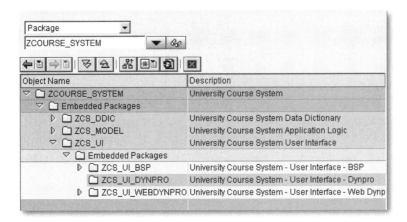

Figure 11.4 Package Hierarchy

11.2.2 Basic Program Coding

Since working with the ALV Object Model is a new experience for Russel, he decides to code the bare minimum in order to display the ALV output first, and then go back and add other functionality later.

Data Declarations

Russel needs to create an internal table (see Listing 11.1). The internal table definition will do two things:

▶ First, it will hold the data, which will be passed to the ALV tool.

▶ Second, it will be used by the ALV tool to build the columns of the ALV output.

Russel was used to having to build a field catalog in his SAP R/3 4.6C system; now, he is very excited to know that this is no longer necessary when using the ALV Object Model.

```
REPORT  zcs_course_rpt.

TYPES: BEGIN OF t_zcs_course,
         course_id       TYPE zcs_course-course_id,
         course_sdesc    TYPE zcs_course-course_sdesc,
         faculty_id      TYPE zcs_course-faculty_id,
         semester        TYPE zcs_course-semester,
         course_year     TYPE zcs_course-course_year,
         major           TYPE zcs_course-major,
         credit_hrs      TYPE zcs_course-credit_hrs,
         student_limit   TYPE zcs_course-student_limit,
         deletion_flag   TYPE zcs_course-deletion_flag,
         start_time      TYPE zcs_course-start_time,
         end_time        TYPE zcs_course-end_time,
         course_schedule TYPE zcs_course-course_schedule,
         cost            TYPE zcs_course-cost,
         currency        TYPE zcs_course-currency,
         pre_req         TYPE zcs_course_preq_att_tbl,
       END OF t_zcs_course.

DATA: gt_zcs_course TYPE STANDARD TABLE OF t_zcs_course.
DATA: gs_zcs_course LIKE LINE OF gt_zcs_course.
FIELD-SYMBOLS: <gs_zcs_course> LIKE LINE OF gt_zcs_course.
```
Listing 11.1 Internal Table Declaration

You might be wondering why Russel created two work areas for the same internal table: one work area as a regular data variable and the other as a field symbol. Well, first of all, Russel is adhering to modern ABAP syntax and declaring his internal table, GT_ZCS_COURSE, as a table without a header line.

But there are two different ways to read data into an explicit header line. You can either directly read data into a data variable or you can assign the data to a field symbol. The latter approach, as seen in Listing 11.2, is generally the preferred method.

```
LOOP AT gt_zcs_course ASSIGNING <gs_course_obj>.
ENDLOOP.
```
Listing 11.2 Loop Using Assigning

Unlike the first method (i.e., directly reading data into a data variable), in the second method (i.e., assigning the data to a field symbol), the memory does not physically get copied from the internal table row into the header area variable. Instead, the field symbol directly references the data row of the internal table. This has certain performance benefits, particularly when you need to update the data in an internal table a row at a time. When changing the data via the field symbol, you are directly accessing the internal table. Therefore, you don't need a MODIFY statement to copy the contents back into the internal table.

Still, there are times when the "direct read into a data variable" approach, as seen in Listing 11.3, can still have the performance advantage over the field symbol assignment. There is a certain amount of overhead associated with the setup of a field symbol. For that reason, when you know you're performing a read-only operation and will be accessing only one or very few rows, the "direct read into...." becomes the preferred alternative.

```
READ TABLE gt_zcs_course INTO gs_course_obj INDEX ls_rows.
```

Listing 11.3 Loop Using Into

Object References

1. At this point, Russel knows that he will be using the two-dimensional tool, so he defines a reference variable for the class CL_SALV_TABLE. This reference variable will be used throughout the rest of the program to provide access to the subclass objects of the ALV tool:

```
DATA: gr_table TYPE REF TO cl_salv_table.
```

Data Retrieval

2. Next, Russel knows that he must fill the internal table with some data. To access the data, he leverages the Business Object classes (see Listing 11.4), which were created in Chapter 3.

```
DATA: gt_courses_obj TYPE zcs_courses_tbl.
FIELD-SYMBOLS: <gs_course_obj> TYPE zcs_course_obj.
FIELD-SYMBOLS: <gs_zcs_course> LIKE LINE OF gt_zcs_course.

START-OF-SELECTION.

  gt_courses_obj = zcl_cs_course=>read_all_courses( ).
  LOOP AT gt_courses_obj ASSIGNING <gs_course_obj>.
    APPEND INITIAL LINE TO gt_zcs_course
         ASSIGNING <gs_zcs_course>.
    MOVE-CORRESPONDING   <gs_course_obj>-course->course
```

```
            TO <gs_zcs_course>.
    ENDLOOP.
```

Listing 11.4 Data Retrieval

Object Instantiation

3. Next, Russel needs to create an instance of the class CL_SALV_TABLE. He knows that in order to do this, he must call the static method, FACTORY. This method is new to Russel, so he decides to use the **Pattern** button in transaction SE80 to help him call the FACTORY method, and enters the class name, instance name, and method name as shown in Figure 11.5.

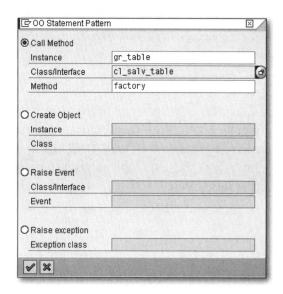

Figure 11.5 ABAP Object Pattern

4. The ABAP Workbench has now inserted the template (shown in Listing 11.5) that will create the instance of the ALV object and initialize the object by passing it a reference to the main data internal table.

```
    TRY.
        cl_salv_table=>factory(
*   EXPORTING
*     list_display    = if_salv_c_bool_sap=>false
*     r_container     = r_container
*     container_name  = container_name
          IMPORTING
            r_salv_table    = gr_table
          CHANGING
```

```
        t_table         = gt_zcs_course
            ).
    CATCH cx_salv_msg .
  ENDTRY.
```

Listing 11.5 Calling the Factory Method

5. Russel needs to uncomment some of the code and specify a few parameters. In this case, the EXPORTING parameters are not needed, but Russel likes to leave them commented out as opposed to removing them completely.

6. Immediately following the FACTORY method call, Russel needs to call the DISPLAY method to display the output.

   ```
   gr_table->display( ).
   ```

7. Russel activates and runs his newly created program. The result is shown in Figure 11.6. He is impressed that the system is clever enough to know the columns of the output just by the definition of the internal table, but he also notices that there are some things about this simple, initial display that he doesn't feel comfortable with and would like to improve, such as adding the ALV toolbar.

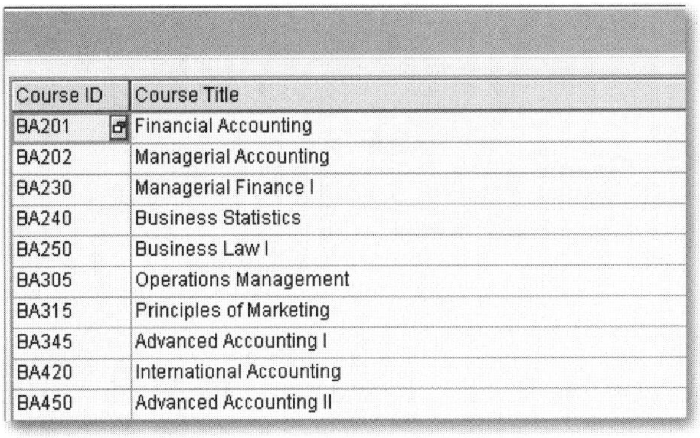

Course ID	Course Title
BA201	Financial Accounting
BA202	Managerial Accounting
BA230	Managerial Finance I
BA240	Business Statistics
BA250	Business Law I
BA305	Operations Management
BA315	Principles of Marketing
BA345	Advanced Accounting I
BA420	International Accounting
BA450	Advanced Accounting II

Figure 11.6 ALV Output

11.3   Modifying the ALV Output

In the last section, Russel was successful in creating his very first application by leveraging the new ALV Object Model. Russel must now make some modifications to the ALV output in order to fulfill all of his business requirements. Simply displaying the data without offering any functionality to manipulate the data does not make for a very user-friendly application. The whole point in using the ALV toolset is to put the reporting power into the hands of the user.

There are many subclasses of the ALV Object Model, which can be used to manipulate the ALV tool. Basically, you create a reference variable for the subclass and use the corresponding GET method of the main class to return an object reference for that subclass. Each ALV tool provides certain GET methods, which you can use to retrieve the object references of the subclasses. Some of the more common methods are:

- GET_FUNCTIONS
- GET_SORTS
- GET_SELECTIONS
- GET_EVENTS
- GET_AGGREGATIONS
- GET_FILTERS
- GET_COLUMNS
- GET_DISPLAY_SETTINGS
- GET_FUNCTIONAL_SETTINGS
- GET_LAYOUT
- GET_PRINT

Once the object reference is retrieved, you can call the appropriate methods of the subclass to manipulate the attributes.

11.3.1 ALV Functions

The first thing that Russel wants to add is the standard ALV function toolbar. When developing ALV applications in his SAP R/3 4.6C system, using the function module REUSE_ALV_GRID_DISPLAY or the class CL_GUI_ALV_GRID, the toolbar displayed automatically. This is not the case when using the ALV Object Model. The subclass CL_SALV_FUNCTIONS can be used to manipulate the functions of the ALV tool. The SET_ALL method of this class is used to make all of the standard ALV functions visible on the application toolbar.

In order to use the subclasses, Russel needs to retrieve the object reference from the main object reference that he has already instantiated, GR_TABLE.

Russel creates another reference variable; this time, the class CL_SALV_ FUNCTIONS is the reference type:

```
DATA: gr_functions TYPE REF TO cl_salv_functions.
```

Russel now calls the method GET_FUNCTIONS to retrieve the object reference for GR_FUNCTIONS. The object reference is sent back using a RETURN parameter. Immediately after calling this method, he then calls the method SET_ALL, which will make the standard functions visible on the application toolbar:

```
gr_functions = gr_table->get_functions( ).
gr_functions->set_all( abap_true ).
gr_table->display( ).
```

Russel then runs the program again. This time, he can see the standard ALV functions on the application toolbar (see Figure 11.7).

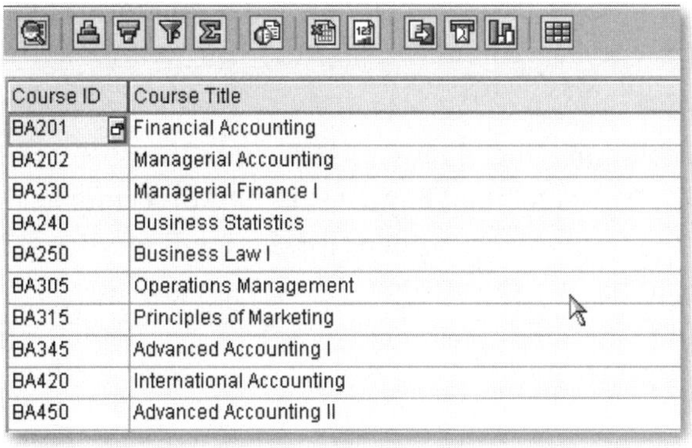

Course ID	Course Title
BA201	Financial Accounting
BA202	Managerial Accounting
BA230	Managerial Finance I
BA240	Business Statistics
BA250	Business Law I
BA305	Operations Management
BA315	Principles of Marketing
BA345	Advanced Accounting I
BA420	International Accounting
BA450	Advanced Accounting II

Figure 11.7 ALV Output with the Standard Toolbar

11.3.2 Modifying Column Attributes

Russel now faces a few more problems with the output display. First, he would like the COURSE_ID and the COURSE_SDESC columns to be fixed on the left side of the display. Doing so will ensure that when the user scrolls to the right, the COURSE_ID and the COURSE_SDESC columns will always remain visible on the left. Also, the COURSE_SDESC column is too wide. The column output length is defined by the data element used in the data dictionary. Russel needs to find a way to change this attribute without modifying the data element in the data dictionary.

Russel discovers that he can use the subclass CL_SALV_COLUMNS_TABLE and the subclass CL_SALV_COLUMN_TABLE to accomplish this task. He uses the CL_SALV_COLUMNS_TABLE subclass to retrieve the object reference, which will allow him to manipulate all columns of the ALV output. In other words, this object contains the objects of each column. He uses the subclass CL_SALV_COLUMN_TABLE to manipulate the attributes of these single column objects. These classes allow you to change many attributes of each column — including heading text, column color, visibility, output length, and alignment — as well as many other attributes.

1. Russel begins modifying his program by adding two new reference variables, one for CL_SALV_COLUMNS_TABLE and the other for CL_SALV_COLUMN_TABLE:

```
DATA: gr_columns TYPE REF TO cl_salv_columns_table.
DATA: gr_column TYPE REF TO cl_salv_column_table.
```

2. Russel then adds the code to retrieve the object reference for GR_COLUMNS using the method GET_COLUMNS of the object GR_TABLE. He can now set the attribute, which will fix the key columns using the SET_KEY_FIXATION method.

3. In order to modify the columns, Russel must first retrieve the object reference by calling the GET_COLUMN method of the GR_COLUMN object for each column that he wants to modify. He can then use the methods SET_KEY and SET_OUTPUT_LENGTH to modify the attributes (see Listing 11.6).

```
gr_columns = gr_table->get_columns( ).
gr_columns->set_key_fixation( abap_true ).

TRY.
    gr_column ?= gr_columns->get_column(
          columnname = 'COURSE_ID' ).
    gr_column->set_key( abap_true ).
  CATCH cx_salv_not_found.
ENDTRY.

TRY.
    gr_column ?= gr_columns->get_column(
          columnname = 'COURSE_SDESC' ).
    gr_column->set_output_length( 20 ).
    gr_column->set_key( abap_true ).
  CATCH cx_salv_not_found.
ENDTRY.
```

Listing 11.6 Setting Column Attributes

4. Russel tests his program again and sees that the color of the key columns has changed and the output length of the course description is much shorter than before. The shorter column length allows the other fields of the output to be displayed without scrolling (see Figure 11.8).

Course ID	Course Title	Faculty ID	...	Year	Ma..	Cre..	Siz..
BA201	Financial Accounting	LOUEYLI	1	2007	BA	3	25
BA202	Managerial Accounting	LOUEYLI	2	2007	BA	3	25
BA230	Managerial Finance I	LOUEYLI	1	2007	BA	3	25
BA240	Business Statistics	LOUEYLI	2	2007	BA	3	25
BA250	Business Law I	LOUEYLI	1	2007	BA	3	25
BA305	Operations Management	LOUEYLI	2	2007	BA	3	25
BA315	Principles of Marketing	LOUEYLI	1	2007	BA	3	25
BA345	Advanced Accounting I	LOUEYLI	2	2007	BA	3	25
BA420	International Accounting	LOUEYLI	1	2007	BA	3	25
BA450	Advanced Accounting II	LOUEYLI	2	2007	BA	3	25

Figure 11.8 ALV Output with Modified Column Attributes

11.3.3 Modifying Display Settings

Russel wants to further modify certain aspects of the display, such as the title bar and the row color. He finds that he can use the subclass CL_SALV_ DISPLAY_SETTINGS to modify these attributes.

1. First, the method SET_STRIPED_PATTERN enables him to set the alternating color pattern for the output lines. By adding the striped pattern to the detail lines, the output becomes more readable to the end user.

2. Russel also finds the appropriate method, SET_LIST_HEADER, which allows him to change the title on the title bar. By default, the title from the program attributes is displayed here.

3. By applying what Russel has learned so far, he knows that he must create a reference variable for the class CL_SALV_DISPLAY_SETTINGS and retrieve the object reference using the GET_DISPLAY_SETTINGS method from the GR_TABLE object. Then, he can call the appropriate methods to change the display settings attributes (see Listing 11.7).

```
DATA: gr_dspset TYPE REF TO cl_salv_display_settings.

gr_dspset = gr_table->get_display_settings( ).
gr_dspset->set_striped_pattern( abap_true ).
gr_dspset->set_list_header( 'Course Report' ).
```

Listing 11.7 Setting Display Attributes

4. Once again, Russel runs his program to test his recent changes. He can see that the title bar now reflects the new title instead of the title from the program attributes. Also, the rows now have the striped pattern applied to them (see Figure 11.9).

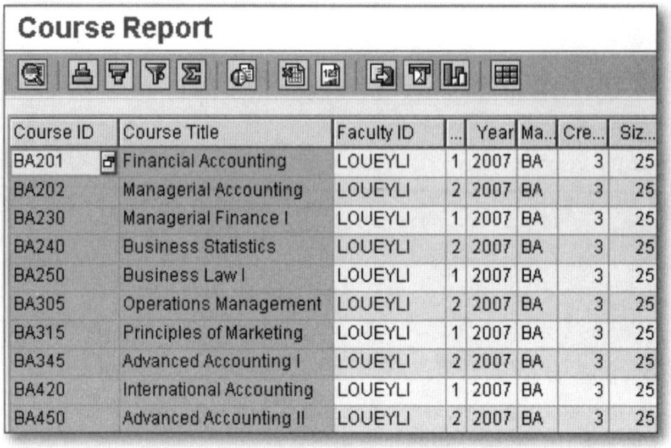

Course Report

Course ID	Course Title	Faculty ID	...	Year	Ma...	Cre...	Siz...
BA201	⊞ Financial Accounting	LOUEYLI	1	2007	BA	3	25
BA202	Managerial Accounting	LOUEYLI	2	2007	BA	3	25
BA230	Managerial Finance I	LOUEYLI	1	2007	BA	3	25
BA240	Business Statistics	LOUEYLI	2	2007	BA	3	25
BA250	Business Law I	LOUEYLI	1	2007	BA	3	25
BA305	Operations Management	LOUEYLI	2	2007	BA	3	25
BA315	Principles of Marketing	LOUEYLI	1	2007	BA	3	25
BA345	Advanced Accounting I	LOUEYLI	2	2007	BA	3	25
BA420	International Accounting	LOUEYLI	1	2007	BA	3	25
BA450	Advanced Accounting II	LOUEYLI	2	2007	BA	3	25

Figure 11.9 ALV Output with Modified Display Settings

11.3.4 Saving Layout Variants

Of course, the end users will want to be able to change the layout of the ALV output and save these layout changes as variants. This is standard functionality, which is handled entirely by the ALV tool. But, in order to use it, Russel must write some code that will turn on this functionality.

1. He notices that the subclass CL_SALV_LAYOUT provides methods for manipulating the layout variants of the ALV output. He also knows — very well by now — that he needs to define a reference variable for the subclass, retrieve the object from the main object GR_TABLE, and call the appropriate methods for setting the values (see Listing 11.8).

```
DATA: key TYPE salv_s_layout_key.
key-report = sy-repid.

gr_layout = gr_table->get_layout( ).
gr_layout->set_key( key ).
gr_layout->set_save_restriction( ).
gr_layout->set_default( abap_true ).
```

Listing 11.8 Setting Layout Attributes

2. By calling the layout methods, two new icons appear on the ALV application toolbar. The first icon, **Select Layout**, allows the user to select layout

variants that have been previously saved. The second icon, **Save Layout**, allows the user to save the current layout variant.

When calling the method SET_SAVE_RESTRICTION, the default value is RESTRICT_NONE, which means that the user will be able to save global layouts as well as user-specific layouts. Also, by calling the method SET_DEFAULT and setting the value to true, the user is allowed to save the layout variant as the default layout (see Figure 11.10).

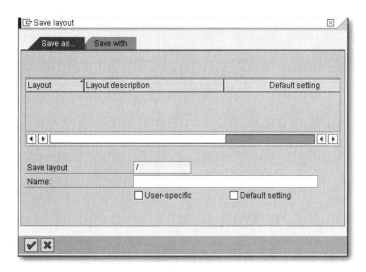

Figure 11.10 Save Layout Variant

11.4 Making the ALV Interactive

Russel has completed the initial coding of his new application. So far, the application displays a basic list, which enables end users to view data about courses. All of the basic functions, such as sorting and filtering, are already handled by the standard ALV application toolbar.

However, the business requirements specify that a bit more interactive functionality is needed. The university administrators want the ability to select a course and click on a button, which will display the course prerequisites, as well as a button that when clicked will display the registered students.

11.4.1 Adding Buttons

Since Russel has decided to use the full-screen display type, he must add the buttons to the application toolbar by adding them to the GUI status. The ALV tool implements the default GUI status automatically, but allows you to override it.

1. Russel begins by copying the standard status SALV_TABLE_STANDARD from the main program SAPLSALV_METADATA_STATUS as seen in Figure 11.11. The SAPLSALV_METADATA_STATUS program is actually the main program for the function group SALV_METADATA_STATUS.

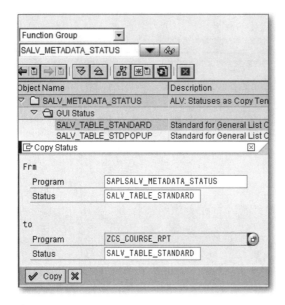

Figure 11.11 Copy GUI Status

2. Now that the GUI status has been copied to Russel's program, he can modify it and add the two new buttons (see Figure 11.12). There are various buttons in the standard GUI status that will not be used and can simply be removed in order to make room for the new buttons. Russel then adds a new button for displaying the course prerequisites, as well as one for displaying the course registrations.

Figure 11.12 Modified GUI Status

3. Russel now needs a way to override the default GUI status with the newly created one. He finds that there is a method of the main ALV class called SET_SCREEN_STATUS to accomplish this task. As shown in Listing 11.9, Russel is simply calling the method, and passing the name of the new GUI status, which is to be used instead of the standard GUI status.

```
DATA: repid TYPE sy-repid.
* Set the GUI status.
  repid = sy-repid.
  gr_table->set_screen_status(
        pfstatus      = 'SALV_TABLE_STANDARD'
        report        = repid
        set_functions = gr_table->c_functions_all ).
```

Listing 11.9 Setting Screen GUI Status

4. When testing his program, Russel sees the new buttons (see Figure 11.13) that have been added to the application toolbar. All of the other standard buttons work as before, with no additional coding required.

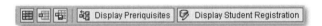

Figure 11.13 New Buttons on Application Toolbar

11.4.2 Defining Selections

For the actions tied to the new custom buttons to work properly, they will require logic to determine which row of the data the user wants to work with. In order for the ALV tool to recognize that a row has been selected in the ALV output, Russel must set the selection mode using the method SET_SELECTION_MODE of the subclass CL_SALV_SELECTIONS.

There are four possible selection modes that allow the user to select single rows, multiple rows, rows and columns, or even a particular cell. The constant attributes, SINGLE, MULTIPLE, ROW_COLUMN, and CELL of the class CL_SALV_SELECTIONS, can be used to set the value when calling the SET_SELECTION_MODE method. For this program, Russel chooses to use the single selection mode, because later he will attach an action to the selection that can only be performed on one record at a time:

```
DATA: gr_selections TYPE REF TO cl_salv_selections.
gr_selections =  gr_table->get_selections( ).
gr_selections->set_selection_mode( gr_selections->single ).
```

11.4.3 Event Handling

Russel has completed the programming that allows the user to select a single row from the ALV output. He must now add the event handling to the program; otherwise, nothing happens when the user clicks on a custom button. This is done using a local event handler class.

1. You can create templates of a class definition and implementation by right-clicking on the program name from the Object Navigator and choosing **Create • Class (Definition)** or **Create • Class (Implementation)** (see Figure 11.14).

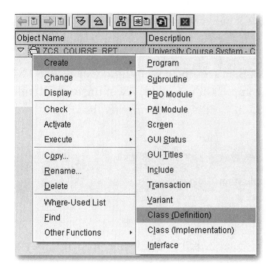

Figure 11.14 Create Local Class

The main program is then updated with the class definition source code containing the names and locations specified as seen in Figure 11.15. The same procedure is used to generate the class implementation template. The class implementation source code is appended to the end of the program.

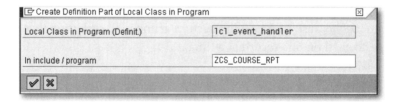

Figure 11.15 Local Class Creation Parameters

The ALV Object Model takes an object-oriented approach to all the event handling. Therefore, we will need this local class to register itself as the event handler for the events that we want to catch.

2. Now Russel can add the code to handle the events raised by the ALV tool. For this report, the event ADDED_FUNCTION of the subclass CL_SALV_ EVENTS_TABLE will be thrown when the user clicks on one of the buttons that Russel added to the application toolbar earlier. In the implemenation of his event handler method, a simple CASE statement is inserted to handle the different function codes (see Listing 11.10).

```
CLASS lcl_event_handler DEFINITION.

  PUBLIC SECTION.
    METHODS:
      on_user_command FOR EVENT added_function
                OF cl_salv_events_table
                    IMPORTING e_salv_function.
  ENDCLASS.                   "LCL_EVENT_HANDLER

CLASS lcl_event_handler IMPLEMENTATION.
  METHOD on_user_command.
    CASE e_salv_function.
      WHEN 'DSPPREQ'.
      WHEN 'DSPREG'.
    ENDCASE.
  ENDMETHOD.                        "on_user_command
ENDCLASS.                     "lcl_event_handler
```

Listing 11.10 Event Handler Implementation

3. The next task is to create an instance of the event handler class and register the handler method for the event (see Listing 11.11).

```
DATA: gr_events TYPE REF TO cl_salv_events_table.
gr_events = gr_table->get_event( ).
CREATE OBJECT  gr_event_handler.
SET HANDLER
      gr_event_handler->on_user_command
                        FOR gr_events.
```

Listing 11.11 Registering the Event Handler Method

4. Russel wants to make sure that the events are being fired correctly, so he sets a breakpoint on the CASE statement inside the ON_USER_COMMAND event handler method and runs his program. When he clicks on one of the cus-

tom buttons, the ABAP Debugger is launched and he sees that the program has stopped at the breakpoint (see Figure 11.16). This definitly means that the event is being fired and handled correctly by the application.

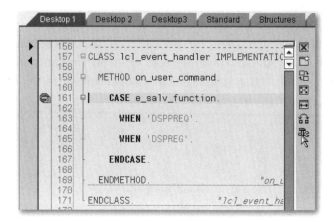

Figure 11.16 ABAP Debugger Stopping in the Event Handler

5. Russel can now begin to add the logic to the event handler method, ON_ USER_COMMAND, which will display the additional data. The data will be displayed in a separate simple two-dimensional ALV grid via a popup dialog.

This is easily done by simply calling the SET_SCREEN_POPUP method of the main ALV class (see Listing 11.12). Russel wants to be consistent with regard to how the data is extracted, so he decides to use the Business Object classes once more to retrieve the data. For the complete implementation of the ON_USER_COMMAND method, including the data retrieval logic, please refer to the sample program ZCS_COURSE_RPT on the CD provided with this book.

```
CLASS lcl_event_handler IMPLEMENTATION.

  METHOD on_user_command.
* Data Retrieval Logic - See Source Code on CD for Details
    CHECK <lt_table> IS ASSIGNED.
* Create instance of ALV Tool
    TRY.
        cl_salv_table=>factory(
            IMPORTING r_salv_table = lr_dialog_table
            CHANGING  t_table      = <lt_table> ).
      CATCH cx_salv_msg .
    ENDTRY.
```

```
* Set column length for course description
    lr_columns = lr_dialog_table->get_columns( ).
    lr_columns->set_key_fixation( abap_true ).
    TRY.
        lr_column ?= lr_columns->get_column(
                columnname = 'COURSE_SDESC' ).
        lr_column->set_output_length( 20 ).
      CATCH cx_salv_not_found.
    ENDTRY.

* Set functions ALL
    lr_functions =  lr_dialog_table->get_functions( ).
    lr_functions->set_all( abap_true ).

* Set to popup display
    lr_dialog_table->set_screen_popup(
                start_column = 1
                end_column   = 70
                start_line   = 1
                end_line     = 20 ).
    lr_dialog_table->display( ).
  ENDMETHOD.                          "on_user_command
ENDCLASS.                    "lcl_event_handler
```

Listing 11.12 Event Handler Implementation

6. One final test run of the application reveals that the additional buttons are working well and the data is being retrieved successfully (see Figure 11.17).

Faculty ID	...	Year	Ma...	Cre...	Siz...	...	Start Time	End Time	S...	Course Cost
LOUEYLI	1	2007	BA	3	25		08:00:00	09:30:00	02	4,500.00
LOUEYLI	2	2007	BA	3	25		08:00:00	09:30:00	02	4,500.00

Course Report

Student ID	First name	Last name	Cre...	GPA	Current Date	Time
BURKSST	Steven	Burks	33	3.887	01/14/2007	18:44:02
ANDREWGA	Gavin	Andrew	127	3.800	01/14/2007	18:44:02
LEIGHKE	Kearston	Leigh	15	3.800	01/14/2007	18:44:02
BONILLAMA	Max	Bonilla	43	3.661	01/14/2007	18:44:02
FRANKLIN...	Jose	Franklin	142	3.606	01/14/2007	18:44:02
HOLLOWA...	Sean	Holloway	128	3.507	01/14/2007	18:44:02
DOVEBI	Billy	Dove	131	3.458	01/14/2007	18:44:02
JONESMI	Mike	Jones	126	3.402	01/14/2007	18:44:02

Figure 11.17 Display Student Registrations in a Popup ALV

11.5 Object Orientiation with Classic Dynpro

After showing the nearly finished report to his end users, Russel receives one final requirement. The users would like to be able to view the course syllabi. The problem, however, is that the syllabi are stored as HTML files in order to allow faculty to maintain them using rich formatting. Russel will not be able to add just one more field to the ALV output for the syllabi. He will need to integrate another screen control, the *HTML Viewer*, into his application.

To make matters even more complex, the end users have rejected his initial suggestion of opening the syllabi in a popup window, similar to the way it displays course registrations and prerequisites. What Russel will ultimately end up creating is a screen layout that hosts both the ALV Object Model Control and the HTML Viewer Control in the same window canvas (see Figure 11.18).

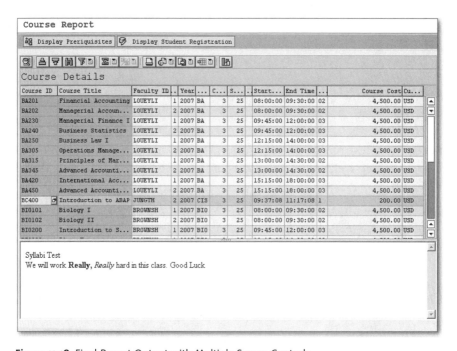

Figure 11.18 Final Report Output with Multiple Screen Controls

11.5.1 Restructuring the Dialog Program

In order to accomplish what the end users want to see in this report, Russel will have to do some major restructuring of his application. First, he has decided to change which ALV Object Modeldisplay type that he is using.

Instead of the ALV full screen, he will need to use the control based display mode. That way, he can control which screen control he will host the ALV output within. But more importantly to the overall program flow, he will also have to start using a full dialog screen program.

Theoretically, he could just throw a screen into his existing program and then move much of his current logic to the PBO/PAI module flow (Process Before Input/Process After Input). However, there is no reason not to follow a good Model View Controller (MVC) logic structure, even when working in classic Dynpro screen development. The whole concept is to separate the layers of logic from one another in order to afford better maintainability and reusability. This can be accomplished within Dynpro if you map the old PBO/PAI flow to a more robust object-oriented event process.

The first step in this process will remove nearly all logic from the main program itself. We only want to keep the absolute minimum coding in the procedural program flow that is necessary to support the legacy format of Dynpro (see Listing 11.13). Everything else will be moved over to a controller class.

```
REPORT  zcs_course_rpt_oo.
DATA: controller TYPE REF TO zcl_cs_course_rpt_dynp_cont.
DATA: ok_code TYPE syucomm.

START-OF-SELECTION.

  CREATE OBJECT controller.
  CALL SCREEN 100.

MODULE status_0100 OUTPUT.
  SET PF-STATUS 'MAIN'.
  SET TITLEBAR '100'.
ENDMODULE.                 " status_0100  OUTPUT

MODULE user_command_0100 INPUT.
  controller->pai(
  EXPORTING
    ok_code = ok_code ).
  CLEAR ok_code.
ENDMODULE.                 " user_command_0100  INPUT

MODULE pbo_0100 OUTPUT.
  controller->pbo( ).
ENDMODULE.                 " pbo_0100  OUTPUT
```

```
MODULE exit_dynp_0100 INPUT.
  CASE ok_code.
    WHEN 'BACK' OR 'CANC' OR 'EXIT'.
      CLEAR ok_code.
      controller->free_controls( ).
      LEAVE TO SCREEN 0.
  ENDCASE.
ENDMODULE.                         " exit_dynp_0100   INPUT
```

Listing 11.13 Dialog Program — OO Version

If you peruse Listing 11.13, you can see that there is not much left to the original dialog program:

▶ Only elements that must be connected to the dialog program, such as the screen models, the call screen and the title and status bar setting, are left.

▶ You map the PBO and PAI events directly into your controller class and pass in the OK_CODE field so that it can be used to trigger corresponding OO events within the controller.

▶ The screen itself is filled with one full size custom container. In this way, all the screen controls can be initialized by the controller class.

11.5.2   Creating the Controller Class

Fortunately, much of the coding from our original program can simply be cut and pasted right into our new controller class. But first, all of the global data and type declarations from the original program need to be made into global attributes for our class.

Back on SAP R/3 4.6C, Russel would have had to input these all manually via the global class builder attribute screen. But now, as of SAP NetWeaver 2004, you can directly access the definition structure of a global class from the menu option **Goto • Public Section** or **Goto • Protected Section** or **Goto • Private Section**, depending on which level of visibility you are working with. Figure 11.19 shows the code based definition area above and the resulting generated attributes below.

One of the major advantages to using this MVC/OO approach is the ability to break your logic down into small units. Instead of one large block of logic in the main section of the original program, you now have several small methods as shown in the **Methods** tab in Figure 11.20.

```
Private Section       Active
    22            pre_req         TYPE zcs_course_preq_att_tbl,
    23          END OF t_zcs_course .
    24
    25      data GR_TABLE type ref to CL_SALV_TABLE .
    26      data GR_FUNCTIONS type ref to CL_SALV_FUNCTIONS .
    27      data GR_COLUMNS type ref to CL_SALV_COLUMNS_TABLE .
    28      data GR_COLUMN type ref to CL_SALV_COLUMN_TABLE .
    29      data GR_DSPSET type ref to CL_SALV_DISPLAY_SETTINGS .
    30      data GR_LAYOUT type ref to CL_SALV_LAYOUT .
    31      data GR_SELECTIONS type ref to CL_SALV_SELECTIONS .
    32      data GR_EVENTS type ref to CL_SALV_EVENTS_TABLE .
    33      data CUSTOM_CONTAINER type ref to CL_GUI_CUSTOM_CONTAINER .
    34      data HTML_CONTROL type ref to CL_GUI_HTML_VIEWER .
    35      data SPLITTER type ref to CL_GUI_EASY_SPLITTER_CONTAINER .
    36      data:
    37        gt_zcs_course  TYPE STANDARD TABLE OF t_zcs_course .
    38      data GT_COURSES_OBJ type ZCS_COURSES_TBL .
    39
    40      methods INITIALIZE_ALV .
    41      methods CREATE CONTROLS .
```

Class Interface	ZCL_CS_COURSE_RPT_DYNP_CONT	Implemented / Active				
Properties	Interfaces	Friends	Attributes	Methods	Events	Types	A

Attribute	Level	Vis	Rea	Typing	Associated Type		Description
GR_TABLE	Instanc	Prive	☐	Type Ref	CL_SALV_TABLE	⇨	Basis Class for Simpl
GR_FUNCTIONS	Instanc	Prive	☐	Type Ref	CL_SALV_FUNCTIONS	⇨	
GR_COLUMNS	Instanc	Prive	☐	Type Ref	CL_SALV_COLUMNS_T	⇨	
GR_COLUMN	Instanc	Prive	☐	Type Ref	CL_SALV_COLUMN_TA	⇨	
GR_DSPSET	Instanc	Prive	☐	Type Ref	CL_SALV_DISPLAY_S	⇨	
GR_LAYOUT	Instanc	Prive	☐	Type Ref	CL_SALV_LAYOUT	⇨	
GR_SELECTIONS	Instanc	Prive	☐	Type Ref	CL_SALV_SELECTION	⇨	
GR_EVENTS	Instanc	Prive	☐	Type Ref	CL_SALV_EVENTS_TA	⇨	
CUSTOM_CONTAINER	Instanc	Prive	☐	Type Ref	CL_GUI_CUSTOM_CON	⇨	Container for Custom
HTML_CONTROL	Instanc	Prive	☐	Type Ref	CL_GUI_HTML_VIEWE	⇨	HTML Viewer
SPLITTER	Instanc	Prive	☐	Type Ref	CL_GUI_EASY_SPLIT	⇨	Reduced Version of Sp
GT_ZCS_COURSE	Instanc	Prive	☐			⇨	
GT_COURSES_OBJ	Instanc	Prive	☐	Type	ZCS_COURSES_TBL	⇨	

Figure 11.19 Direct Input of Class Attributes and Types

The main change to the original logic will revolve around the creation of the screen controls. Russel must now have a splitter control within the custom container, and place the ALV object in the top of the splitter and the HTML viewer in the bottom.

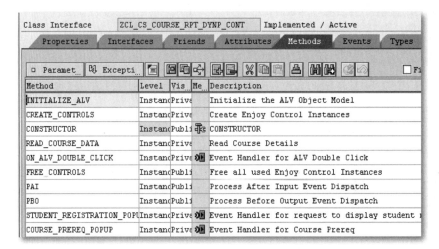

Method	Level	Vis	Me	Description
INITIALIZE_ALV	Instanc	Prive		Initialize the ALV Object Model
CREATE_CONTROLS	Instanc	Prive		Create Enjoy Control Instances
CONSTRUCTOR	Instanc	Publi	⛭	CONSTRUCTOR
READ_COURSE_DATA	Instanc	Prive		Read Course Details
ON_ALV_DOUBLE_CLICK	Instanc	Prive	»	Event Handler for ALV Double Click
FREE_CONTROLS	Instanc	Publi		Free all used Enjoy Control Instances
PAI	Instanc	Publi		Process After Input Event Dispatch
PBO	Instanc	Publi		Process Before Output Event Dispatch
STUDENT_REGISTRATION_POPU	Instanc	Prive	»	Event Handler for request to display student
COURSE_PREREQ_POPUP	Instanc	Prive	»	Event Handler for Course Prereq

Figure 11.20 Controller Class Methods

Thanks to the flexibility of the ALV Object Model, there are very few changes that Russel has to make to the coding in order to switch from using the full screen display mode to the control based display mode.

1. Russel must pass a reference to the hosting container (in bold) during the initialization of the ALV Object Model (see Listing 11.14).

```
TRY.
    cl_salv_table=>factory(
      EXPORTING
        r_container    = me->splitter->top_left_container
      IMPORTING
        r_salv_table   = gr_table
      CHANGING
        t_table        = gt_zcs_course ).
    CATCH cx_salv_msg .
  ENDTRY.
```

Listing 11.14 Object Model Factor Method Adjustments

2. The only other change that Russel has to make is the removal of the section of code that used to set the custom GUI status (see Listing 11.9). Russel simply doesn't need to pass a status through the ALV Object Model, because it no longer controls the entire screen. Instead, he has complete control over the screen and what GUI status it uses.

11.5.3 Enjoy Control Events

In Russel's original program, he had created a local class within his executable program for handling the control events that were raised by the ALV. Although there is nothing wrong with using local classes, they can be more difficult to maintain, especially when not properly separated from the procedural code of the main program. Keeping this in mind, Russel has the opportunity to use his global controller class as his event handler.

1. The process simply involves creating a method. Then, he clicks on the **Detail view** button (see Figure 11.21).

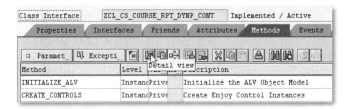

Figure 11.21 Triggering the Detail View Maintenance for a Method

2. This brings up a dialog where Russel enters the class and event that this event handler will support (see Figure 11.22)

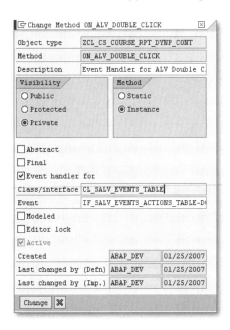

Figure 11.22 Method Detail View Dialog

This approach makes it even easier to define the parameters for the event handler. With the local class method approach, you had to manually define the event parameters, which proved to be a potential place for errors, as well as a bit time-consuming.

3. Instead, Russel just goes to the **Parameters** view of the method and clicks on the **Copy event parameters** button (see Figure 11.23). The ABAP editor then inserts all the available event parameters with their correct signatures.

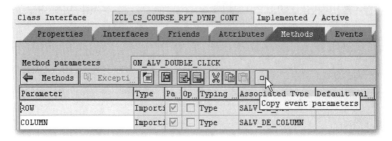

Figure 11.23 Copy the Event Parameters

4. The registration process for the event handler remains the same when using the local class. Now, during the control initialization, the controller class will just declare itself through the use of the alias ME, as the registered event handler:

```
* Set event handlers
  gr_events = gr_table->get_event( ).
  SET HANDLER me->on_alv_double_click FOR gr_events.
```

11.5.4 Dynpro Events

The final change that Russel has to tackle is how to deal with those pesky old PAI OK_CODE events. He has already used the dialog model of the screen to call a method in the controller class during a PAI. This method call will contain the value of the OK_CODE. He could stop there and just map method calls directly off a CASE of the OK_CODE, but Russel decides to try a full OO event approach even for his OK_CODE events.

1. The first step is to define events in his controller class corresponding to each of the possible OK_CODE values that he is expecting to receive from the screen (see Figure 11.24).

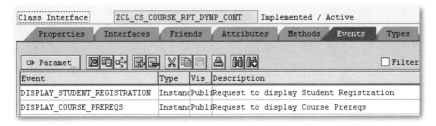

Figure 11.24 Controller Events

2. The logic of his controller's PAI method is now significantly simpler since all it must do is raise the corresponding event. It no longer needs to know what logic will actually respond to the event (see Listing 11.15).

```
METHOD PAI.
   CASE ok_code.
      WHEN 'DSPREG'.
         RAISE EVENT display_student_registration.
      WHEN 'DSPPREQ'.
         RAISE EVENT display_course_prereqs.
   ENDCASE.
ENDMETHOD.
```

Listing 11.15 PAI Event Mapping

With this change, the old PAI-based events now look exactly like control events to any outside class. Now, any class can register its own event handlers for these events.

3. For the purpose of this application, the controller class will contain the event handlers for these events. It simply needs to register itself as the handler, just like it did earlier with the ALV Object Model double-click event (see Listing 11.16).

```
* Set event handlers
  gr_events = gr_table->get_event( ).
  SET HANDLER me->on_alv_double_click FOR gr_events.
  SET HANDLER me->student_registration_popup FOR me.
  SET HANDLER me->course_prereq_popup FOR me.
```

Listing 11.16 Event Registration

4. Russel is now ready to turn this application over to the user community for rigorous testing. He knows that with all good applications come further enhancements. But, he also knows that the ALV Object Model provides a good API in which enhancements can be applied easily.

In this chapter, Russel will explore Web Dynpro ABAP, SAP's new, primary user interface development tool. Russel will follow SAP's lead and develop the majority of his user interfaces in this technology.

12   Web Dynpro ABAP

Web Dynpro ABAP is SAP's new UI strategy, which was introduced in SAP NetWeaver 7.0. It is based on the Model View Controller (MVC) paradigm that separates business logic from the user interface logic. Developers, like Russel, can use this tool to develop robust business applications quickly and easily, without ever having to deal with the inner coding of the user interface elements.

The Web Dynpro ABAP framework provides a WYSIWYG view editor (*What You See Is What You Get*) where the developer simply drags and drops the UI elements into the view. This means that there is no coding of the UI elements. This is not the case when working with *Business Server Pages* (BSP), where the developer must know some HTML or JavaScript in order to code the user interface.

The Web Dynpro framework approach can be viewed in a number of ways. If a developer is not proficient in HTML or JavaScript, the Web Dynpro ABAP tool looks pretty good. He doesn't have to worry about coding the UI and he can focus more on the business application logic. On the other hand, if the developer wants to add his own look and feel or some additional UI functionality to the Web Dynpro ABAP UI, he can't. The UI implementation is hidden from the developer and cannot be manipulated, such as adding your own HTML or JavaScript. The reason for this protection is that Web Dynpro was developed to provide a standard business application user interface across all applications that leverage this tool.

There is another advantage to the client abstraction approach that Web Dynpro takes. When you design a user interface in Web Dynpro, what is saved is just a metadata representation of the layout and elements. In other words, Web Dynpro is not tied to just HTML and JavaScript as its output medium. The Web Dynpro runtime analyzes the type of client that is making a request and responds with the appropriate rendering output. Today that means web browsers are making the request and receiving HTML and JavaScript. But, in the future, when the next great UI revolution occurs, you won't necessarily have to recreate your applications to take advantage of it. Already you can see examples of a smart client and Adobe Flex based rendering engines for Web Dynpro. Switching to these alternative presentation tools requires no coding changes within the applications themselves.

> **Note**
>
> Web Dynpro ABAP is a huge topic and cannot be adequately covered in one chapter. If you want to know more about this subject, we suggest that you check out the SAP Developer Network website (*http://sdn.sap.com*) as well as the book *Web Dynpro for ABAP* (SAP PRESS, 2006), covering all of the basic topics regarding Web Dynpro ABAP.
>
> We will assume that you understand the basic framework of the tool and know how to create simple Web Dynpro ABAP applications. You should also understand such concepts as basic UI elements, component controller, and view contexts, as well as inbound and outbound plugs.
>
> This chapter will focus on how Russel will use Web Dynpro ABAP to create separate components and fuse them together into one application. We will also cover some of the more powerful and advanced features of Web Dynpro ABAP.

12.1 Overview of the Components

Russel's requirement is to develop an application that can be accessed by the faculty members via the university's portal site. This application must allow them to maintain course details and faculty data. The faculty members have also requested that they have the ability to upload course assignments and to email those assignments to the students who are registered for the course.

One of the clear advantages of using the Web Dynpro ABAP tool is component reuse. Most of the tutorials that have been published only work with one Web Dynpro component. This is not a realistic scenario in a real world application. Instead, many actual applications are broken up into smaller reusable components that can be combined together into one application. Russel will take this same approach when developing his application for the university course system.

Russel will develop four separate components. All of the components will use the model class ZCL_CS_MAIN_MODEL as an assistance class of the component. Three of the components will supply the overall content of the application, while the fourth will be more of the application framework. This is a good practice as it allows Russel to reuse the components in other applications if the need arises. In this section, we'll take a quick look at the components that make up Russel's application and see how they all fit together.

12.1.1 Course Frame Component

The ZCS_COURSE_FRAME component is the application framework component. This is where all of the detail components come together in one application. This component uses links on the left side of the page in a ContextualPanel, and the corresponding content is presented in a ViewContainerUIElement on the right side (see Figure 12.1).

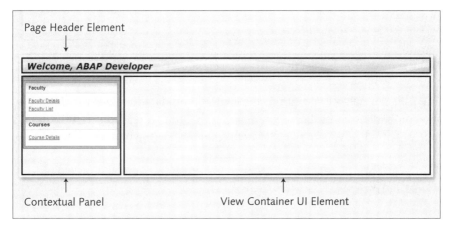

Figure 12.1 ZCS_COURSE_FRAME Component

The ViewContainerUIElement is a very special UI control that allows you to reserve a spot in your design for the embedding of another inner component. This is sort of like a subscreen area in classic Dynpro.

12.1.2 Faculty Detail Component

The first inner component is the ZCS_COURSE_FACULTY_DTL component. This component will be used to maintain and display faculty data (see Figure 12.2).

The user can enter a **Faculty ID** and click on the **Submit** button to view the faculty details. There is also a **Change** button (see the pencil icon at the top of the **Select Faculty** tray toolbar) to switch into change mode that makes all of the fields in the view editable.

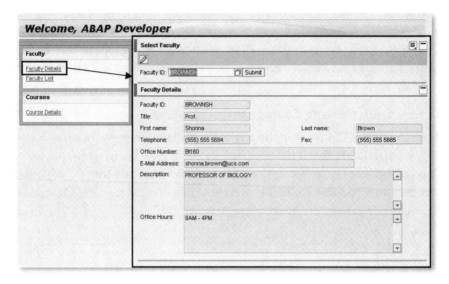

Figure 12.2 ZCS_COURSE_FACULTY_DTL Component

The user can then click on the **Save** button to update the database. Basically, the component controller implements a method to read the faculty details and a method to save the faculty details by interacting with the model class.

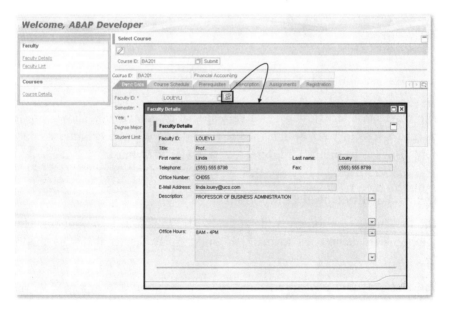

Figure 12.3 ZCS_COURSE_FACULTY_DTL Component in a Dialog

As you can see in Figure 12.3, this component is used in more than one place. It can be used in full edit mode within the main `ViewContainerUI-Element` space, but Russel will also reuse the same component in a dialog box during his course maintenance in order to display more details about the assigned faculty member. This is a good illustration of the power of component reuse.

12.1.3 Faculty List Component

The `ZCS_COURSE_FACULTY_LIST` component will be used to show a list of faculty members (see Figure 12.4).

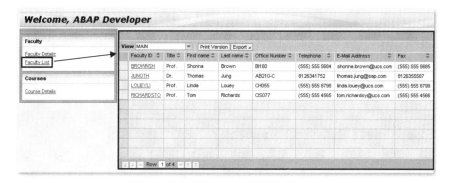

Figure 12.4 ZCS_COURSE_FACULTY_LIST Component

This component also defines a component usage relationship with the `ZCS_COURSE_FACULTY_DTL` for viewing the faculty details (see Figure 12.5). This is the second place where Russel was able to reuse this same detail component. This view is fired within a popup window when a **faculty ID** is selected from the list.

The `ZCS_COURSE_FACULTY_LIST` component also uses the standard component `SALV_WD_TABLE` to present the list in SAP List Viewer (ALV) grid format. Later, we will explore the ALV functionality in more depth.

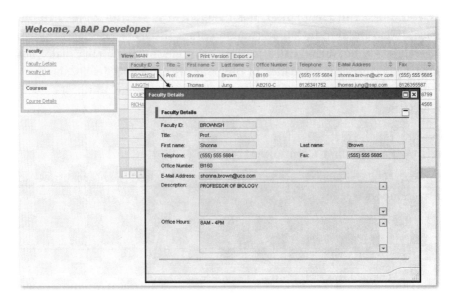

Figure 12.5 ZCS_COURSE_FACULTY_LIST and ZCS_COURSE_FACULTY_DTL

12.1.4 Course Details Component

The ZCS_COURSE_DETAILS component will be used to view and maintain courses (see Figure 12.6).

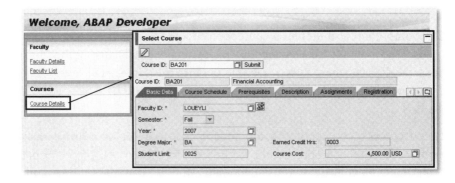

Figure 12.6 ZCS_COURSE_DETAILS Component

It uses a TabStrip UI element that includes all of the subobjects of the course details including prerequisites, assignments, and the student roster. The faculty members will be able to upload course assignments, as well as email those assignments to the students who are registered for the course.

12.2   Component Usage

To better understand component usage, let's take a closer look at Russel's ZCS_COURSE_FRAME component. First, all of the content components are defined as **Used Components** in the component overview screen as shown in Figure 12.7.

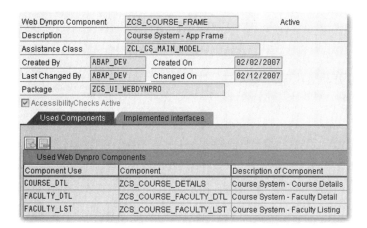

Figure 12.7 Used Components

This allows Russel to embed the windows of these components into the W_ MAIN window of the ZCS_COURSE_FRAME component. Figure 12.8 shows the hierarchy. Here you can see that the main view V_MAIN of the component ZCS_COURSE_FRAME is embedded into the main window W_MAIN. The V_MAIN view contains a view container in which all of the main windows of the content components have been embedded.

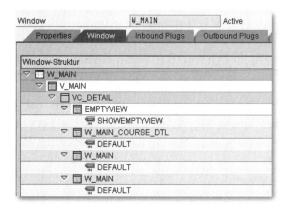

Figure 12.8 ZCS_COURSE_FRAME Main Window

The layout of view V_MAIN is very basic; there are links on the left and the view container on the right. Each link in the layout has a corresponding action assigned to it. These actions then have an associated event handler method. For instance, the **Faculty List** link is attached to the action LNK_FACULTY_LISTS, which has a corresponding event handler ONACTIONLNK_FACULTY_LISTS. This event handler method checks for an instance of the inner component. If one does not exist, it creates it and passes the instance of the assistance class to it. Finally, the outbound plug to the inner component is fired (see Listing 12.1).

```
METHOD ONACTIONLNK_FACULTY_LISTS .
  DATA: l_ref_cmp_usage TYPE REF TO if_wd_component_usage.
  l_ref_cmp_usage =   wd_this->wd_cpuse_faculty_lst( ).
  IF l_ref_cmp_usage->has_active_component( ) IS INITIAL.
    l_ref_cmp_usage->create_component(
      assistance_class = me->wd_assist ).
  ENDIF.
    wd_this->fire_outto_faculty_list_plg(
    ).

ENDMETHOD.
```
Listing 12.1 Event Handler Implementation

This passing of the assistance class is the key to powerful component reuse. All of these components are connected in that they have defined the same class as their assistance class, namely, the course model object, ZCL_CS_MAIN_MODEL.

But passing the instance of the assistance class goes even farther. Now all the component instances share the same instance of the assistance class. This means that any changes made to the model instance in the framework component are immediately available within any of the children components and vice versa. This is an excellent mechanism to allow for cross-component data sharing.

The outbound plugs are then tied to the inbound plugs of the content components using *Navigational Links*. This is done in the main window W_MAIN of the ZCS_COURSE_FRAME component. For example, Figure 12.9 shows that the outbound plug OUTTO_COURSE_DETAILS is linked to the inbound plug DEFAULT of the ZCS_COURSE_DETAILS component.

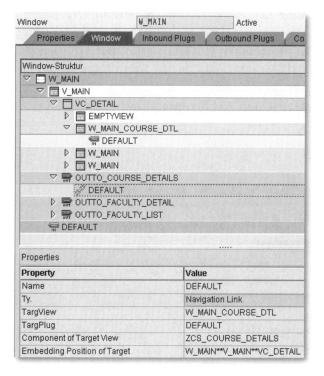

Figure 12.9 Navigational Links

12.3 General UI Features

As you can see from the screenshots, the Web Dynpro application that Russel built has a lot of functionality. Unfortunately, we cannot describe the creation of every UI element in the application, as that would exceed the scope of this book. Moreover, it wouldn't necessarily be helpful. Instead, we will focus our attention on some of the more interesting aspects of the application. The source code for the complete application is available on the CD that accompanies this book, so you can study the application in its entirety to whatever level you choose.

12.3.1 Value Help

The built-in value help capabilities in the ABAP environment are probably often taken for granted by most ABAP developers. This powerful feature is so tightly integrated in classic Dynpro that a developer hardly has to do anything in order to take advantage of it.

Fortunately, this is a feature that has been brought over to Web Dynpro ABAP with great success. The functionality, quite amazingly, is very much on a par with its classic Dynpro counterpart. This means that Web Dynpro ABAP has support for both *Elementary* and *Collective Search Helps*. As you can see from Figure 12.10, the custom Collective Search Help that Russel created (see Chapter 2) works just as well in Web Dynpro ABAP.

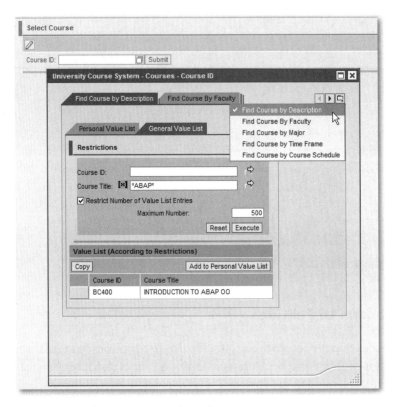

Figure 12.10 Web Dynpro ABAP Value Help

End users who are already familiar with value helps from classic Dynpro transactions won't require any additional training to become masters of the same constructs in Web Dynpro ABAP. When an InputField has a value help attached to it, the Web Dynpro ABAP framework will render it different. It will have an icon output to the right of the InputField. This icon, when clicked, will open the value help in a popup window (there are more details on how developers can create their own popup windows in Section 12.5). This popup window runs in the same browser of the original application, but floats above it. This is known as a *modal dialog*. The popup window can be moved around the screen, resized, or minimized/maximized.

The basic search helps within a collective search help are all represented as individual tabs in a TabStrip UI element. The inner element search help supports a **Personal Value List** for quick retrieval of user-specific FAVORITE values. But the **General Value List** is where most users will interact with the search help. Any field restrictions will be listed first as select-options. By implementing the restrictions as select-options, users already have powerful search capabilities for a single criterion or multiple criteria.

The output of a restricted or unrestricted search will be displayed in a Table element at the bottom of the **General Value List**. The key column of the output table will be a **Link** field, allowing the selected value to be copied back to the source field. Users can also select the row and then click on the **Copy** button.

So what did Russel have to do to get all of this functionality into his application? The good news is that he didn't have to do anything! Figure 12.11 shows the context definition of Russel's component. When he defined the attribute COURSE_ID, he declared it as having the data dictionary type ZCS_COURSE_ID. The Web Dynpro design tools looked up the metadata for the given data dictionary type and found the association to the search help, ZCS_COURSE_SHLP.

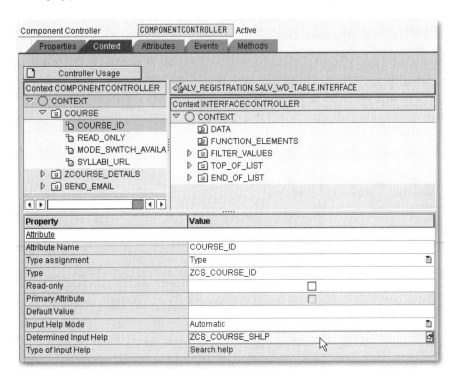

Figure 12.11 Context Attribute Definition of the Used Input Help

Because the search help was determined from the existing data dictionary definitions, the **Input Help Mode** was set to **Automatic**. By changing the value of this field to **Dictionary Search Help**, you can override the data dictionary proposal or define a search help association for a field that doesn't have a data dictionary link.

12.3.2 Required Fields

After seeing how easy it was to build the search help in his application, Russel feels like he's off to a pretty good start. Next, he wants to code some of the input field validations for the basic data maintenance of his university course system. He wants validations in order to ensure that all the required fields have values in them before saving the data to the database. In classic Dynpro, you can set the properties of a screen field to REQUIRED and an automatic message will be triggered on *Process After Input* (PAI) if any field was not filled in.

Web Dynpro ABAP offers a slightly different approach. Instead of the framework automatically checking the required fields, a helper method does the checking. This gives the application developer more freedom to control how and when the checking is done, without having to code the technical details of the checks themselves.

As Figure 12.12 shows, the end result for the user is relatively the same. A message is generated and placed into the Message Area (*Fill in all required entry fields*). Also, all required fields that generated the message are highlighted. Clicking on the error message will position the cursor on the first required field without a value in it.

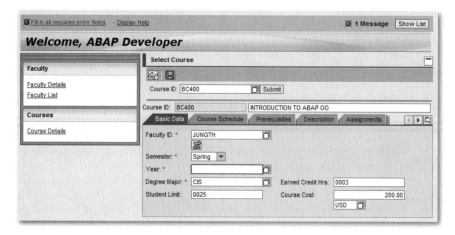

Figure 12.12 Required Field Check

There are two parts to creating a required field:

▶ First, in the **Layout tab**, as Russel is creating the UI elements for his application, he needs to set the **state** property of the InputField to **required** (see Figure 12.13). This will cause the red asterisk to be rendered at the end of the connected field label, signifying that this is a required field. It will also make the field available to the Web Dynpro utility for checking mandatory fields.

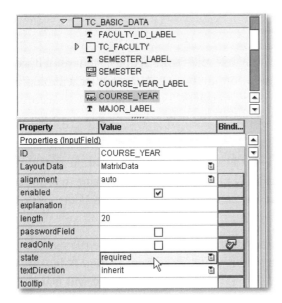

Figure 12.13 Required Field UI Property

▶ Now Russel needs a call to the Web Dynpro helper method to actually perform the validation check. Setting the field property alone will do nothing but render the asterisk.

Russel could place the coding in any of the standard action handler methods (see Listing 12.2). He chooses to use the WDDoBeforeAction event handler. This event handler is called before any of the other action event handlers.

```
METHOD wddobeforeaction .
  DATA: node_course        TYPE REF TO if_wd_context_node,
        elem_course        TYPE REF TO if_wd_context_element,
        stru_course        TYPE if_v_details=>element_course ,
        item_read_only     LIKE stru_course-read_only.
  node_course = wd_context->get_child_node(
      name = if_v_details=>wdctx_course ).
```

```
elem_course = node_course->get_element( ).
elem_course->get_attribute(
  EXPORTING  name =  `READ_ONLY`
  IMPORTING  value = item_read_only ).
CHECK item_read_only NE abap_true.
DATA l_view_controller TYPE REF TO if_wd_view_controller.
l_view_controller = wd_this->wd_get_api( ).
cl_wd_dynamic_tool=>check_mandatory_attr_on_view(
    view_controller = l_view_controller ).
ENDMETHOD.
```
Listing 12.2 Required Field Validation

In other words, if he has separate save and create actions, he doesn't have to link them both to the validation routine because this handler will be called before either of them. Any error messages issued within the WDDoBefore-Action event handler will keep processing from continuing to the other handlers.

For the logic, he first wants to read from the context to see if the application is in display mode. If it is in display mode, there is no real value in producing an error message that should never really occur; and even if the error did occur, the user couldn't correct it.

Finally, Russel gets access to the view's controller object. He then passes this instance into the Web Dynpro utility for checking mandatory fields, CL_WD_DYNAMIC_TOOL=>CHECK_MANDATORY_ATTR_ON_VIEW. This utility will manage all of the remaining work, including the issuing of any error messages.

You might be looking at the large block of coding at the beginning of the method in Listing 12.2 that Russel used to read the context. Although the logic for navigating through the context to read an attribute is not difficult, it can be a bit verbose. But, as it turns out, Russel didn't have to write all the code manually. There are a series of very helpful code generation wizards in Web Dynpro ABAP (see Figure 12.14). They can be accessed by clicking on the **Wizard** icon that appears on the ABAP Workbench toolbar in the coding window of a Web Dynpro method. You can also access these wizards via the menu path **Edit • Web Dynpro Code Wizard**.

These wizards are especially helpful when reading from the context. Choosing the **Read Context** wizard will bring up a screen with the graphical representation of the context. Then, all you have to do is double-click on the level of the context that you want to access. All of the code is generated and inserted into the method.

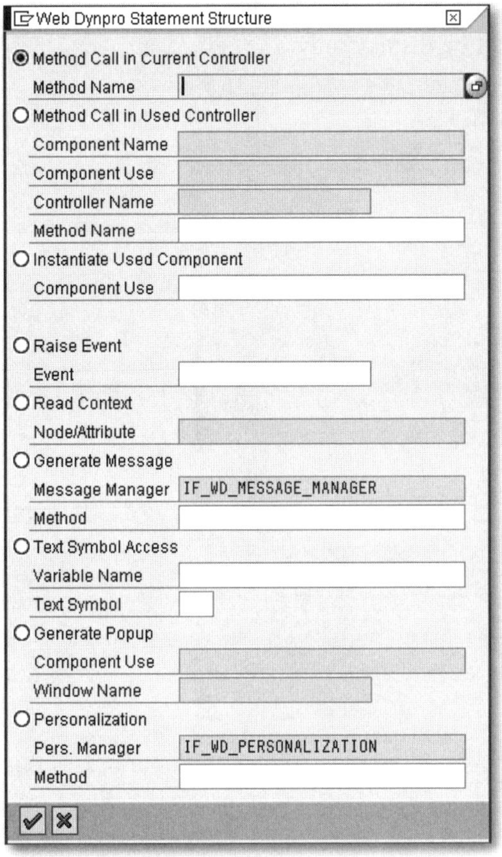

Figure 12.14 Web Dynpro ABAP Code Wizards

12.3.3 Change/Display Mode

Switching between change and display mode is another area where Web Dynpro offers some nice improvements over the mechanisms in classic Dynpro. In classic Dynpro, you could create screen groups to simplify the process, but you still had the cumbersome activity of looping through the screen elements in order to individually set their ready for input status.

Web Dynpro ABAP takes advantage of the UI element ability to bind properties to context attributes. A developer only needs to update a value of a context attribute, and all UI elements bound to that attribute will automatically adjust their status. Russel decides to create a single context attribute, READ_ ONLY, which controls his ready for input status on all of his UI elements (see Figure 12.15). He declares this attribute as WDY_BOOLEAN with a default value of true (**X** as shown in the **Value** column is the boolean value for TRUE in ABAP) since his default mode will be display only.

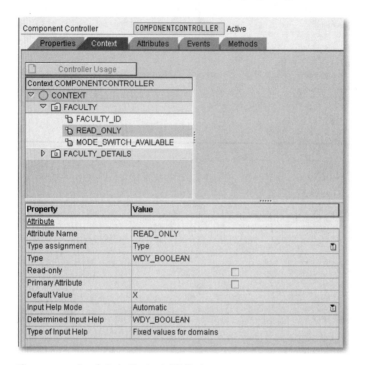

Figure 12.15 Read-Only Context Attribute

The ABAP coding that controls the switch between modes never has to interact with any of the UI elements. In fact, this logic doesn't really care which, if any, UI elements are even responding to the mode switch. All this logic needs to concern itself with is the changing of the value of the context attribute. Thanks to the code wizard, it only takes Russel about 1 minute to create the coding for this method (see Listing 12.3), since it primarily involves updating the context attribute.

```
METHOD set_read_only_mode .
  DATA: node_faculty  TYPE REF TO if_wd_context_node,
  elem_faculty   TYPE REF TO if_wd_context_element,
  stru_faculty   TYPE if_componentcontroller=>element_faculty ,
  item_read_only LIKE stru_faculty-read_only.
  node_faculty = wd_context->get_child_node(
    name = if_componentcontroller=>wdctx_faculty ).
  elem_faculty = node_faculty->get_element(  ).
  item_read_only = i_read_only.
```

```
elem_faculty->set_attribute(
  EXPORTING  name =  `READ_ONLY`
             value = item_read_only ).
IF i_read_only = abap_true.
  wd_this->read_details( ).
ENDIF.
ENDMETHOD.
```

Listing 12.3 Read-Only Mode Switch Method

So, all that remains now is to set the individual UI elements to use this context attribute as their binding. Russel double-clicks on the button in the **Binding** column of the property box for the property **readOnly**. This launches another graphical representation of the context (see Figure 12.16) that is similar to the code wizard. Russel just has to double-click on the attribute and the binding string will be inserted into the property value.

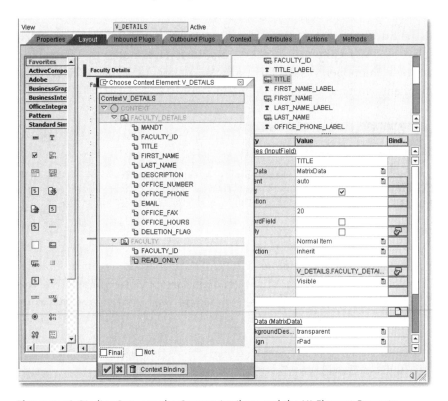

Figure 12.16 Binding Between the Context Attribute and the UI Element Property

In Russel's example, he used one attribute to control all of his UI elements. However, if he wanted, he could simulate the functionality of the screen groups from classic Dynpro by defining multiple context attributes that could be controlled separately.

12.4 ALV Component

Russel has become quite comfortable with programming reports using the ALV technology. Before the upgrade, Russel had written a lot of custom programs, which used the function module REUSE_ALV_GRID_DISPLAY, as well as some programs that used the class CL_GUI_ALV_GRID. The ALV tool provides a lot of functionality to the user, while requiring little programming effort from the developer. Realizing this fact, SAP has brought this technology to Web Dynpro ABAP via a reusable component SALV_WD_TABLE.

12.4.1 ALV Component Usage

Let's take a closer look at the ZCS_COURSE_FACULTY_LST component, which displays a list of faculty members in ALV format. First, notice that Russel has declared a component usage for the ALV component in the Web Dynpro component overview screen as shown in Figure 12.17.

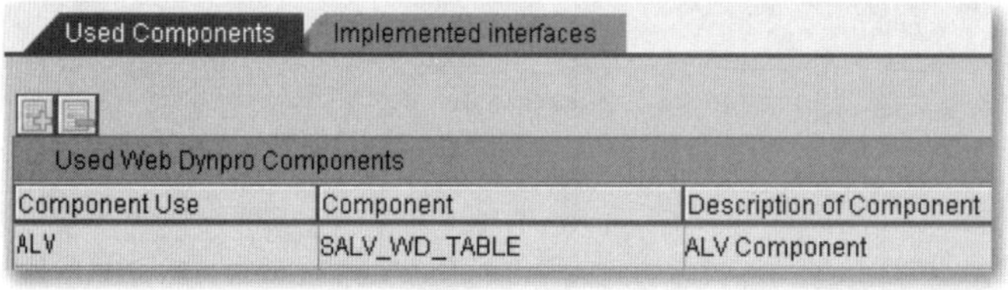

Figure 12.17 ALV Component Usage

If you navigate to the Component Controller properties screen by double-clicking on the COMPONENTCONTROLLER node in the object tree on the left, you will see that it also defines the used component SALV_WD_TABLE as well as its INTERFACECONTROLLER (see Figure 12.18).

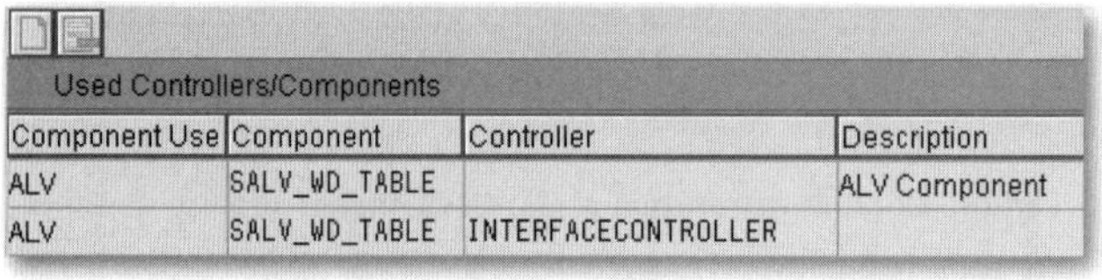

Figure 12.18 Component Controller — Used Components/Controllers

12.4.2 Context Mapping

Russel has also created a context node FACULTY_LIST in the component controller context (see Figure 12.19). This node includes some context attributes taken from the data dictionary table ZCS_FACULTY and has a cardinality of 0..n, or zero to many. This allows for a node that could be bound to an ABAP internal table, yet still allows for the situation where the internal table is empty.

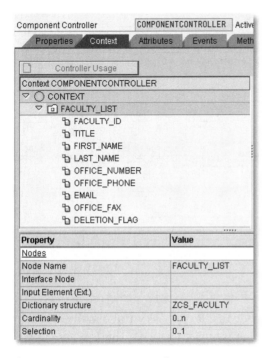

Figure 12.19 Component Controller Context

By double-clicking on the INTERFACECONTROLLER_USAGE node of the ALV component under the **Component Usages** node (see Figure 12.20), we can see the mapping of the DATA context node of the ALV component to the FACULTY_LIST context node of the ZCS_COURSE_FACULTY_LST component (see Figure 12.21). This provides a link between the data of the FACULTY_LIST context node and the columns of the ALV component.

Figure 12.20 Component Usages

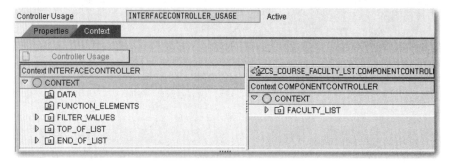

Figure 12.21 ALV Interface Controller

12.4.3 ALV Implementation

Finally we can take a look at the code that Russel has written in the WDDOINIT method of the component controller (see Listing 12.4). This is where Russel has used the assistance class to retrieve the faculty data and has bound this data to the FACULTY_LIST context node.

```
DATA faculty_listing TYPE STANDARD TABLE OF zcs_faculty.
DATA x_faculty      TYPE REF TO zcx_cs_faculty.
TRY.
  faculty_listing = wd_assist->read_faculty_listing( ).
  CATCH zcx_cs_faculty INTO x_faculty.

  DATA: l_current_controller TYPE REF TO if_wd_controller,
       l_message_manager TYPE REF TO if_wd_message_manager.
    l_current_controller ?= wd_this->wd_get_api( ).
    l_message_manager =
        l_current_controller->get_message_manager( ).
    l_message_manager->report_exception(
```

```
        message_object            = x_faculty ).
  ENDTRY.

  DATA: node_faculty_list  TYPE REF TO if_wd_context_node.
   node_faculty_list = wd_context->get_child_node(
        name = if_componentcontroller=>wdctx_faculty_list ).

  IF ( node_faculty_list is initial ).
    EXIT.
  ENDIF.
  node_faculty_list->bind_table( faculty_listing ).
```

Listing 12.4 Data Retrieval and Context Binding

Now that Russel has a working ALV list, he can start manipulating the ALV configuration, as well as bring some additional functionality to the output.

▸ Russel has already discovered some advantages to using ALV as opposed to the TableView UI element. The ALV is delivered with the basic functionality of sorting and filtering, which is not the case when working with the table view. There is no need for Russel to code this functionality separately.

▸ Another useful feature is that you can manipulate the ALV by setting the configuration settings. The class CL_SALV_WD_CONFIG_TABLE can be used to set all of these attributes. It implements simple getter and setter methods for manipulating all kinds of ALV attributes, such as showing or hiding certain buttons on the ALV toolbar.

Listing 12.5 shows that Russel is using the configuration class and setting a few attributes. For example, he definitely wants to be able to generate a PDF document with the data from the ALV, so he is sure to set the attribute, using the method SET_PDF_ALLOWED, to show the button on the toolbar.

```
  DATA l_salv_wd_table TYPE REF TO iwci_salv_wd_table.
  l_salv_wd_table = wd_this->wd_cpifc_alv( ).
  DATA l_table TYPE REF TO cl_salv_wd_config_table.
  l_table = l_salv_wd_table->get_model( ).
 l_table->if_salv_wd_std_functions~set_bi_broadcasting_allowed(
    abap_false ).
 l_table->if_salv_wd_std_functions~set_dialog_settings_as_popup(
    abap_true ).
 l_table->if_salv_wd_std_functions~set_graphic_allowed(
    abap_true ).
 l_table->if_salv_wd_std_functions~set_pdf_allowed( abap_true ).
```

Listing 12.5 ALV Configuration

Russel now wants to modify the first column of the ALV output. He wants to make the faculty ID a link, which the user can use to show the faculty details. The class CL_SALV_WD_COLUMN can be used to modify the columns of the ALV. Listing 12.6 shows that Russel simply gets an object of the column and changes the column type from a TextView column to a LinkToAction column via the CL_SALV_WD_UIE_LINK_TO_ACTION class.

```
DATA: lr_column TYPE REF TO cl_salv_wd_column,
      lr_link   TYPE REF TO cl_salv_wd_uie_link_to_action.
lr_column = l_table->if_salv_wd_column_settings~get_column(
      'FACULTY_ID' ).
CREATE OBJECT lr_link.
lr_link->set_text_fieldname( 'FACULTY_ID' ).
lr_column->set_cell_editor( lr_link ).
```
Listing 12.6 ALV Column Settings

Now that the column is of type LinkToAction, the event ONCLICK, which is fired from the ALV component, can be handled in the V_ALV_MAIN view. The ONCLICK event handler method then implements all the logic for retrieving the faculty details based on the faculty ID as well as firing the dialog popup window to display the data. In the next section, the implementation of dialog popup windows will be discussed in detail.

Figure 12.22 shows the final result. Notice that the column headings have up and down arrows. This is the sorting functionality that is automatically provided by the ALV component. Also, the first line with the filter icon is used to filter the data. You can simply enter the value that you want to filter by and press the **Enter** key. This filter row also accepts wildcards.

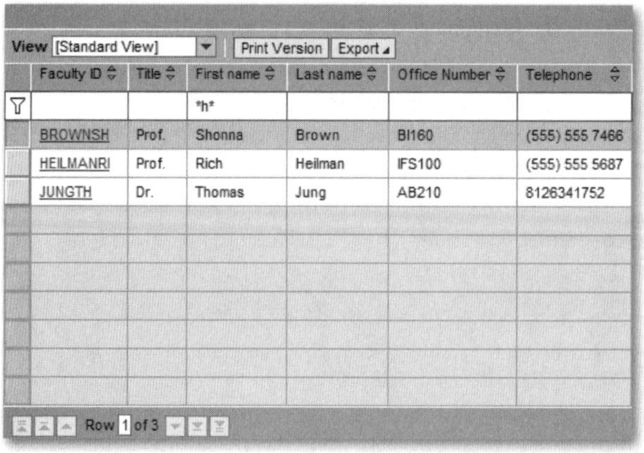

Faculty ID ⇕	Title ⇕	First name ⇕	Last name ⇕	Office Number ⇕	Telephone ⇕
		h			
BROWNSH	Prof.	Shonna	Brown	BI160	(555) 555 7466
HEILMANRI	Prof.	Rich	Heilman	IFS100	(555) 555 5687
JUNGTH	Dr.	Thomas	Jung	AB210	8126341752

Figure 12.22 ALV Output

12.5   Dialog Popup Window

Earlier when we looked at the integration of the search help in Web Dynpro ABAP (see Section 12.3.1), we got our first glimpse of the dialog window. The value help implementation sits in a modal window that can be resized, moved around the screen, and minimized or maximized. But this functionality for dialog popup windows is not limited to just the search help functionality. This is a generic capability of Web Dynpro ABAP that is available to the application developer. Russel plans to use this function in several places within his application.

12.5.1   Windows from the Same Component

There are several ways that you can place content into one of these dialog popup windows. The first way is to reuse content that exists within the same component. It is possible to have multiple windows and views within a component. That is precisely what Russel wants to do in his application. When a user clicks on the **Upload Attachment** button, Russel wants to load a dialog for the process of uploading a file (see Figure 12.23).

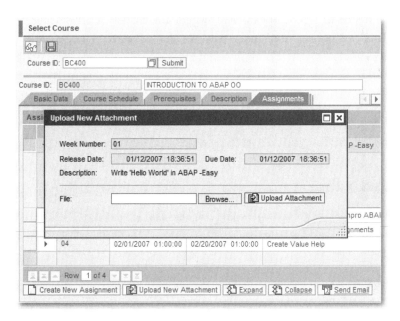

Figure 12.23 Dialog Window Example

The content that appears in the dialog is defined as a separate window, W_NEW_ATTACHMENT, in the same component (see Figure 12.24). Although the main window, W_MAIN_COURSE_DTL, loads with the component and displays the default view, V_DETAILS, these additional windows can be used for alternative displays such as dialog popups.

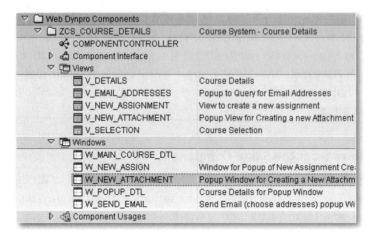

Figure 12.24 Multiple Windows in the Same Component

The easy part was defining a new window with a separate view within it. Now Russel needs to figure out how to trigger the display of this separate window. This can be accomplished easily via the window manager object (see Listing 12.7).

```
METHOD onactionupload_attachment .
  DATA: l_window_manager TYPE REF TO if_wd_window_manager,
        l_cmp_api         TYPE REF TO if_wd_component,
        l_window          TYPE REF TO if_wd_window.
  DATA: l_text_p01 TYPE string.
  l_text_p01 =
    wd_assist->if_wd_component_assistance~get_text( 'P01' ).
  l_cmp_api        = wd_comp_controller->wd_get_api( ).
  l_window_manager = l_cmp_api->get_window_manager( ).
  l_window         = l_window_manager->create_window(
        window_name           = 'W_NEW_ATTACHMENT'
        title                 = l_text_p01
        message_display_mode  =
              if_wd_window=>co_msg_display_mode_selected
        button_kind           = if_wd_window=>co_buttons_none
        message_type          =
              if_wd_window=>co_msg_type_none
        default_button        =
              if_wd_window=>co_button_close ).
```

```
  l_window->open( ).
ENDMETHOD.
```

Listing 12.7 Coding to Launch a New Window

The window manager will create an instance of a new window, given the input criteria that Russel supplies. Since he is using an existing window in the same component, he mainly supplies the window name. The window, in turn, will display its default view. The remaining options are used to control the appearance of the dialog window. The interface, if_wd_window, contains constants for the possible values of most of these options.

That small amount of code was all that was needed to get the dialog window displayed. Once active, the window can be closed via the button supplied by the Web Dynpro ABAP framework, but Russel also wants to be able to programmatically close the dialog as well.

In this case, once the user has clicked on the **Upload Attachment** button, there is no reason for the dialog window to remain open. From the view controller object, Russel can get access to the window controller that the view is currently hosted within. The window controller allows access to the inner window object, which, in turn, is used to close the dialog.

```
METHOD close_popup .
  DATA l_api_v_new_attachment TYPE REF TO if_wd_view_controller.
  l_api_v_new_attachment = wd_this->wd_get_api( ).
  DATA window_controller TYPE REF TO if_wd_window_controller.
  window_controller =
     l_api_v_new_attachment->get_embedding_window_ctlr( ).
  DATA window TYPE REF TO if_wd_window.
  window = window_controller->get_window( ).
  window->close( ).
ENDMETHOD.
```

Listing 12.8 Programmatically Closing the Window

12.5.2 Windows from an External Component Usage

Obviously, you would not want to be limited to only accessing windows in your own component for dialogs. Part of the power of component reuse is that it gives you the ability to create small, autonomous user interface building blocks that can be combined in different ways. Dialogs support this reuse by having an easy method to also embed external components via their component usage.

If you recall, Russel's application has two places where the faculty details can be displayed in one of these dialog popup windows; however, faculty details is a separate component from both the faculty list component and the course details component, where these dialogs are triggered (see Figure 12.2, Figure 12.3, and Figure 12.5).

1. First, the component that is going to host the dialog popup needs to declare a component usage for the inner component, which will be placed within the popup (see Figure 12.25).

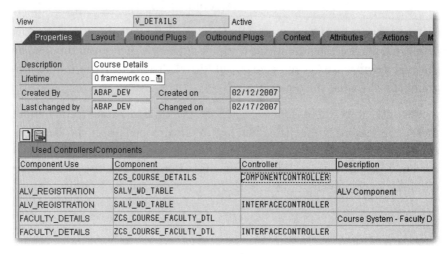

View		V_DETAILS		Active			

Properties | Layout | Inbound Plugs | Outbound Plugs | Context | Attributes | Actions | M

Description	Course Details
Lifetime	0 framework co...
Created By	ABAP_DEV	Created on	02/12/2007
Last changed by	ABAP_DEV	Changed on	02/17/2007

Used Controllers/Components

Component Use	Component	Controller	Description
	ZCS_COURSE_DETAILS	COMPONENTCONTROLLER	
ALV_REGISTRATION	SALV_WD_TABLE		ALV Component
ALV_REGISTRATION	SALV_WD_TABLE	INTERFACECONTROLLER	
FACULTY_DETAILS	ZCS_COURSE_FACULTY_DTL		Course System - Faculty D
FACULTY_DETAILS	ZCS_COURSE_FACULTY_DTL	INTERFACECONTROLLER	

Figure 12.25 Definition of the Component Usage of the Faculty Details within the Course Details

2. Next Russel has to code the logic to launch the popup dialog. This example is going to be somewhat different from the previous examples, because he needs some way to pass some initial data into the component usage that will be in the dialog window.

He is displaying the faculty details, so he will need to pass the desired faculty ID from the current component into the inner component usage. Therefore, he begins the coding by reading the local component's context to get the selected faculty ID:

```
METHOD onactiondisplay_faculty_dtl .
  DATA: node_zcourse_details TYPE REF TO
          if_wd_context_node,
        elem_zcourse_details TYPE REF TO
          if_wd_context_element,
        stru_zcourse_details TYPE
          if_v_details=>element_zcourse_details ,
```

```
        item_faculty_id LIKE
          stru_zcourse_details-faculty_id.
  node_zcourse_details = wd_context->get_child_node(
        name = if_v_details=>wdctx_zcourse_details ).
  elem_zcourse_details =
    node_zcourse_details->get_element( ).
  elem_zcourse_details->get_attribute(
    EXPORTING   name = `FACULTY_ID`
    IMPORTING   value = item_faculty_id ).
```

3. Next Russel codes the process to initialize the faculty details component. He first queries his current component to get the reference to the component usage for the faculty details. The method WD_CPUSE_FACULTY_DETAILS is generated as part of the component class based on whatever you specify as the component usage name (see Figure 12.25 to see where the component usage name is specified).

```
DATA: l_ref_cmp_usage TYPE REF TO if_wd_component_usage.
l_ref_cmp_usage =   wd_this->wd_cpuse_faculty_details( ).
```

4. Once Russel has a reference to the component usage, he then needs to verify whether the usage has an active component. In other words, the component usage is just a way of accessing another component. Having a component usage does not immediately create an instance of the component objects for that usage. Therefore, before you access the actual component of a component usage, you should always check to see if the instance exists, yet via the HAS_ACTIVE_COMPONENT method.

5. If the inner component has already been initialized somewhere else during the application flow, then the logic can just move on. Otherwise, it needs to create an instance of the component via the CREATE_COMPONENT method:

```
IF l_ref_cmp_usage->has_active_component( ) IS INITIAL.
  l_ref_cmp_usage->create_component( ).
ENDIF.
```

6. Every component automatically generates a component interface. This interface is what exposes context nodes and methods of the component controller to the outside world. In this case, Russel has designed his faculty details component with external usages in mind. He has declared a special interface method (as you will see in Figure 12.27), called EXTERNAL_INITIALIZATION, as part of the faculty details component. This method can now be accessed from either the faculty list component or the course

details component to pass in the faculty ID that needs to be displayed in the faculty details component:

```
DATA: l_ref_interfacecontroller
        TYPE REF TO ziwci_cs_course_faculty_dtl .
l_ref_interfacecontroller =
        wd_this->wd_cpifc_faculty_details( ).
l_ref_interfacecontroller->external_initialization(
        faculty_id = item_faculty_id ).
```

7. Like the local window example that we looked at previously, he will still use the window manager to create the window. But this time, he will use a different method, CREATE_WINDOW_FOR_CMP_USAGE, which is designed for this external scenario. He must pass in the component usage name, in addition to which window he wants to have initially displayed (see Listing 12.9).

```
DATA: l_window_manager TYPE REF TO if_wd_window_manager,
      l_cmp_api         TYPE REF TO if_wd_component,
      l_window          TYPE REF TO if_wd_window.
DATA: l_text_t01 TYPE string.
l_text_t01 =
  wd_assist->if_wd_component_assistance~get_text( 'T01' ).
l_cmp_api        = wd_comp_controller->wd_get_api( ).
l_window_manager = l_cmp_api->get_window_manager( ).
l_window = l_window_manager->create_window_for_cmp_usage(
                interface_view_name    = 'W_POPUP_DTL'
                component_usage_name   = 'FACULTY_DETAILS'
                title                  = l_text_t01
                message_display_mode   =
            if_wd_window=>co_msg_display_mode_selected ).
l_window->open( ).
ENDMETHOD.
```

Listing 12.9 Code to Open a Window from Another Component

Now that you have seen the process that Russel took to initialize the external component within the dialog window, let's look at the aspects of the hosted component, ZCS_COURSE_FACULTY_DTL, that were designed in advance to support this scenario.

▸ First, there was the design of the secondary window, W_POPUP_DTL. The main window hosts both views: V_DETAILS and V_SELECTION (see Figure 12.2). By breaking up the **Faculty ID** selection and the resulting detail fields into two separate views, Russel has managed to give himself a lot of flexibility.

▶ In the dialog popup, there is no reason to display the selection fields. The faculty ID key will be passed into the component from the calling component. In fact, Russel only wants his faculty details dialog to be display only, so he doesn't want the save button or the mode switch options.

▶ He can easily reuse just the details view by using the second window of the component and embedding only the single view that he needs (see Figure 12.26).

Figure 12.26 Faculty Detail Component with a Special Window for External Use

▶ The only remaining step for Russel's component reuse scenario is to add the interface method. Any method added to a component can be exposed via the component interface simply by checking the **Interface** option in the **Methods** tab (see Figure 12.27).

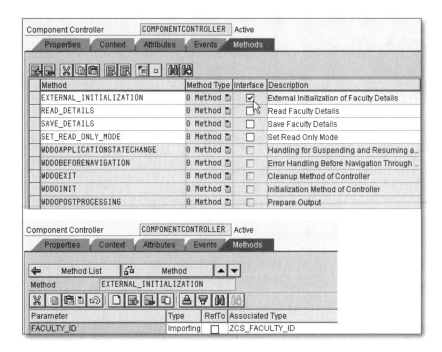

Figure 12.27 Component Controller Interface Method

12.6 Table Popins

The most visually complex section of Russel's application is undoubtedly the **Assignments** tab. In this tab, Russel has a Table UI element to display each of the assignment weeks; however, for each week there can be multiple file attachments.

12.6.1 What Is a Table Popin?

Traditionally, he might have considered using a tree UI element to accomplish this data layout, but Russel saw an example of the TablePopin element in one of SAP's delivered Web Dynpro applications. It was in LORD_MAINTAIN, the Web Dynpro ABAP version of the Sales Order Entry transactions VA01, VA02, VA03. SAP has used the table popin to display multiple scheduling details for schedule lines that have split requirements.

After examining the SAP examples, Russel sees this approach as an opportunity to design an inner table within each row of his main table (see Figure 12.28). When Russel looks at the finished product, he is amazed that creating this table popin was relatively simple. Initially, he expected that implementing such a complex UI construct would be rather difficult.

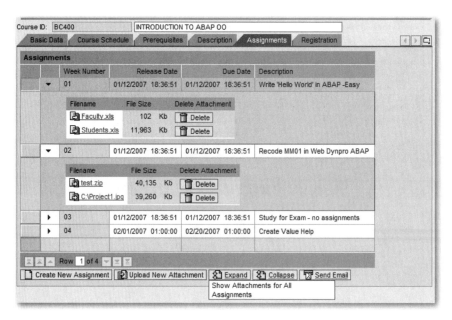

Figure 12.28 Example of a Table Popin

12.6.2 Designing the Table Popin

Russel starts out by creating his main table.

1. He fully defines the data binding, and then designs each of the columns. He even tests the first version of the table with just the assignment week-level data before he begins to build his table popin.

2. Now he is ready to add the popin to his existing table. He just has to right-mouse click on the table element in the View Designer. The context menu provides all the elements that can be added to a standard table element. He chooses **Insert Table Popin** (see Figure 12.29).

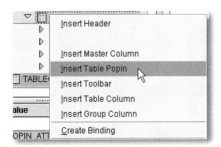

Figure 12.29 Insert a New Table Popin

This creates a subelement that will live within the definition of the main table. The TablePopin element that Russel has added is basically a blank canvas. When he right-mouse clicks on this element, there is a menu option to **Insert Content**. This means that you can assign only one UI element within a popin.

3. This isn't really a problem, however, even though Russel wants to display an entire inner table. He adds a TransparentContainer, named TC_POPIN_CONTENT, as his single content item. He can add whatever grouping of inner UI elements that he wants to the TransparentContainer (see Figure 12.30).

4. He does make one other addition. He returns to the main table definition and adds one more column. This declares this column as the special type TablePopinToggleCell. This is what generates the column with an arrow in it, which allows the user to expand or collapse the display of the popin.

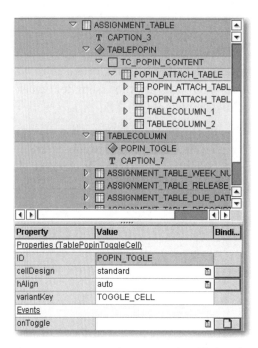

Figure 12.30 Popin and Popin Toggle Added to the Table Element

12.6.3 Context Design

It might seem like the data population of the popin inner table would be complex. Actually, thanks to the robust nature of the context design, it turns out to be really simple. Russel just has to define a nested structure within his context. Each element of the COURSE_ASSIGN context node will have a subnode called COURSE_ASS_ATT (see Figure 12.31).

Normally, this nesting of nodes would not create the structure needed to keep a separate selection of course assignment attachment records per course assignment, but Russel has unchecked the **Singleton** property on the COURSE_ASS_ATT node. This option creates a new instance of the COURSE_ASS_ATT node for each element in the higher level node. In traditional ABAP constructs, this is like nesting an internal table as a cell within a higher level internal table.

Because of the context structure that Russel has defined, he only has to bind his highest level table to the COURSE_ASSIGN node. Then, the inner table within the popin will be bound to the COURSE_ASS_ATT node. Without having to write a single line of code to keep the two levels of tables in sync, the relationships defined within the context will do all the work of presenting the correct assignment attachments for each week's popin.

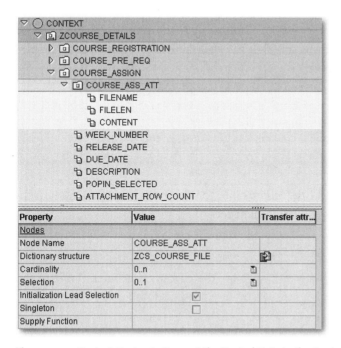

Figure 12.31 Context Design to Support the Nested Data in the Popin

Because of the context structure that Russel has defined, he only has to bind his highest level table to the COURSE_ASSIGN node. Then, the inner table within the popin will be bound to the COURSE_ASS_ATT node. Without having to write a single line of code to keep the two levels of tables in sync, the relationships defined within the context will do all the work of presenting the correct assignment attachments for each week's popin.

12.6.4 Logic to Populate the Context for a Popin

The coding to populate the nested contexts is only slightly complicated by the change to the **Singleton** node type.

1. The model class method that reads the data will return the assignment records with the attachments as a nested internal table. The course assignments can be directly bound to the COURSE_ASSIGN node:

```
node_course_assign =
  node_zcourse_details->get_child_node(
```

```
    name = if_componentcontroller=>wdctx_course_assign ).
  node_course_assign->bind_table( course_ass_att ).
```

2. To populate the inner node, Russel has to first loop through the elements of the COURSE_ASSIGN node. This is done by requesting an element set from the node. The element set is an internal table where each row is an element object instance:

```
DATA: element_set TYPE wdr_context_element_set.
FIELD-SYMBOLS: <wa_set> LIKE LINE OF element_set,
               <wa_ass> LIKE LINE OF course_ass_att.
element_set = node_course_assign->get_elements( ).
DATA node_course_ass_att TYPE REF TO if_wd_context_node.
LOOP AT element_set ASSIGNING <wa_set>.
```

3. Russel can then read the inner table for the course assignments attachments from the course assignment record:

```
READ TABLE course_ass_att INDEX sy-tabix
  ASSIGNING <wa_ass>.
```

4. Finally he performs a BIND_TABLE for the current attachment table to the instance of the COURSE_ASS_ATT node within his loop:

```
node_course_ass_att = <wa_set>->get_child_node(
  name = if_componentcontroller=>wdctx_course_ass_att ).
node_course_ass_att->bind_table( <wa_ass>-attachments ).
ENDLOOP.
```

12.7   File Upload/Download

We have already seen that in the maintenance screen of the course details there are options to download course assignment attachments, as well as the ability to upload new attachments (see Figure 12.28). These are important aspects of the application and certainly worth a closer examination.

12.7.1   File Downloads

There are two ways to download a file in Web Dynpro ABAP:

▶ The first option involves a dedicated FileDownload UI element. Bind this UI element to context nodes that contain the MIME type and binary content for the file that you want to download, and it will do the rest of the work for you.

▶ Russel, however, chooses to go with the second option. He will use a utility method of the Web Dynpro ABAP framework to attach content directly to the response object. This approach gives you greater flexibility in coding so you can determine how the download will work.

1. Before Russel can trigger the download code, however, he needs a UI element. In the table that lists the course assignment attachments, he has defined one of the columns with the `LinkToAction` cell type. This will create hyperlinked text that can trigger the server side event, `DOWNLOAD_ATTACHMENT` (see Figure 12.32).

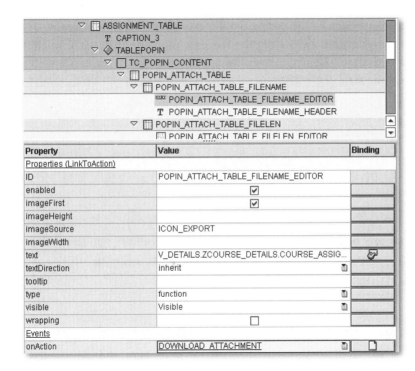

Figure 12.32 LinkToAction for the File Download

2. The coding of the event handler for this action begins by using the method input parameter, `WDEVENT`, to read the context element that is associated with the action. This makes it easy to determine which data was the selected item that the user wants to download.

```
METHOD onactiondownload_attachment .
  DATA: elem_course_ass_att TYPE REF TO
          if_wd_context_element,
        stru_course_ass_att
```

```
          TYPE if_v_details=>element_course_ass_att.
elem_course_ass_att = wdevent->get_context_element(
        `CONTEXT_ELEMENT` ).
IF ( elem_course_ass_att IS INITIAL ).
  EXIT.
ENDIF.
elem_course_ass_att->get_static_attributes(
   IMPORTING   static_attributes = stru_course_ass_att ).
```

3. The business data for a course assignment attachment stores only the full filename. In order for a browser to know what application needs to be used to open a file attachment, it needs a MIME type. Luckily, the MIME type can be determined using the file extension. Russel first needs to split the full filename away from the file extension. He uses what he already learned about Regular Expressions (see Section 6.5) to easily split the filename string:

```
DATA dot_offset TYPE i.
DATA extension TYPE mimetypes-extension.
DATA mimetype TYPE mimetypes-type.
FIND FIRST OCCURRENCE OF REGEX '\.[^\.]+$'
   IN stru_course_ass_att-filename
     MATCH OFFSET dot_offset.
ADD 1 TO dot_offset.
extension = stru_course_ass_att-filename+dot_offset.
```

Now that he has just the file extension, he can call the standard SAP function module, SDOK_MIMETYPE_GET, to perform the mapping:

```
CALL FUNCTION 'SDOK_MIMETYPE_GET'
   EXPORTING   extension = extension
   IMPORTING   mimetype  = mimetype.
```

4. Finally, the Web Dynpro Runtime Services method, ATTACH_FILE_TO_ RESPONSE, is used to prepare the content for download:

```
data l_mimetype type string.
l_mimetype = mimetype.
cl_wd_runtime_services=>attach_file_to_response(
     i_filename      = stru_course_ass_att-filename
     i_content       = stru_course_ass_att-content
     i_mime_type     = l_mimetype
*    i_in_new_window = abap_false
*    i_inplace       = abap_false
        ).
ENDMETHOD.
```

12.7.2 File Uploads

For the file upload, the only choice is to use the `FileUpload` UI element. This element allows data binding for retrieval of the file content, as binary string, and the filename.

1. The **Browse** button is generated by the `FileUpload` element and allows for searching for a single file to use in the upload process (see Figure 12.33).

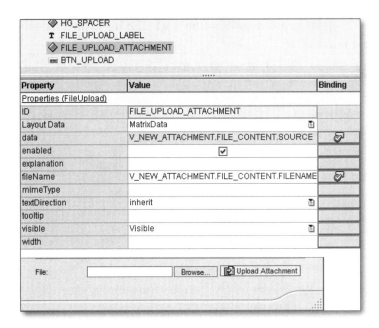

Figure 12.33 File Upload UI Definition and Corresponding Output

2. A `FileUpload` element is designed to bring back any content specified with the response object during any server request. Therefore, there is no action that can be attached directly to the `FileUpload` element. Consequently, Russel just has to add his own button following the `FileUpload` element, and code his file upload processing within an action tied to this button.

The content from the `FileUpload` has automatically been loaded into the bound context attributes. Therefore, Russel needs to start his processing logic by reading from the context:

```
METHOD onactionupload_attachment .
  DATA: node_file_content TYPE REF TO if_wd_context_node,
    elem_file_content TYPE REF TO if_wd_context_element,
    stru_file_content
```

```
        TYPE if_v_new_attachment=>element_file_content .
   node_file_content = wd_context->get_child_node(
      name = if_v_new_attachment=>wdctx_file_content ).
   elem_file_content = node_file_content->get_element(  ).
   elem_file_content->get_static_attributes(
      IMPORTING static_attributes = stru_file_content ).
```

3. Russel had declared a local context structure just for the upload view. This kept the data binding for the FileUpload UI element simple. Now that he has uploaded content, he needs to map this back into his main data controller context nodes:

```
DATA: node_course_assign  TYPE REF TO if_wd_context_node,
      elem_course_assign  TYPE REF TO
       if_wd_context_element,
      node_course_ass_att TYPE REF TO if_wd_context_node,
      elem_course_ass_att TYPE REF TO
       if_wd_context_element,
      stru_course_ass_att
        TYPE if_v_new_attachment=>element_course_ass_att .
   node_course_assign = wd_context->get_child_node(
      name = if_v_new_attachment=>wdctx_course_assign ).
   IF ( node_course_assign IS INITIAL ).
     EXIT.
   ENDIF.
   elem_course_assign = node_course_assign->get_element(  ).
   node_course_ass_att = node_course_assign->get_child_node(
      name = if_v_new_attachment=>wdctx_course_ass_att ).
   IF ( node_course_ass_att IS INITIAL ).
     EXIT.
   ENDIF.
```

4. For the new content, Russel creates a new element within the COURSE_ASS_ ATT node via the BIND_ELEMENT method:

```
CHECK stru_file_content-source IS NOT INITIAL.
MOVE stru_file_content-source
     TO stru_course_ass_att-content.
stru_course_ass_att-filelen = XSTRLEN(
   stru_course_ass_att-content ).
MOVE stru_file_content-filename
   TO stru_course_ass_att-filename.
node_course_ass_att->bind_element(
   new_item = stru_course_ass_att
   set_initial_elements = abap_false ).
```

5. He then wants to expand the popin of the corresponding row so that the newly uploaded file will be displayed in the assignments table:

```
elem_course_assign->set_attribute(
  EXPORTING name =  `POPIN_SELECTED`
            value = `TABLEPOPIN` ).
```

6. The file upload view was displayed within a dialog window. Now that the content has been uploaded and processed, there is no reason to keep this dialog window open:

```
  wd_this->close_popup( ).
ENDMETHOD.
```

12.8   Web Dynpro Debugger

Web Dynpro ABAP has another important feature. When debugging a Web Dynpro application, the *ABAP Debugger* has an additional view that can be used to analyze all attributes of the Web Dynpro component, including the view context and layout.

1. Once in debug mode, choose the **New Tool** icon as show in Figure 12.34.

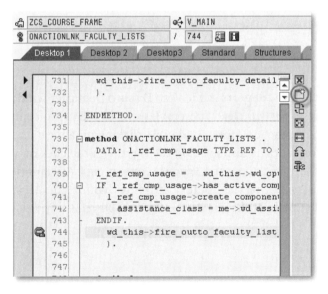

Figure 12.34 ABAP Debugger

2. The **New Tool** dialog opens, which gives you access to various tools within the Debugger (see Figure 12.35). Under the **Special Tools** node, double-click on **Web Dynpro**.

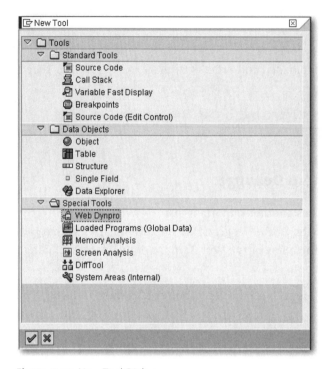

Figure 12.35 New Tool Dialog

3. The new debugging view appears in the Web Dynpro Debugger window. The tree structure to the left clearly resembles the Web Dynpro component structure in transaction SE80. By double-clicking on a view on the left, the view information is displayed on the right. You can click on various tabs in the view, including the **Layout**, **Context**, and **Attributes**. In Figure 12.36, the values of the context attributes within the GLOBAL_ATTRIBUTES context node of the V_MAIN view are displayed.

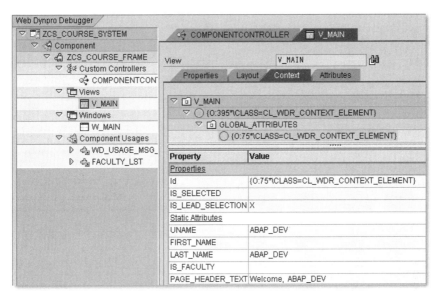

Figure 12.36 Web Dynpro Debugger

Business Server Pages is a technology that was introduced with SAP Web AS 6.10 to offer a similar server-side web page scripting environment to ASP and JSP, only utilizing the ABAP language. Turning away from the idea of the Internet Transaction Server and its external web server, BSP first brought true web page creation capabilities to ABAP. Russel will explore this tool as he develops the external facing part of the university course system user interface.

13   Business Server Pages

You might ask where *Business Server Pages* (BSP) fits in with all the other ABAP UI technologies that you have seen so far in this book. After all, Russel just finished building some fairly impressive Web Dynpro ABAP applications that run in the browser.

It's true that Web Dynpro ABAP will become the primary user interface for the majority of ABAP applications. These applications are generally replacements or enhancements to the existing business transactions, and Web Dynpro ABAP is well suited to their design. Web Dynpro is always stateful, making the programming model very similar to what developers are used to when creating business transactions. Also, the rendering abstraction layer means that developers can focus on the business coding and user interface design without having to use or even learn HTML or JavaScript. They also don't have to worry about creating a unique look and feel for each application since the design is delivered as part of the Web Dynpro ABAP framework.

Nevertheless, these very strengths that make Web Dynpro ABAP the perfect tool for building business transactions also make it inappropriate for certain other types of applications. This is where BSP makes an excellent addition to any ABAP developer's toolset. Unlike Web Dynpro ABAP, BSP applications can be either *stateful* or *stateless*. This makes BSP appropriate for very light pages that must scale to a large number of simultaneous users. BSP is also completely web page centric, which means that there is no client abstraction, as in Web Dynpro ABAP, thereby giving developers complete freedom to innovate and create custom designs and use all the latest techniques in HTML and JavaScript, such as AJAX (*Asynchronous JavaScript and XML*).

These are precisely the kinds of strong points that Russel plans to take advantage of in the next phase of his project. He has reached the phase of the project where he must begin to build the Internet facing section of the university course system.

> **Note**
>
> The area of BSP development is a vast subject. There have been entire volumes of work devoted just to this topic. Therefore, it doesn't make sense to try and rehash any of the basic topics that have already been covered in other sources. Instead, we have opted to continue with the theme of this book and focus on the application of BSP in real world scenarios.
>
> We assume that you will already be familiar with the basic constructs of BSP such as page layout, page events, MVC, and BSP extensions. This allows us to channel our energy into sharing new techniques with you, our readers, for putting these core elements to use.

13.1 Internet Facing BSP Application

Russel is ready to undertake the job of creating the Internet facing section of his application. His requirements are to create web pages that can be accessed on the Internet, which have a similar look and feel to the existing university Internet website. The purpose of these web pages will be to list the course offerings and the details about each course. Potential students for these courses will use this site as a course catalog in which they can then register for a particular course.

13.1.1 Stateless versus Stateful

The first decision that Russel must make is whether he wants his application to be *stateful* or *stateless*. Before he can arrive at the best choice, it is important to understand something about how web browsers and HTTP work at a low level:

▶ Internet browsers and the web servers that supply the content that they display are inherently disconnected. When you're on the web and attempt to a load a page, your browser sends an HTTP Request to the appropriate server.

► The web server processes this request and then sends back an HTTP Response that contains the content the browser will display. After sending the response back to the client, the web server basically forgets about that particular client and releases any resources needed to process the request.

► A user may view a particular web page for five seconds or five hours. During that time, the browser has no connection to the server that provided the content. When the user causes an event to occur in the page that needs more data from the server, a new request is sent.

► The server doesn't remember anything about this client however, so the request will need to include any relevant data that is carried over from the previous step. The server may also have to repeat certain processing steps, such as reading data from the database that was already performed in the previous step.

It is this mechanism that allows large Internet sites to scale to thousands or even millions of simultaneous users. Only enough hardware on the servers is needed to process the individual requests.

Business applications, like SAP ERP, have traditionally taken a different approach because they have tightly connected clients that can utilize a stateful mechanism. If the SAP GUI disconnects or the user closes it, the server knows right away that this connection is gone and can close the corresponding session on the server. This makes business transactions operate more efficiently, because related data can be loaded just once at the beginning of the transactions. It also makes managing locks in the database very easy, because the lock lifetime can be tied to the session lifetime. The downside is that if a user goes to lunch without exiting an application, all the memory on the server for that session will continue to be held in memory.

Russel decides that a *stateless* approach would best meet the requirements of the particular website that he is creating:

► There will be very little business logic in these pages. The logic that is present will be read-only access to the course data. That means there will be no database locks to manage.

► Also he can utilize the shared memory object that is part of his course business object (see Chapter 5), and table buffering (see Chapter 2), to ensure that he is getting maximum efficiency for the reads of the course data. The course shared memory object will cache all the course data in memory once, and then each stateless page request can read the data from that memory cache instead of returning to the database. Likewise, the table buffering settings on the Degree Majors tables, ZCS_MAJORS and ZCS_MAJORS_T, will ensure that redundant reads caused by the stateless setting will be performed on the buffered data in memory and not sent to the database.

In BSP, it is relatively simple to control whether or not an application is stateful — see the **Stateful** checkbox on the **Properties** tab of the BSP application as shown in Figure 13.1.

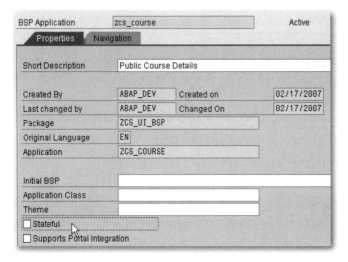

Figure 13.1 BSP Application Properties: Stateful Setting

13.1.2 Application Layout

Russel begins the process of building the first page of his application. Although stateless, he will still follow the Model View Controller (MVC) design paradigm for his application. He therefore creates the default.do controller as the entry point into this application. This will be the main page that contains links to other pages and has some static content, such as news items about the university's new course offerings.

This page will contain only static content, so there is no need to have any logic that links to the model class. The controller in this case, default.do, is also quite simple. Although there are currently no events handled by this controller, it is still a good idea to put in the DISPATCH_INPUT method call and navigation logic that is needed to process events in a high level controller. There is also no branching logic to process, so the controller only needs to link to the single view, default.bsp, which will be displayed with this controller:

```
DATA: view TYPE REF TO if_bsp_page.
dispatch_input( ).
IF is_navigation_requested( ) IS NOT INITIAL.
  RETURN.
ENDIF.
view = create_view( view_name = 'default.bsp' ).
call_view( view ).
```

The view, default.bsp, will contain all the visualization for this page. This page will be static content so it will only have HTML, images, and a style sheet. All of these objects are uploaded from the developers' machines and stored with the BSP application on the ABAP server (see Figure 13.2). Also, these images and style sheet objects are included in the development transport (and for the reader, they are also contained on the CD that accompanies this book), so they are easily migrated through the development landscape like any other objects.

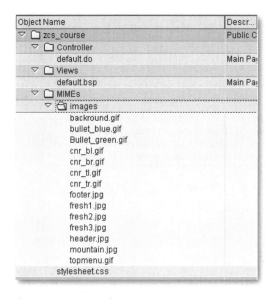

Figure 13.2 BSP Application Contents

13.1.3 Custom Style Sheets

Russel inserts his static content into the layout of the view and runs the first test of his application (see Figure 13.3). This first test is successful. All of his content appears, but the basic HTML tags that he used to output the content certainly leave a little to be desired from a design standpoint.

Campus Events:

National Testing Day
Spring Festival
Book Sale

Menu:

- Home
- Academics
- Employment
- Community
- Resources
- Contact

University News:

The University to offer Online Courses

Presidents breakfast April 1st

Book Fees due

The University

The University is a progressive learning institution that is focused on learning techniques that combine the best from the business and technology fields. We strive to bring an educational experience to our students that is above and beyond that of the traditional University. Our faculty all have years of practical experience working in the business world and bring thoes

Figure 13.3 default.do without Any Style Sheet Formatting

This is where *Cascading Style Sheets* (CSS) comes into play. CSS files provide a simple mechanism for applying styles on top of HTML code. This separates the HTML elements from the direct definition of the style information.

Russel has no experience with website design. He can hack his way through basic HTML, but creating a nice looking CSS design is a little beyond his reach. Fortunately, CSS is a technology that is not specific to the SAP environment. As it turns out, the current Internet pages on the university website are created in PHP. The website designers have already created CSS files for these existing PHP pages; however, there is no reason why these exact same CSS files cannot be used in a BSP application as well.

Russel's curiosity prompts him to look at the CSS file that was provided (see Figure 13.4). After studying it, he believes that he understands CSS well enough to use it in his BSP application. Different styles, like `body` and `box_right`, are named in the file. Then visual properties, like the font size and type, are set. Styles have a hierarchy; for instance, `box_right` is a child of `body` and inherits all the attributes of its parent style. It can also override style attributes as it does with the `background` value.

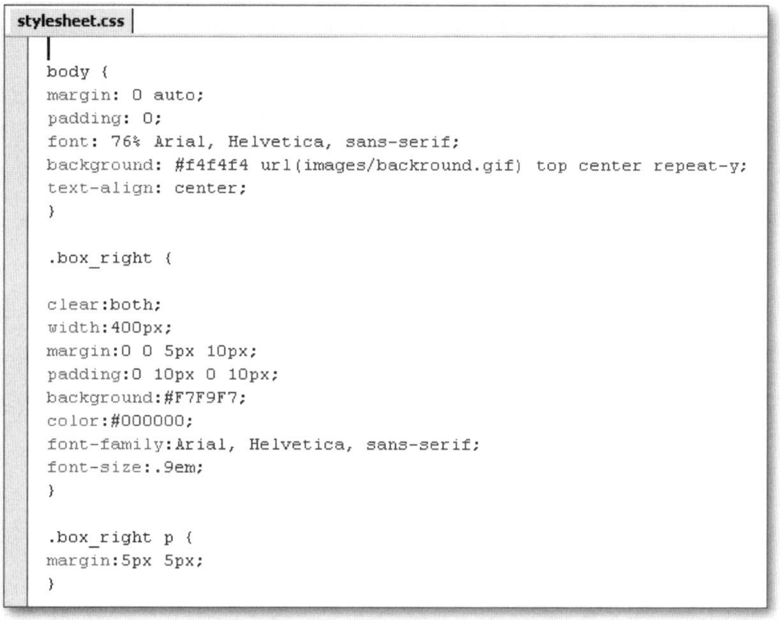

```
stylesheet.css

body {
margin: 0 auto;
padding: 0;
font: 76% Arial, Helvetica, sans-serif;
background: #f4f4f4 url(images/backround.gif) top center repeat-y;
text-align: center;
}

.box_right {

clear:both;
width:400px;
margin:0 0 5px 10px;
padding:0 10px 0 10px;
background:#F7F9F7;
color:#000000;
font-family:Arial, Helvetica, sans-serif;
font-size:.9em;
}

.box_right p {
margin:5px 5px;
}
```

Figure 13.4 Content of the CSS File

Now Russel only has to change his HTML coding slightly to adjust for the use of the CSS. He needs to insert division elements, `<DIV>`, with class attributes that connect back to sections of the CSS file. Standard HTML elements, like the `<BODY>`, will directly use the corresponding elements from the CSS (see Listing 13.1):

```
<div id="leftsidebar">
<img id="header" src="images/University_Logo_Small.jpg"
  width="760" height="185" alt="header" />
<div id="topmenu"></div>
<div class="rightnews">
    <img src="images/grounds1.jpg" alt="The University Grounds"
      width="90" height="60" /><br />
    <br />
    <img src="images/faculty1.jpg" alt="Our Faculty at Work"
      width="90" height="60" />
```

```
    <br />
    <br />
    <img src="images/great_hall1.jpg" alt="The Great Dining
      Hall" width="90" height="60" />
    <br />
    <br />
    <span class="style3">Campus Events:</span>
<br />
    <img src="images/bullet_blue.gif" alt="blue" width="19"
      height="16" /><br />
    <a href="">National Testing Day</a>
    <br />
    <a href="">Spring Festival</a>
    <br />
    <a href="">Book Sale</a><br />
    <br />
<br />
  </div>
<div id="menu">
<h2 class="hide">Menu:</h2>
<ul>
<li><a href="default.do">Home</a></li>
<li><a href="course_overview.do">Academics</a></li>
<li><a href="#">Employment</a></li>
<li><a href="#">Community</a></li>
<li><a href="#">Resources</a></li>
<li><a href="#">Contact</a></li>
</ul>
```

Listing 13.1 HTML Coding Fragment with Style Links for the default.bsp

As Figure 13.5 shows, the CSS has had a huge impact on this web page when compared with the earlier version in Figure 13.3. Thanks to changes introduced by the CSS file, the entire page contents are now centered in the browser window instead of being right-aligned.

Also, the main content area has been divided into three separate columns. Consistent fonts and colors have been applied to all areas of the page. Lastly, the menu on the left side of the page has received the most dramatic changes. What used to be a simple listing of hyperlinks now functions more like a dynamic menu, thanks to styles that change as the user positions the mouse over individual entries.

Figure 13.5 BSP Application with Custom HTML and CSS

13.1.4 Course Overview Page

Now Russel comes to his Course Overview page. This is the page that is linked off of his main page when a user chooses **Academics** and is the main purpose of what he is developing. For this page, Russel will use MVC again. He starts by creating the controller `course_overview.do` with implementation class `ZCL_CS_BSP_CTRL_COURSE_OVR`. This controller will have more logic than the previous page, because it needs code to call the model and read the course list.

1. Once more, Russel can reuse his existing model class. He returns the course list and the possible value for the course majors into attributes of the controller class. Then he calls the only view, `course_overview.bsp`, attached to this controller:

```
METHOD do_request.
  DATA view TYPE REF TO if_bsp_page.
  DATA model TYPE REF TO zcl_cs_main_model.
  CREATE OBJECT model.
  TRY.
```

```
        model->read_course_listing(
          IMPORTING
            e_courses = me->courses
            e_majors  = me->majors ).
      CATCH zcx_course_system .
    ENDTRY.
    view = create_view( view_name = 'course_overview.bsp' ).
    call_view( view ).
  ENDMETHOD.
```

The view is always visible to the controller object instance. By default, however, the controller class definition is left at the base controller class, CL_BSP_CONTROLLER, thereby not giving you access to methods and attributes that you need to add to your specific controller implementation.

2. This is where Russel likes to use a little trick that he devised, whereby he changes the controller class to the more specific implementation, ZCL_CS_BSP_CTRL_COURSE_OVR, via the **Properties** tab of the view (see Figure 13.6). This will give him the ability to directly access the attributes of the controller that he populated during the DO_REQUEST method within the layout of his view.

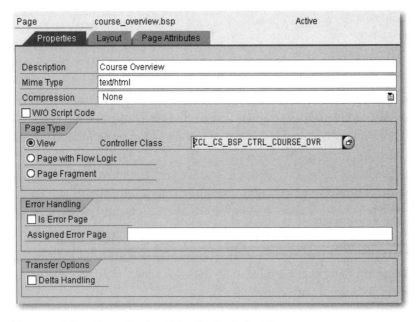

Figure 13.6 Page Properties Specifying the Controller Class

3. The coding of the `course_overview.bsp` view shows how ABAP can be used as the server-side scripting language to build the output HTML. Russel just loops at the internal tables that are exposed as attributes of the controller to output data in the layout. He can mix HTML content directly with ABAP, because the ABAP coding blocks are separated by `<% %>` and the ABAP variables are separated by `<%= %>`:

```
<%
  FIELD-SYMBOLS:
    <Wa_major> LIKE LINE OF controller->majors,
    <Wa_course> LIKE LINE OF controller->courses.
  LOOP AT controller->majors ASSIGNING <wa_major>.
%>
<%= <wa_major>-MAJOR %> - <%= <wa_major>-major_desc %><br/>
<%
  LOOP AT controller->courses ASSIGNING <wa_course>
  WHERE major = <wa_major>-major.
%>
   
<%= <Wa_course>-course_id %> -
<%= <Wa_course>-course_sdesc %>
<br/>
<%  ENDLOOP. "Loop at Courses %>
<%  ENDLOOP. "Loop at Majors %>
```

4. Russel likes to get the coding of his dynamic content pages working before he tries to apply any visual styles or more complex client-side functionality. If he runs his application now, he'll see that his server-side ABAP code works fine (see Figure 13.7). The formatting obviously needs some work, but that will just involve the simple process of applying the CSS classes, much like he did for his static page.

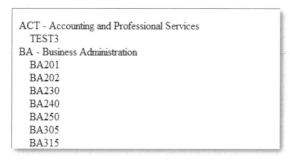

Figure 13.7 Course Output without Formatting

Still, even after Russel applies some visual styles to improve the appearance of the fonts, he won't be officially done with this page. Although initially the page will display only a listing of courses grouped by major, the requirement is to expand the display when a user clicks on the course ID in order to display the rest of the course details.

13.1.5 AJAX

Russel could do this the old-fashioned way and just have a hyperlink around the course ID that triggers a server event. The entire page would have to be rebuilt and sent again to the client for display. Instead, Russel decides that he wants to try to build his first *AJAX application*.

Russel has read a fair amount about AJAX, but this is really the first time he has had an opportunity to code an application that uses the technique. His idea is to send an asynchronous request to the server for just the new information about a single course, which is required when the user clicks on the link. Then, the page can be updated dynamically with the new information, without the server having to do a complete page reload. This has the advantage of requiring less redundant operations on the server, because it doesn't have to constantly rebuild the entire page. More importantly, this provides a nicer user experience on the frontend. The new information simply pops into place, instead of the user having to see the entire page rebuild in the browser. Another benefit is that the user doesn't lose his or her scroll position. Russel assumes that all of this should be perfectly done with AJAX.

So, the first thing Russel wants to do is to ensure that he really understands how AJAX works inside and out. AJAX is not really a technology. Rather, it is more of a technique for using existing technologies (JavaScript and XML) in new ways. AJAX is also not a standard. There are many different ways to combine these technologies to achieve the same effects. Regardless of the technical implementation, AJAX is quintessentially about breaking from the traditional model of performing full-page refreshes when only a portion of the page content needs to be updated. Besides, being a more efficient model, this also opens up the possibility to a lot of new visual techniques such as tree controls that only preload the first level of the hierarchy, drag and drop interactivity, and data sections that "pop in" or "float" over the main page.

But you should know that there are disadvantages to using AJAX as well. The JavaScript coding required to parse XML and to dynamically manipulate the *Document Object Model* (DOM) of the page can be quite complex. JavaScript is also unfortunately not implemented exactly the same way across all browsers. Therefore, the increased use of JavaScript can require more intense testing. These negatives can largely be avoided through the use of an AJAX framework. The idea of a framework is that it hides many of the technical implementation details of the XML parsing and the more complex JavaScript. In this way, these complex parts can be written once in a highly generic library that already has logic to support different browsers. This abstraction layer also simplifies the use of AJAX for the application developer.

Luckily, there is an Open Source AJAX engine, *ABAP JavaScript* (AJS), which is built on top of the *scriptaculous* library for BSP development and can be downloaded from *http://code.google.com/p/abapjs*.[1] Although Russel thinks AJS looks amazingly simple to use, he wants to use this first project as a learning experience to determine what is going on in low level AJAX. Therefore, he decides to leave AJS for a future project and instead write his own JavaScript for this business requirement.

Call back to the server via AJAX

1. Russel's first step in adding AJAX to his application will be to adjust the layout of his view. He needs to add a JavaScript function that will be responsible for initializing the XMLHTTPRequest object. It is this client- side object that makes it possible to have the asynchronous HTTP communications. Notice the conditional logic based on which browser the script is running within:

```
<script>
function createRequestObject() {
    var ro;
    var browser = navigator.appName;
    if(browser == "Microsoft Internet Explorer"){
        ro = new ActiveXObject("Microsoft.XMLHTTP");
    }else{
        ro = new XMLHttpRequest();
    }
    return ro;}
var http = createRequestObject();
```

---

1 This tool was built and contributed by Dan McWeeney and Ed Herrmann, who basically took what they liked from the *Ruby on Rails* environment and brought it to BSP. McWeeney and Herrmann also gave the SAP developer community *SAPlink*, which is an open source solution for the exchange of ABAP development objects. It can be downloaded from *http://SAPlink.org*.

2. Next Russel needs a JavaScript function that can be attached to the hyperlink of each course ID. This is the function that will trigger the asynchronous request. This link refers to a different controller, `course_detail.do`, and passes the selected `COURSE_ID` along as a URL parameter. This demonstrates that any normal BSP controller can be the target of an AJAX call and doesn't need any special functionality:

```
function sndReq(course_id) {
    http.open('get',
      'course_detail.do?course_id='+course_id);
    http.onreadystatechange = handleResponse;
    http.send(null);
}
```

In the previous function, Russel specified that when the state of the HTTP Request changed, another function, `handleResponse`, should be called. The function, `handleResponse`, essentially becomes a callback handler. It will be fired when a response is received. It can then extract the new data or content out of the response and process it into the current page.

3. In a minute, you'll see the content that Russel built to be passed back in the response object, but basically he is passing back the content already formatted as HTML and ready to be inserted as the new inner content of a `<DIV>` tag. Also, in order to retrieve the course ID key of the area that this response is for, the controller has passed back a header field in the response. Therefore, this JavaScript function just needs the method `getResponseHeader` to extract that data on the client:

```
function handleResponse() {
    if(http.readyState == 4){
        var response = http.responseText;
        var course_id = http.getResponseHeader(
            'course_id' );
        document.getElementById(course_id).className =
            'bluebox';
        document.getElementById(course_id).innerHTML =
            response;
    }
}
</script>
```

4. Finally, Russel needs to adjust his hyperlink in the basic data output. The hyperlink will trigger the JavaScript function, `sndReq`, and pass the course ID as a parameter of the function:

```
<a href="javascript:sndReq('<%= <Wa_course>-course_id
    %>');"><%= <Wa_course>-course_id %></a>
<div id="<%= <Wa_course>-course_id %>"></div>
```

AJAX Handler on the Server

Now Russel is ready to create his AJAX handler controller. There is really nothing special about this controller. It will be designed to take in the course ID as a URL parameter and then call a view. This view will output the course ID and the content that needs to be included in the main page. You should note that both of these objects don't know anything about the object they are included within, nor do they know anything about AJAX.

1. Russel is even able to test the handler as a standalone page in the browser (see Figure 13.8). All he has to do is to manually supply the COURSE_ID URL parameter.

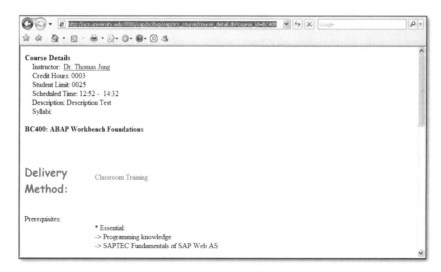

Figure 13.8 Standalone Testing of the AJAX Handler Controller

2. The DO_REQUEST method of the COURSE_DETAIL controller will be called automatically whenever a request is made. It will extract the course ID from the request URL parameter via the method GET_FORM_FIELD. It then reuses the model class to retrieve the necessary details and place them in controller attributes. Lastly, it sets the course ID back into the response header so that it can be read by the AJAX callback handler function:

```
METHOD do_request.
  DATA view TYPE REF TO if_bsp_page.
  DATA model TYPE REF TO zcl_cs_main_model.
  CREATE OBJECT model.
  DATA course_id TYPE zcs_course_id.
  course_id = request->get_form_field( 'course_id' ).
  TRY.
      model->read_course_details(
      EXPORTING   i_course_id  = course_id
      IMPORTING   e_course_att = me->course_att  ).
    CATCH zcx_course_system .
  ENDTRY.
  DATA s_course_id TYPE string.
  s_course_id = course_id.
  response->set_header_field( name = 'course_id'
                                value = s_course_id ).
  view = create_view( view_name = 'course_detail.bsp' ).
  call_view( view ).
ENDMETHOD.
```

The layout is just your standard output of the details that Russel wants displayed in the updated area. The only thing specific to the hosting page used within this layout is the reuse of the CSS style class names on the <SPAN> object.

3. You might notice the use of the PAGE->TO_STRING method to output the start and end times. If the ABAP variables were output directly, they would appear in their internal format. However, the PAGE->TO_STRING method will format dates, times, and currencies much like the ABAP WRITE statement would do in list processing:

```
<%@page language="abap" %>
<span class="style3"> <strong>Course Details </strong>
<br />
    Instructor:  
<A HREF="mailto:<%= controller->course_att-faculty->
  faculty_att-email %>?subject=Inquiry about Course:
  <%= controller->course_att-course_id %>">
   <%= controller->course_att-faculty->faculty_att-TITLE %>
       <%= controller->course_att-faculty->
     faculty_att-first_name %>   <%= controller->
     course_att-faculty->faculty_att-last_name %></a><br />
    Credit Hours:   <%= controller->
  course_att-CREDIT_HRS %><br />
    Student Limit:   <%= controller->
  course_att-student_limit %><br />
```

```
    Scheduled Time:   <%= page->to_string
  ( controller->course_att-start_time ). %>
    -    <%= page->to_string( controller->
    course_att-end_time ). %><br />
    Description:   <%= controller->
  course_att-description %><br />
    Syllabi:   <br />
<%= controller->course_att-syllabi %>
</span>
```

4. The output, once merged with the Course Overview page (see Figure 13.9), creates one seamless presentation to the end user. Although this may not be the most dramatic use of AJAX, it certainly has given Russel an opportunity to try out the technology, and now it is one more tool he has in his developer's toolbox that he can use.

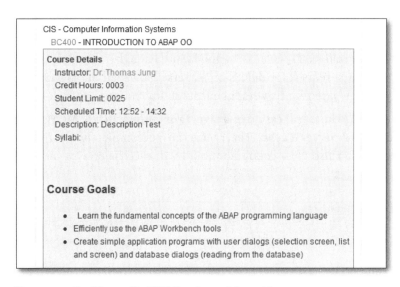

Figure 13.9 Final Page with AJAX Handler and Formatting

Caching of the AJAX Response

As Russel is testing his application, he considers caching some of his pages on the server. Thanks to the shared memory object, he's already taking advantage of caching course data in his model class logic, but BSP also offers caching opportunities at the entire page level. His content doesn't change often and has no security concerns, so it seems ideal for caching.

Server caching within BSP has even more performance advantages. This server cache is located in the *Internet Communication Manager* (ICM) of the

ABAP server. The ICM and its cache access are implemented in the C-Kernel and not ABAP. Therefore, accessing data from the ICM cache doesn't require processing to ever drop into the ABAP dialog work process.

1. This caching even works for the asynchronous AJAX requests. All Russel needs to do is set the **Server Cache** option on the controller's property maintenance (see Figure 13.10). The ICM caches individual objects based on their full URL. Because the course ID is passed as a URL parameter, this makes each request per course unique and cached as a separate object.

Figure 13.10 Server Cache Setting at the Controller Level

2. Russel decides to test the caching, so he sets a breakpoint within the COURSE_ DETAIL controller's DO_REQUEST method. Sure enough, the breakpoint gets hit on the first request for details on a course; however, on all subsequent requests, the page returns without encountering the breakpoint.

3. The server cache is still easy to manage. From transaction SMICM, choose **Goto · HTTP Server Cache**. The cache can be completely cleared from here. You can also view details about individual cache entries (see Figure 13.11).

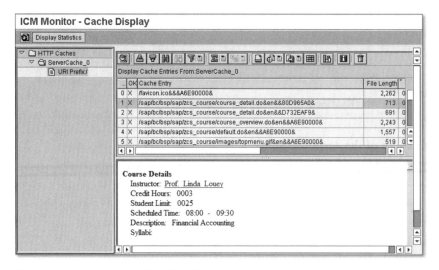

Figure 13.11 Viewing Cache Entry Details

13.2   BSP Extensions

Russel has another business requirement that he thinks might be a good match for BSP. The users need an easy way of editing the HTML content of the course syllabi. Although Russel is editing the rest of the course data with his Web Dynpro ABAP application, Web Dynpro ABAP doesn't have a text edit control rich enough to meet the users' requirements.

This is where the openness of the BSP environment can be quite handy. There are plenty of open source HTML editor solutions available on the web. Most are designed as HTML and JavaScript for easy integration into many different environments. As Russel already discovered with his inclusion of AJAX, BSP is ripe for the use of solutions built on such open standards. Russel searches the Internet and finds an open source project called the *FCKeditor* (*http://www.fckeditor.net*) that appears to meet his needs. The solution primarily involves client-side HTML and JavaScript. All that remains for Russel to do is to integrate these scripts in the BSP development environment.

Although he could code directly against the scripts in his BSP applications, similar to the way he just coded his AJAX solution directly against the `XMLHttpRequest` object, he decides that for long-term reuse of the FCKeditor libraries he would like to wrap the logic within a *BSP extension element*. BSP extension elements are basically custom tags. They can be used in your layouts just like regular HTML tags, except their implementation is coded on the server in ABAP. This allows a developer to create reusable sets of HTML and JavaScript that can all be encapsulated within a single extension element.

13.2.1   Upload of Open Source Solution

Before Russel can even start building the BSP extension element for the editor, he has to get the source editor uploaded to the ABAP server. On other web servers, this process might involve just copying the downloaded project folders and libraries to the server's file system.

The SAP NetWeaver Application Server ABAP however, doesn't use the file system to store its web content. Given the common practice of having multiple application servers in production systems, this could get rather complex. To complicate matters further, it is possible to have heterogeneous mixtures of operating systems used across these different application servers. Therefore, in order to simplify things, ABAP simply stores its entire web content in the database. This storage is commonly referred to as the *MIME Repository*. It can be viewed and accessed as a folder/file hierarchy, making it compatible with solutions that expect a file- system approach.

Therefore, Russel can upload the folders and files that he downloaded as part of the FCKeditor project directly to the MIME Repository. There is a standard SAP program called BSP_UPDATE_MIMEREPOS. Since it doesn't have a transaction code, it must be run directly from the ABAP development environment. All Russel has to do is specify the name of the path where he wants to upload the files to and then choose to **Import from Disk** and **Process Whole Structure** (see Figure 13.12). This will upload all subdirectories in the main directory. When he executes this application, it will ask him to supply the import directly on his front-end machine.

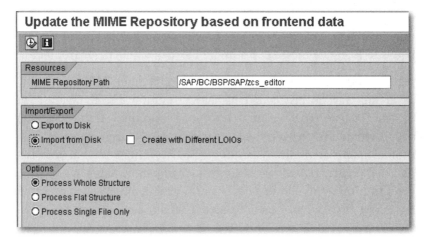

Figure 13.12 Application to Import Mimes from the Frontend

After uploading all the files and folders associated with the project, they are visible from within transaction SE80 as parts of a BSP application (see Figure 13.13). They are also ready to use in a BSP application or extension element, without your having to change a single line of code in any of the files.

```
▽ 🗀 zcs_editor              Opensoure FCKEditor (HTML Editor)
   ▽ 🗀 MIMEs
      ▷ 🗀 _samples
      ▷ 🗀 _testcases
      ▷ 🗀 editor
        _documentation.htm  _documentation.html
        _upgrade.html        _upgrade.html
        _whatsnew.html       _whatsnew.html
        fckconfig.js         fckconfig.js
        fckeditor.afp        fckeditor.afp
        fckeditor.asp        fckeditor.asp
        fckeditor.cfc        fckeditor.cfc
        fckeditor.cfm        fckeditor.cfm
        fckeditor.js         fckeditor.js
        fckeditor.lasso      fckeditor.lasso
        fckeditor.php        fckeditor.php
        fckeditor.pl         fckeditor.pl
        fckeditor.py         fckeditor.py
        fckeditor_php4.php   fckeditor_php4.php
        fckeditor_php5.php   fckeditor_php5.php
        fckstyles.xml        fckstyles.xml
        fcktemplates.xml     fcktemplates.xml
        htaccess.txt         htaccess.txt
        license.txt
```

Figure 13.13 Open Source Solution in a BSP Application

13.2.2 Creating the BSP Extension

All BSP elements have to be assigned to an *extension*. Extensions are basically just libraries or groupings of elements. For what Russel needs to accomplish, in order to wrap the FCKeditor for use in BSP, he will need a header element and an editor element. Therefore he will group together these two items into their own extension called `zfckeditor` (see Figure 13.14).

```
BSP Extension    zfckeditor                        Inactive(revised)
 ╱ Properties ╲

Short Description         BSP Extension for the FCKEditor
Default Prefix           zfckeditor
BSP Extension Class
BSP Element Basis Class  CL_BSP_ELEMENT|


 ╱ General Data ╲
Created by          ABAP DEV
Created On          02/18/2007
Last Changed        ABAP DEV
Changed On          02/18/2007
Time changed        14:50:09
Package             ZCS UI BSP
Original Language   E
```

Figure 13.14 BSP Extension Definition

Besides the description and the name, there really isn't much to define when creating the extension. The main point is the selection of the **BSP Element Basis Class**. As Russel will see shortly, BSP elements are implemented as an ABAP class. This class is generated by the ABAP development environment with its inheritance preconfigured. The inheritance defines what extension framework methods will be available to the element class.

It is entry of the Basis Class that controls what class will be used as the superclass in this inheritance hierarchy. Although specifying a custom Basis Class is possible if you wanted to extend the base capabilities of the extension framework, for what Russel wants to do to implement the FCKeditor, that really won't be necessary. For that reason, Russel can just choose the standard SAP element class, CL_BSP_ELEMENT.

13.2.3   Creating the BSP Extension Element

Before any page can use the FCKeditor, it must declare a SCRIPT statement that links to the main JavaScript library of the solution. This is what Russel wants to wrap up in his first BSP element. This way, he can ensure that uses of the FCKeditor library all point to the same JavaScript and he is not left with multiple copies of the library floating around.

1. This is a pretty simple element since it needs no attributes or special processing settings. Russel only has to supply the description and the name of his **Element Handler Class** (see Figure 13.15).

2. When he clicks on the **Activate** button, the handler class and the basis class will both be generated for him.

3. Without attributes, there is nothing to code in the element handler class except for the main rendering implementation. This will be done in the method DO_AT_BEGINNING. All Russel really needs to do is output the SCRIPT statement.

   But he knows that it would be foolish to hard code the URL or path to the location of the script. Therefore, he uses a class of all constants so that he has one place to maintain all the configuration values of these two elements (see Figure 13.16).

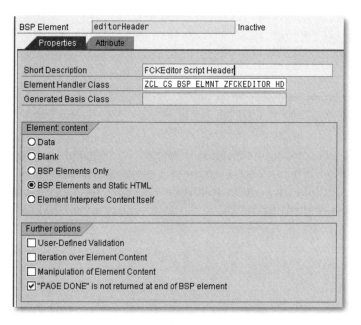

Figure 13.15 editorHeader Element Properties

Attribute	Level	Visi...	Re...	Typing	Associat...		Description	Initial value
BSP_APPLICATION	Consta..	Publ..	☐	Type	STRING	⇨	BSP Application that hold...	'zcs_editor'
HEADER_SCRIPT	Consta..	Publ..	☐	Type	STRING	⇨	Name of the main heade...	'fckeditor.js'
SKIN_VALUES	Consta..	Publ..	☐	Type	STRING	⇨	Possible Skin Values	'default/office2003/silver'
TOOLBAR_VALUES	Consta..	Publ..	☐	Type	STRING	⇨	Possible Toolbar Values	'Default/Basic'
SKIN_DEFAULT	Consta..	Publ..	☐	Type	STRING	⇨	Default Skin	'default'
TOOLBAR_DEFAULT	Consta..	Publ..	☐	Type	STRING	⇨	Default Toolbar	'Default'

Figure 13.16 Element Constants

4. For instance, now he can use the constant, HEADER_SCRIPT, in his call to the SAP delivered static method, CL_BSP_RUNTIME=>CONSTRUCT_BSP_URL, to generate the necessary link to the header script:

```
METHOD if_bsp_element~do_at_beginning.
  DATA script_url TYPE string.
  DATA html_out TYPE string.
  cl_bsp_runtime=>construct_bsp_url(
    EXPORTING   in_application =
        zcl_cs_bsp_elmnt_editor_cnst=>bsp_application
            in_page        =
        zcl_cs_bsp_elmnt_editor_cnst=>header_script
```

```
        IMPORTING   out_local_url  = script_url  ).
    CONCATENATE `<script type="text/javascript" src=""`
                script_url
                `"></script>`
                INTO html_out.
    me->print_string( html_out ).
    rc = co_element_done.
ENDMETHOD.
```

5. Next Russel will start on the creation of the editor element (see Figure 13.17). The main difference between the two elements is that this one will have input attributes that need validation. In order for the validation methods to be called, Russel must check the **User-Defined Validation** option.

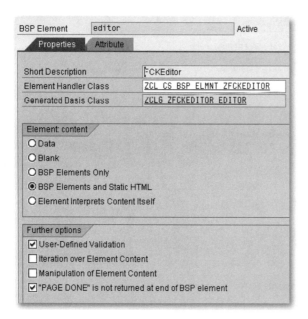

Figure 13.17 editor Element Properties

6. Now Russel can start to define the attributes of the element (see Figure 13.18). These are different settings that can be made on the editor object via JavaScript. By defining them as attributes of the element, Russel can validate them with ABAP coding at design time and runtime, before passing anything to JavaScript and possibly generating a cryptic error on the frontend.

Attribute	Dy..	C...	Bi..	Typing met..	Associated Type	Dflt value	Description
browse	✓	☐	✓	1 TYPE	🗎 STRING	FALSE	Allow Broswing on the Server
fullPage	✓	☐	✓	1 TYPE	🗎 STRING	FALSE	Edit Full HTML Page (including Heade..
height	✓	☐	☐	1 TYPE	🗎 STRING	400	Height
id	✓	☐	☐	1 TYPE	🗎 STRING		Element ID
skin	✓	☐	✓	1 TYPE	🗎 STRING		Editor Skin
textDirection	✓	☐	☐	1 TYPE	🗎 STRING		Text Direction (LTR, RTL, INHERIT)
toolbar	✓	☐	✓	1 TYPE	🗎 STRING		Toolbar (Default or Simple)
upload	✓	☐	✓	1 TYPE	🗎 STRING	FALSE	Allow Upload to the Server
value	✓	☐	✓	1 TYPE	🗎 STRING		Editor Content
width	✓	☐	☐	1 TYPE	🗎 STRING	100%	Width

Figure 13.18 editor Element Attributes

Russel is also able to support data binding on attributes. This is functionality of the BSP framework that allows binding of element attributes to model class attributes, similar to the way Web Dynpro binds to a context.

13.2.4 Design Time Validation

There are two types of validation that can occur on element attributes and each has its own method within the element handler class:

The first type of validation is design time and is implemented in the COMPILE_TIME_IS_VALID method. The ABAP development environment calls this method automatically when someone activates a page or view that contains the element.

This is really like being able to write your own syntax checks specific to the element you are creating. The element handler class has already created an instance of the VALIDATOR object to assist with the checks and handle all the error situations. All Russel's coding needs to do is to call the correct method of the VALIDATOR object for each attribute.

For any of the attributes that have a fixed set of possible values, he will use the TO_ENUM method. This requires passing in the enumerated value set to the method call. Once again, Russel will rely on his set of constants that he has defined to avoid hard coding any values. The true/false values are even easier because there is a TO_BOOLEAN validator method as well (see Listing 13.2).

```
validator->to_enum( name = 'skin'
  enums = zcl_cs_bsp_elmnt_editor_cnst=>skin_values ).
validator->to_enum( name = 'toolbar'
```

```
    enums = zcl_cs_bsp_elmnt_editor_cnst=>toolbar_values ).
  validator->to_boolean( name = 'fullPage' ).
  validator->to_boolean( name = 'upload' ).
  validator->to_boolean( name = 'browse' ).
  validator->to_enum( name = 'textDirection'
    enums = cl_htmlb_textview=>c_textview_textdirections ).
  valid = validator->m_all_values_valid.
```

Listing 13.2 Element compile_time_is_valid Method

13.2.5 Runtime Validation

Obviously, catching errors for incorrect attribute values at design time is the ideal situation, but what happens when the value of an attribute is supplied dynamically via a variable or model binding? The compiler can't possibly check these values in advance since they will only be known at runtime.

To perform validations at runtime, there is a separate method, RUNTIME_IS_ VALID. In addition to performing validations, this method also maps all the input runtime parameters to attributes of the element handler class. This allows you to apply default values to an attribute.

Russel uses the VALIDATOR object again to perform the actual checks and produce any errors if necessary (see Listing 13.3).

```
  m_validator->id( value = me->id required = abap_true ).
  IF runtime_parms = '/*/' OR runtime_parms CS 'skin'.
    DATA l_skin TYPE string.
    l_skin = m_validator->to_enum( name = 'skin'
     enums = zcl_cs_bsp_elmnt_editor_cnst=>skin_values
     value = me->skin
     default = zcl_cs_bsp_elmnt_editor_cnst=>skin_default ).
    IF me->skin IS INITIAL.
      me->skin = l_skin.
    ENDIF.
  ENDIF.
...
  IF runtime_parms = '/*/' OR runtime_parms CS 'upload'.
    me->upload = m_validator->to_boolean( name = 'upload'
        value = me->upload ).
  ENDIF.
```

Listing 13.3 Element runtime_is_valid Method

13.2.6 Element Rendering

With all the validation complete, Russel can now move on to the implementation of the element rendering in the method `DO_AT_BEGINNING`.

1. It will start off similarly to the element handler rendering of the `editor-Header` element in that it will first create a link to the JavaScript library:

```
DATA html_out TYPE string.
DATA script_url TYPE string.
cl_bsp_runtime=>construct_bsp_url(
  EXPORTING   in_application =
      zcl_cs_bsp_elmnt_editor_cnst=>bsp_application
  IMPORTING   out_local_url  = script_url ) .
CONCATENATE script_url '/' INTO script_url.
me->resolve_model_binding( ).
CONCATENATE
  `<script type="text/javascript">`
  `var sBasePath = '` script_url `';`
```

2. Now Russel creates the instance of the `FCKeditor` object on the front-end using the same ID as the BSP element to ensure uniqueness. He can then start mapping the attribute values of his element to the attributes of the front-end control:

```
  `var oFCKeditor = new FCKeditor( '` me->id `' ); `
  `oFCKeditor.BasePath = sBasePath; `
  `oFCKeditor.Height = '` me->height `'; `
  `oFCKeditor.Width = '` me->width `'; `
  `oFCKeditor.ToolbarSet = '` me->toolbar `'; `
  INTO html_out.
```

One of the advantages of wrapping the JavaScript of the editor within a BSP extension is to hide some of the inner complexities. This next section is a perfect example of this. Russel is able to use the system logon language as an automatic parameter to the language settings of the front-end control and map the ABAP Boolean values to the JavaScript ones:

```
DATA slang TYPE char10.
WRITE sy-langu TO slang.
TRANSLATE slang TO LOWER CASE.
CONCATENATE html_out
  `oFCKeditor.Config["AutoDetectLanguage"] = false; `
  `oFCKeditor.Config["DefaultLanguage"] = '` slang `'; `
  INTO html_out.
IF me->skin IS NOT INITIAL.
  CONCATENATE html_out
```

```
        `oFCKeditor.Config['SkinPath'] = sBasePath +
        'editor/skins/' + '`
          me->skin `' + '/'; `
            INTO html_out.
    ENDIF.
    IF me->fullpage = abap_true.
      CONCATENATE html_out
        `oFCKeditor.Config['FullPage'] = true; `
        INTO html_out.
    ELSE.
      CONCATENATE html_out
        `oFCKeditor.Config['FullPage'] = false; `
        INTO html_out.
    ENDIF.
```

3. Now we come to the content string for the editor. This string will contain HTML formatted text. Because of this, it cannot just be passed directly into the JavaScript stream. The special formatting of HTML tags would likely be interpreted as JavaScript and could well lead to errors in the page.

   To avoid this situation, the special characters in HTML must be safely encoded for JavaScript. For example, all instances of quotation marks (") must be replaced with the escape sequence \". Developers don't have to worry about the details of this process however, since SAP supplies a method to encode the string:

   ```
   me->value = cl_bsp_utility=>encode_string(
     in        = me->value
     encoding = if_bsp_writer=>co_javascript ).
   CONCATENATE html_out
     `oFCKeditor.Value = '` me->value `'; `
     `oFCKeditor.Create(); `
     `</script>`
     INTO html_out.
   ```

4. Finally, the scripting for the editor is output into the surrounding page:

   ```
   me->print_string( html_out ).
   rc = co_element_done.
   ```

13.2.7 Testing the New Extension

Russel is ready to test his new extension.

1. He'll create a simple page that just has the editor in it with a button. He'll tie a server event on the button so he can test the logic for capturing the editor content during an event:

```
<%@page language="abap" %>
<%@extension name="htmlb" prefix="htmlb" %>
<%@extension name="zfckeditor" prefix="zfckeditor" %>
<htmlb:content design="design2003" >
  <htmlb:page title="Basic Test" >
    <htmlb:form>
      <zfckeditor:editorHeader />
      <zfckeditor:editor id    = "test"
                         value = "<%= me->value %>" />
      <br>
      <htmlb:button text    = "Press Me"
                    onClick = "myClickHandler" />
    </htmlb:form>
  </htmlb:page>
</htmlb:content>
```

2. The BSP extension for the editor has the added benefit that Russel can now use the HTMLB Event Manager for retrieving the stored data in the editor:

```
DATA event TYPE REF TO cl_htmlb_event.
event ?= cl_htmlb_manager=>get_event(
    runtime->server->request ).
DATA data TYPE REF TO zcl_cs_bsp_elmnt_zfckeditor.
data ?= cl_htmlb_manager=>get_data(
      request = runtime->server->request
      name    = 'zfckeditor:editor'
      id      = 'test' ).
IF data IS NOT initial.
  value = data->value.
ENDIF.
```

3. With this simple page, Russel brings the open source editor into the BSP environment (see Figure 13.19).

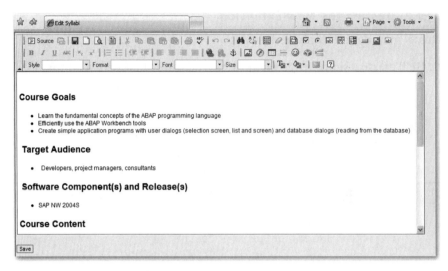

Figure 13.19 Open Source Editor Running in Business Server Pages

As part of his project, Russel has requirements for some print and interactive, yet paper-like forms. Russel decides to turn to one of the major new capabilities of SAP NetWeaver, the Forms technology powered by Adobe, to meet these requirements based on the existing standards of PDF and the Adobe LifeCycle Designer.

14   Adobe Forms

Russel has been around the SAP world for a good many years, so he's had the opportunity to use both of SAP's previous forms technologies — SAPscript and SAP Smart Forms. Good, old SAPscript, being the first of the technologies, is a solid print form tool, but lacks functionality found in many of the modern design tools. Most ABAP developers, Russel included, were not overly dismayed to move on to a slightly more user-friendly design environment when SAP introduced Smart Forms in the SAP R/3 4.6x releases. In addition to providing an improved design tool, SAP Smart Forms also introduced the first steps toward creating interactive forms that could be run in a web browser.

But, even with the advances that SAP Smart Forms introduced, the SAP technology still lagged behind products created by companies that specialized in forms development and output rendering. Therefore, SAP decided to partner with the leader in this field, Adobe. Forms technology powered by Adobe offers an alternative user interface technology that generates PDF documents and runs in the familiar Adobe Reader. With over 200 million existing PDF documents on the World Wide Web today (see *http://www.adobe.com/products/acrobat/adobepdf.html*), this makes an excellent choice for creating nicely formatted print output or paper-like interactive forms.

This new toolset uses the *Adobe LifeCycle Designer* embedded within the SAP development environment to create forms. The rendering of the form itself is performed in native PDF format. And of course the output of forms, even interactive ones, is hosted in the widely installed and used Adobe Reader.

14.1 Infrastructure and Setup

As part of his project, Russel has requirements for some print and interactive forms. But, before he even starts working with the design tools to fulfill those requirements, he thinks that it would be a good idea to learn a little about the underlying infrastructure of the Adobe-based forms solution.

14.1.1 Adobe Document Services Infrastructure

The core of the Adobe Forms technology is the PDF rendering engine. This software component is referred to as the *Adobe Document Services* (ADS). This software was developed by Adobe and written in Java. Therefore, the use of any of SAP's delivered forms or the development of custom forms requires that ADS is installed into a *SAP NetWeaver Application Server Java* (AS Java).

As is common with SAP ERP 6.0 systems, during the upgrade, the system administrators added the Java Stack to Russel's systems. This is sometimes called an "ABAP+J2EE add-in instance," meaning that both the ABAP and Java runtimes are installed into the same instance of software. They may well live within the same database, but they have separate schemas. Therefore, communication between the ABAP system and any software running on the Java Stack, including the ADS, must be done via external communication services like Remote Function Calls (RFC) or Web Services.

The ADS solution uses Web Services and the exchange of XML to communicate during forms rendering. When a developer designs a form from the ABAP environment, the XML representation of the form is saved in the ABAP repository. This means that it is still transported and treated like any other ABAP development object.

At runtime when the form needs to be rendered, the definition and data are sent by the ABAP system to the ADS running on an AS Java via Web Services. The rendering to PDF is done within the ADS and the output is returned to the ABAP system. From there, if the document is printed, the output is still funneled through the ABAP print spooler. Consequently, the use of the Adobe solution for printing doesn't require duplication of your printer or print spooler setup. Furthermore, all the normal ABAP spool monitoring tools can be used against Adobe-based print jobs.

14.1.2 Exposing the Service from the J2EE Engine

There are several steps that Russel and his Basis coworkers went through to set up the connection between their ABAP and Java engines to make the Adobe scenario work. The first few steps involve using the Java *Visual Administrator* to set up the security on the exposed Web Services.

SAP provides complete set-up instructions for the ADS. Following these instructions, Russel's team was able to easily set up the new security roles for the ADS within the J2EE Engine. Next, these roles had to be assigned to the Web Service Endpoint.

The final setting that they needed to do was to install a certificate for *Reader Rights*. Normally, Adobe Reader is a read-only tool. It can't be used to edit just any PDF document. In order to utilize the Adobe Reader client for working with interactive forms, a special certificate called the Reader Rights has to be sent down to the client with the form. This certificate is what indicates to the Adobe Reader application that there has been a proper license granted to allow interactive forms. This Reader Rights key is specific to the customer and has to be acquired from SAP. Then, the certificate is loaded into the file system of the SAP NetWeaver AS Java, generally by the system administrator. Lastly, a configuration setting in the Visual Administrator (see Figure 14.1) must be made to tell the ADS which certificate to use.

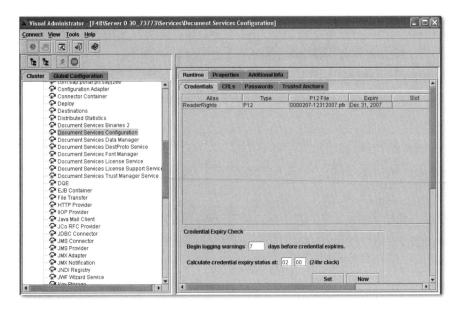

Figure 14.1 Certificate Installation for Reader Rights

14.1.3 Configuring the Service Interface from ABAP

Now that everything is exposed properly from the Java side of the system, all that is left to do is configure the ABAP system to be able to call the ADS.

1. Russel and the Basis team go to transaction SM59. In the past, this transaction was primarily associated with only RFC-based connections. However, in SAP NetWeaver. It can also be used to create HTTP(S)-based connections that can be employed by Web Services.

2. That is precisely what Russel must do to connect to the ADS. He creates a connection of type **G, HTTP Connection to External Server** (see Figure 14.2) with the name **ADS**. This is the default name that will be used in the system whenever a call for an Adobe form is needed. When working with the ADS API directly in code, you can supply an alternative destination name. You can also supply certain performance settings per destination by maintaining entries in the configuration table FPCONNECT.

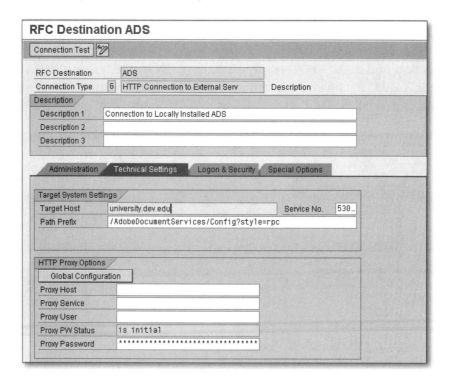

Figure 14.2 RFC Destination Technical Settings

3. Within this connection, Russel only needs to specify the URL, hostname, and service port of the AS Java he is connecting to. Although Russel's installation uses the shared Java and ABAP dual stacks, it is possible to connect to a completely separate installation of the AS Java and ADS that could be running on a different set of hardware.

4. Next on the **Logon & Security** tab (see Figure 14.3), Russel needs to specify the user name and password that will be used to connect to the ADS. Since this is only a development system, he is using **Basic Authentication** without SSL (*Secure Sockets Layer*). However, for production he will follow the complete ADS set-up guide and configure a secure connection. For the **User** and **Password**, he uses the account, "ADSUser", which the system administrators created within the J2EE earlier in the ADS setup.

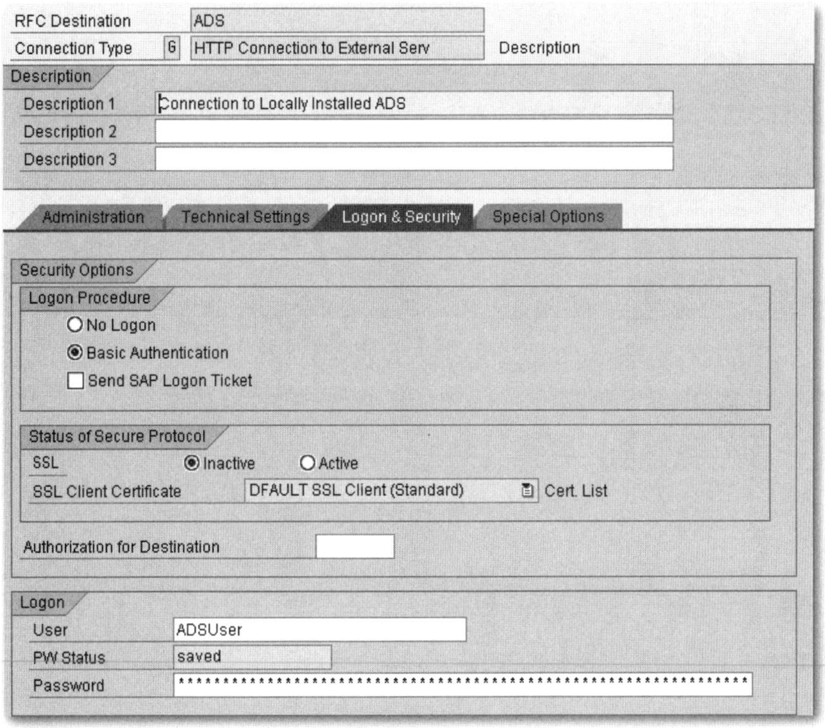

Figure 14.3 RFC Destination Logon & Security

After completing this configuration, Russel tests the setup by trying to print one of the sample SAP delivered Adobe Forms. But his first attempt to print a form is met with a cryptic connection error message. Russel turned to the SAP Service Marketplace (*http://service.sap.com*) to look for answers. He quickly found the OSS note 944221 with lots of ADS-specific troubleshooting techniques and tools.

It turns out that later support packages of SAP NetWeaver 7.0 had made some changes to the communication interface to allow for a single ADS to be used for multiple ABAP systems. Previously, the ADS configuration used a single callback destination named **FP_ICF_DATA** to communicate with the requesting ABAP system. Now this is a configurable destination that must also be maintained from the Visual Administrator. Figure 14.4 shows the location of this configuration and the connection settings for the callback destination that Russel's team used.

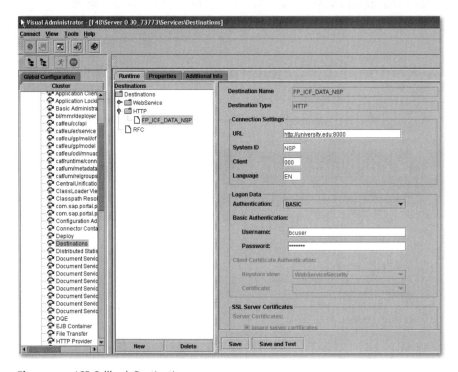

Figure 14.4 ICF Callback Destination

14.2 Function Module Based Forms

Now that Russel has everything set up and working properly, he can get back to the activity that he really loves — development. He has several different requirements for forms:

▶ First he has the requirement to be able to print the details of a course, but this printing might have to be done in the background. Users also want to be able to save course details as a PDF document.

▶ Next he needs some kind of print mode for the Web Dynpro ABAP application that he has already created. Using tabstrips and other formatting options doesn't make printing from the browser a very reliable option. Therefore, he will need a way to produce a PDF document in Web Dynpro.

▶ Finally, the users have requested an interactive offline form that can be used to request the creation of a new course. Currently, this is a paper form that must be sent via interoffice mail and then typed into the system. By switching to an offline interactive form, he can simplify this process tremendously.

Fortunately, the Adobe Forms solution has methods that will meet each of these requirements. Although all three methods use the same Adobe LifeCycle Designer tool for building the actual form, the type of form you choose has a considerable affect on the form's interface.

14.2.1 Creating the Interface

Russel decides to start with the simplest solution, which is the course detail form that only needs to be printed. For this solution, he uses the function module based Adobe Form. The Function Module based form will create a form interface very similar to that of SAP Smart Forms. The designer dynamically generates a function module that matches the interface that you design for the form. This makes the technical conversion from SAP Smart Forms to Adobe Forms a much simpler task.

1. Russel starts this process by creating a form interface from within transaction SE80 (see Figure 14.5). During this process, he must choose the **Interface Type**. The **ABAP Dictionary-Based Interface** is the type that he will use for this solution. This will allow him to pass native ABAP data types, such as internal tables, directly into the form interface.

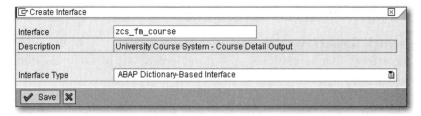

Figure 14.5 Create Interface Dialog

The other interface type, **XML-Based Interface**, will be used later for Web Dynpro integration since the context in Web Dynpro is easily converted to XML.

2. The next screen that Russel arrives at is the **Interface** design screen (see Figure 14.6). The process for creating an interface is very similar to the same activity in SAP Smart Forms. You name the interface parameters and give them data dictionary references. Whatever you specify as the interface parameters will later be exposed as the parameters of the generated function module.

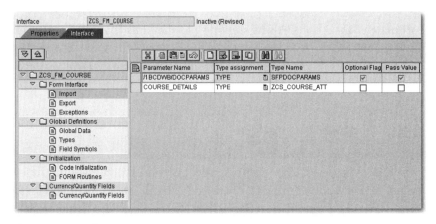

Figure 14.6 Interface Maintenance

3. To ensure compatibility with SAP Smart Forms, there are also options for creating form routines and local variable definitions. But even in SAP Smart Forms, Russel has never been a big fan of inserting a lot of coding into the form. He has always felt that this logic is difficult to maintain with the form and is better suited to a wrapper application surrounding the form, which is exactly how he plans to build this form. So, all he needs are importing parameters for the data that he wants to pass into the form.

14.2.2   Form Interface to Context Mapping

Now that Russel has a form interface, it is time to start creating the form.

1. He chooses to create the **Form** with the same name as the **Interface** (see Figure 14.7). That way, if the interface is used only with the one form, it makes it very easy to see the relationship between the two objects from the Object Browser.

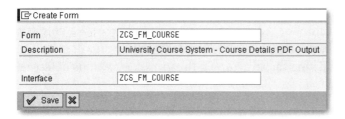

Figure 14.7 Create Form Dialog

2. When Russel first enters the Form Maintenance perspective, the first screen that Russel sees is the context mapping screen (see Figure 14.8). On the left side of the screen, Russel has all the elements of the interface that he just built. On the right side of the screen, he has all the elements that have been defined for the context of his form.

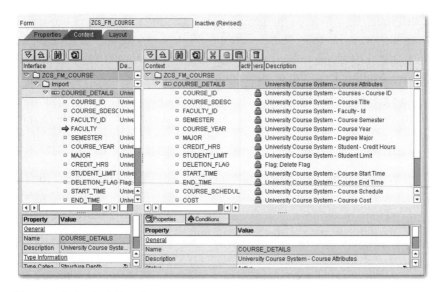

Figure 14.8 Context Mapping

3. In order to connect elements of the interface to the form context, all Russel has to do is drag and drop them between these two views. In fact, all he did is drag and drop his entire COURSE_DETAILS structure and all inner elements were automatically copied over as well.

You might notice that within the interface in the COURSE_DETAILS structure there is the FACULTY object reference. It is identified as an object reference via the blue arrow icon. You should note that having object references in your form interface and even using them in form modules is all well and good; however, within the Adobe Form, you can only use data objects that the form environment understands. Therefore, during the drag and drop operation used to define the structure in the form context, this object reference was dropped.

Images and Icons

Not all context elements have to come directly from the form interface. One excellent example of this is the use of images or system icons in a form.

1. In this case, Russel will be choosing which system icon he wants to print on the page from within his logic and then passing that selection into the form interface. This task is therefore more complex than just placing a static image in the form via the form designer.

2. Although he will have the binary content and the MIME type for the icon in his form interface, Russel needs to create a special kind of graphic node within the form context by right-clicking on the context and selecting **Create • Graphic** from the context menu (see Figure 14.9).

The graphic node by itself doesn't do much. It needs some of its special attributes to be mapped to other nodes in the context to be able to supply the content of the graphic itself. There are two different types of graphic nodes: **Graphic Reference** and **Graphic Content**:

▸ With **Graphic Reference**, only a URL needs to be supplied via the form interface that points back to the image content that you want to include in the form. The URL will be resolved at runtime in order to place the graphic in the form output.

▸ With **Graphic Content**, the entire graphic is passed through the form interface and is embedded in the form. This does make the form larger, but it also eliminates the possibility that the image may not be accessible at runtime. Therefore, this is the solution that Russel chooses for his application.

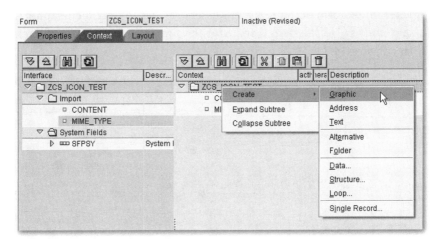

Figure 14.9 Create a Graphic Context Node

3. When setting the **Graphic Type** to **Graphic Content**, two new attributes appear in the **Graphic** element property box: **Field** and **MIME Type** (see Figure 14.10). Each of these properties must be supplied with the name of another node in the context that contains the corresponding information.

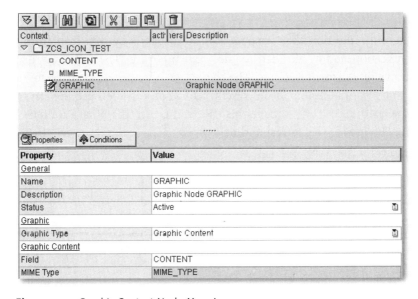

Figure 14.10 Graphic Context Node Mapping

4. Later in the form designer itself, Russel only has to drag the **Graphic** context node on to the design area and the proper mappings are all created (see Figure 14.11).

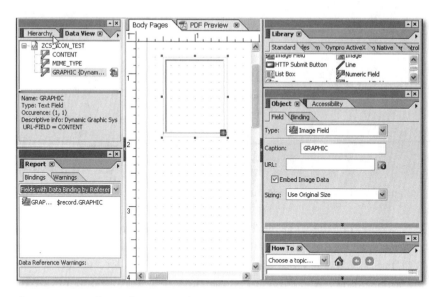

Figure 14.11 Graphic Node Usage in the Form

5. The only question that remains is how to pass a system icon from the application coding through to the form interface. The following listing shows just such an example. The class CL_BSP_MIMES can be used to build a full URL that points to the system icon. You can then use the class CL_MIME_REPOSITORY_API to take this URL and return the binary content and MIME type for the corresponding icon:

```
DATA: l_icon TYPE string,
      url TYPE string,
      content TYPE xstring,
      mime_type TYPE string.
DATA: mr_api TYPE REF TO if_mr_api.
mr_api = cl_mime_repository_api=>get_api( ).
l_icon = `ICON_PRINT`.
url = cl_bsp_mimes=>sap_icon( l_icon ).
mr_api->get( EXPORTING i_url = url
             IMPORTING e_content = content
                       e_mime_type = mime_type ).
```

14.2.3 Form Layout Editor

Russel finally gets to play with the new tool when he arrives at the Designer. As you can see in Figure 14.12, the Adobe LifeCycle Designer is integrated right into the ABAP development environment.

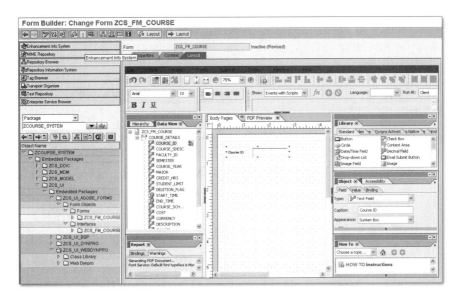

Figure 14.12 Form Layout Editor Integrated in Transaction SE80

The enhanced design tool is a huge departure from the previous design tools in SAPscript and SAP Smart Forms:

▶ The left column in the Designer shows the form context as it was defined in the previous section. You can simply drag and drop elements from the content onto the design area and UI elements with the correct data binding will be created automatically.

▶ The middle of the tool is the design area. This provides an area where you arrange your elements in a near-WYSIWYG (*What You See Is What You Get*) editor. There are lots of tools for the automatic arrangement and alignment of elements. There is also a real-time **PDF Preview** tab that shows you what the output rendering will actually look like. You can also create multiple "pages," including header pages that can be merged with body pages to create reusable headers and footers. Each "page" appears as a separate tab in this area.

▶ Finally, on the right are the toolbox and element property windows. At the top is a toolbox of all possible UI elements. You can also drag and drop elements from this toolbox onto the design area and then create the binding to the context via the element properties. The bottom of this area shows the properties for the currently selected UI element. In this box, you can change the data binding as well as other visual design attributes.

One of the major new and powerful aspects of this form design environment is the ability to create *subforms*. Subforms are groupings of elements that allow for easy mass manipulation of the inner elements.

1. In the form that Russel is designing, he had copied over several context elements onto the form, but the spacing and alignment between the elements is fairly haphazard at this point.

2. This is easy to correct by placing a subform around the elements. First he selects the area with all of his elements and then right-clicks. From the context menu, he chooses **Wrap in Subform** (see Figure 14.13).

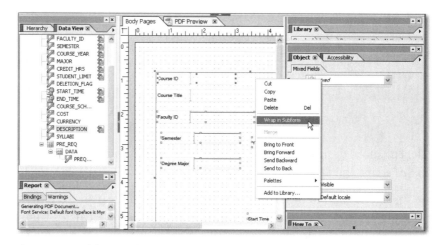

Figure 14.13 Subforms Offer Easy Organization of Form Elements

3. Now that he has all of his elements wrapped in a subform, he can set visual properties for all elements in the subform via the property box of the subform. Figure 14.14 shows how he uses the **Content** attribute of the subform to switch from **Positioned** to **Flowed**. This will automatically align each field in the subgroup, placing one item per line.

4. To complete his first form, he adds a static image to the header of the page. He chooses to embed the image data in the form so that no reference to a URL has to be performed at runtime. At this point, he can switch to the **PDF Preview** tab to see how the form looks so far (see Figure 14.15).

Figure 14.14 Content Positioning Options

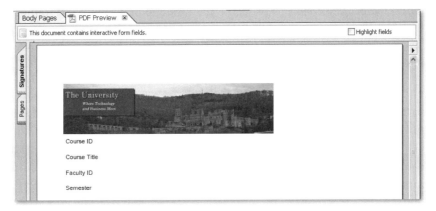

Figure 14.15 PDF Preview from the Layout Editor

5. The **PDF Preview** is an accurate representation of how the final rendering will look; however, none of the data being fed via the context is processed during the preview. Consequently, Russel can only see the field labels for the output and not his data fields.

   This is the only drawback to the **PDF Preview** in the ABAP forms space. Usually, you're working primarily with dynamic data in your form. If you have looping data structures being populated by an internal table, the PDF Preview can become almost useless, because it will only show you the general position of the table and its headers, and not the entire table and its contents.

14.2.4 Coding Against the Form Function Module

Russel has a lot of experience with integrating custom SAP Smart Forms into his applications, and, as it turns out, the generated function modules for Adobe Forms are actually quite similar to those of the old SAP Smart Forms. This makes converting from using SAP Smart Forms to Adobe Forms in existing applications relatively straightforward. It also means that much of what Russel already knows from working with SAP Smart Forms will make his job of processing the newly designed Adobe Form into his course application that much easier.

Logic Added to the Model Class

To make forms processing available to all of his applications, Russel will add all the logic to the existing model class. He could use this type of function model based processing to print the form online or in the background. He can also use it to generate a downloadable version of the form. Another nice option is to generate the form and use the PDF output as an attachment in an email.

Therefore, he will build the model method in a way that fits all these possible uses. Because he is in his model class, he can build on the data retrieval methods that already exist. So he will read all the course data from the global attributes of the model class. You should note that before form generation could be executed, these attributes would have to be initialized by another model method via the calling application.

With all data selection occurring outside of the method, he only has one input parameter, GET_BINARY_OUTPUT, which is an optional parameter that, when set to true, will not send the rendered output to the print spooler. Instead, it will return a binary string with the generated PDF output. This binary string is the only returning parameter of the method.

1. Russel begins the method's logic by first checking this binary output parameter. If the calling application has selected this option, he only needs to pass that flag through to the Adobe Document Services via the OUTPUT-PARAMS variable. There are other fields in the OUTPUTPARAMS structure that can control many of the output options such as the default print or the timing of the print output:

```
METHOD render_course_pdf.
  DATA outputparams TYPE sfpoutputparams.
  IF get_binary_output = abap_true.
    outputparams-getpdf = abap_true.
  ENDIF.
```

2. Russel now calls the function module FP_JOB_OPEN to mark the start of his forms processing. He could process multiple forms in one job for improved performance. In this case he will only output one form per job.

Note that the options that he specified via the OUTPUTPARAMS are applied to the entire job, not the individual form output:

```
CALL FUNCTION 'FP_JOB_OPEN'
  CHANGING
    ie_outputparams = outputparams.
```

3. Like SAP Smart Forms, Adobe Forms generates a function module for each form. These function module names can differ from system to system since they use a simple number range for assigning a unique name. For that reason, Russel knows that you never want to directly call the generated function module.

Instead you call FP_FUNCTION_MODULE_NAME and pass in the form name. This function will return the correct corresponding generated function module name that can be called dynamically:

```
DATA: fpname   TYPE fpname,
      funcname TYPE funcname.
      fpname = `ZCS_FM_COURSE`.
  CALL FUNCTION 'FP_FUNCTION_MODULE_NAME'
    EXPORTING
      i_name     = fpname
    IMPORTING
      e_funcname = funcname.
```

In this block of code, Russel calls the generated function module. By generating the function module, SAP can provide a fixed interface based on the form interface instead of some generic data types.

4. However, it is important to note that because the function module name is supplied dynamically, no syntax checks can be performed on the parameters. If you specify something incorrectly, you probably will not find the error until the application creates a short dump during testing:

```
DATA: fp_docparams  TYPE sfpdocparams,
      fp_formoutput TYPE fpformoutput.
  CALL FUNCTION funcname
    EXPORTING
      /1bcdwb/docparams  = fp_docparams
      course_details     = me->course_obj->course
    IMPORTING
      /1bcdwb/formoutput = fp_formoutput
    EXCEPTIONS
      usage_error    = 1
      system_error   = 2
      internal_error = 3.
```

5. Although the function group can produce an error if there is a serious error communicating with the Adobe Document Services, it might be helpful to be able to trap additional information about an error. Therefore you can call the additional function modules, FP_GET_LAST_ADS_ERRSTR and FP_GET_LAST_ADS_TRACE, to receive more detailed information about the error state:

```
DATA error TYPE string.
  CALL FUNCTION 'FP_GET_LAST_ADS_ERRSTR'
    IMPORTING
      e_adserrstr = error.
  IF error IS NOT INITIAL.
    MESSAGE  error TYPE 'I'.
  ENDIF.
  CALL FUNCTION 'FP_GET_LAST_ADS_TRACE'
    IMPORTING
      e_adstrace = error.
```

6. The final step is to close the job with FP_JOB_CLOSE. Russel then extracts the PDF content as well from the exported parameter FP_FORMOUTPUT:

```
  CALL FUNCTION 'FP_JOB_CLOSE'
    EXCEPTIONS
      usage_error    = 1
      system_error   = 2
      internal_error = 3
      OTHERS         = 4.
  r_content = fp_formoutput-pdf.
ENDMETHOD.                         "render_course_pdf
```

Form Output Test Program

Now that he has integrated the print-only Adobe function module into his model class, Russel wants to create a simple test application to either print or download the form he has created.

1. He will have a basic dialog report that has a parameter to choose the course to output and to set the option to download the output as a PDF file as well:

```
REPORT  zcs_adobe_course_print.
PARAMETER p_course TYPE zcs_course_id OBLIGATORY.
PARAMETER p_down   TYPE boolean AS CHECKBOX.
START-OF-SELECTION.
  DATA: model TYPE REF TO zcl_cs_main_model,
        content TYPE xstring,
```

```
        o_exception TYPE REF TO cx_root.
    CREATE OBJECT model.
```

2. He will use the model class to read the data that will be used in the form. He will then request the form processing logic to be executed. If the download parameter was set, the binary string, CONTENT, will be filled with the PDF output of the form:

```
TRY.
    model->read_course_details( p_course ) .
    content = model->render_course_pdf( p_down ).
  CATCH cx_root INTO o_exception.
    MESSAGE o_exception TYPE 'I'.
    EXIT
ENDTRY.
```

3. To download the form as a PDF file, he will first query the user for the file save location:

```
IF p_down = abap_true AND content IS NOT INITIAL.
    DATA: filename TYPE string,
          path     TYPE string,
          fullpath TYPE string,
          default_extension TYPE STRING VALUE 'PDF'.
    cl_gui_frontend_services=>file_save_dialog(
        EXPORTING
          default_extension    = default_extension
        CHANGING
          filename             = filename
          path                 = path
          fullpath             = fullpath ).
    CHECK fullpath IS NOT INITIAL.
```

4. Binary strings cannot be downloaded directly with the SAP provided classes. So before the download can occur, the content in the returned binary string must be converted to a simple binary table:

```
DATA data_tab TYPE STANDARD TABLE OF x255.
CALL FUNCTION 'SCMS_XSTRING_TO_BINARY'
  EXPORTING
    buffer     = content
  TABLES
    binary_tab = data_tab.
```

5. Now the content can be downloaded to the frontend. With the extra call to the EXECUTE method, the newly downloaded file will immediately be opened in Adobe Reader on the frontend:

```
cl_gui_frontend_services=>gui_download(
    EXPORTING
        filename                 = filename
        filetype                 = 'BIN'
    CHANGING
        data_tab                 = data_tab ).
    cl_gui_frontend_services=>execute(
        EXPORTING
            document             = filename ).
ENDIF.
```

6. If the user doesn't select the `preview` parameter, the standard print dialog, which offers a **Print Preview** option, will be displayed (see Figure 14.16). This is similar to the print preview offered by SAPscript and SAP Smart Forms, except here the output is displayed by an instance of the Adobe Reader running within the SAP GUI.

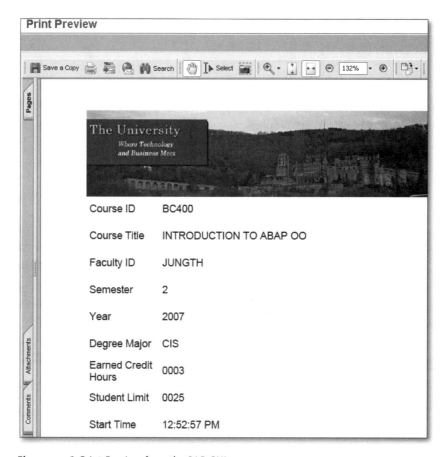

Figure 14.16 Print Preview from the SAP GUI

14.3   Web Dynpro Based Forms

The integration of Web Dynpro and Adobe Forms offers a very different approach than the function module based example that Russel first started with. Because the Web Dynpro context is XML based, there's another option for interfacing to the Adobe Form content. By interfacing between both contexts using XML, it can make communication between the two technologies much easier.

That is not the only aspect that is easier. When working in Web Dynpro, Russel has already seen how all changes in data in either the context or the screen elements are automatically reflected in the corresponding object via data binding. The Web Dynpro integration with Adobe Forms brings this same ease of use thanks to data binding between the Web Dynpro context and the form context. This is especially important for interactive forms where updates to the form are automatically bound back into the Web Dynpro context.

Keeping with the Web Dynpro approach of UI element abstraction, all the coding for calling the Adobe Form is also hidden from view. This makes Adobe Forms (even interactive ones) integration a code free venture.

14.3.1   Web Dynpro View Creation

Web Dynpro offers a great feature, in that the tool can automatically generate an Adobe Form context and interface for the developer based on the existing Web Dynpro context. Therefore Russel takes a different approach to meet the requirement that he will create his objects in the same way that created the function module based form.

1. He starts by creating his Web Dynpro application. All of his data retrieval logic is housed in the model class and accessed via the Web Dynpro controller. Results are held in the controller context.

2. After working with the Web Dynpro tools to populate the data and build the context, Russel turns to the layout of his view. He simply adds the **InteractiveForm** UI element to his layout

3. From here, he specifies the display options for the form via the **Properties** of the UI element (see Figure 14.17). The **templateSource** property is used to specify which Adobe Form he wants to use in this interactive form area.

   Russel supplies the **templateSource** value of ZCS_WD_COURSE. Although this form does not exist yet, he knows this is what he will want to name the form. He can start the form creation process from within Web Dynpro by double-clicking on the aforementioned value that he supplied to the **templateSource**.

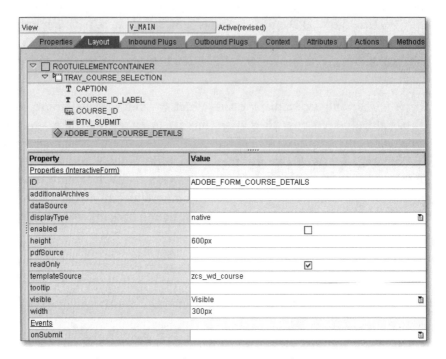

Figure 14.17 Web Dynpro View with an Interactive Form Element

4. The dialog that the system proposes (see Figure 14.18) not only allows you to supply the name of the interface that will be generated as well, but also allows you to use a **Context Node** to create the interface.

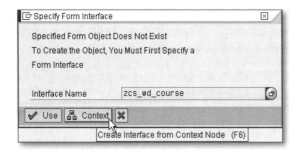

Figure 14.18 Form Interface Creation from the Web Dynpro Context

14.3.2 Form Design from Web Dynpro

The generation of the form context from the Web Dynpro context has several advantages that go beyond just being a time-saving measure. Figure 14.19 shows the two contexts juxtaposed for better comparison. The left side shows the context as it is defined in Web Dynpro. The right side, on the other hand, is the corresponding context that was generated in the forms environment:

▸ First, we have the COURSE_PRE_REQ subnode of our COURSE_DETAILS main node. Because the source node in Web Dynpro had a cardinality of **0:n** (allows multiple instances or corresponds to an ABAP internal table), a table element was created in the form context.

▸ Likewise the special data types of DELETION_FLAG, **Boolean**, and START_TIME, **time**, were carried over into the forms context. Notice the icons next to each attribute in the form context. These denote the type of UI element that will be generated if the attribute is dropped onto the form's designer area. The Boolean based attribute will produce a checkbox and the time-based attributes will create a time-specific input field.

▸ Finally notice the icons next to the SEMESTER and COURSE_SCHEDULE attributes in the form's context. They denote that these attributes will create drop-down list boxes within the form. As you can see, more than just the UI element has been brought over from the Web Dynpro context.

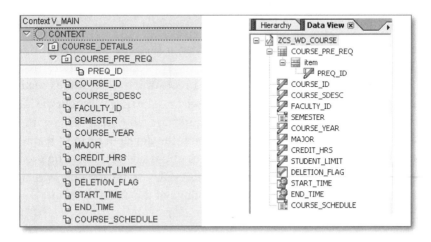

Figure 14.19 Automatic Generation of a Matching Form Context

The value set for an attribute, even if originally populated from the data dictionary, is part of a Web Dynpro context. This information also flows through to the Adobe Form and provides the possible values for the drop-down list box. This allows for a simple type of value help to automatically flow from the data dictionary all the way through to the interactive form without any coding on the developer's part.

14.3.3 Table Output in Forms

Although not specific to working in Web Dynpro, this second application that Russel is working on provides his first opportunity to output a table of data in an Adobe Form. Luckily, Russel did some research on the Adobe Life-Cycle Designer prior to starting this task. The version of the Adobe LifeCycle Designer that was installed on his machine during his SAP GUI installation was 7.0. This is the version of the design tool most commonly used against a SAP NetWeaver 7.0 system. It is possible, however, to update the Adobe LifeCycle Designer Software to a newer version, even against a SAP NetWeaver 7.0 system.

Russel follows the upgrade instructions that he found on the SAP Service Marketplace (*http://service.sap.com*) in OSS note 962763 and updates his Adobe LifeCycle Designer to Version 7.1. Although this is a minor level change, this update brings with it an important feature that many ABAP developers will find very useful, namely, a table wizard. So when Russel starts the process of outputting the course prerequisites on his form, he chooses the new toolbar option for **Insert Table**. This starts the **Table Assistant** (see Figure 14.20).

The Table Assistant makes it simple to design the look and flow of a data table by having the user work through a series of simple selections. It also turns more complex operations, such as a repeating header or area section, into just another option in the assistant's wizard-like flow. Without the Table Assistant and some of the other new features for tables that come with the 7.1 update to the Adobe LifeCycle Designer, the developer had to manually design the layout of the table using a series of nested subforms. The process became less difficult after studying a few examples, but it certainly was more cumbersome than using the enhanced options of the Table Assistant.

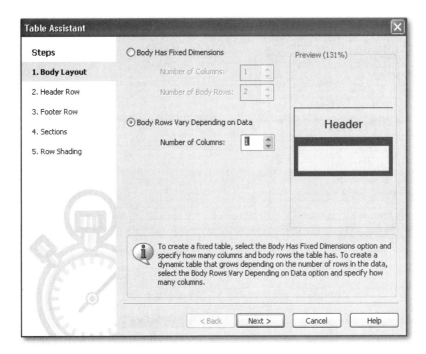

Figure 14.20 Table Assistant

Figure 14.21 shows the settings that would have to be manually created for the three separate subforms in versions before the 7.1 update to the Adobe LifeCycle Designer.

▶ On the **Table Subform**, you would want to be sure to use the **Flow Content** type.

▶ Also the **Column Widths** option was where you set your overall columns for the whole table. They had to be specified by size and separated by commas.

▶ Next there are the separate subforms for the table header and the table body. Each needed a special flow direction of **Header** and **Table row** respectively.

▶ The real difficulty came however in the binding settings of the table body subform (see Figure 14.22). In order to get more than one row of the bound data attribute output, you had to select the **Repeat Subform for Each Data Item** option, which enabled you to set minimum and maximum row output options.

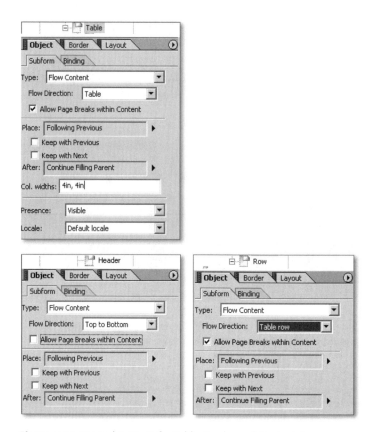

Figure 14.21 Manual Settings for Table Header and Content Areas

▶ Finally, if you wanted the table header to be repeated when the table overflowed onto a second page, you could set the **Overflow Leader** to the name of the table header subform.

Figure 14.22 Manual Setting for Row Processing in a Table

Now that Russel has his form layout completed, he saves and activates it. Upon returning to the Web Dynpro application, he is ready to test what he has created so far. The initial output is shown in Figure 14.23. Without writing a single line of code, he has the form running in his Web Dynpro application with the data being populated between the two contexts.

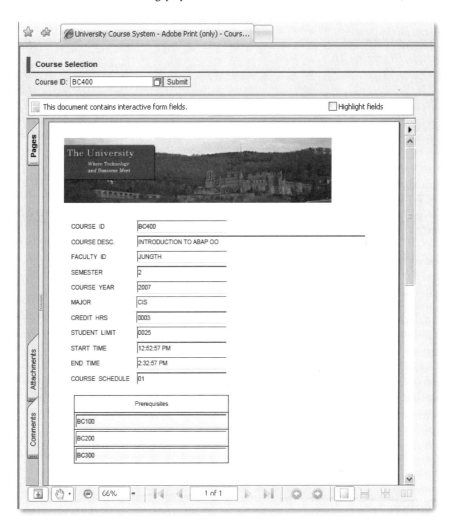

Figure 14.23 Form Output from Web Dynpro

14.3.4 Making the Form Interactive

The only question that remains is how to make this form interactive. As it turns out, the Web Dynpro runtime will take care of all the complexities involved with this task. All Russel has to do is return to the properties of the

`InteractiveForm` UI element in his Web Dynpro view (see Figure 14.24), where he checks the **enabled** property. This simple action is all that is required to make the form interactive.

Property	Value	Binding
Properties (InteractiveForm)		
ID	ADOBE_FORM_COURSE_DETAILS	
additionalArchives		
dataSource	V_MAIN.COURSE_DETAILS	
displayType	activeX	
enabled	☑	
height	600px	
pdfSource		
readOnly	☐	
templateSource	ZCS_WD_COURSE_CREATE	
tooltip		
visible	Visible	
width	600px	
Events		
onSubmit	SUBMIT_PDF	
Layout Data (FlowData)		
cellDesign	padless	
vGutter	none	

Figure 14.24 Element Settings for Creating an Interactive Form

He can also now attach an event handler to the **onSubmit** event of the form. There is a special **Toolbox** tab in the forms designer for Web Dynpro. In this **Toolbox** is a **Submit** button. This button, when pressed within the form, will trigger the corresponding event in the hosting Web Dynpro application.

Russel will use this event handler that is triggered in the form to call an update method of his model class. However, just like the print form's output was automatically populated by the values of the Web Dynpro Context, the opposite is true is well. When working with an interactive form and submitting an event, all the updated form values are automatically copied back into the Web Dynpro Context.

14.4   Offline Forms

Russel's final business requirement around forms is for an offline form that can be used to create new courses. The process of creating the form itself, for use in an offline scenario, doesn't require any additional steps. In fact, Russel decides to reuse much of the interactive form he has already created. He creates a simple Web Dynpro application to display an empty version of the form. He can then perform a **File • Save As** to create an offline version of this same form. Users can then complete the form offline and save it for a later upload into their system.

There are many ways in which you can get the completed forms back into the system. You can use inbound email processing or some form of file upload. Russel elects to create another simple Web Dynpro application. This application will just have a FileUpload UI element, where the user can choose which completed form he or she wants to load into the system. All the processing for the uploading occurs in the event handler for the File Upload element. Although he is performing this action in Web Dynpro, Russel isn't using any special Web Dynpro features. You can adjust this sample example so it can be used in classic Dynpro or BSP.

1. Russel starts the event handler logic by reading the binary content of the uploaded object:

```
METHOD onactionupload_form.
 DATA: node_pdf_source_node TYPE REF TO if_wd_context_node,
       elem_pdf_source_node
           TYPE REF TO if_wd_context_element,
       stru_pdf_source_node
           TYPE if_v_upload=>element_pdf_source_node,
      item_pdf_source LIKE stru_pdf_source_node-pdf_source.
     node_pdf_source_node = wd_context->get_child_node(
         name = if_v_upload=>wdctx_pdf_source_node ).
     elem_pdf_source_node =
         node_pdf_source_node->get_element( ).
     elem_pdf_source_node->get_attribute(
       EXPORTING name =  `PDF_SOURCE`
       IMPORTING value = item_pdf_source ).
```

2. The programming interface to the Adobe Forms processing is exposed through the classes CL_FP*. For this processing, Russel needs to create a reference to the PDF Object Class:

```
DATA: i_course TYPE zcs_course_att,
      o_except TYPE REF TO cx_root.
TRY.
    DATA fp TYPE REF TO if_fp.
    fp = cl_fp=>get_reference( ).
    DATA pdf TYPE REF TO if_fp_pdf_object.
    pdf = fp->create_pdf_object( ).
```

3. Now he will take the binary context that has been uploaded and set that as the source of the PDF object:

```
pdf->set_document( pdfdata = item_pdf_source ).
```

4. To process the interactive fields, Russel doesn't need the entire source of the PDF document. There is lot of information, like images, labels, and screen positioning, that simply is not relevant. The ADS provides a method for extracting only those values stored in the interactive fields:

```
pdf->set_extractdata( ).
pdf->execute( ).
```

5. Russel needs this data to be in a format that is easy to work with from ABAP. For that, he asks the ADS to return it as XML:

```
DATA pdf_data TYPE xstring.
pdf->get_data( IMPORTING formdata = pdf_data ).
DATA: ixml TYPE REF TO if_ixml,
      streamfactory
          TYPE REF TO if_ixml_stream_factory,
      istream TYPE REF TO if_ixml_istream.
ixml = cl_ixml=>create( ).
streamfactory = ixml->create_stream_factory( ).
istream = streamfactory->create_istream_xstring(
          pdf_data ).
DATA document TYPE REF TO if_ixml_document.
document = ixml->create_document( ).
```

6. Now Russel parses the XML Document in order to access its individual elements and attributes easily:

```
DATA parser TYPE REF TO if_ixml_parser.
parser = ixml->create_parser(
  stream_factory = streamfactory
  istream        = istream
  document       = document ).
parser->parse( ).
DATA node TYPE REF TO if_ixml_node.
```

7. Next, Russel uses the XML document methods to extract the particular fields that he needs for processing:

```
node = document->find_from_name(
    name = 'course_id' ).
i_course-course_id = node->get_value( ).
...
node = document->find_from_name(
    name = 'course_schedule' ).
i_course-course_schedule = node->get_value( ).
```

8. With the XML data moved to a flat ABAP structure, Russel calls a method of his model object to perform the create operation:

```
wd_assist->create_course( i_course_att = i_course ).
```

9. If everything has worked fine so far, Russel just wants to fire an outbound plug. This will take his Web Dynpro application to a different view that will display the results of the uploaded form:

```
wd_this->fire_outto_success_plg( ).
```

10. If any errors occurred when the ADS processed the input form, or when the XML data was extracted and processed, or when the model object performed the business logic validations and updates, they would all be caught and output by this final block of logic:

```
    CATCH cx_root INTO o_except.
      DATA: l_current_controller
                 TYPE REF TO if_wd_controller,
            l_message_manager
                 TYPE REF TO if_wd_message_manager.
      l_current_controller ?= wd_this->wd_get_api( ).
      l_message_manager =
            l_current_controller->get_message_manager( ).
      l_message_manager->report_exception(
          message_object          = o_except ).
    ENDTRY.
ENDMETHOD.
```

The SAP NetWeaver Portal constitutes the foundation of SAP's User Interface strategy. It is the primary method for accessing all of your business processes. It provides role-based access to the individual parts of your business process and the technology that helps to bridge these parts. For Russel, the SAP NetWeaver Portal is the unifying tool that brings all of the UI elements of his project together.

15   SAP NetWeaver Portal

The university that Russel works for is actually new to the SAP NetWeaver Portal. They've had a custom intranet for several years. With the upgrade to SAP ERP 6.0, they have realized the value of having a unified method for accessing their ERP content and they therefore need a tool that can be more than just a place to display their company and department news. For that reason, Russel wants to ensure that everything that he has developed for the new online course system can run well in the portal via role-based access.

15.1   Creating a System Configuration

Before Russel can set up his individual roles and applications in the new portal, he has to define his ERP system within the portal's **System Configuration**. When creating portal elements for SAP objects, you never directly reference the URLs or other system connection information within the object definition itself. Instead, you should only reference a system alias that points to a reusable set of system connection options. This gives you the freedom you need to make system configuration changes and then have those changes become effective immediately across all elements that use that system.

Russel starts out by navigating to the **System Administration** role within the portal. Then he chooses **System Configuration • System Landscape** from the portal navigation menu. This provides a series of folders. These folders make up the *Portal Content Repository*.

This is the same repository that all portal objects will be stored in. So before creating anything, Russel decides to create a folder that is specific to the project that he is working on. Then, by right-clicking on this new folder, he chooses **New • System (from template)** (see Figure 15.1). This starts the *New System Wizard*.

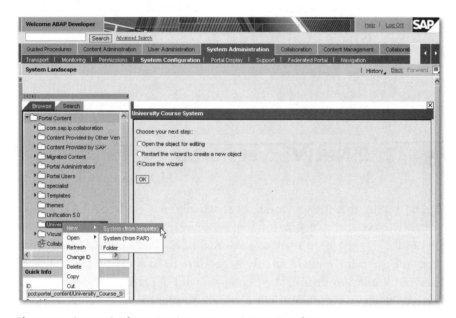

Figure 15.1 System Configuration Creation via a System Template

1. The New System Wizard provides Russel with many potential templates to choose from (see Figure 15.2). There are templates specific to Business Intelligence and Knowledge Management. For ABAP-based applications like SAP Enterprise Resource Planning (SAP ERP) or SAP Customer Relationship Management (SAP CRM), there are three specific templates to consider:

   ▶ **SAP system using connection string**
   The connection string is used in more exotic landscapes where it is necessary to pass communications through SAProuter in order to connect through multiple networks or firewalls.

   ▶ **SAP system using dedicated application server**
   This option is perhaps the simplest of the three and can be useful for test and development systems where you traditionally only have one application server. In this setup, you will primarily be required to specify the hostname of the application server that you want to connect to. In a system with multiple application servers, no load balancing will occur, because you will always connect to whichever application server is specified in the configuration.

▷ **SAP system with load balancing**
The final option for ABAP-based applications is probably the most commonly used for production systems. With this option, you will configure the connection to communicate via the Message Server, which, in turn, will load balance requests across all available application servers.

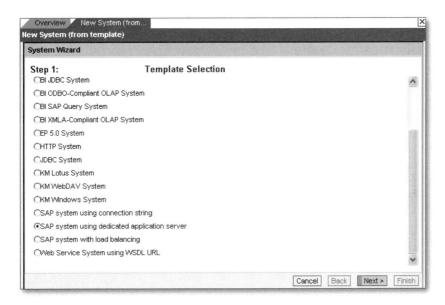

Figure 15.2 New System Configuration — Template Selection

For Russel's purposes, choosing the dedicated application server option makes the most sense, because he is only setting up his development system at this time. Later, when he sets up his production system, he will use the load balancing option instead.

2. Next, Russel has to give this new connection a name (see Figure 15.3). The first field, **System Name**, is really more of a free form description. You can use special characters and spaces. The **System ID**, on the other hand, is more restrictive and must be unique.

Optionally Russel could have used a **System ID Prefix**, which can be used to make object names more unique. This is very similar to a namespace in ABAP development. There are also different divisions within the university and each division could potentially be assigned separate prefixes so as to avoid name clashes and to keep their objects separated.

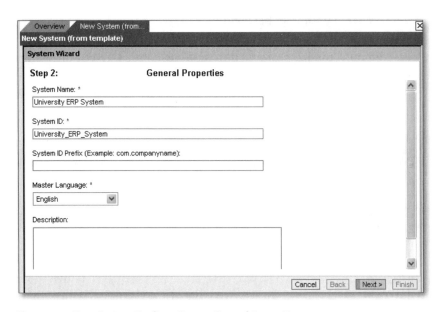

Figure 15.3 New System Configuration — General Properties

3. In the next step, Russel must contend with the first of the core configuration properties for his new system configuration (see Figure 15.4). This maintenance screen is actually multilayered, although it may not appear that way at first glance.

   ▸ The highest level of configuration set options is controlled by the value in the **Display** drop-down field at the top, on the right of the screen. You can think of this value as controlling different blocks of configuration options. For now, Russel will work with the largest block, the **Object** options.

   ▸ The second level of options is controlled by the **Property Category** drop-down field near the top, on the left of the screen. There are well over 100 possible configuration fields on this system template and this option reduces the number of fields you see at one time. You can also use this option to group these fields into related sets. There is also an option to display all the fields at once.

4. It makes sense for Russel to start with the **Connector Property Category**. This particular category controls the main options that will be used to connect to the ABAP-based portions of the ERP system via remote function call (RFC) and SAP GUI. It is also the category that varies the most, depending on which of the three templates you chose earlier.

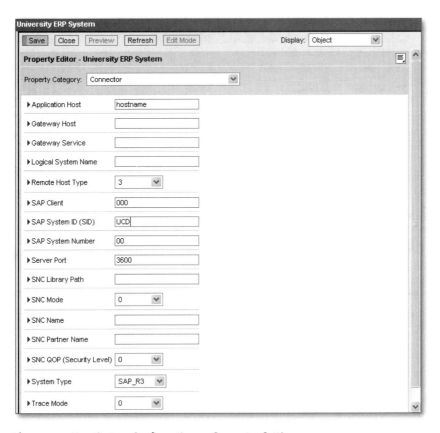

Figure 15.4 New System Configuration — Connector Settings

Most of the configuration options constitute technical information that is required to establish a connection to the system. These same options are probably used in your SAP Logon in order for you to connect to the system via the SAP GUI. Russel already knew most of the answers, simply by checking the configuration in his SAPLogon. The **Server Port** was the only configuration option that he wasn't sure about, so he asked his Basis Administrator.

5. The next **Property Category** is the **User Management** section (see Figure 15.5). This group of options controls how the user will log on to the backend systems.

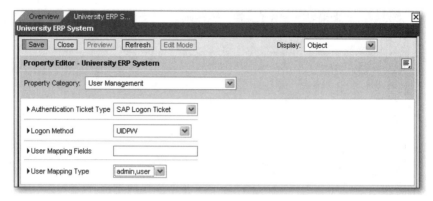

Figure 15.5 New System Configuration — User Management

There are two main options that could potentially be used for the **Logon Method**:

▶ The first is direct passing of **User Name and Password via User Mapping (UIDPW)**. Without the use of HTTPS for the connection to the back-end system, the password will be transmitted in clear text. This makes this type of connection quite insecure and should really only be used for testing and development systems if possible.

▶ The more secure method is to use **Single Sign-On**. This does require more setup between the systems in question. These steps are well documented in the SAP online guides and consist mostly of loading the portal's certificate into the ERP system via transaction STRUSTSSO2.

The portal generates a Single Sign-On (SSO) ticket in the form of a session browser cookie. If the certificate embedded within this ticket matches a portal certificate that has been loaded and configured in the back-end system, that system will allow access without the need to transmit any passwords.

6. For Russel's purposes, his system administrators have not configured SSO between the new portal and their ERP back-end system yet. Therefore, he must resort to using **UIDPW** (see Figure 15.5). He can choose, via the **User Mapping Type** option, who can maintain the user mapping. He decides to allow both administrators and individual users to maintain their own mapping. Before he can use this connection, he will have to create a user mapping for his own account later.

7. The final main **Property Category** that Russel needs to set up is the **Web Application Server (Web AS)** configuration set. The settings that he entered earlier in the **Connector category** will only be used for connections that use the SAP GUI or RFC. More importantly, for the majority of iViews he will be creating, he will need to access Business Server Pages (BSP) and Web Dynpro ABAP applications via a URL. That is precisely what this configuration set allows him to specify (see Figure 15.6).

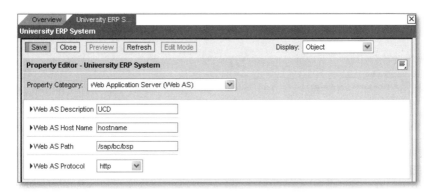

Figure 15.6 New System Configuration — Application Server

You might notice that the **Web AS Path** is specific to BSP. Originally, this category was only used for BSP applications. However, with the introduction of Web Dynpro ABAP, rather than have two very similar property categories, the system just ignores the path when building URLs for Web Dynpro. Instead, it substitutes a path built from the attributes that must be supplied during iView creation.

8. Although there are many other configuration options, Russel has entered enough options to start using this system configuration. He can always return later and set up secondary sets of configuration like those for accessing the *Integrated Internet Transaction Server* (ITS) of his ERP system.

   Before this system configuration can be used in iView creation, or even for user mapping, it must be assigned a *System Alias*. Although you can create numerous system aliases for a single system configuration, you must have at least one default alias.

9. Russel changes the **Display** type to **System Aliases** so he can enter an **Alias Name** (see Figure 15.7).

10. If everything is configured correctly, the **User Mapping Status** should now change to a green checkmark.

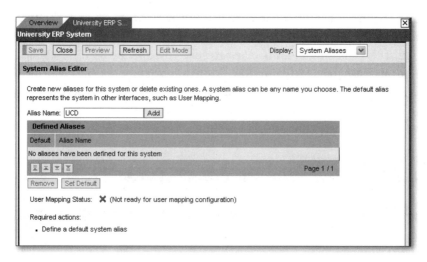

Figure 15.7 New System Configuration — System Alias

15.1.1 User Mapping

Before Russel can test his new system configuration, he needs to complete the user mapping. The nice thing about user mapping is that it allows users to have different user IDs between the portal and the various back-end systems.

Russel accesses the **User Maintenance** application in the portal. He then navigates to the **User Mapping for System Access** tab (see Figure 15.8). Here he can choose any system alias that has been configured to allow for user mapping. He only needs to enter his username and password for this ERP system and it will be used automatically any time content accesses this system for him via the system configuration alias.

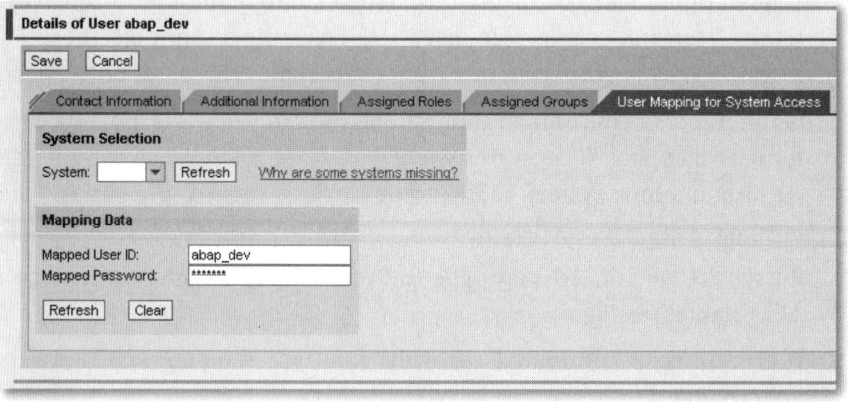

Figure 15.8 User Maintenance — User Mapping

15.1.2 System Test

Before using the system configuration in any iViews, Russel thinks it would be a good idea to test it. That way he knows he has a good, working system configuration. It also eliminates the possibility of a problem, if he needs to troubleshoot any newly created iViews. So he returns to the **System Configuration** maintenance. He just needs to change the **Display** option to **Connection Tests**.

There are choices for the different types of connections that could have been set up in the system configuration. It is important to note that these connection tests are little more than simple pings against the back-end systems. They will tell you if you made a major mistake during the configuration and test basic user authentication; however, they might not uncover all existing configuration issues (see Figure 15.9).

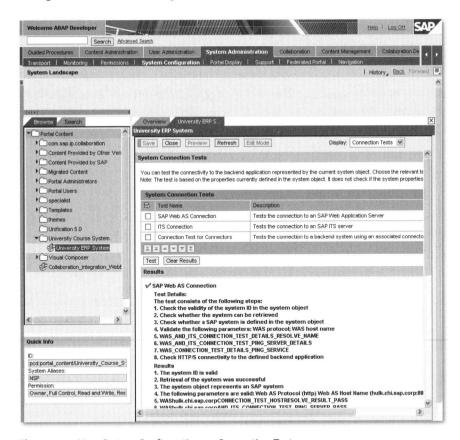

Figure 15.9 New System Configuration — Connection Tests

15.2 Creating Portal Content

Now that Russel has completed all of his system configuration steps, he is ready to get some of his applications running in the portal. Content within the portal can all be set up from the standard role, **Content Administration**. Then he chooses **Portal Content** from the role navigation menu.

The first question that Russel faces is what kind of portal content does he want to create. The *iView* is the most atomic type of content. It acts as a "wrapper" around remote content so that it can be managed within the portal context. So, if you have a Web Dynpro application on your ERP system, it needs an iView created for it before it can be used within the portal. Each Web Dynpro application would be represented by its own iView.

iViews, however, don't have to take up the entire portal workspace. Multiple iViews, even those from very different source technologies, can be combined in one workspace. The portal content that controls this grouping of iViews is called a *Page*.

The navigational structure within the portal is all role based. The options in the role-based menu are built automatically via assignments of portal content to the role. Although Pages can be assigned directly to roles, it is often more efficient to group similar Pages together. This grouping can be accomplished via the third type of portal content called the *Workset*.

15.2.1 iView Creation

On the left side of the **Portal Content** maintenance application is the same set of **Portal Content** folders that we saw earlier when creating the system configuration. Once again, Russel is going to create all of his new content within the folder that he created earlier to hold the system configuration.

1. He starts creating an iView by right-clicking on the **University Course System** folder and choosing **New • iView**. This action loads the iView Wizard. Then, Russel starts the wizard with the **iView template** option. (see Figure 15.10)

2. There are several different types of iView templates to choose from based on the type of content that you want to display (see Figure 15.11). For ERP development, some of the more common templates to use are the BSP, Web Dynpro, and Transaction iView.

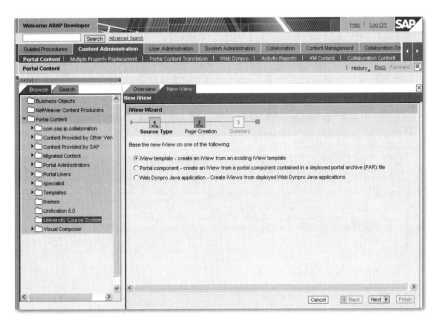

Figure 15.10 iView Creation via Template

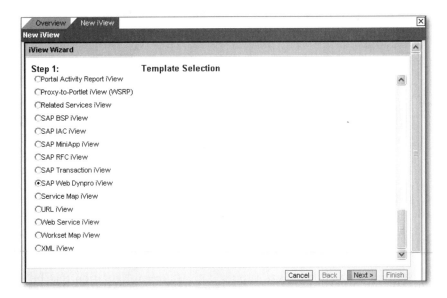

Figure 15.11 iView Creation — Template Selection

Since Russel wants to start with one of his new Web Dynpro ABAP applications, the **SAP Web Dynpro iView** template is the one he will choose in

Step 1 of the iView Wizard. Notice that there is no distinction yet between Web Dynpro Java and Web Dynpro ABAP.

3. Next, Russel must supply the **General Properties** for his new iView (see Figure 15.12). This step (Step 2) in the wizard is the same, regardless of what template type is being processed. The rules are basically the same as when setting up the general properties on the system configuration earlier.

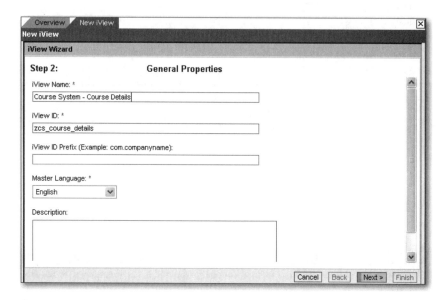

Figure 15.12 iView Creation — General Properties

The **iView Name** is a free form description that will show up in the navigation tree and frame around the iView. This value can be edited later. The **iView ID**, on the other hand, is the unique key for the iView and cannot be changed.

4. Step 3 of the iView Wizard is a fairly simple one. Russel just has to specify whether he is using **Web Dynpro for ABAP** or **Web Dynpro for Java** (see Figure 15.13). This will affect several background settings, such as how the portal theme is applied to the Web Dynpro application.

5. The final step (Step 4) is to supply the system configuration that he created earlier for his ERP system. You will notice that at no point does Russel have to supply the URL for his Web Dynpro application. He only has to supply the application name and, optionally, the configuration name. These values will be combined with the settings in the system configuration to assemble the full URL at runtime (see Figure 15.14).

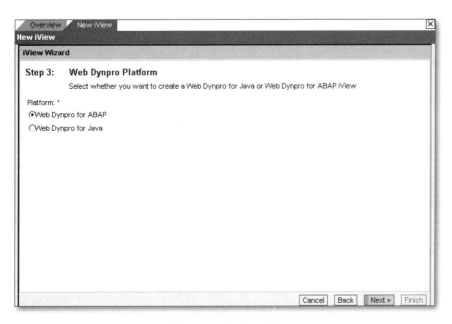

Figure 15.13 iView Creation — Web Dynpro Platform Choice

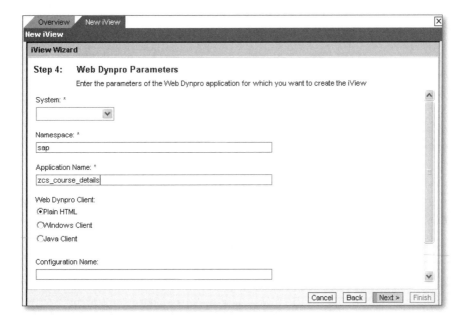

Figure 15.14 iView Creation — Web Dynpro Parameters

15.2.2 Role Assignment

This particular iView will take up the full workspace. Therefore, it doesn't need to be placed in a page. So now Russel can proceed with creating the role. The process of creating the role can vary by system configuration. Some portals will be configured to read their roles from external directories; however, in Russel's portal, he creates the **Role** directly in the content directory via the context menu, like all the other objects he has created so far (see Figure 15.15).

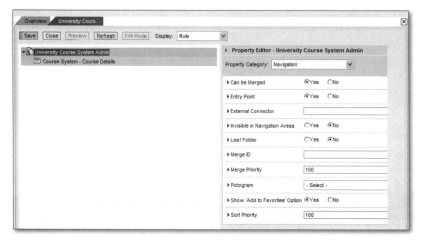

Figure 15.15 iView Assignment to a Role

Notice that in the **Property Editor** on the right side of the screen, there are options for the role that is being edited. Russel is going to keep all the default values except for the **Entry Point** parameter. Setting this value to **Yes** allows the role to appear directly on the role-based navigation bar. Without this value, this role could only be used within other roles. In order to assign the iView to the role, the role needs to be loaded in change mode in the **Portal Content** maintenance application as seen in Figure 15.15.

From the **Browse** tab of the **Portal Content** folders, Russel can still select any of the other objects he has created. When he right-clicks on the iView, the context menu will now have extra options, because a role is open in the edit window. He will choose the **Add iView to Role • Delta Link** menu option. This will create the assignment of the iView to this role and the display in the role maintenance window will be updated to reflect this new relationship.

Before this role and objects attached to it show up on the navigation bar, the role must be assigned to Russel's user account. Once again, this is a step that can vary greatly, depending on how your portal is configured. A portal that uses an external directory for its user store would likely also delegate role assignment to the directory. Russel's portal, on the other hand, uses the local Java *User Management Engine* (UME) of the portal for its directory. Therefore, he only has to return to the **User Administration • Identity Management** role menu and edit his own user account.

On the **Assigned Roles** tab, as seen in Figure 15.16, Russel can maintain what roles are currently assigned directly to his user. Normally, it might be more likely that roles are assigned to groups and that users are members of groups. However, the SAP NetWeaver Portal at the university is just getting set up and doesn't have all of its groups defined yet. Anyway, the process of assigning roles to groups, or groups to users, is comparable.

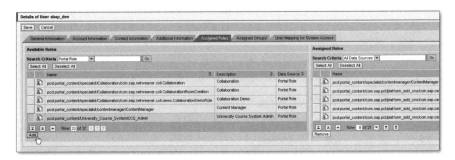

Figure 15.16 Role Assignment to a User

Russel changes the **Search Criteria** to **Portal Role** so that he only sees those roles directly created within the *Portal Content Directory* (PCD). He can then select the role that he created just a few minutes ago and add it to the selection of roles assigned to his user account.

15.2.3 Running Examples

With the new iViews created and all the role assignments finished, Russel is ready to test everything that he has been working on for the past few hours. He logs out of the portal and then logs back in again so that the new role assignments will be displayed in his role menu. Figure 15.17 shows his initial Web Dynpro ABAP iView, now running nicely in the portal:

▶ If you look at the main navigation bar, you'll see the new item called **University Course System Admin**. This entry is the role that has now been attached to his user account. The description on the navigation bar comes directly from the text description of the role that can be maintained from the PCD.

▶ On the second level navigation bar, you'll notice the entry **UCS Admin Activities**. This is the title of the workset that Russel created in order to group together all of his administrative iViews. He could eventually create more than one Workset and assign them all to his role. Multiple worksets, or other objects attached directly to the role, are what would make up the entries on this second level navigation bar.

▶ On the line directly below the second level navigation bar is the title **Course System — Course Details**. This is the name of the currently selected iView. This name comes directly from the iView properties and overrides anything that the inner application might propose as its page name.

▶ Under this line, you'll see the **Detailed Navigation** section. This is the listing of the iViews or pages that are attached to the selected workset.

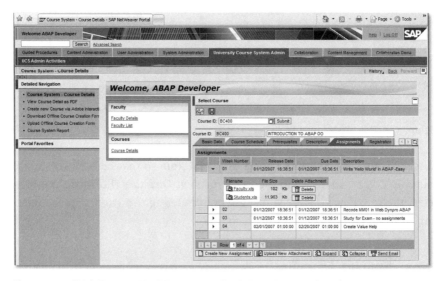

Figure 15.17 Web Dynpro ABAP Running in the SAP NetWeaver Portal

The iView technology makes it possible to integrate all of SAP's various UI technologies directly into the portal. Figure 15.18 and Figure 15.19 show two possible other technologies:

▶ Figure 15.18 shows an Adobe Interactive Form that was created in Chapter 14.

▶ Figure 15.19 is the classic Dynpro application that was created in Chapter 11. This was brought into the portal via the SAP transaction iView.

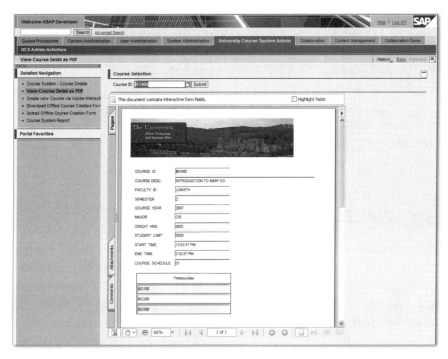

Figure 15.18 Adobe Forms Running in the Portal

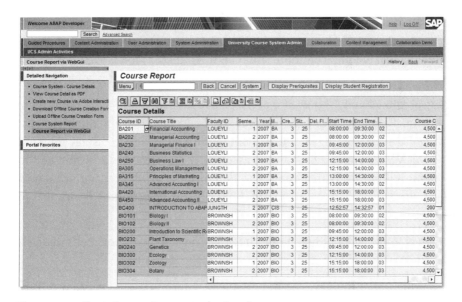

Figure 15.19 Classic Dynpro Running in the Portal

When creating an SAP Transaction iView, Russel had the choice of the GUI he wanted to use to open the transaction. The Transaction iView supports either the SAP GUI for Windows, SAP GUI for Java, or the Web GUI using the ITS. Both the SAP GUI for Windows and the SAP GUI for Java require installations on the client machine. However, the Web GUI requires no front-end installation, and with the introduction of the *Integrated ITS* in SAP NetWeaver 2004, no additional servers on the backend. This makes it an excellent choice for easily bringing classic Dynpro transaction to the portal to run side-by-side with newer UI technologies.

15.3 Portal Eventing

So far, Russel has been completely focused on getting his existing content running as is in the portal. Now he wants to look at how he might take advantage of some of the unique features of the portal. Earlier we discussed how multiple iViews can be placed in a single page. This allows for iViews comprised of different technologies to sit side-by-side within the same portal workspace. For instance, Russel might want to combine two existing iViews, one of which is implemented in Web Dynpro ABAP and the other in BSP.

This is where the power of the portal really comes through. These two separate iViews don't have to be islands cut off from one another. The portal framework that they are running in provides a technology called *Portal Eventing* that enables communication between these iViews, even if they run on different systems using completely different programming languages.

Russel immediately thinks of a perfect example that would allow him to use this functionality. Because a syllabus for a course was maintained and displayed as formatted HTML, he had not found a good way to display this content in Web Dynpro ABAP and consequently, had resorted to using BSP to output it. But ideally, he would like to utilize the validation and value help that already exist in Web Dynpro ABAP for the selection of the course to view.

Thanks to portal eventing, he can now take advantage of both technologies. Figure 15.20 shows this in action:

▶ At the top of the page, he has his Web Dynpro iView. This iView will be responsible for the user selecting a course. Once a course is selected, the Web Dynpro ABAP application will raise a portal event and send the selected course ID through with the event as supporting data. Raising the portal event does not require any knowledge of what subscribers, if any, there are for the event. It only hands off the event to the portal framework.

▶ The bottom half of the screen has the iView for the BSP application. It will register itself with the portal as an event listener. When the portal receives any event that matches the registered ID, it will inform the BSP application that the event occurred. The BSP will receive the event like any other front-end event and process it as it would a standard BSP extension.

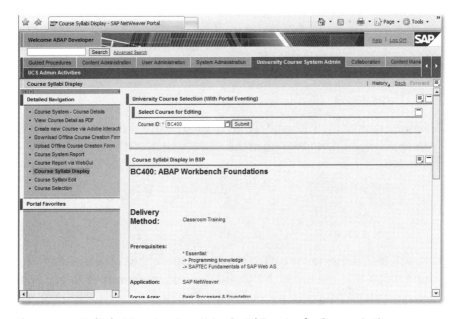

Figure 15.20 Multiple iViews in a Page Using Portal Eventing for Communication

Of course, this is just one possible combination. Technologies like BSP, Web Dynpro Java, Web Dynpro ABAP, and SAP NetWeaver Visual Composer can all be event subscribers and event receivers.

15.3.1 Throwing a Portal Event

In order to adjust his existing applications to support portal eventing, Russel will have to make a few minor modifications. Within the Web Dynpro ABAP view, a Web Dynpro action is already being triggered when the user clicks on the **Submit** button. The event handler for this action, `ONACTIONSELECT_COURSE`, is where he will place his portal eventing coding.

1. First he needs to read the context to get the currently selected course ID so that he can send the value along with the event:

```
METHOD onactionselect_course .
   DATA:
 node_course_details TYPE REF TO if_wd_context_node,
 elem_course_details TYPE REF TO if_wd_context_element,
 stru_course_details TYPE
   if_v_main=>element_course_details,
 item_course_id      LIKE stru_course_details-course_id.
   node_course_details = wd_context->get_child_node(
       name = if_v_main=>wdctx_course_details ).
   elem_course_details =
     node_course_details->get_element( ).
     elem_course_details->get_attribute(
       EXPORTING   name =  `COURSE_ID`
       IMPORTING   value = item_course_id ).
```

2. Now he uses a call to the model class to validate that the course ID that was entered is valid. If it is not, then the ZCX_COURSE_SYSTEM exception will be thrown:

```
DATA o_except TYPE REF TO zcx_course_system.
TRY.
    wd_assist->read_course_details(
       EXPORTING   i_course_id   = item_course_id ).
```

3. Now Russel comes to the coding that is specific to the portal eventing. The first action is to use the Web Dynpro Component Controller to get a reference to the Web Dynpro Portal Manager object:

```
DATA l_api_component   TYPE REF TO if_wd_component.
DATA l_portal_manager TYPE REF TO
   if_wd_portal_integration.
   l_api_component = wd_comp_controller->wd_get_api( ).
   l_portal_manager =
     l_api_component->get_portal_manager( ).
```

4. Next is the logic necessary to trigger the portal event. The fire method has three parameters: the event name, namespace, and a parameter string. The name and namespace form the keys of the event to be raised. These are the values that must be the same between the portal event sender and the receiver. By using a portal event namespace, Russel is assured that an event he named will not conflict with an event used in a standard SAP application.

Remember that Russel wants to send along the selected course ID with the event. When raising an event, you can send along a single string as the event parameter. Since he only has one value to send, it is easy to just move that value to a string field and pass that through. However, if you had multiple values, you might want to come up with a good way to place them all in the single string, perhaps using some form of delimited string. Keeping in mind that you might be crossing platforms and programming languages, you'll find that converting your parameters to XML will provide you with the most portability and be an easy way of processing the individual elements from the event string:

```
DATA portal_event_parameter TYPE string.
portal_event_parameter = item_course_id.
l_portal_manager->fire(
  portal_event_namespace = 'edu.university'
  portal_event_name      = 'course_select'
  portal_event_parameter = portal_event_parameter   ).
```

5. With the portal eventing specific coding completed, all that is left to do is catch the exception condition and issue a message to the user:

```
CATCH zcx_course_system INTO o_except.
  DATA: l_current_controller
             TYPE REF TO if_wd_controller,
        l_message_manager
             TYPE REF TO if_wd_message_manager.
  l_current_controller ?= wd_this->wd_get_api( ).
  l_message_manager =
      l_current_controller->get_message_manager( ).
  l_message_manager->report_exception(
      message_object              = o_except ).
  ENDTRY.
ENDMETHOD.
```

15.3.2 Catching a Portal Event

From the BSP side, Russel needs to first register the fact that his application wants to receive certain portal events. All the portal interaction elements are contained in the *BSP Extension Library*. During the view layout, Russel only needs to include a call to the `bsp:portalEvent` BSP extension element. Here he matches the same name and namespace as the Web Dynpro ABAP application uses to raise the event.

1. The only other UI elements being output during the layout make up the display of the syllabi itself. The field `syllabi` is a page attribute that can

contain the HTML content of the syllabi from the database. Because it is already in HTML format, it simply needs to be output directly in the layout as shown:

```
<%@page language="abap" %>
<%@extension name="htmlb" prefix="htmlb" %>
<%@extension name="bsp" prefix="bsp" %>
<htmlb:content design="design2003" >
  <htmlb:document>
    <htmlb:documentBody>
      <htmlb:form>
        <bsp:portalEvent name        = "course_select"
                         namespace = "edu.university" />
        <%= syllabi %>
      </htmlb:form>
    </htmlb:documentBody>
  </htmlb:document>
</htmlb:content>
```

The BSP extension element, `bsp:portalEvent`, really serves two purposes:

▸ First, it will register the event with the portal framework.

▸ Second, it will generate JavaScript coding that runs in the client to receive the portal event.

When this JavaScript gets an event from the portal framework, it will forward the event as a server event back to the BSP Framework.

2. Therefore, from the BSP side of the world, this ends up acting just like any other BSP extension event. In this case, Russel is trapping the event in his page's `onInputProcessing` event handler:

```
DATA event TYPE REF TO if_htmlb_data.
event ?= cl_htmlb_manager=>get_event_ex(
    runtime->server->request ).
IF event IS BOUND.
```

3. Since all portal events will have the same BSP extension server event name, the actual portal event ID will be passed back as an extension event attribute called `EVENT_ID`. The logic just needs to split the `EVENT_ID` into the event namespace and the event name:

```
IF event->event_name EQ 'portalEvent'.
   data event_dataobject TYPE string.
   data event_sourceid   TYPE string.
   data event_namespace  TYPE string.
   data event_name       TYPE string.
   event_sourceid   = event->event_defined.
```

```
    SPLIT event->event_id AT ':'
      INTO event_namespace event_name.
    IF event_namespace = 'edu.university' and
        event_name      = 'course_select'.
```

4. Another extension event attribute, the EVENT_SERVER_NAME, will contain the event parameter string. In this case, Russel will place the event parameter into a page attribute:

```
      event_dataobject = event->event_server_name.
      me->course_id = event_dataobject.
    ENDIF.
  ENDIF.
ENDIF.
```

Because this BSP application is stateless, the onInitialization event will fire on every page refresh. The server event triggered for the portal event will cause just such a refresh.

5. If the event handler logic was able to extract the course ID from the server event, it will now be available in the page attribute. The logic of the onInitialization event reuses the model class to load course attributes and extract the syllabi. Any exceptions are simply ignored since the Web Dynpro ABAP application is responsible for all error output:

```
DATA model TYPE REF TO zcl_cs_main_model.
CREATE OBJECT model.
DATA course_att TYPE zcs_course_att.
TRY.
    model->read_course_details(
       EXPORTING i_course_id  = course_id
       IMPORTING e_course_att = course_att ).
    syllabi = course_att-syllabi.
  CATCH zcx_course_system .
ENDTRY.
```

15.4 SAP NetWeaver Visual Composer

Another tool in the portal that ABAP developers, like Russel, will certainly want to try out is the *SAP NetWeaver Visual Composer*. The Visual Composer is an integrated part of the SAP NetWeaver Portal in SAP NetWeaver 7.0 and has been gathering attention, because it is a code-free modeling environment.

This means that people with little or no programming experience can build simple transactions and reports with this tool. This does not mean, however, that it won't have value to the hard-core ABAP developer as well. Visual Composer can be used by a programmer to build quick transaction prototypes or even complete applications. Furthermore, given its powerful abilities to consume data from BI systems and its robust charting capabilities, Visual Composer is particularly well suited to analytic applications.

It is exactly these kinds of features that attracted Russel to experiment with Visual Composer. He has a new requirement — to support members of the faculty with an additional report that shows the Grade Point Average (GPA) spread of the students who are enrolled in their respective courses. He could of course build this report in any of the UI technologies that we have already looked at, but instead he decides that this is the perfect opportunity to give Visual Composer a spin.

Visual Composer's design tool runs completely within the web browser. Only an SVG Viewer plug-in for the browser is a necessary addition. Visual Composer is also integrated into the SAP NetWeaver Portal. You access the designer via the URL for the J2EE Engine of the Portal with the additional string /VC/:

http://<j2ee engine url>:<j2ee engine port>/VC/ or

http://ucs.university.edu:50000/VC/

Within Visual Composer, you build models. This would be comparable to a project in other environments and should not be confused with the type of model that we have already discussed as part of the Model View Controller (MVC) design paradigm. Models are stored in the underlying database of the portal system.

1. Russel begins building his report by selecting the **New Model** option from the **Model Menu** after opening SAP NetWeaver Visual Composer in his browser (see Figure 15.21).

2. After choosing a name for his model (University_Course_Report) and a folder (University_Course_System) in which to store the model, he is brought to the main design area of Visual Composer.

3. Because Visual Composer is a code-free environment, he can't just start typing code into this application for data retrieval. Visual Composer can only consume existing services and then visualize them. Luckily, Russel has already built plenty of services around his system.

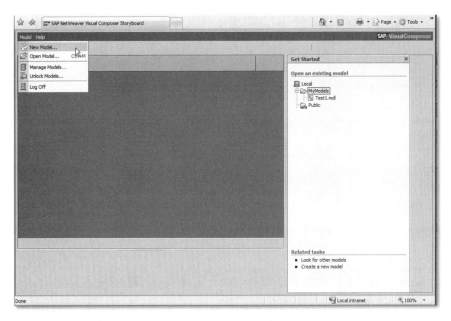

Figure 15.21 Visual Composer Designer — Running in the Browser

15.4.1 Consuming a Web Service

There are two types of service consumption in Visual Composer that Russel wants to explore. The first is the ability to consume Web Services. Russel already has several Web Services as part of his project. He also has learned just how easy it is to Web Service enable any RFC.

Although Visual Composer technically uses the portal connection service and system configurations like he setup at the beginning of this chapter, Russel doesn't have to leave the Visual Composer to create a new Web Service system configuration.

1. If he chooses **Tools • Define Web service system...** (see Figure 15.22), this will start a simplified wizard in Visual Composer.

2. This is basically a compressed and simplified version of the full system configuration process that Russel went through in the first section of this chapter. He still must supply a unique system name and alias to the system configuration that will be generated.

3. The rest of the configuration is fairly straightforward. First, he must supply the full URL for accessing the Web Service Definition Language (WSDL) of the Web Service. Also, if the Web Service requires authentication, Russel must supply a username and password (see Figure 15.23).

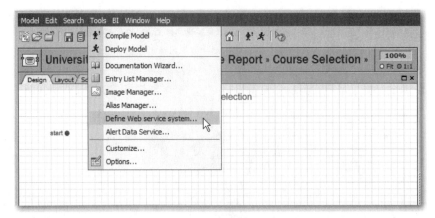

Figure 15.22 Menu Path to Define a Web Service System

Figure 15.23 Web Service System Definition

The ability to consume Web Services in Visual Composer obviously opens the tool to more than just the SAP environment. You could just as easily consume a third-party service written in various other programming languages.

4. Once connected to the Web Service, it will be displayed on the Visual Composer **Design** board as a service. Before moving on with designing the application based on this type of service, let's look at another type of service that would be of particular interest to the ABAP developer.

15.4.2 Consuming an RFC

Visual Composer also has the native ability to consume RFCs as a service. Once again, the portal connector and the system configurations are reused.

1. Russel only has to select the **Find Data** icon in the Task Panel Toolbar on the right side of the screen to bring up the **Find Data Services** search (see Figure 15.24). In the **System** drop-down field, he finds only entries for existing system configurations. Therefore, there is nothing new he needs to set up here since he can just reuse the system configuration that he already created for use in his iViews.

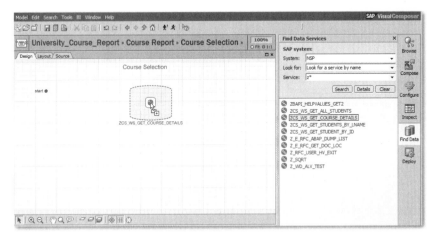

Figure 15.24 Find RFC-Based Data Services

2. There are two different ways that Russel can search for RFCs. The types of searches can be selected via the **Look for** option:

   ▷ He could search via service hierarchy. This would display the well know Business Application Programming Interface (BAPI) Service Tree just like in the SAP GUI transaction BAPI.

   ▷ Instead Russel will use the search by name option. He narrows down his selection to just RFCs in the customer name range. Then, to add the service to his model, all he needs to do is drag and drop it onto the Design board.

3. Upon dropping the service within the Design board, the **Define Data Service** dialog will pop up (see Figure 15.25). This dialog shows you all the input and output parameters exposed by the RFC. This way you can reduce the interface to just the elements that you absolutely need.

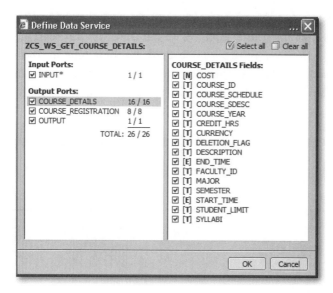

Figure 15.25 Defining the Data Service

4. As it turns out, Russel was having a bit of a problem with the currency field, COST. It was causing an error in Visual Composer when he tried to execute the application, even though he had not used it anywhere on the screen.

To fix the problem, Russel devised a workaround. All he had to do was to go into the **Define Data Service** dialog and uncheck the COST and CURRENCY fields. Now, they no longer will be processed during the service call.

5. After the **Define Data Service** dialog has been passed through, the service is displayed on the design board. Each of the selected inputs and outputs are displayed as their own items within the data service.

You can also right-click on the service to open a context menu of options. For instance, from here you can rerun the **Define Data Service...** option. However the menu option that catches Russel's eye is **Test Data Service...** (see Figure 15.26).

6. When Russel selects this option (see Figure 15.27), a screen that is a simple, yet nice test tool opens. There are input fields on the left to supply values for all the possible input parameters of the service. As he scrolls down on the right side of the screen, each of his separate output parameters are all displayed.

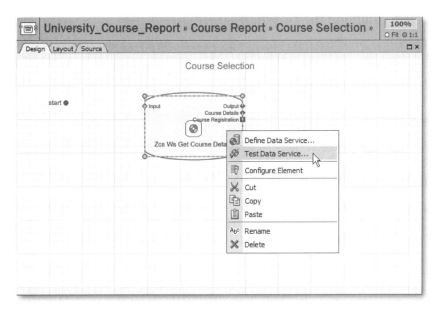

Figure 15.26 Data Service on the Designer

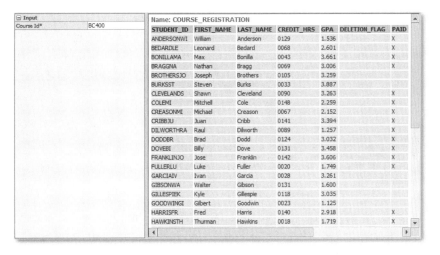

Figure 15.27 Testing a Data Service

This is an excellent way for you to quickly test the service to ensure that it will work correctly in the Visual Composer environment and that there are no issues with the portal system configuration. It is also a nice way to preview the data so you can tailor the user interface according to the actual data.

15.4.3 Building the User Interface

Regardless of which type of service you use, the act of building a user interface around the service is the same. For Russel's purpose, he had an RFC that already exposed all the data that he would need for this report so he decided to stick with that service type.

To say that user interfaces can be built quickly in Visual Composer would be a bit of an understatement. In order to visualize service parameters, all you have to do is click on the parameter name and drag it. A context menu will pop up with the possible types of visualizations.

For example, when Russel selects **Course Registration**, which is a table populated with data, he has two options: **Add Table View** or **Add Chart View**. On the other hand, when he selects the **input** port he only has the option to **Add a Form View**. Visual Composer analyzes the parameter direction and data type to only propose visualizations that match (see Figure 15.28).

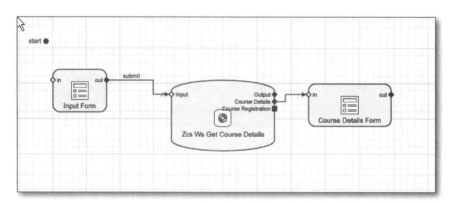

Figure 15.28 Drag and Drop from the Inputs and Outputs to Generate User Interface Elements

But even more than just a type proposal, Visual Composer will generate the basic layout for the developer. All Russel has to do is create an Input Form and a Course Details Form by dragging out from the respective ports. The designer automatically creates the framework of a user interface with input fields and a **Submit** button. The basic generated User Interface can be seen in Figure 15.29.

Not bad for what amounted to three minutes' worth of work. The generated UI could use some refining at this point. Russel can change the alignment, titles, and size of the input fields in the **Layout** tab to get everything just the way he wants it. However, the tedious work of getting all the input fields into the form has already been taken care of for him.

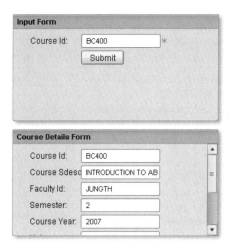

Figure 15.29 Quick Preview of the UI That Has Been Built

15.4.4 Building Value Help

Value Help is a fairly essential part of any user-friendly application. Russel knows that he would like to include some form of value help for the input of the course ID. Unfortunately, Visual Composer does not yet have the same level of automatic support for complex and elementary search helps as Web Dynpro ABAP. Still, there is the functionality necessary to build a custom search view with a fair amount of ease.

1. Russel turns to the **Layout** tab in the designer view. When he right-clicks on the **Course Id** input field, he has options to change the properties and the position of the field. But there is also the important **Add Value Help** option (see Figure 15.30), which, when selected, will start a wizard that will generate most of the components of a Value Help dialog.

2. The first step of the **Value Help Configuration Wizard**, shown in Figure 15.31, allows you to choose the **Type** of selection for the input field. For a normal RFC service, the only choice you will probably be presented with is a **Single selection**. But, when consuming a Business Intelligence (BI) service, there are more advanced options that allow for multiple selections and even input selections that are very close in functionality to SELECT-OPTIONS.

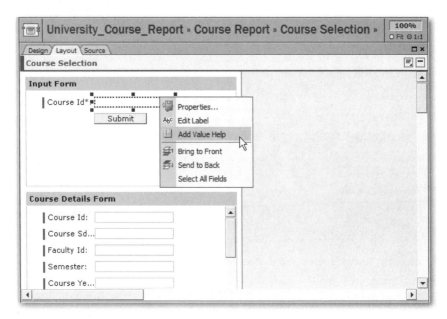

Figure 15.30 Starting the Value Help Wizard

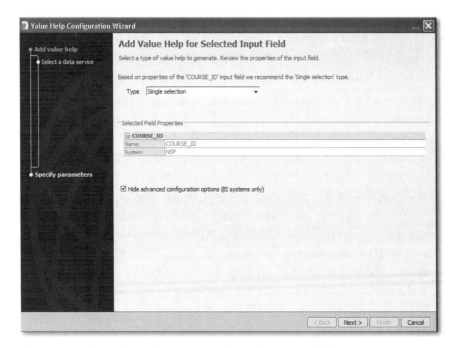

Figure 15.31 Value Help Configuration Wizard — Select Input Field Options

3. In the second step of the wizard (see Figure 15.32), we reach the heart of the value help functionality. Russel must supply another service to function as the value help processor. This might very well mean creating a specialized function module to process the value help for the given input field. That is precisely what Russel decides to do. He switches back to the ABAP Workbench and creates a new function module called ZCS_RFC_VC_ COURSE_LIST that will work as the value help service.

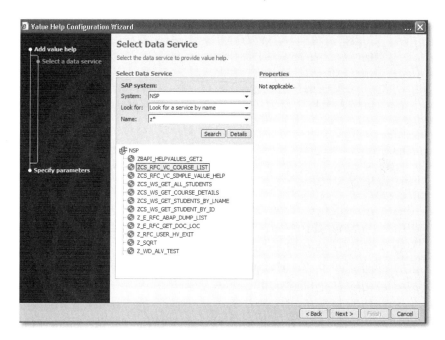

Figure 15.32 Value Help Configuration Wizard — Select Data Service

4. The coding of the value help service is rather simple because once again, Russel is able to reuse his existing model class. His output is not restricted to just a value and a description like a drop-down list would be.

He defines a structure that has several output fields to make the value help more robust, as well as more comparable to the collective search help used in Web Dynpro ABAP (i.e., in terms of the amount of information included):

```
FUNCTION ZCS_RFC_VC_COURSE_LIST5.
*"--------------------------------------------------------
*"*"Local Interface:
*"  IMPORTING
*"     VALUE(COURSE_ID) TYPE  ZCS_COURSE_ID OPTIONAL
*"  EXPORTING
```

```
*"      VALUE(E_VALUE_HELP) TYPE  ZCS_COURSE_ATT_RFC_TBL
*"-----------------------------------------------------------
  DATA model TYPE REF TO zcl_cs_main_model.
  CREATE OBJECT model.
  TRY.
      DATA courses TYPE zcs_course_att_tbl.
      model->read_course_listing(
          IMPORTING   e_courses = courses ).
      FIELD-SYMBOLS:
          <wa_course> LIKE LINE OF courses,
          <wa_help>   LIKE LINE OF e_value_help.
      LOOP AT courses ASSIGNING <wa_course>.
        APPEND INITIAL LINE TO e_value_help
            ASSIGNING <wa_help>.
        MOVE-CORRESPONDING <wa_course> TO <wa_help>.
      ENDLOOP.
    CATCH zcx_course_system .
  ENDTRY.
  SORT e_value_help BY course_id.
ENDFUNCTION.
```

5. The final step of the **Value Help Configuration Wizard**, shown in Figure 15.33, requires Russel to map the **Input** and **Output** fields of the value help service. The **Search field ID** is optional. This would have allowed Russel to map the source field to an input field of the value help service, in order to pass through an initial search value; however, Russel didn't build this functionality into his service.

At the bottom of the screen, you'll see that Russel has the option to map the output from the value help service back into the calling screen. Keep in mind that there could be a lot of output values from the value help service, and the names of the fields don't need to match the field that the value help is for. Nevertheless, you do have to select one field from the value help service output to match up with the original input field.

6. After finishing the **Value Help Configuration Wizard**, the Design view of Russel's model looks somewhat different (see Figure 15.34). He now has a new action emanating out of the Input Form. This action points to a **Popup Signal**.

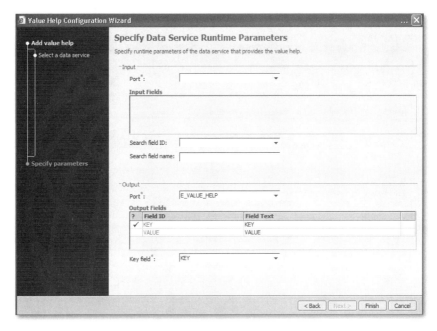

Figure 15.33 Value Help Configuration Wizard — Runtime Parameters

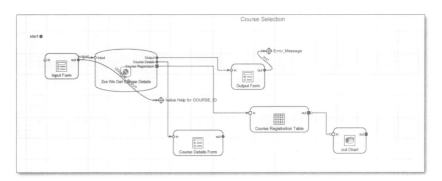

Figure 15.34 Design View of the Entire Model After Value Help Generation

7. Russel can double click on the **Popup Signal** and view the secondary popup iView that has been generated by the Value Help Configuration Wizard based on the selected service. Without needing to adjust any of the objects that were generated by the Value Help Configuration Wizard, Russel runs his application again (see Figure 15.35). Now, the **Value Help** button appears next to his **Course Id** input field.

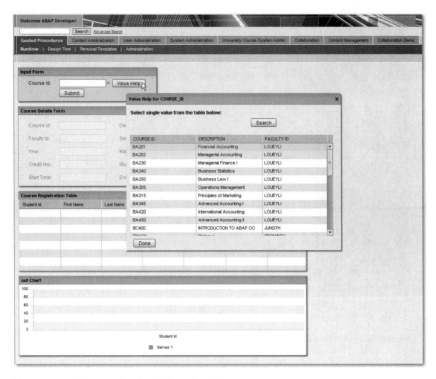

Figure 15.35 Generated Value Help at Runtime

When pressing this button, his value help service will be invoked. The results are displayed in a dialog window that floats above the main application. He can then select a value and press the **Done** button to return the value to the **Course Id** input field.

With little more than a half hour's worth of effort, Russel is quite pleased with his first application built in Visual Composer. He was especially pleasantly surprised with how easy it was to create the chart of Grade Point Averages (see Figure 15.36, **Student GPA**). All he had to do was drag off of the output of the Course Registration table and choose **Add Chart View**. Then there was the simple process of just setting the properties of the chart to supply the type of chart, the fields to use for the X and Y axis, and the type of data animation.

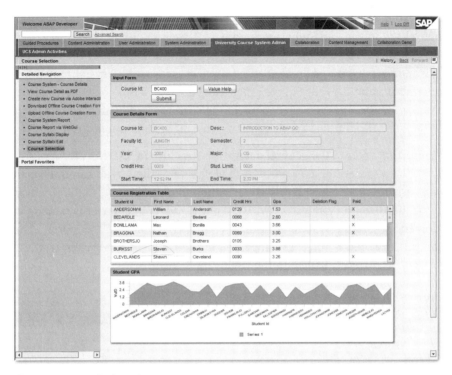

Figure 15.36 Finished Application

15.5 SAP NetWeaver Business Client

If Russel had a crystal ball and could gaze into his own near future, he may very well see one additional tool in use at his company related to the portal, namely, the SAP NetWeaver Business Client. The SAP NetWeaver Business Client or as many people may have first heard about it under the larger internal code name for a SAP Project called *Project Muse*, is a new client technology that is just about ready for release at the time of this writing.

The whole idea of the SAP NetWeaver Business Client is not to replace the portal, but to provide an alternative user client for accessing the portal's services. Today, the only way to access the portal is via a web browser like Internet Explorer or Firefox. However, these tools are generalized browsers designed more for surfing the Internet than running enterprise applications.

Even with the more common use of the technologies like AJAX for browser-based applications, it is difficult for anything running with a browser to achieve the same levels of performance, interactivity, and security of an application running on the desktop. This may be fine for casual portal users, but what about people who work with SAP transactions all day, every day? The whole concept of the SAP NetWeaver Business Client is to reuse the existing portal services or standalone services from an ERP system for roles, navigation, portal eventing, etc. That way companies can continue to leverage the investment they have made in the current environment, while gaining the enhanced user experience of a rich, smart client application.

Figure 15.37 shows the general navigation structure in SAP NetWeaver Business Client, called the *L-Frame*. On the left side of the screen running vertically are the two highest levels of navigation that correspond to the first two horizontal levels of navigation with the portal today. You have the same role, **University Course System Admin**, which was present in the portal. The items that would before have appeared in the **Detailed Navigation** window in the portal are displayed on the right side at the top.

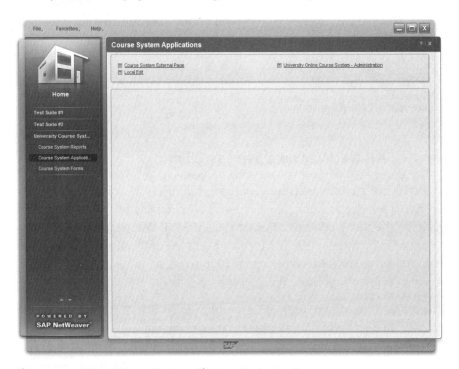

Figure 15.37 SAP NetWeaver Business Client — Navigation Bar

Without any changes to the existing applications, SAP GUI transactions, BSP pages, Web Dynpro applications, and Adobe Forms all run just fine from within the SAP NetWeaver Business Client. Thanks to the client abstraction theory of Web Dynpro, this even allows for enhanced capabilities to immediately be rendered when the Web Dynpro application knows that it is running in the SAP NetWeaver Business Client.

You can see in Figure 15.38 that the interface changes once an application has been selected. The left side navigation bar has collapsed, although it can be expanded again at any time by clicking on the **Home** button in the top, left corner. The Web Dynpro application itself runs within the canvas area, giving it most of the application space. Notice that what would have been the title bar in the browser automatically becomes the header for this application window within the Business Client.

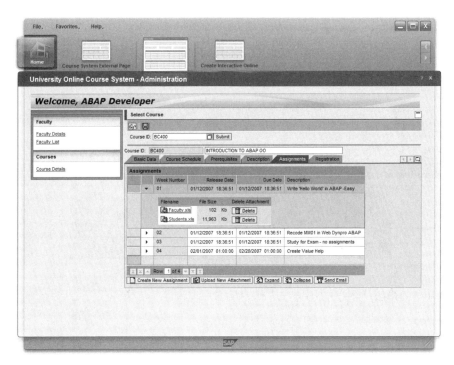

Figure 15.38 Web Dynpro ABAP Running in the SAP NetWeaver Business Client

The top bar next to the **Home** button shows all the applications that are currently running in the Business Client. This allows the user to run a mulitple of applications and easily switch between them. The other "hidden" applications are still running and don't have to be reloaded or reset when switching to them. It is also possible to run applications from different technologies, like Web Dynpro and classic Dynpro, at the same time.

The SAP NetWeaver Business Client is also responsible for the session management of the applications running within it. This is a common problem with browser-based applications that are stateful. Internet browsers are generally designed for stateless web pages. They do not by default notify the server when the user closes the browser or navigates away from the current page. This can cause stateful applications to continue to consume resources long after the user has moved on to something else. The SAP NetWeaver Business Client, being a specialized application, can perform just such a notification and make sure that if the user closes a single application or the entire client that all resources and locks are released on the server.

The final two figures of this chapter, Figure 15.39 and Figure 15.40, demonstrate some of the various types of applications that can also run in the SAP NetWeaver Business Client. The first is the Internet facing stateless BSP application. Actually, any web page can be run from within the SAP NetWeaver Business Client, not just those built in SAP's User Interface technologies.

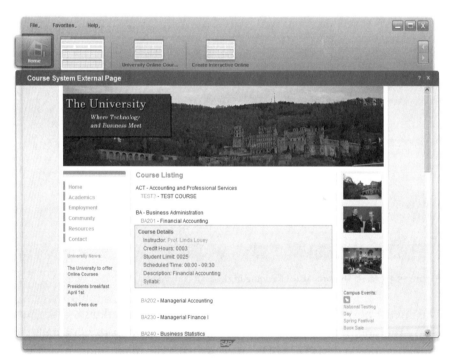

Figure 15.39 BSP Application Running as a Standard Web Page

Figure 15.40, shows a classic Dynpro application running in the SAP GUI. Yes, even the SAP GUI can run comfortably in the SAP NetWeaver Business Client.

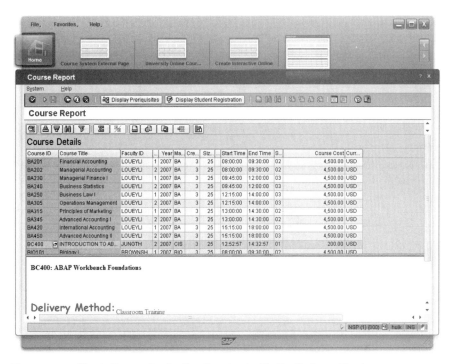

Figure 15.40 Classic Dynpro Application Running Inside the Business Client

You might even notice that the look of the SAP GUI transaction has changed from how it appeared when running standalone. The SAP GUI can sense when it is running in the SAP NetWeaver Business Client and it consequently adopts a special theme that makes it look more like Web Dynpro. This creates a more unified approach for end users who may be interacting with both classic Dynpro and Web Dynpro, for many years to come.

Understanding the underlying structure of the Internet Connection Framework and its inner implementation through handler classes is a powerful addition to any developer's toolbox. For Russel's project, handler classes will be used as an important supplement, allowing for direct access and complete control over the HTTP Request and Response objects. This low level access is perfect for meeting his final requirement, an RSS feed.

16 RSS Feed Using an ICF Service Node

Russel's project is nearly complete. He has only one major business requirement remaining — to expose course assignments as an RSS feed. This will allow students to subscribe to the assignments for the courses they are enrolled in, and receive updates and assignment attachments via a push mechanism.

RSS is an acronym that can stand for *Really Simple Syndication*, *RDF Site Summary*, or *Rich Site Summary*. Whichever definition of this acronym you use, RSS — an XML format for syndicating web content — is integral to the modern Internet. So much information is available on the Internet that the most important tools are those that help people sift through the madness to find the information they want. RSS is one of those tools. RSS also takes a different approach than the standard *go-and-find-it* or pull approach. Instead of users having to search for updates to their selected information, they can subscribe to RSS feeds. In this way, updates to the information can be pushed out to all interested parties. RSS, at its core, is built on top of established technologies such as HTTP and XML. Fortunately, these technologies are readily available in the ABAP world as well.

There are several different approaches that Russel could take to build an RSS feed. For example, he could expose the XML as a Business Server Page (BSP) application. Ultimately, he decides to use this final phase of the project as another learning opportunity and use a custom *Internet Communication Framework* (ICF) *Service Node*. ICF service nodes are the underlying technology for Business Server Pages, Web Dynpro ABAP, and Web Services in the ABAP environment. This lowest level of the HTTP communication layer is available to customers for programming their own ICF handlers, thus allowing them direct access to the HTTP request and response objects. The lightweight nature of ICF handlers combined with their freedom of implementation make them an excellent candidate for Russel's RSS feed requirement.

16.1 What Is an ICF Service Node?

A web server is like a large shopping center, with thousands of incoming customers, all asking for a specific shop. However, with a web server, there are thousands of incoming requests as well, all asking to be processed. The problem is how to dispatch each HTTP request to the correct handler.

This is where the Internet Communication Framework comes in. The ICF takes the URL from the HTTP request and splits it into tokens, which are used to direct the HTTP request through a tree of services.

Each node in the ICF tree can be configured to contain zero or more HTTP handlers. The handlers are processed in sequence, until one handler signals that it has processed the request completely. Next, the HTTP response is returned to the browser. The sequence of processing is primarily from the root node down and then, secondarily, in sequence for each node. Effectively, it processes all handlers for the specific node (one can use the expression that "the handlers are chained"), and then goes to the next deeper node. A node doesn't require a handler. If no handler is found on a specific node, the next deeper node is checked.

For example, in Figure 16.1, the nodes `sap` and `bc` have no handlers. The node `bsp` contains the BSP runtime handler. It will look at the incoming HTTP request and completely process it. Because the BSP runtime indicates to the ICF that the request has been fully processed, no further searching is done through lower levels of the ICF tree. Everything below the node `bsp`, in this example `/sap/absenceform_new/default.htm`, will be used within the processing of the handler class itself.

It is important to note that ICF uses the tokens one at a time to navigate deeper into the handler tree until one handler signals that the HTTP request has been processed. The rest of the URL is then not considered. You can also use this feature to embed data into the URL as part of the URL segments. It's simply a question of what the receiving handler will do with the rest of the URL, which is considered to be actual data (one string) passed to the handler.

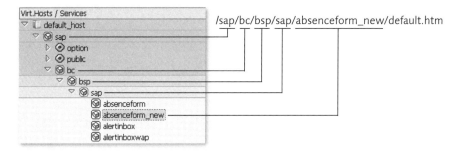

Figure 16.1 URL to ICF Node Mapping

16.2   Handler RSS Feed

An HTTP handler is a normal ABAP class, which implements the interface IF_HTTP_EXTENSION with one method HANDLE_REQUEST. Once the ICF has found a node that contains a handler, the class is instantiated and called to process the request. As an input parameter, this method gets a server object, which is a wrapper object containing the HTTP request and response objects.

Russel's application will accept the name of the course, which this feed will provide data for, passed in via a URL parameter. Then, Russel will query the records via the model class, convert the results from an ABAP internal table to a binary XML stream, and return this XML stream with the HTTP response. Therefore, using the following URL would generate the output in:

http://<host>/university/course_rss/bc400

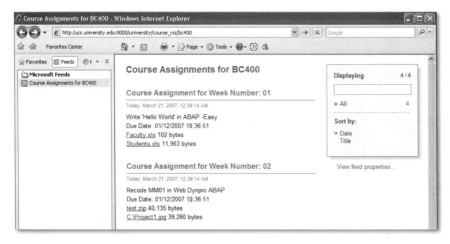

Figure 16.2 RSS Feed in Internet Explorer

16.2.1 HTTP Handler Class Test Implementation

For the actual HTTP handler, Russel starts his work by creating the class ZCL_CS_COURSE_ASSIGNMENT_RSS and specifying that it implements the interface IF_HTTP_EXTENSION. It is this interface that signifies that this class can be used as a service node handler.

There is a single method, HANDLE_REQUEST, which is part of this interface. This method will be called when the ICF finds a request that is mapped to this service node handler. For the HANDLE_REQUEST method, he will start with some very simple placeholder coding to test so he can ensure that he has all the pieces in order:

```
METHOD if_http_extension~handle_request.
  if_http_extension~flow_rc = if_http_extension=>co_flow_ok.
  server->response->set_status( code = 200 reason = 'OK' ).
  server->response->set_cdata(
                  '<html><body>Hello World!</body></html>' ).
ENDMETHOD.
```

The flow return code informs the ICF that he has finished processing the request, and written a complete response. For this simple example, he doesn't set any of the content-specific headers, relying instead on the default behavior of the *Internet Communication Manager* (ICM). You should note that this is not recommended for actual production programs. The only value that he sets explicitly is the HTTP return code (value 200 implies OK for HTTP traffic). The last line is the classic "Hello World!" for web servers.

16.2.2 ICF Node Creation and Handler Association

He now has a handler class that will respond with valid HTML coding when called.

1. He must decide where he wants to place this handler in the ICF tree. The handler is not a BSP or a Web Dynpro application and therefore should not be placed under /sap/bc/.

2. Initially, Russel creates the first level node, university. This is the namespace for all the custom development created at his organization. Then he creates a node beneath his namespace called course_rss by right-clicking and choosing **New Sub-Element** from the context menu, in order to create an association to the handler class (see Figure 16.3).

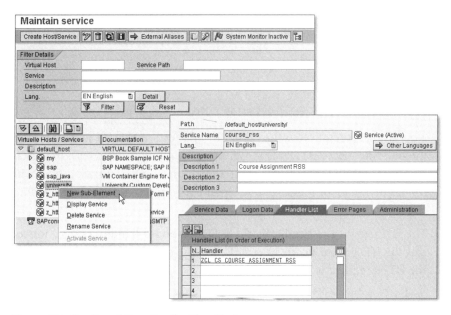

Figure 16.3 Creation of New Handler Class Node

3. With this, he has defined a new HTTP handler. Once he activates the node, he can use the context menu to start a test for this node. In the output, he sees the simple "Hello World" placeholder, which proves that everything has been set up correctly.

453

16.2.3 RSS Handler Implementation

Russel begins the processing of his actual handler implementation much the same way as he did his first test implementation. But this time, he has to process the request header fields so he can pull the course ID out of the URL.

The ~path_info header field contains the part of the string that has not yet been used by the ICF. Keep in mind that the beginning of the URL was used to find this node in the ICF. The string is determined and manipulated a little: uppercase conversion, strip leading /-character, etc.

1. To avoid hard coding the name of the ~path_info header field, Russel uses the interface IF_HTTP_HEADER_FIELDS_SAP. SAP actually offers two interfaces, IF_HTTP_HEADER_FIELDS_SAP and IF_HTTP_HEADER_FIELDS, to cover all the possible header field names via public constants:

```
* Determine table name from URL ~path_info (= Table Name)
  DATA: name TYPE string.
  name = server->request->get_header_field(
      name = if_http_header_fields_sap=>path_info ).
  TRANSLATE name TO UPPER CASE.
  IF strlen( name ) >= 1 AND name(1) = '/'.
    SHIFT name LEFT.
  ENDIF.
  server->request->get_form_fields(
                    CHANGING fields = m_parameters ).
```

Now all that is required is the call to the application-specific logic and then the building of the HTTP response. Error handling is done with the usual ABAP exceptions. The ICF has an exception handler installed and will render out an error message if he should encounter any problems loading the course content.

2. The last part of the handler is the HTTP response handling. First, Russel sets the HTTP return code to 200. This is the defined code to indicate that the HTTP request was processed correctly:

```
* Application logic
  DATA: content TYPE xstring.
  content = me->load( name ).
  IF xstrlen( content ) IS INITIAL.
    RAISE EXCEPTION TYPE cx_http_ext_exception
          EXPORTING msg = 'Invalid URL!'.
  ENDIF.
* Set up HTTP response
  server->response->set_status( code = 200
    reason = 'OK' ).
```

HTTP status code descriptions can be found in the global interface IF_ HTTP_STATUS.

3. The final statement places the content into the HTTP response. Notice that there are methods for handling both XSTRING — SET_DATA and APPEND_ DATA — as well as STRING — SET_CDATA and APPEND_CDATA:

```
server->response->set_data( content ).
```

16.2.4 RSS Handler Application Logic

Let's take a closer look at the application logic that Russel implemented in the load method.

1. He starts the application logic by using the course ID, which was previously extracted from the URL as the input parameter into a call to his model class. This will return all the data necessary for building the RSS feed.

2. He also catches any exception that might be thrown by the model class. He maps the error message associated with the inner exception into the handler-specific exception, CX_HTTP_EXT_EXCEPTION:

```
DATA model TYPE REF TO zcl_cs_main_model.
  CREATE OBJECT model.
  DATA course_id  TYPE zcs_course_id.
  DATA course_ass TYPE zcs_course_assign_att_tbl.
  DATA course_att TYPE zcs_course_att.
  data o_excpt    type ref to zcx_course_system.
  course_id = i_name.
  TRY.
      CALL METHOD model->read_course_details
        EXPORTING  i_course_id      = course_id
        IMPORTING  e_course_att     = course_att
                   e_course_ass_att = course_ass.
    CATCH zcx_course_system INTO o_excpt.
      DATA error_msg TYPE string.
      error_msg = o_excpt->get_text( ).
      RAISE EXCEPTION TYPE cx_http_ext_exception
              EXPORTING msg = error_msg.
  ENDTRY.
```

3. Next Russel needs to begin to build the XML in the RSS format. From a technical standpoint, there are several different ways that he could build the XML stream:

▶ The simplest form would be to *concatenate strings* together; this low-tech approach has the advantage of not requiring interaction with any of the special XML processing tools. This approach quickly becomes cumbersome and error-prone for anything more than the most basic XML structures.

▶ Another approach would be to use an *XSL Transformation* program to convert from the ABAP data to the RSS XML. *Extensible Stylesheet Language Transformations* (XSLT) are a standards-based language for the manipulation of XML data. ABAP has full support for XSLT and transformations. They can be called directly with the CALL TRANSFORMATION keywords. XSL Transformations are great for highly complex manipulations of XML based data. They also support tools to transform XML data to and from HTML and ABAP.

▶ *iXML libraries* are special ABAP classes designed for the direct creation of and interaction with XML. If you need complete control of the XML creation process in ABAP, this is definitely the way to go.

4. Ultimately, Russel decides to use the iXML libraries. By doing so, Russel will start his coding by creating a stream factory that will render the resulting XML as a binary string with Unicode encoding directly into his returning parameter, r_content:

```
DATA: g_ixml TYPE REF TO if_ixml,
      g_stream_factory TYPE REF TO
        if_ixml_stream_factory,
      g_encoding TYPE REF TO if_ixml_encoding,
      xml_doc    TYPE REF TO if_ixml_document.
CONSTANTS encoding TYPE string VALUE 'UTF-8'.
DATA: resstream TYPE REF TO if_ixml_ostream.
****Create an instance of the iXML Processor
  g_ixml = cl_ixml=>create( ).
****Create the Stream Factory
  g_stream_factory = g_ixml->create_stream_factory( ).
****Create an Endcoding and Byte Order
  g_encoding = g_ixml->create_encoding(
    character_set = encoding
    byte_order = if_ixml_encoding=>co_little_endian ).
****Create the output stream with a pointer to our binary
  resstream = g_stream_factory->create_ostream_xstring(
    r_content ).
****Set the Encoding into a stream
  resstream->set_encoding( encoding = g_encoding ).
```

Up to this point, Russel has only created the technical channel with which to render the final XML output. The definition of the XML structure is done independently of the rendering. He is now ready to build his XML according to the format of the RSS 2.0 specification. To get details on the format of the specification, Russel went directly to the people who set the specification standards — the RSS Advisory Board at *http://www.rssboard.org/rss-specification*.

1. Russel begins by creating an XML document:

```
xml_doc = g_ixml->create_document( ).
xml_doc->set_encoding( g_encoding ).
xml_doc->set_standalone( abap_true ).
```

The RSS XML structure is really quite lean:

- ▸ You must start with a mandatory element called RSS that needs only the details of the version of RSS that this stream was created for.

- ▸ The RSS element can have one or many subelements called CHANNELS. Russel will structure his RSS feeds so that each channel corresponds to one course.

- ▸ The CHANNEL element must have at least a TITLE subelement to display as the name of the feed.

- ▸ As children of the CHANNEL element, you can have one or many ITEM elements. These are the individual weekly course assignments in Russel's application.

This represents the basic structure of an RSS feed. There are many optional elements that can be added to the XML as well. Because RSS is an open standard, there are countless places to go on the Internet, in addition to the RSS Advisory Board, to find complete documentation on all the optional parameters as well as samples.

2. Russel continues by adding the RSS element to his XML document. This element will be the root node; therefore, its parent specification is the document object:

```
DATA: rss     TYPE REF TO if_ixml_element,
      channel TYPE REF TO if_ixml_element,
      c_dtls  TYPE REF TO if_ixml_element,
      item    TYPE REF TO if_ixml_element,
      i_dtls  TYPE REF TO if_ixml_element.
  DATA: t_string TYPE string,
        t_date   TYPE c LENGTH 22.
  FIELD-SYMBOLS <wa_file> TYPE zcs_course_file.
```

457

```
rss = xml_doc->create_simple_element(
        name = 'rss' parent = xml_doc ).
rss->set_attribute(
        name = 'version' value = `2.0` ).
```

Since Russel's RSS handler is structured so that the course ID is specified within the URL, he will be processing only one course at a time. Therefore, he will only have a single channel in each RSS XML document.

3. He creates the CHANNEL element and specifies the RSS element object as the parent. This will cause the iXML library to create the nesting structure as shown in Figure 16.4.

```
channel = xml_doc->create_simple_element(
        name = 'channel' parent = rss ).
DATA title TYPE string.
CONCATENATE 'Course Assignments for'(t01) ` ` i_name
        INTO title.
c_dtls = xml_doc->create_simple_element(
        name = 'title' parent = channel
        value = title ).
```

```
<?xml version="1.0" encoding="utf-8" standalone="yes" ?>
- <rss version="2.0">
  - <channel>
      <title>Course Assignments for BC400</title>
      <link>/sap/bc/webdynpro/sap/zcs_course_system</link>
      <description>INTRODUCTION TO ABAP OO</description>
      <ttl>10</ttl>
    - <item>
        <title>Course Assignment for Week Number: 01</title>
        <description>Write 'Hello World' in ABAP -Easy<br />Due Date: 01/12/2007 18:36:51<br /><a
          href="/university/course_file/BC400?week=01&file=001" target="_blank">Faculty.xls</a> 102
          bytes<br /><a href="/university/course_file/BC400?week=01&file=002"
          target="_blank">Students.xls</a> 11,963 bytes<br /></description>
      </item>
    - <item>
        <title>Course Assignment for Week Number: 02</title>
        <description>Recode MM01 in Web Dynpro ABAP <br />Due Date: 01/12/2007 18:36:51<br /><a
          href="/university/course_file/BC400?week=02&file=001" target="_blank">test.zip</a> 40,135
          bytes<br /><a href="/university/course_file/BC400?week=02&file=002"
          target="_blank">C:\Project1.jpg</a> 39,260 bytes<br /></description>
      </item>
    - <item>
        <title>Course Assignment for Week Number: 03</title>
        <description>Study for Exam - no assignments<br />Due Date: 01/12/2007 18:36:51<br /></description>
      </item>
    - <item>
        <title>Course Assignment for Week Number: 04</title>
        <description>Create Value Help<br />Due Date: 02/20/2007 01:00:00<br /><a
          href="/university/course_file/BC400?week=04&file=001" target="_blank">C:\IMG_0657.JPG</a>
          42,113 bytes<br /></description>
      </item>
    </channel>
  </rss>
```

Figure 16.4 Raw RSS XML

4. RSS allows you to hyperlink to other web content. It makes sense to pull up the Web Dynpro application that can be used to view all the informa-

tion about a course. Russel uses one of the Web Dynpro utility classes to build the URL dynamically:

```
DATA url TYPE string.
CALL METHOD cl_wd_utilities=>construct_wd_url
   EXPORTING   application_name = `ZCS_COURSE_SYSTEM`
   IMPORTING   out_local_url    = url.
c_dtls  = xml_doc->create_simple_element(
        name = 'link' parent = channel
        value = url ).
```

5. Next Russel takes advantage of some of the optional parameters of the channel element to add a description and a *Time To Live* (TTL) value. The TTL value tells RSS feed readers how long they should cache their current values before checking the server for updates:

```
t_string = course_att-course_sdesc.
c_dtls  = xml_doc->create_simple_element(
        name = 'description' parent = channel
        value = t_string ).
c_dtls  = xml_doc->create_simple_element(
        name = 'ttl' parent = channel
        value = '10' ).
```

6. For each item in the RSS, Russel will loop through the course assignment records. He only wants to send out items that have a release date greater than the current time. In this way, the faculty can create course assignments, without allowing them to be seen by students until these assignments are ready:

```
FIELD-SYMBOLS <wa_ass> LIKE LINE OF course_ass.
  LOOP AT course_ass ASSIGNING <wa_ass>.
    DATA now TYPE timestamp .
    CONVERT DATE sy-datlo TIME sy-timlo
        INTO TIME STAMP now TIME ZONE sy-zonlo.
    IF <wa_ass>-release_date <= now.
      item  = xml_doc->create_simple_element(
        name = 'item' parent = channel ).
    CONCATENATE
          'Course Assignment for Week Number:'(t02) ` `
          <wa_ass>-week_number INTO t_string.
      i_dtls = xml_doc->create_simple_element(
        name = 'title' parent = item
        value = t_string ).
      WRITE <wa_ass>-due_date TO t_date.
      CONCATENATE <wa_ass>-description `<br />`
```

```
            'Due Date:'(t03) ` ` t_date `<br />`
        INTO t_string.
```

7. Russel's business requirements state that he has to provide a link to all assignment attachments so that students can download them directly from the RSS feed. It would not make sense to send the assignment attachment content with the RSS feed, even if that was technically possible. Instead, he decides that what would be most useful is to create another service handler that is specifically designed for the downloading of attachments. For now, all he needs to do is reference the URL for this new service handler:

```
DATA file_num TYPE n LENGTH 3.
    CLEAR file_num.
    LOOP AT <wa_ass>-attachments ASSIGNING <wa_file>.
      file_num = file_num + 1.
      WRITE <wa_file>-filelen TO t_date.
      CONCATENATE t_string `<a href="`
                 `/university/course_file/` i_name `?week=`
                 <wa_ass>-week_number
                 `&file=` file_num `" target="_blank">`
                 <wa_file>-filename `</a>` ` `
                 t_date ` bytes` `<br />` INTO t_string.
    ENDLOOP.
    i_dtls = xml_doc->create_simple_element(
      name = 'description' parent = item
      value = t_string ).
  ENDIF.
ENDLOOP.
```

8. The final step is to tell the document object that he is ready for it to render itself into the output stream. The association made earlier will actually cause the data to be passed back through the R_CONTENT parameter.

Although what is returned to any RSS reader is raw XML, as seen in Figure 16.4, different readers will interpret this XML and render it in different ways. Both Internet Explorer 7.0 (IE7) and Firefox 2.0 have built-in support for processing RSS feeds. Figure 16.2 shows this exact same RSS content running within IE7. There are also dedicated RSS readers available. One of the popular utilities is *SharpReader*. Figure 16.5 shows what the same content rendered in this tool looks like as opposed to how it looked in IE7.

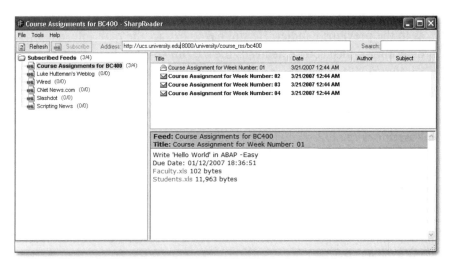

Figure 16.5 SharpReader — Popular Windows-Based Feed Reader

16.2.5 Handler for Attachment Downloads

Russel has decided to implement the attachment download in a separate Service Handler class. He can leverage the functionality that he already wrote for his Web Dynpro application to offer attachment downloading within the handler class as well.

1. He begins by copying his existing handler class to a new name, ZCL_CS_ COURSE_ASSIGNMENT_FILE. He then assigns this new handler to a separate node, named course_file, in the service hierarchy (see Figure 16.6).

Path:	/default_host/university/		
Service Name	course_file		Service (Active)
Lang.	EN English		Other Languages

Description	
Description 1	Course Assignment File Attachment Download
Description 2	
Description 3	

Service Data | Logon Data | Handler List | Error Pages | Administration

Handler List (in Order of Execution)

N..	Handler	
1	ZCL CS COURSE ASSIGNMENT FILE	

Figure 16.6 File Download Service Handler

2. The logic in the HANDLE_REQUEST method is going to be virtually the same as in the previous handler. He still has to extract the path information to determine which course he needs the attachments for, but he now has the additional URL parameter to specify the assignment week and file attachment ID:

http:/<host>/university/course_file/BC400?week=04&file=001

3. Russel uses the following logic to pull out all the additional URL parameters and place them in a class attribute:

```
server->request->get_form_fields(
        changing fields = me->m_parameters ).
```

4. Most of the changes that Russel must make are in the LOAD method that contains the application logic. He still starts by reading the course data via the model class:

```
DATA model TYPE REF TO zcl_cs_main_model.
CREATE OBJECT model.
DATA course_id TYPE zcs_course_id.
DATA course_ass TYPE zcs_course_assign_att_tbl.
DATA course_att TYPE zcs_course_att.
course_id = i_name.
TRY.
    CALL METHOD model->read_course_details
        EXPORTING   i_course_id      = course_id
        IMPORTING   e_course_ass_att = course_ass.
    CATCH zcx_course_system .
ENDTRY.
```

5. Next Russel pulls the individual URL parameters out of their storage in the class attribute for use in narrowing the course assignment and attachment to the correct records he must process:

```
FIELD-SYMBOLS: <wa_parameter> LIKE LINE OF  m_parameters.
    DATA file_num TYPE n LENGTH 3.
    DATA week TYPE zcs_course_ass_week.
    LOOP AT m_parameters ASSIGNING <wa_parameter>.
      IF <wa_parameter>-name = `file`.
        file_num = <wa_parameter>-value.
      ENDIF.
      IF <wa_parameter>-name = `week`.
        week = <wa_parameter>-value.
      ENDIF.
    ENDLOOP.
```

It would be easy to just return the content of the attachment as the body of the response object. But the content by itself would not make much sense to the browser. For most file types, the browser would typically make the user select a filename and would not be able to propose a file extension, making the process of opening the attachment less than user friendly.

6. To help the browser determine the correct application with which to open the attachment, Russel also needs to send along the MIME type. For this, he'll use a regular expression to strip the file extension off the attachment filename. He can then use the SAP supplied function module, SDOK_MIMETYPE_GET, to look up the corresponding MIME type for the extension:

```
FIELD-SYMBOLS: <wa_ass> LIKE LINE OF course_ass,
               <wa_file> TYPE zcs_course_file.
  READ TABLE course_ass ASSIGNING <wa_ass>
      WITH KEY week_number = week.
  IF sy-subrc = 0.
    READ TABLE <wa_ass>-attachments ASSIGNING <wa_file>
      INDEX file_num.
    IF sy-subrc = 0.
      r_content = <wa_file>-content.
      DATA dot_offset TYPE i.
      DATA extension TYPE mimetypes-extension.
      DATA mimetype TYPE mimetypes-type.
      " Find out file name extension
      FIND FIRST OCCURRENCE OF REGEX '\.[^\.]+$'
        IN <wa_file>-filename MATCH OFFSET dot_offset.
      ADD 1 TO dot_offset.
      extension = <wa_file>-filename+dot_offset.
      " Get mime type
      CALL FUNCTION 'SDOK_MIMETYPE_GET'
        EXPORTING   extension = extension
        IMPORTING   mimetype  = mimetype.
      me->mimetype = mimetype.
    ENDIF.
  ENDIF.
```

7. The MIME type needs to be passed back as a header field of the response object. Luckily, the handler class provides direct access to both the request and response objects, and the header fields can be updated as follows:

```
server->response->set_header_field(
    name = if_http_header_fields=>content_type
```

```
      value = me->mimetype ).
    server->response->set_data( content ).
```

So now when users click on the attachment names, regardless of what tool they're using to view the RSS feed, they'll have the option of downloading the attachment files (see Figure 16.7).

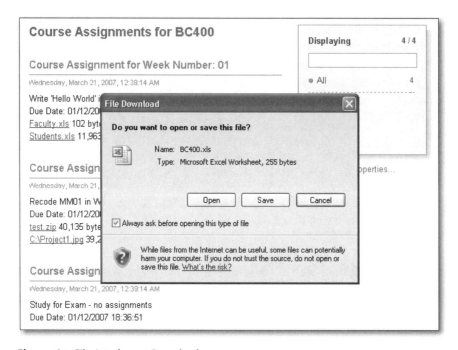

Figure 16.7 File Attachment Download

17 Closing

Russel may have been a fictional character working on a fictional project, but hopefully you have seen a little bit of yourself reflected in the main character of this book. The world of application development is an ever-changing, yet highly competitive place. Every year, it becomes increasingly important that all application developers keep their skills up to date. But with the right basic skill sets, there is no reason why every project that a developer embarks on can't be viewed as a learning experience. We encourage all of you to embrace these learning opportunities in order to expand your knowledge and to have fun in the process.

Hopefully, you've encountered just such a learning experience in reading this book. We started with a project in its very early stages, when it was nothing more than the raw business requirements. Then, we explored the lower level design areas, not just creating data dictionary objects, but also encapsulating the lowest layer of the application logic in a good object-oriented framework. Later in the project, we saw that there was real value in this encapsulation. Reusability and the opportunity to localize changes to small sections of code were critical to our being able to complete the sample project on time.

Contrary to many other learning materials, we didn't restrict ourselves to staying within the comfort zone of the ABAP Development Workbench. If you followed the scenario of the project's development, then you got a glimpse of several of the touch points between the ABAP development environment and the vast SAP NetWeaver platform. SAP NetWeaver Process Integration, SAP NetWeaver Master Data Management, the SAP NetWeaver Portal, and SAP NetWeaver Visual Composer are all important tools that are just beginning to emerge as parts of the average ABAP developer's toolbox. Learning about these tools and how they can enhance your core ABAP development adds tremendous value to your overall worth as a developer and what you can contribute to an enterprise.

As we look to the future, people often ask about where ABAP development tools are headed. In the past few years, a lot of attention has focused on the introduction of Java as a development tool in the SAP environment. ABAP developers have sometimes grown anxious about this, not knowing if their current skill set would soon become obsolete. We would like to assure you that ABAP has a long and prosperous future in the SAP environment. ABAP will remain the business logic language for the majority of SAP applications. In addition, it will also supply the user interface layer, via Web Dynpro ABAP, for SAP ERP and other solutions of the SAP Application Suite that are already heavily based on ABAP.

But service enablement does open ABAP up to the rest of the world. Business logic and data are no longer confined to the SAP and ABAP-only worlds. It is a simple exercise, as we have seen throughout this book, to both expose ABAP via Web Services and consume Web Services from various other platforms.

We will see a new age of composite applications built using the SAP NetWeaver Composition Environment. Many of these applications will use Visual Composer or Web Dynpro Java for their user interface, yet consume business services written in ABAP. So, although ABAP has a strong future, anyone who is passionate about development in the SAP space would naturally be interested in some of these new tools. If Java development doesn't interest you, then look to some of the other SAP NetWeaver platform aspects, like SAP NetWeaver MDM or SAP NetWeaver PI, to add to your capabilities.

Appendix

A   Code Samples

Disclaimer

Although the authors have tested the code samples that accompany this book, we can make no guarantee to their use in your SAP system. We also cannot be held responsible for any damage done by installing them. Therefore, we strongly encourage you to always implement the code samples in a sandbox system first, so you can analyze any impact that they might have.

Support for this code will be provided on a "best effort" basis. The authors will strive to answer questions about the source code, although we obviously are not in a position to offer production critical support levels.

Release Level

The code contained here was developed entirely on SAP NetWeaver 7.0 SP10. The target platform for installing the code samples is SAP NetWeaver 7.0 with at least SP10. Although the vast majority of the samples would function properly on any support package level of SAP NetWeaver 7.0, there were some enhancements made to Web Dynpro and Adobe Forms Integration that are only available with this support package level.

The ideal system into which to install the code samples is the SAP NetWeaver 7.0 ABAP Trial Version, available for download from SAP Developer Network (SDN):

https://www.sdn.sap.com/irj/sdn/downloaditem?rid=/library/uuid/cfc19866-0401-0010-35b2-dc8158247fb6

This is the same system image that we used to develop the code samples on. SDN already offers a version of the trial software with SP11 embedded; therefore, the proper release level is already met.

Lastly, this trial edition is designed to run on the average developer's desktop or laptop. So, even if your organization does not yet have a SAP NetWeaver 7.0 system, you can install a personal version of the software to examine our code samples.

Installation Options

The source code that we deliver here is available in three different formats:

▸ First, all samples are available as text files and screenshots. Using this generic format, you can choose which samples you want to install. This also allows you to rename or change objects as you implement them. Due to the sheer number of objects contained in these samples (nearly 1,000), however, it is quite time-consuming to recreate all code samples by hand.

▸ To help with this problem, we also offer all source code as a transport file. The SAP transport mechanism was designed for delivery of code from SAP to customers and through a customer's own landscape, but not necessarily for the type of delivery that we are doing. Therefore, before you import these transport files, we must stress certain points:

  ▸ First, the objects contained in this transport were created in the custom name range (typically Z and Y named objects). Therefore, it is conceivable that we would deliver an object with a name that you have already used. In this situation, your object will likely be overwritten. Once again, please import this transport first in some non-critical sandbox system to ensure that none of your own development items are lost.

  ▸ Another factor to consider is that by transporting these objects, your system will see them as foreign objects. Therefore, if you need to change them, you will first need to change their transport group assignment or use the modification assistant.

  Here are more reasons why importing the code samples into the SDN provided trial system is the best option:

  ▸ You will avoid the possibility of overwriting anything important.

  ▸ Also, because we did our development on the same system image, the objects will be delivered thinking NSP (the system ID for the trial system) is the home location, thus allowing full editing of the objects.

  ▸ Lastly, there is already a document available on SDN that details how to import the transport files into the trial edition: *https://weblogs.sdn.sap.com/pub/wlg/6380*.

▸ The final format is a new option based on the open source project, SAPlink (*http://saplink.org*). SAPlink is a tool that was developed by the ABAP community for the easy exchange of development objects. It exports development objects into an XML file. This solution has the advantage that you can still view the source of the objects from the XML file, yet have an easy way to import the objects into your system. All objects are delivered into the local private package and are inactive.

The only downside to SAPlink is that it, as yet, does not include plugins to support all possible ABAP development objects. We have exported as many object types as were supported when the book/CD was printed. We have the Slinkee and Nugget files for the development objects on the CD; however, to use them, you will need to download the latest version of SAPlink and all of its plugins from the SAPlink project page.

One important note to consider, regardless of which import mechanism you choose, has to do with the SAP NetWeaver Master Data Management (MDM) related objects. The MDM code samples will only import into your system if you have the MDM ABAP API Add-on installed in your system. Without the Add-on (which is only available from the SAP Service Marketplace to customers who are licensed for MDM), these objects will not compile and can lead to import errors during the transport process. These errors are unavoidable and can be ignored.

B The Authors

Rich Heilman is a Software Engineer/Analyst currently working for an SAP customer. He has a total of 10 years' experience in software development. He started his career working with RPG/IV on the AS/400 and transitioned into ABAP when his company implemented SAP in 2001.

Rich has been involved in many projects over the past six years, developing custom ABAP and Java applications to satisfy business requirements. For the past few years, he has presented at the annual ASUG Spring Conference as well as the SAP TechEd Conference. He is also one of the Top Contributors on SDN, spending much of his time answering questions in the ABAP forums.

Thomas Jung is a SAP NetWeaver Product Manager focusing on the Custom Development IT Practice, particularly as it applies to Enterprise Information Management. More specifically, he is the Product Manager for SAP NetWeaver Master Data Management APIs, Knowledge Management APIs, SAP NetWeaver Discovery System, and SAP NetWeaver Voice. He is a frequent presenter at SAP events and can often be found on SDN.

Before joining SAP Labs in 2006, Thomas was an applications developer for an SAP customer. He was involved in SAP implementations as an ABAP Developer for almost 10 years. He is also the co-author of the book *Advanced BSP Programming* (SAP PRESS, 2006).

Index

T

ABAP Objects

www.sap-press.com

H. Keller, S. Krüger

ABAP Objects

ABAP Programming in SAP NetWeaver

Describes the complete SAP UI libraries and how to use them

Explains the process starting with design through development and test up to system configuration

approx. 400 pp., with CD, 79,90 Euro / US$ 79,90
ISBN 978-1-59229-112-0, July 2007

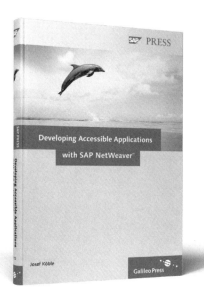

Accessible Applications with SAP NetWeaver

www.sap-press.com

Josef Köble

Developing Accessible Applications with SAP NetWeaver

This comprehensive reference book is a developer's complete guide to programming accessible applications using SAP NetWeaver technology. Readers get step-by-step guidance on the requirements and conceptual design and development using ABAP Workbench, NW Developer Studio, and Visual Composer. The authors provide you with a detailed presentation of all relevant design elements for Dynpro, WebDynpro (ABAP and Java), and Adobe Interactive Forms. In addition, you'll learn the ins and outs of testing applications, as well as configuration techniques for both front-end interfaces and back-end apps. With this unique approach, developers get a thorough introduction to all interface elements along with best practices for how to use them, and QA managers gain exclusive, expert insights on testing accessibility features.

>> www.sap-press.de/1362

Learn to design intuitive business applications with SAP Visual Composer for NetWeaver 2004s

Best practices for configuration settings and advice to master the development lifecycle

A comprehensive reference, providing you with complete A-to-Z details— directly from SAP

524 pp., 2007, 69,95 Euro / US$ 69,95
ISBN 978-1-59229-099-4

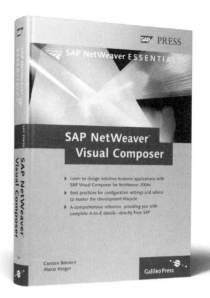

SAP NetWeaver Visual Composer

www.sap-press.com

C. Bönnen, M. Herger

SAP NetWeaver Visual Composer

Instead of conventional programming and implementation, SAP NetWeaver Visual Composer (VC) enables you to model your processes graphically via drag & drop—potentially without ever having to write a single line of code. This book not only shows you how, but also serves as a comprehensive reference, providing you with complete details on all aspects of VC. You learn the ins and outs of the VC architecture—including details on all components and concepts, as well as essential information on model-based development and on the preparation of different types of applications. Readers quickly broaden their knowledge by tapping into practical expert advice on the various aspects of the Development Lifecycle as well as on selected applications, which have been modeled with the VC and are currently delivered by SAP as standard applications.

Comprehensive introduction to
the basic principles and tools of
the Adobe Flex Application
Framework

ActionScript and MXML, data
communication, chart
generation, dynamic screens,
and much more

298 pp., 2007, 69,95 Euro / US$ 69,95
ISBN 978-1-59229-119-9

SAP Applications
with Adobe Flex

www.sap-press.com

Armin Lorenz, Gunther Schöppe, Felix Consbruch,
Daniel Knapp, Frank Sonnenberg

Developing SAP Applications with Adobe Flex

This book provides you with the practical guidance
needed to develop intuitive user interfaces for SAP
NetWeaver Portal, using Adobe's Flex Application
Framework. First, you'll get a concise introduction to
the details on the development environment for Flex
applications: Adobe Flex Builder. Using clearly
structured examples you'll quickly learn to
understand the syntax of the Flex programming
languages, ActionScript and MXML. Readers get
detailed coverage of the backend connection to the
SAP system, data communication functions, and learn
how best to generate charts.

>> www.sap-press.de/1379

Basic principles, architecture, and configuration

Development of dynamic, reusable UI components

Volumes of sample code and screen captures for help you maximize key tools

360 pp., 2006, 69,95 Euro / US$
ISBN 1-59229-078-7

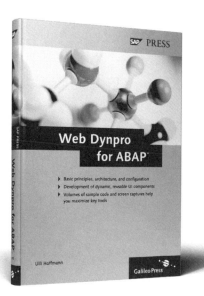

Web Dynpro for ABAP

www.sap-press.com

U. Hoffmann

Web Dynpro for ABAP

Serious developers must stay ahead of the curve by ensuring that they are up-to-date with all of the latest standards. This book illustrates the many benefits that can be realized with component-based UI development using Web Dynpro for ABAP. On the basis of specifically developed sample components, readers are introduced to the architecture of the runtime and development environment and receive highly-detailed descriptions of the different functions and tools that enable you to efficiently implement Web Dynpro technology on the basis of SAP NetWeaver 2004s. Numerous code listings, screen captures, and little-known tricks make this book your indispensable companion for the practical design of modern user interfaces.

The Official ABAP Reference

Horst Keller

The Official ABAP Reference

Thoroughly revised and significantly extended, this all-new edition of our acclaimed reference, contains complete descriptions of all commands in ABAP and ABAP Objects, Release 6.40.

Not only will you find explanations and examples of all commands, you'll also be able to hit the ground running with key insights and complete reviews of all relevant usage contexts. Fully updated for the current Release 6.40, many topics in this new book have been revised completely. Plus, we've added full coverage of ABAP and XML, which are now described in detail for the very first time. The book comes complete with a test version of the latest Mini-SAP System 6.20!

>> www.sap-press.de/946

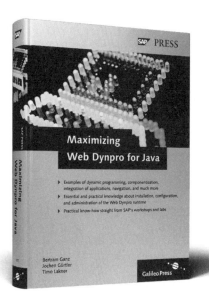

Examples of dynamic programming, componentization, integration of applications, navigation, and much more

Essential and practical knowledge about installation, configuration, and administration of the Web Dynpro runtime

497 pp., 2006, 69,95 Euro / US$
ISBN 1-59229-077-9

Maximizing
Web Dynpro for Java

www.sap-press.com

B. Ganz, J. Gürtler, T. Lakner

Maximizing Web Dynpro for Java

Standard examples of Web Dynpro applications can leave SAP developers with many questions and severe limitations. This book takes you to the next level with detailed examples that show you exactly what you need to know in order to leverage Web Dynpro applications. From the interaction with the Java Developer Infrastructure (JDI), to the use of Web Dynpro components, to the integration into the portal and the use of its services—this unique book delivers it all. In addition, readers get dozens of tips and tricks on fine-tuning Web Dynpro applications in terms of response time, security, and structure. Expert insights on the configuration and administration of the Web Dynpro runtime environment serve to round out this comprehensive book.

Comprehensive guide to end-to-end process integration with SAP XI—from a developer's perspective

Practical exercises to master system configuration and development of mappings, adapters, and proxies

341 pp., 2007, 69,95 Euro / US$ 69,95
ISBN 978-1-59229-118-2

SAP Exchange Infrastructure for Developers

www.sap-press.com

V. Nicolescu, B. Funk, P. Niemeyer, M. Heile

SAP Exchange Infrastructure for Developers

This book provides both experienced and new SAP XI developers with a detailed overview of the functions and usage options of the SAP NetWeaver Exchange Infrastructure. The authors take you deep into the system with a series of practical exercises for the development and configuration of mappings, adapters, and proxies: RFC-to-File, File-to-IDoc, ABAP-Proxy-to-SOAP, and Business Process Management. Each exercise is rounded off by a description of relevant monitoring aspects and is combined in a comprehensive case study.

Interested in reading more?

Please visit our Web site for all
new book releases from SAP PRESS.

www.sap-press.com